PHILOSOPHERS ON FILM
FROM BERGSON TO BADIOU

PHILOSOPHERS ON FILM FROM BERGSON TO BADIOU

A Critical Reader

EDITED BY CHRISTOPHER KUL-WANT

Columbia University Press
New York

Columbia University Press
Publishers Since 1893
New York   Chichester, West Sussex
cup.columbia.edu

Library of Congress Cataloging-in-Publication Data
Names: Want, Christopher, editor.
Title: Philosophers on film from Bergson to Badiou : a critical reader /
    edited by Christopher Kul-Want.
Description: New York : Columbia University Press, [2019] | Includes
    bibliographical references and index.
Identifiers: LCCN 2019010032 | ISBN 9780231176026 (cloth : alk. paper) |
    ISBN 9780231176033 (pbk. : alk. paper) | ISBN 9780231549363 (ebk.)
Subjects: LCSH: Motion pictures—Philosophy. | Continental philosophy.
Classification: LCC PN1995 .P4984 2019 | DDC 791.4301—dc23
LC record available at https://lccn.loc.gov/2019010032

Columbia University Press books are printed
on permanent and durable acid-free paper.
Printed in the United States of America

For Catherine, Enna Thea, and B

CONTENTS

ACKNOWLEDGMENTS

The contents and ideas of the book draw a great deal upon my experience of teaching about art, cinema, and philosophy as the course leader of the MRes Art: Theory and Philosophy course at Central Saint Martins, University of the Arts, London, and I'm especially grateful to colleagues and students on the course who have contributed to my thinking and writing about these subjects. I'd like to thank my college for the investment that it has put into developing this book, awarding me a sabbatical term of research study as well as grants to cover the copyright purchases and to curate a program of films and discussions at the Close-Up Film Centre in London in July 2018 that drew upon the ideas of the book. I'd like to thank Damien Sanville, the director of Close-Up Film Centre, and Oliver Dickens, the program and events manager at the center, for this opportunity as well as for their generosity in allowing me open access to the center's extensive film collection. I'm especially thankful to the editorial team at CUP—Wendy Lochner, Susan Pensak, and Lowell Frye—for their advice and help throughout the production of this book. Additionally, I'm grateful to Hilary Knox for her assistance in collating the primary texts of the book and Murad Khan for his help with the final proofing of the manuscript. Most of all, I would like to thank my partner, Catherine Yass, for her support throughout this project.

* * *

Texts in the following chapters are taken from these sources:

"The Work of Art in the Age of Its Technological Reproducibility," from *Walter Benjamin: Selected Writings,* vol. 3: *1935–1938,* edited by Howard Eiland and Michael W. Jennings, translated by Edmund Jephcott, Howard Eiland, and others (Cambridge, MA: Belknap Press of Harvard University Press), copyright © 2002 by the President and Fellows of Harvard College, used with permission from Harvard University Press.

"The Culture Industry" (1979), from Theodor W. Adorno and Max Horkheimer, *Dialectic of Enlightenment,* pp. 120–43, used with permission from Verso Books UK.

"Le cinéma et la nouvelle psychologie," from Maurice Merleau-Ponty, *Sens et Non-Sens,* pp. 48–59; originally published in French copyright © 1948 by Editions Nagel. The translation published here is based on the revised third edition, issued by Nagel in 1961. English translation copyright © 1964 by Northwestern University Press. First published 1964 by Northwestern University Press. All rights reserved.

"On Contemporary Alienation or the End of the Pact with the Devil," from Jean Baudrillard, *The Consumer Society: Myths and Structures,* 1998, used with permission from Sage Publications Ltd.

"The Looking Glass, from the Other Side," from Luce Irigaray, *This Sex Which Is Not One*, pp. 9–22, trans. Catherine Porter and Carolyn Burke; translation copyright © 1985 Cornell University, reprinted by permission of Georges Borchardt, Inc.

"Acinema," from Jean-François Lyotard, *Wide Angle* 2, no. 3 (1978): 52–59, translated by J-F. Lyotard and Paisley N. Livingston, used with permission from the Ohio University School of Film.

Cinema I: L'Image-Mouvement, Gilles Deleuze, copyright © 1983 Les Editions de Minuit, used with permission from Les Editions de Minuit.

Cinema II: L'Image-temps, Gilles Deleuze, copyright © 1985 Les Editions de Minuit, used with permission from Les Editions de Minuit.

"Notes on Gesture," Georgio Agamben, from *Means Without End: Notes on Politics,* translated by Vincenzo Binetti and Cesare Casarino (UMP, 2000), pp. 49–60, plus notes on p. 144, used with permission from University of Minnesota Press.

"In His Bold Gaze My Ruin Is Writ Large," from Slavoj Žižek, ed., *Everything You Always Wanted to Know About Lacan (But Were Afraid to Ask Hitchcock),* 1992, pp. 211–50, plus notes used with permission from Verso Books UK.

"And Life Goes On: Life and Nothing More," from Jean Luc Nancy and Yves Gevaert, *The Evidence of Film,* 2001, pp. 58–78 (English text), used with permission from Editions Klincksieck.

Contesting Tears: The Hollywood Melodrama of the Unknown Woman, Stanley Cavell, 1996, pp. 3–21, plus notes, copyright © by the University of Chicago.

"From One Manhunt to Another: Fritz Lang Between Two Ages," from
Jacques Ranciere, *Film Fables,* 2006, translated by Emiliano Battista,
copyright © Jacques Ranciere and Emiliano Battista, pp. 45–61, Berg
Publishers, an imprint of Bloomsbury Publishing Plc, used with permission from Bloomsbury Publishing Plc.

"Cinema as Philosophical Experimentation," from Alain Badiou, *Cinema,*
2013, pp. 202–32, used with permission from Polity Books.

Technics and Time, 3: Cinematic Time and the Question of Malaise, 2011,
Bernard Stiegler, pp. 8–26, plus notes, copyright © by the Board of
Trustees of the Leland Stanford Jr. University for the English translation,
used with permission from Stanford University Press.

The Miracle of Analogy: or, The History of Photography, Part I, 2015, Kaja
Silverman, pp. 87–88, 124–34, plus notes, copyright © by the Board of
Trustees of the Leland Stanford Jr. University for the English translation,
used with permission from Stanford University Press.

INTRODUCTION

Philosophers on Film

This book is for those who want to know what philosophers have said about cinema and film and how their ideas relate historically and conceptually. The book is devised as a companion to my book *Philosophers on Art from Kant to the Postmodernists: A Critical Reader*, also published by Columbia University Press (2010); both books comprise a chronologically arranged series of primary texts written by seminal philosophers informed by the continental tradition of philosophy as this was developed originally in Germany and France. The texts in the present book encompass approaches to cinema informed variously by the Marxist intellectual tradition, phenomenology, philosophies of affect, as well as psychoanalytic and gender theories. In the hope of enhancing the enjoyment of the texts, their extraordinary qualities of writing and radicality, each of these texts is prefaced with an introduction elucidating their concepts and thinking about film As will be seen, the philosophical genealogy that the texts draw upon stem from two founding texts of continental philosophy by Immanuel Kant: the *Critique of Pure Reason* (1781), which is concerned with a priori (that is, pregiven) forms of categorizing and understanding phenomenological experience, and the *Critique of Judgment* (1790), which, in contrast, is about phenomenologies of experience that exceed understanding. The ways in which these influential *Critique*s inform the philosophies of cinema covered in this book, and their consequences for appreciating film's radical innovations as an art form and as a philosophy, as well as its relations to power and ideology, underpin the selection of the texts and form the basis of this general introduction.

The majority of the philosophers in the book either belong to, or have helped shape, the intellectual movements of the late twentieth century known variously as postmodernism, poststructuralism, and postphenomenology. This book is a historical and retrospective inquiry into these intellectual movements, offering an understanding of their legacy for both philosophy and cinema now and in the foreseeable future; thus, the texts included here are selected as much for their ongoing currency as for their historical significance. This is for the purpose of highlighting what the twin concepts of cinema and film—with their attendant issues of mass consumption, technological innovation and modes of affectivity—meant in the past as well as what it can, or could, mean today. The dynamic of the book, therefore, works in cross-directions, drawing upon a history of postmodern thought with regard to film that also provides the coordinates for a speculative understanding of the cinematic image in our own hyperindustrial age of informatics and telecommunications.[1]

Cinema and Mass Audience

Midway through the twelfth and last tableaux scene of Jean Luc-Godard's film *Vivre sa vie* (1962), as the film reaches its denouement, the camera pans down a long line of people queuing, two and three abreast, on a Parisian boulevard to see François Truffaut's film *Jules et Jim*, which had been released at the same time as the shooting of *Vivre sa vie*. The camera shot is a brief aside in the movie's plot, one of a series of reflexive devices introducing a distantiation that call attention to the film's means of production and sense of artifice, achieved in this instance by several knowing references to the context for Godard's own film practice and philosophy. In the first instance, the sequence refers to contemporary developments in filmmaking in France and the rise of *la Nouvelle Vague* ("the New Wave" of filmmakers), that counted Truffaut and Godard among its chief exponents and, second, it points to the mass appeal of cinema continuing at that time, a point that had a particular resonance for Godard, who believed, like many filmmakers and theorists, in the power of cinema to help activate the masses in effecting sociopolitical change.

Subsequently, over twenty years later, in his extended video work *Histoire(s) du cinéma* (1988–1998), Godard reproached cinema for not fulfilling this potential to play its part in shaping mass consciousness and mobilization owing to a failure to acknowledge its own historicity. This overlooked or forgotten historicity of cinema, to which Godard dedicated his work, and with which he never entirely lost faith, was bound up with several interconnected elements that relate to cinema's early popularity in the silent and modern eras. These elements form the background not only to Godard's philosophy, but also to many of the philosophers included in this book who use the term *cinema* to denote the fact that they are writing not simply about film, but about the interrelationship between film and its audience, as a collective experience. Although this understanding of cinema was most explicit in the years before the Second World War, nevertheless, it remained immanent within philosophical approaches to cinema after the war, too. In this context, it should be noted that the word *cinema* is derived from the French *cinématographe*, which comes in part from the Greek *kinema*, meaning movement (hence the popular term *the movies*). So, the word *cinémato* plus the suffix *graphe* means variously imaging, tracing, or writing movement. Given the etymology of the word *cinema*, this explains the reason why many of the philosophers in the book address *cinema* as a term not only to denote the activities of filmmaking and film viewing, but also as a term that designates, in connection with these activities, the experience of movement, whether affective or sociopolitical movement or a combination of both. Such are the traits and attributes that many of the thinkers in the *Reader* invest in the concept of cinema as the context for the experience of filmgoing and watching.

It was in the silent and modern periods of its history that cinema's extraordinary mass appeal as a form of public entertainment and consumption arose, especially in the metropolitan areas of Europe and North America. This social and cultural phenomenon, which is now largely confined to the past, at least in the West, is illustrated by the statistics for the number of cinemas and cinema attendance over this period. In the latter stages of the German Reich in the 1930s, about two million people went to the movies every day.[2] A comparable situation was reflected in America where it was estimated that by 1927 an average of 110 million people went to the cinema on a weekly basis. Despite the Depression in the 1930s, cinema remained a huge attraction, and it was this and the following decade that became known as "the golden age" of Hollywood.

Writing in "The Work of Art in the Age of Its Technological Reproducibility" in 1935–36 (*Reader* text 2), Walter Benjamin observed that "the masses are a matrix from which all customary behavior towards works of art is today emerging newborn" (section 18). Like other writers on cinema at the time, Benjamin developed his philosophy of film (the "works of art" to which he refers) believing that an entirely new aesthetic sensibility of affectivity had emerged with the advent of cinema that cut across distinctions of gender and age and, for the first time in history, incorporated the masses as its addressee. In similar vein, the German critic Eugen Tannenbaum wrote a decade earlier in 1923:

> The many millions who sit every night in their movie theaters, mesmerized by the life that flickers across the screen in uncounted kilometers of celluloid, the many millions who were a minute ago businessmen, workers, handymen, academics, secretaries, snobs, and ladies of the night—they all have become, after

just a few scenes a homogeneous mass, their attention focused on a story or a star and hypnotized by the suggestiveness of passion.[3]

Tannenbaum's description of the moviegoing public in Berlin as a "homogeneous mass," which merges different professions and classes and, collectively, is held in thrall to desire and the cult of the glamorous movie star, echoes an observation by Siegfried Kracauer, another important critic in Germany of the same period. In his essay "Cult of Distraction: On Berlin's Picture Palaces" (1926), Kracauer notes that in a city such as Berlin, composed of four million people, class distinctions are absorbed through the popular activity of cinema going, and, at the same time, new cultural and aesthetic tastes seem to be in process of formation through the experience of cinema. No longer, Kracauer says, are the masses "thrown scraps" of pretentious culture by the bourgeoisie such as literature, classical music, and drama,

> they demand instead to be served at set tables. There is little room for the so-called educated classes who must either join in the dining or maintain their snobbish aloofness. Their provincial isolation is, in any case, at an end. They are being absorbed by the masses and this gives rise to the *homogeneous cosmopolitan audience* in which everyone has the same responses, from the bank director to the sales clerk, from the diva to the stenographer.[4]

Cinema as a form of collective, citywide experience began in the 1890s, and, by the time of Tannenbaum's and Kracauer's writing on cinema some thirty years later, it was widely agreed that it possessed a radically new aesthetic that was different from the traditional visual art forms and which required commentary and theorization, not least because of its mass appeal. This project aimed to characterize and discern cinema's ideological as well as affirmative, even revolutionary, tendencies, which were shaped implicitly by the wider question of the consciousness and mobilization of the masses through both aesthetic and sociopolitical means. In this respect, Kracauer and Benjamin put down a marker in their respective essays on cinema in the form of a fundamental question to which many of the writings in this book can be seen to return. Kracauer states that through cinema, "the audience encounters itself";[5] and Benjamin adds that it enables "the masses [to] come face to face with themselves."[6] The idea of the audience's encounter with themselves through the medium of cinema led Kracauer to ask whether there was a political element involved in this experience that was bound up with imminent social change. Alternatively, Kracauer was anxious that the experience of cinema could reinforce the audience's narcissistic and ideological tendencies through a misconceived nostalgia for a purported organic and social unity supported by the orthodoxy of the cinematic image's spatial depth.[7] Although Kracauer's question about cinema's sociopolitical efficacy was expressed in Germany amidst the political tensions of the Reich prior to the Second World War, it continued to have a resonance through subsequent history for the philosophers writing in this book, especially for the generation of cinephiles, such as Alain Badiou, Gilles Deleuze, Julia Kristeva, Jean-François Lyotard, Jean-Luc Nancy, and Jacques Rancière, who encountered cinema in the late 1950s and 1960s in France. Like Benjamin and Kracauer before them, these philosophers believed that it was necessary to analyze cinema's aesthetic and affective qualities so as to come to a fuller understanding of its political potential and transformative value.

By the 1960s, scenes of queues outside cinemas, such as that captured by Godard's passing camera on the boulevards of Paris in *Vivre sa vie*, were some of the last that were to be seen in the Western world. Subsequently, such crowds would endure only in the hypercommodified form of the movie industry's spectacular opening nights and galas. The rise of television from the 1950s onward and the advent of home video in the 1980s and 1990s guaranteed the death of cinema as a mass, citywide form of entertainment, and, as a consequence, the majority of the movie theaters were shut down. Today, "a night at the movies" as a choice of entertainment lags a long way behind watching film on television and DVD or Blu-ray at home, with online streaming set to cap these formats as the principal means by which to access and purchase film. A number of the texts in the book reach beyond this watershed moment in the history of cinema. The essays written after the 1960s were shaped by the passing of the "golden age of cinema" and, subsequently, the innovation of new forms of transmission and distribution for film. More widely, the rise of new kinds of intersubjectivities, and control, that are effected through the web in conjunction with capital informs many of the philosophers' ideas in a profoundly contemporary way (see especially the texts in the *Reader* by Jean Baudrillard, Deleuze, Rancière, and Bernard Stiegler). These sociopolitical factors force the philosophers to approach Benjamin's and Kracauer's founding question about cinema's efficacy and the, as yet to be realized, consciousness of the masses in new philosophical ways. However, what still remains in their writings, as was the case in the essays by Benjamin as well as Adorno and Horkheimer in the 1930s and 1940s, are the issues of ideology and the formative legacies of Enlightenment rationalism in the West for understanding, if only by default, the sociopolitical and affective stakes of cinema's aesthetic.[8]

Cinema and the Legacy of the Enlightenment I:
Walter Benjamin, Theodor Adorno, and Max Horkheimer

Two seminal, yet largely opposed, discussions of cinema as a form of mass media and entertainment in the modern period follow the opening text of the book by Henri Bergson (*Reader* text 1): Walter Benjamin's essay "The Work of Art in the Age of Its Technological Reproducibility" (*Reader* text 2) and Theodor W. Adorno's and Max Horkheimer's coauthored chapter "The Culture Industry: Enlightenment as Mass Deception" (1944; *Reader* text 3). Adorno's and Horkheimer's book *Dialectic of Enlightenment*, in which the essay on the culture industry appears, begins with a grim assessment of the modern West, "the Enlightenment has always aimed at liberating men from fear and establishing their sovereignty. Yet the fully enlightened earth radiates disaster triumphant."[9] While Adorno and Horkheimer endorse the original program of the Enlightenment established at the dawn of modernity in the eighteenth century, with its aim of dissolving ideologies by substituting "knowledge for fancy,"[10] they posit that the Enlightenment's faith in rationality as the chosen path leading toward humankind's emancipation achieved the very opposite of what was promised. Far from obtaining social and political liberation, rationality created the circumstances in which the ideologies of capitalism and fascism could flourish and, together, engender more absolute forms of social domination and repression than hitherto known in Western history. Having escaped from Nazi Germany and the Holocaust to the safe haven of the U.S. in the 1930s, Horkheimer and Adorno were all too aware of the deleterious effects of rationalist ideology placed in the service of war and genocide. However, their critique was not only aimed at the Nazi's instrumentalization of technology in the name of rationalism but also at what they perceived to be the governing ideology over-determining rationality itself. This ideology, they claimed, lay at the core of Enlightenment philosophy, the principles of which were articulated most fully by Immanuel Kant in his philosophy of knowledge.

In the *Critique of Pure Reason*, Kant set out to establish the necessary categories of understanding by which all forms of possible experience, now or in the future, are capable of being transformed into objects of immanent knowledge.[11] Famously, Kant described his project in the *Critique of Pure Reason* as a "Copernican revolution" involving a shift from the question "what must the mind be like in order to know?" to the question "what must objects be like in order to be known?" Ultimately, Kant's answer to this latter question was that objects are conformable to the categories of understanding that he established in the *Critique*. Governed by concepts of Euclidian space and linear time, these categories of quantity, quality, relation and modality, and their respective subsets,[12] Kant believed, provided the framework by which so-called manifold— that is, phenomenological—experience is organized in the mind, thus providing the basis for thinking such experience under the aforementioned categories in the form of a determinant judgment. Contrary to Kant, Adorno and Horkheimer argued that to put the universal before the particular—that is, to subsume experience under the classification of the categories—is to occlude what is singular and particular about such experience, replacing its intrinsic alterity with an a priori notion of identity. For Adorno and Horkheimer, the legacy of determinant reasoning found in the presuppositions of Kantian Enlightenment ideology has its counterpart in capitalism's system of exchange, by means of which commodities and labor power are subsumed under a general system or principle of monetary value and exchange. Adorno and Horkheimer conceded that in Kant's theory of determinant judgment a certain space is left for individual will and an inner intuitive sense by which to relate phenomena and experiences to universal concepts and categories, but, as modernity has developed, they observe that capitalism's commercial interests have forced its own mediated experiences upon the individual, leaving no room for the will since "there is nothing left for the consumer to classify. Producers have done it for him." In the introduction to *Dialectic of Enlightenment,* Adorno and Horkheimer state that "the essay on the 'culture industry' demonstrates the regression of enlightenment to ideology which finds its typical expression in cinema and radio."[13] They go on to define the Enlightenment's legacy in the twentieth century for culture, saying it "consists above all in the calculation of effectiveness and of the techniques of production and distribution."[14] This is apparent, Adorno and Horkheimer argue, in the culture industry's promulgation of hit songs, the creation of singing and movie stars, and a reliance on a series of invariant types, slogans, and repetitive formulas. The contents of mass culture, they say, are interchangeable across different media, each of which is subject to the same positivist forms of calculation and planning. Gags, formulas, and clichés are calculated for their effects by special teams of experts, the lengths of stories rigidly adhered to, and the endings of films wholly predictable from the outset. Standardization as a species of technical rationality purges culture of all spontaneity and originality. Intrinsic worth is calculated in advance, supported by market research, for the sole purpose of achieving maximum profitability.

Like Adorno and Horkheimer, Benjamin believed that much of what is wrong with modernity lay in the damaging influence of the Enlightenment's ideology of rationality exemplified, but by no means confined to, Kant's philosophy of the subsumption of experience in the *Critique of Pure Reason.* Benjamin opposed this Kantian form of ideology acting upon the cultural sphere of society, although not by highlighting its pervasiveness as was the case with Adorno and Horkheimer. Rather, Benjamin sought to expose its limits seeking areas of affective experience that, he believed, remained beyond the grasp of ideology. Through the 1920s and 1930s an important part of Benjamin's work was directed at fundamentally altering Kant's categories of understanding—which he declared as a "type of insane consciousness"[15]—so as to replace them with a new form of affectivity. Specifically, what this entailed was a rethinking of the Kantian system by which a purported synthesis occurs between manifold sensate experience and the respective categories of the understanding. In place of Kant's notion of synthesis, Benjamin proposed a "nonsynthesis" that negates the subsumption of experience within an a priori system of understanding so as to affirm the fluidity of experience as the film comes alive once more each time it is screened through the audience's receptivity to the film.

Behind his seminal essay "The Work of Art in the Age of Technological Reproducibility" (*Reader* text 2) lay Benjamin's concerns about the instrumentalization of technology by the combined forces of capitalism and fascism at a time of rising sociopolitical tension in Germany and Europe. While Benjamin sought freedom from the technological oppression of society, he did not reject technology per se. Indeed, what cinema revealed, for Benjamin, was the very possibility of the liberation of technology from ideology and its determinate use through the development of a wholly new conception of the work of art. Inspired by the films of Sergei Eisenstein and Dziga Vertov of the post-1917 revolutionary period and the 1920s, Benjamin believed that cinematic montage contained a radical affect that resulted in a viewing experience of shock (*schocken*),[16] a "tactile" (*taktisch*) experience, "based on successive changes of scene and focus which has a percussive effect" (section 17). Such an experience of shock, Benjamin says, interrupts cognition (of the type assumed, for instance, by Kant), and leads the spectator to conclude, "I can no longer think what I want to think. My thoughts have been replaced by moving images."[17] Benjamin claimed that such a radical experience is accompanied by the audience's recognition that films are technological constructs, lacking a specific origin in the same way that their own class identity is a sociopolitical construct. This idea underlies Benjamin's use of the term *reproduzierbarkeit* in the title to his essay, meaning not simply reproduction but reproducibility or transmissibility. Given his sympathies with the communist party and its revolutionary cause, Benjamin hoped that this challenging experience of spectatorship posed by cinema to presumed understanding and thought (that is, ideology) would lend itself to the revolutionary mobilization of the masses.[18]

Cinema and Mass Deception: After Adorno and Horkheimer

Cinema is marked by the heaviest and the most ambiguous of signs—myth, mass, power, money, vulgarity, circus games, exhibitionism and voyeurism.

—Jean-Luc Nancy (*Reader* text 13)

Like Adorno and Horkheimer, philosophers writing in the period after the Second World War had few illusions about the power of the mass media to pacify the masses, its collusion in promoting the "societies of control" that Deleuze identified as the paradigm for hegemonic power and domination in Western society today, "Individuals have become '*dividuals*,' and masses, samples, data, markets, or *'banks.'*"[19] In "Cinema II: The Time-Image" (*Reader* text 9), published in 1985, Deleuze recognized that the hopes and aspirations for a truly mass art realizable through cinema were over in the sense that Benjamin, as well as the great filmmakers of the early modern period, had hoped for. What has come to pervade film production in his own time, Deleuze says, is a general mediocrity, a "mediocrity of products,"[20] that goes hand in hand with a certain "fascism of production."[21] Deleuze brings to bear a similar argument to that of Adorno and Horkheimer in their essay "The Culture Industry: Enlightenment as Mass Deception" to explain why Benjamin's revolutionary hopes for the relationship of cinema and the masses failed. The masses, he says, were denied access to their status as true subjects because the link that connected them to cinema as a mass art was severed by fascist and capitalist ideology:

> the mass-art, treatment of masses, which should not have been separable from an accession of the masses to true subject, has degenerated into state propaganda and manipulation, into a kind of fascism which brought together Hitler and Hollywood, Hollywood and Hitler. The spiritual automaton[22] became fascist man. As Serge Daney says, what has brought the whole of cinema of the movement-image into question are "the great political *mises-en-scène*, state propaganda turned *tableaux vivants*, the first handlings of masses of humans," and their backdrop, the camps. This was the death knell for the ambitions of "the old cinema": not, or only, the mediocrity and vulgarity of current production but rather Leni Riefenstahl, who was not mediocre.[23]

As Benjamin observed in "The Work of Art in the Age of Its Technological Reproducibility," documentary cinema and photography in Germany in the 1930s represented the masses as a unified—and, ultimately, fascist—body. This is what Daney's *tableaux vivants* refer to in the foregoing quotation by Deleuze, the archetypal examples of which were the documentary images of Nazi rallies produced by Leni Riefenstahl that were staged with the camera in mind or, as Benjamin put it, "fed into the camera" (*Reader* text 2, note 40TK). Benjamin was opposed to this representational tendency, for, as he pointed out, the masses are only assigned such representations of themselves, "from the outside, in the minds of its oppressors" (*Reader* text 2, note 29). However, Deleuze's understanding of the succeeding historical events, following Benjamin's essay "The Work of Art in the Age of Its Technological Reproducibility," is that the masses were ensnared by this representational tendency, thus fulfilling Kracauer's warning concerning the dangers of narcissism and the allures of glamou that could bedevil cinema's mass audiences. As a consequence, Benjamin's hopes for cinema's reproducibility as an affective form for mobilizing mass movement were curtailed, and this led Deleuze to pronounce a harsh verdict upon cinema, "When grandeur is no longer that of the composition, but a pure and simple inflation of the represented, there is no cerebral stimulation or birth of thought."[24]

Deleuze's judgment about the cinema of his time as a "mediocrity of products" is endorsed by Badiou, in his essay "Cinema as Philosophical Experimentation" (2003; *Reader* text 16), who understands the "impure art" of cinema as *"first and foremost* an industry," defined by commercialism and deeply informed by the modern social imaginary: "so, in any film at all," he says, "you will find banal images, trite materials, stereotypes, images that have already been seen elsewhere, clichés." Badiou suggests that it is owing to the perennial presence in film of this phantasmatic material, rooted in violence and pornography, as well as the importance of money to the industry, that it is impossible for cinema to attain the same degree of purity as was once possible in the other six arts. "In any film, there are whole bits of it that are banal, images that are pointless, lines that could disappear, over-done colors, bad actors, rampant pornography, and so on."[25]

Badiou's argument that cinema "shares the social imaginary with the masses"[26] echoes Kracauer's theory that cinema is a mirror of the masses' desires, albeit in this case in a reactionary mode. According to Stiegler, in "Cinematic Time" (2011; *Reader* text 17), the Western film industry today exploits the public's desire for stories—an age-old human desire—by investing in the development of audiovisual technics at the same time as expanding transmission networks and the distribution of mass entertainment to audiences. Owing to the velocity with which data and information can be transmitted today (reaching the speed of light), Stiegler believes that this severely limits the mind's capacities to "play" with the repeated inputs it receives. In another register, what particularly concerns Stiegler is the promulgation by Hollywood of "the American way of life" supported by stories of a mythologized past that repress heterogeneity. In this connection Stiegler writes:

What Horkheimer and Adorno call "cultural industries" now constitute the very heart of economic development. . . . Global commerce now develops by mobilizing techniques of persuasion owing everything to the narrative arts. There is no event, no moment, independent of the desire for stories. Media networks and the programming industries exploit this *fictionalizing* tendency by systematizing the specific resources of audiovisual technics. And within the horizon of these immense technological and social issues, *cinema* occupies a unique place. Its technics of image and sound—now including informatics and telecommunications—re-invent our belief in stories that are now told with remarkable, unparalleled power. But at the same time, these technical powers cast doubt on and sow incredulity into the future of a world to whose disruption they have already contributed.

Adorno and Horkheimer proposed that the commodification of the subject is almost total under capital—"There is nothing left for the consumer to classify. Producers have done it for him"—leaving little room for the will or resistance. However, both Stiegler and Baudrillard (*Reader* text 5) go further than this, with the latter proposing that Marx's theory of alienation, which formerly informed the work of Adorno and Horkheimer, is no longer relevant to contemporary society. Baudrillard argues that the capitalist system of consumerism is now all-encompassing, from which there are no vanishing points. "Commodity logic," Baudrillard says,

> has become generalized and today governs not only labor processes and material products, but the whole of culture, sexuality, and human relations, including even fantasies and individual drives. Everything is taken over by that logic, not only in the sense that all functions and needs are objectivized and manipulated in terms of profit, but in the deeper sense in which everything is spectacularized or, in other words, evoked, provoked and orchestrated into images, signs, consumable models.

All needs and desires in such a logic of universalized commodification are always already mediated through methods of anticipation and calculation that today match digital trails and personal consumer details with the dictates and predictions of the consumerist market. Thus, Stiegler states, "'*Processes of automated decision making* can then be functionally tied to the *drive-based automatisms* that control consumer markets—initially through the mediation of the mass media, and, today, through the industry of traces that is also known as the data economy (i.e., the economy of *personal data*).'"[27]

For Stiegler, this means that today's society of control is no longer based upon the models of the factory (in the industrial age) or the corporation (the postmodern epoch) but rather the "hegemony of the industry of traces"[28] that dominates the masses' libidinal drives; as a consequence, Stiegler designates today's epoch as that of "the hyper-industrial age" owing to the hypercontrol over the consumer's desires exercised by generalized digital automatization.

Although Baudrillard's text in the *Reader* precedes that of Stiegler's (1970 as opposed to 2011), they possess a comparable understanding of the implications of such generalized automatization of data made possible by the digital revolution. For Baudrillard, this means, among other things, that there is no space or distance left by which to mirror or reflect the exploited subject, alienated or otherwise. In turn, representation and allegory are made redundant, rendering a film such as *The Student of Prague* (1913) or the novella *Peter Schlemihl's Miraculous Story* (1814), both of which are concerned with the alienated self, as irrelevant to today's age. In Baudrillard's opinion, it is the commodified market that manufactures "images, signs, consumable models" (which he calls simulacra), absorbing as well as producing every desire and need. In this respect Baudrillard's text (*Reader* text 5) might seem to return full circle to Adorno's and Horkheimer's argument in "The Culture Industries: Enlightenment as Mass Deception" (*Reader* text 3) of the way in which capital subsumes individual desires for exploitative purposes:

> Everybody must behave (as if spontaneously) in accordance with his previously determined and indexed level, and choose the category of mass product turned out for his type. Consumers appear as statistics on research organization charts, and are divided by income groups into red, green, and blue areas; the technique is that used for any type of propaganda . . . industry robs the individual of his function. Its prime service to the customer is to do his schematizing for him. . . . There is nothing left for the consumer to classify. Producers have done it for him.

And yet, for all the similarities between Baudrillard's and Adorno's and Horkheimer's positions, there are also marked differences, particularly concerning Baudrillard's opinion that Marxist forms of analysis of alienation and class conflict are outmoded today and are no longer applicable to the social. Also, despite Adorno and Horkheimer's pessimism about the possibility of sociopolitical transformation, these thinkers still believed in certain forms of nonconformism and deviation. Thus, in their essay, "The Culture Industry: Enlightenment as Mass Deception, Adorno and Horkheimer highlight the voyeuristic peepshow in the act of watching films, a potentially transgressive element opposed to the social mechanism. There are heroines, too, in Adorno's and Horkheimer's account of cinema, ranging from Greta Garbo, whose image does not fulfill stereotypical Hollywood prescriptions,[29] to the desperate housewife whose adoption of the cinema theater for her own purposes is an aesthetic act of resistance as well as a way of exploiting available commercial resources: "the housewife finds in the darkness of the movie theater a place of refuge where she can sit for a few hours with nobody watching, just as she used to look out of the window when there were still homes and rest in the evening." While Baudrillard acknowledges that forms of rebellion or dissent will still occur, his understanding of the logic of capital today is that it no longer possesses a distinctive and bounded form that could, therefore, be subverted or changed. In Baudrillard's opinion, capital is more akin to an implosive black hole without horizons or vanishing points. Governed by its own self-reproductive logic, capital is endlessly absorbent of dissent.

In his essay "From One Manhunt to Another: Fritz Lang Between Two Ages" (2001; *Reader* text 15), Jacques Rancière provides a historical and epistemological context to Stiegler's and Baudrillard's ideas about the hyperindustrial age today. Through an account of the rise of what Rancière terms "images-that-know," he compares two films directed by Fritz Lang that share the same subject of the hunt for a psychopathic killer: *M*, released in Weimar Germany in 1931, and *While the City Sleeps*, made in Hollywood in 1956. Each film, in Rancière's view, characterizes their respective historico-political regimes ("the ages of the visible") in which they were conceived. *M* characterizes the modern era's epistemological regime and *While the City Sleeps* is representative of today's regime. Rancière shows that in *M* the Weimar republic as a paradigm for modernity is shaped by a calculative mentality, exemplified by both the police and the underworld and the instrumental methods by which they map the city and its buildings in their hunt for the killer. However, in the post-war period this type of calculative rationality is no longer the required mode of control. In *While the City Sleeps* control is now constructed through a set of statistical categories that purport to identify and always already "know" the subject/murderer in terms of his very appearance, tastes, predilections, and desires.

Cinema and the Legacy of the Enlightenment II:
From the 1940s

For Benjamin, as well as Adorno and Horkheimer, what prevented social change and revolutionary movement, to which cinematic experience might contribute, was the subsumption of experience into pregiven forms and categories utilized by capitalism, and given legitimacy as an approach to knowledge in Kant's *Critique of Pure Reason*. Similarly, both Stiegler and Rancière show how this logic is at work today with anticipatory forms of subjectivization built up from data trails harvested through transmission networks. A number of further texts in the book continue to explore the extensiveness of the ideology that Kant's philosophy characterizes. In this respect, the essays by Maurice Merleau-Ponty, Lyotard, and Slavoj Žižek (*Reader* texts 4, 7, and 12) are especially relevant.

Merleau-Ponty; Lyotard; Žižek

Writing to affirm a phenomenology of cinema in *The Film and the New Psychology* (1945; *Reader* text 4), Merleau-Ponty expressly opposes the primacy awarded to the faculty of understanding by Kant in the first *Critique*. Historically, Merleau-Ponty understands Kant's philosophy of knowledge, in which the faculty of understanding subsumes the manifold data of intuition into the categories, to be derived from a Cartesian philosophy of the subject, and, as evidence of this, he cites a passage from Descartes's *Méditations*, "I say that I see men going by in the street, but what do I exactly see? All I see are hats and coats which might equally well be covering dolls that only move by springs, and if I say that I see men, it is because I apprehend 'through an inspection of the mind what I thought I beheld with my eyes.'" While Descartes recognized that a dis-junction exists between perception and mental cognition, nevertheless, he asserted the power of cognition to organize phenomena that otherwise, he says, would appear alien and strange. This power, claimed by Descartes, applied not just to the subject's immediate perception but also to what is hidden from view and what exists beyond individual perception: as Merleau-Ponty states, "for classical thought . . . invisible objects subsist for me . . . because my judgment keeps them present." In this way, according to Cartesian thought, the mind organizes the world into a meaningful whole.

Lyotard, in his essay "Acinema" (1978; *Reader* text 7), expands Merleau-Ponty's understanding of the genealogy of the Kantian philosophy of sub-sumption beyond Descartes, proposing that it underlies the very notion of iden-tity in the West as this pertains to all aspects of subjective experience and thought. To substantiate this, in a section of "Acinema: entitled "The Movement of Return," Lyotard refers to Freud's ideas outlined in his essay *Beyond the Plea-sure Principle* (1920) as well as Nietzsche's concept of "the eternal return of the same." Following these philosophies, Lyotard suggests that all forms of iden-tity are based upon "[the] return . . . of sameness." This ensures the incorpo-ration of "useless expenditures, differences of pure consumption . . . sterile explosions of libidinal discharge," and, in cinema, "aberrant movements," into pregiven ideas of form and similarity. In cinema, Lyotard says, the effective repression or elimination of diversity and difference permeates every aspect of filmmaking and production, including the plot as well as the deployment of "lens, framing, cuts, lighting, shooting, etc." All these elements, "are submit-ted to the same law of a return of the same. . . . In this regard all endings are happy endings, just by being endings, for even if a film finishes with a murder, this too can serve as a final resolution of dissonance."

Underlying Žižek's Lacanian reading of the subject, in his text *In His Bold Gaze My Ruin Is Writ Large* (1992; *Reader* text 12) on Alfred Hitchcock's classic film *Psycho* (1960), is a similar logic to Lyotard's foregoing analysis. At stake in Žižek's interpretation of Hitchcock's film is the question of the subject that is Norman and the subject that is cinema's audience. According to Lacan, the Sub-ject I—"the self"—is a construction, the fundamental coordinates of which are created through, and maintained by, the Symbolic order. As such, "the self" is formed by the linkages of symbolic and linguistic signifiers so as to make a "coherent" chain or series of significations. However, Lacan states that the iden-tity of the self revolves around a depthless void, the nothingness that lies behind the Symbolic order and lurks in the gaps between the linkages that com-pose socialized forms of expression and representation. The individual represses this void—which Lacan calls "the Real"—in order to maintain his/her own consistent identity as the Subject I in an inexorable pursuit of the elusive object of desire: that is, realizable unitary meaning and sense: "'Desire is a metonymic sliding propelled by a lack, striving to capture the elusive lure: it is always, by definition, 'unsatisfied,' susceptible to every possible interpretation, since it ultimately coincides with its own interpretation: it is *nothing but* the movement of interpretation, the passage from one signifier to another, the eternal production of new signifiers which, retroactively, give sense to the preceding chain.'"

In other words, the Symbolic order is maintained by virtue of the subject continually reproducing him-/herself through symbolic, representational language, modifying the alterity of the Real/void into an experience of lack (the lack that propels language along the signifying chain). In this context, the Real can be understood as the alterity of Kant's notion of intuitive experience before it is processed by the categories of understanding; similarly, the Real is comparable to Freud's idea of the unfettered libidinal drives referred to by Lyotard in his essay "Acinema." Žižek's Lacanian understanding of the Symbolic order is that it functions in a similar way to Kant's categories of understanding and Freud's pleasure principle, displacing the void/Other/the drives for the purpose of reproducing subjectivity with the support of the Symbolic order and its movement of significations. Žižek illustrates these ideas with reference to Hitchcock's *The Lady Vanishes* (1938) and the traces of Miss Froy's former presence on the train that simultaneously signify her disappearance. These traces of Miss Froy (her name written on the train window and the Harrimans herbal tea label), left in the wake of her vanishing, are assimilated to language and the Symbolic order with the effect that her absence is overdetermined by the fantasy of (her) presence—that is eventually "achieved" in diegetic, narrative terms through the solving of her mysterious disappearance. Such is the phantasmatic nature of standard detective and mystery stories.

Reevaluating Cinema

A number of pressing and speculative questions about cinema emerge from the writings of the philosophers in this volume concerning its ideology and its status as a form of mass consumption today. To summarize what has already been said, Deleuze claims that cinema in the postwar period degenerated altogether "into state propaganda and manipulation, into a kind of fascism which brought together Hitler and Hollywood, Hollywood and Hitler."[30] Prior to Deleuze, Adorno and Horkheimer judged that all singularities are dissolved through the activities of market calculation and, according to Baudrillard, Stiegler, and Rancière, this has become an all-pervasive reality by virtue of the creation of global transmission networks structuring the subject. Lyotard echoes Stiegler's concern that libidinal drives and unconscious investments—formless movements of *jouissance*—are denied by the culture industries in their relentless interpellation of the consumer (*Reader* text 7). Clearly, the philosophers in this book suggest that it would be naive in the extreme to ignore these ideological and sociopolitical issues in any consideration of the culture industries today, including that of cinema filmmaking. As Stiegler writes, echoing Adorno's and Horkheimer's argument:

> speculative marketing, having become hegemonic, systematically exploits the drives, which are divested of every attachment. . . . It is a matter both of the consumerist model and of those instruments that capture and harness consumer attention, implemented by the culture industries and mass media at the beginning of the twentieth century. These instruments, controlled by marketing, bypass and short-circuit the savoir-vivre of consumers, their knowledge of how to live.[31]

And yet, in defiance of the prevailing hegemonic order, and on account of an ongoing belief in cinema's innovative potential, Stiegler, along with nearly all of the philosophers in this book writing since the 1980s to the present, with the possible exception of Baudrillard, knowingly contradict themselves on this crucial point. Far from judging cinema as ideological through and through, they persist in offering analyses that understand cinema to be inventive, dissensual, and a power for the transformation of thought; this is especially true of Deleuze's writings on cinema, but also those of Luce Irigaray, Giorgio Agamben, Žižek, Stanley Cavell, Badiou, Stiegler, and Kaja Silverman (*Reader* texts 6, 11, 12, 14, 16, 17, 18, respectively).

Given that recent and contemporary continental philosophers believe that the Kantian principle of the a priori synthetic judgment outlined in the *Critique of Pure Reason* is the paradigm by which hegemonic power achieves its dominance through ideology and its deployment of technological automation today, the challenge for the philosophers in the book is to develop accounts of perceptual experience, along with their understandings of cinema, that counter or oppose such a paradigm. Benjamin's phenomenology of movement and time as the two related concepts by which to carry out a reevaluation of Kantian reason and experience foreshadows subsequent philosophical thinking in relation to this challenge; in this respect, the titles to Deleuze's two seminal books, *Cinema I: The Movement-Image* (*L'Image-Mouvement*, 1983) and *Cinema II: The Time-Image* (*L'Image-Temps*) (see *Reader* texts 8 and 9), are indicative of the importance of these concepts of movement and time for the continental philosophy of cinema. While the philosophers in the book offer their own singular interpretations of film, informed by a range of philosophical traditions, they are united in seeking forms of experience and alterity that would seem to defy incorporation within ideology. What follows is an account of the various ways in which philosophers after the Second World War to the present have pursued this subject.

Feminism, Patriarchy, and Cinema: Irigaray and Cavell

Two of the essays in the *Reader* are concerned specifically with the issues of representations of woman in cinema: Irigaray's "The Looking Glass, from the Other Side" (1977; *Reader* text 6) and Cavell's text (*Reader* text 14), which outlines his project on representations of woman in cinema that he has explored in two related books, *Pursuits of Happiness: The Hollywood Comedy of Remarriage* (1981) and *Contesting Tears: The Hollywood Melodrama of the Unknown Woman* (1996). For Irigaray, the basis of patriarchal ideology lies in the ongoing legacy of metaphysics and the persistence of a conceptual structure for shaping notions of identity that relies upon binary oppositions organized in terms of a hierarchy. Thus, Irigaray sees patriarchy as a variation upon the same theme of the classical hierarchical division between Essence (the One) and Appearance (the lack of the One), with masculinity, allied to the Phallus, occupying the former position, and femininity as lack denigrated to the latter position. Irigaray refuses such binary logic for what she describes in its stead as "a different economy . . . one that upsets the linearity of a project, undermines the goal-object of a desire, diffuses the polarization towards a single pleasure, disconcerts fidelity towards a single discourse."[32] Woman, Irigaray claims, "puts into question all prevailing economies [and] their calculations"[33] since "she" does not possess an identity and nor does "she" lack one, "For if 'she' says something, it is not, it is already no longer, identical with what she means. What she says is never identical with anything, moreover, rather, it is contiguous. *It touches (upon).* And when it strays too far from that proximity, she breaks off and starts over at 'zero': her body-sex."[34] Woman, therefore, is equivalent with the concept of zero (naught; no-thing), but irreducible to a binary logic of the One in relation to zero, and vice versa. Thus, in her consideration of Michel Soutter's film *The Surveyors* (1972), and in opposition to the goal-oriented desires of the male characters and even Alice herself, who desires to be desired, Irigaray weaves through her writing an-other elusive Alice. Inspired by Lewis Carroll's story of *Alice in Wonderland*, Irigaray's other Alice impels the diegetic narrative of the film in an economy that resists a rationalist mentality, particularly that of the eponymous surveyor who comes to embody a logic of calculation and a destructive desire for possession.

Following the writing of her foundational books on feminism, *Speculum of the Other Woman* (1974) and *This Sex Which Is Not One* (1977), in which the foregoing essay about *The Surveyors* appeared, Irigaray was criticized for resorting to essentialist ideas about woman's body while attempting to overthrow the metaphysical assumptions underlying Freudian and Lacanian psychoanalytic theory. Irigaray herself countered that her writing about woman's body was a strategy designed not to depose psychoanalysis but to contradict its pretensions to scientific law and thereby rediscover its originality:

> For [Freud and the first analysts], every analysis was an opportunity to uncover some new facet of a practice and a theory. Each analysand was listened to as though he or she had some new contribution to make to that practice and that theory. But once psychoanalytic "science" begins to claim to have discovered the universal law of the workings of the unconscious, and once every analysis is no more than an application or a practical demonstration of that law, the only status the new complete "science" can possibly have is that of an era of knowledge already over.[35]

If Irigaray's work is an attempt to reevaluate psychoanalysis and recuperate its practice for feminist and, more widely, liberatory concerns, Cavell's writing, in turn, is also shaped by a similar desire. In his case, this involves a modification of gender readings of cinema of the late twentieth century as they were informed at the time by theories of fetishism and the voyeuristic gaze. As Cavell describes, his books *Pursuits of Happiness: The Hollywood Comedy of Remarriage* and *Contesting Tears: The Hollywood Melodrama of the Unknown Woman* are concerned with woman's struggle for self-fulfillment and recognition in a group of Hollywood comedies and melodramas of the 1930s and 1940s. In the comedies, the female protagonists desire recognition from their partners not just in the private, domestic sphere of their lives, but in the public realm too (see especially *Adam's Rib* [1949]). As such, the films offer an opportunity for the couples to enjoy a rediscovered sense of friendship as the basis for their marriages. However, in the melodramas, especially the films *Stella Dallas* (1937) and *Now, Voyager* (1942), the female protagonists undertake a form of self-creation that exceeds the approval of both men and society.[36] Cavell proposes that these films are not subject to the dominance of the male gaze in Hollywood cinema and do not fit with Laura Mulvey's arguments about the gaze in her influential essay on gender studies, "Visual Pleasure and Narrative Cinema" (1975).[37] The concluding scenes of *Stella Dallas* are particularly important in this regard for Cavell's argument. In this scene, Stella watches her daughter's wedding through a window that is framed like the proverbial cinematic silver screen. While her daughter fulfills the manufactured fantasies of Hollywood, Stella adopts a distance, both literally and metaphorically, from these fantasies through rediscovering the gaze of the mother, as represented by Helen Morrison (played by Barbara O'Neil), a gaze that encourages and supports her independence even though this involves the pain of separation from her daughter.

Phenomenology and Postphenomenology: Merleau-Ponty; Nancy; Stiegler; Agamben; Silverman

Writing in *The Film and the New Psychology* (*Reader* text 4), Merleau-Ponty states, "Kant's remark that, in knowledge imagination serves the understanding, whereas in art understanding serves the imagination is a profound one." Following this axiom, Merleau-Ponty's own phenomenology, including his phenomenology of film—"A movie is not thought; it is perceived"—recuperates the ideas of Kant's third *Critique*, the *Critique of Judgment* (1790), which aimed to affirm the primacy of experience over cognition. Thus, his account of cinema is dedicated to confounding the position of Kant's first *Critique* with respect to the subservient relationship of the faculty of imagination to the understanding, by reversing this hierarchy in line with the third *Critique* where understanding is not only subservient to imagination but elided altogether. Merleau-Ponty asserts that phenomenological perception negotiates the world prior to and without the support of cognition through an embodied form of perception that has an "intelligence" of its own. Drawing on the Gestalt work of Adhémar Gelb (1887–1936) and Kurt Goldstein (1878–1965) with victims of the First World War at the Frankfurt Institute for Research Into the Consequences of Brain Injuries (1916–1933), Merleau-Ponty proposed that perception proceeds in meaningful, structured, and organized wholes, rather than through the sum of parts, and that the most basic perception of a whole is always in terms of a figure against a ground; the basic tendency of perception moving toward an equilibrium and striving for wholeness where a lack might be perceived or an experience is unclear. These ideas inform Merleau-Ponty's theory of film shaping his holistic understanding of the *Kuleshov Effect* (1929) and *On Borrowed Time* (1939), the meanings of which, Merleau-Ponty claims, emerge through the combination of all aspects of the film's means and over the entire temporal duration of the films.

Toward the end of his life, Merleau-Ponty acknowledged that essays such as "The Film and the New Technology" and his book *The Phenomenology of Perception*, both written in the mid-1940s, were partly flawed by an overemphasis upon the body as a site of consciousness (an inversion of the Cartesian stress upon consciousness as a faculty of cognition). The postphenomenological philosophy of Jean-Luc Nancy remains concerned with the body and sensate experience, but, in this context, such "experience" occurs through forms of withdrawal, separation, and discontinuity, rather than an assumption of affective immediacy of contact, as in Merleau-Ponty's early phenomenology. For Nancy, so-called bodily and sensate affects are unconscious and remain unrepresent-able even while the trace of such affects leave indelible yet constantly shifting marks upon the world of experience. In this respect, Nancy's study of Abbas Kiarostami's film *Life and Nothing More* (1992), in his essay "And Life Goes On: Life and Nothing More" (1995; *Reader* text 13) is apt since it is a road movie, but the journeys that it traces are punctuated by a series of unresolved intervals and delays. With this in mind, Nancy proposes the axiom that life is movement, a movement that precedes and goes ahead and, therefore, is never present bodily, spatially, or temporally. The effect of the spatial and temporal dimensions of *Life and Nothing More* and the continual movements that it follows across, and between, a traumatic past (the film was made in the Manjil-Rudbar region of Iran in 1990, shortly after a devastating earthquake) and future time yet to come is, ultimately, to thwart the subject and the audience of a power to judge and condemn the discontinuities of life, including even those of unexpected acci-dents and fatalities. Transcending the desire to judge life by finding it blame-worthy, lacking in a utopic dimension or future requires, Nancy proposes, a radical new ontology based in nonsynthesis, "'Being is not something; it is that something goes on. It is that it continues, neither above nor below the moments, events, singularities and individuals that are discontinuous, but in a manner that is stranger yet: in discontinuity itself, and without fusing it into a *contin-uum*. It continues to discontinue, it discontinues continuously. Like the images of the film.'"

If Benjamin prioritizes reproducibility over the unique and auratic work of art that can only be experienced in one place at a particular time, in his essay "Cinematic Time" Stiegler wishes to affirm the singular as an outcome of repro-ducibility, itself (2011; *Reader* text 16). Taking issue with Husserl's phenome-nology, Stiegler argues that the experience of watching a film that has already been seen, or of listening to a piece of recorded music once again, is always dif-ferent and can never be exactly the same. What lies at the heart of this differ-ence is the dimension of time that intervenes, and changes, the circumstances of repeated experiences as well as affecting the subject him-/herself, a fact that is supported by reproducible technology. In Stiegler's view, reproducibility in the technological sense reveals not only that things can never be the same (again)—"It is obvious only because of the *fact* of recording: it is the phono-graphic *revelation* of the structure of all temporal objects"—but that, as a con-sequence, there is no origin to which the subject can return. There are com-parisons here with Agamben's "Notes on Gesture" (1992; *Reader* text 11), which is also informed by the reproducible as a singular event involving forgetting and loss. By virtue of this loss, Agamben sees a potential for unlearning bodily forms of gesture, and even bodily movements, thereby eliding a purposiveness in representation.

For Stiegler, the loss of origin that he perceives as an effect of a concept of reproducibility has profound implications for Hollywood and its myths of unity and origin, by means of which the ideology of "the American way of life" is constructed and narrativized. In light of the implications of reproducibility, understood in terms of time, Stiegler reads the language of Hollywood through its own unconscious repetitions of différance and play, traces of an ontological withdrawal of Being similar in some senses to Nancy's own ontology although they remain in the form of a haunting rather than an experience of the threshold, as in Nancy (*Reader* text 13). Thus, Scarlett O'Hara, the stubborn, beautiful Southern belle, "loved and hated by the entire world," in *Gone with the Wind* (1939) is haunted by the psychotic Blanche Dubois in Elia Kazan's *A Streetcar Named Desire* (1951), since both characters are woven together through the performances in each film of Vivien Leigh. Of this deconstruction of Hollywood by Hollywood itself, Stiegler exclaims, "How not to feel insane ourselves, carried along by this exemplar of the great, mad American destiny—that never fails at the same time to sell us, through making us laugh and cry in the face of our own fate, the American Way of Life? *America, America!*" *America, America*, it should be said, is the title of a later film by Kazan of 1963 about his own—and contemporary America's—immigrant background.

Merleau-Ponty, himself, attempted to resolve the contradiction that he perceived in his early phenomenological work between the body and world with his concept of "flesh" and of everything emerging from a shared world bearing the same ontological weight. Merleau-Ponty developed these ideas in his book *The Visible and the Invisible* (1964), and they are taken up by Kaja Silverman in her book *Flesh of My Flesh*[38] and, again, in her history of photography. In the first volume of this history, "The Miracle of Analogy: or, The History of Photography, Part 1" (2015; *Reader* text 18), Silverman discusses Chantal Akerman's films, especially *Je tu il elle* (1974) and *The Captive* (2001), the latter of which is based upon Marcel Proust's fifth volume of *In Search of Lost Time* (1923). In this text, Silverman follows Merleau-Ponty's idea that the subject's interwoven mode of existing in the world overlaps or "crosses" with the mode of existence of the material world and, as such, is the condition for the subject's perception. Rather than supporting a subject/object division, this conception allows for mutually interactive relations and correspondences—chiasmatic crossings—between the subject and the world. Silverman argues that in *The Captive*, especially in its opening scene, although not exclusively, the pronouns *I* and *You* (*Je* and *Vous*) become interchangeable between the three characters of the film, Simon, Ariane, and Andrée, each of whom share in a triadic relationship of desire. In Akerman's film *Je tu il elle* (1974), The 'I' and the 'you,'" Silverman says, "shift positions at a dizzying rate, both literally and metaphorically."

Lacanian Psychoanalysis and Žižek

Silverman's reading of Merleau-Ponty's phenomenology involved a departure from her earlier work in cinema studies, the analyses of which drew upon psychoanalysis, film theory, and feminism. At the same time as interpreting the films under discussion, Silverman read these theories, themselves, "symptomatically," showing them "to be motivated at least in part by the same psychic and ideological forces as the films."[39] Subsequently, Silverman became concerned about certain aspects of psychoanalytic theory, especially the stress that Freud and Lacan place upon difference (sexual difference, the difference between the subject and their ego ideals). And this led Silverman in her later writings to Merleau-Ponty's late work for another account of relationality (*Reader* text 18). While Žižek's ideas continue to owe much to Lacanian psychoanalytic theory, he departs from earlier understandings of Lacan of the 1970s and 1980s that tended to stress the register of the Symbolic and the semiotic idea of signification alone, which is what Silverman, too, finds problematic. Žižek orients his theories around *all three orders* of the psyche as determined by Lacan—the Symbolic, the Imaginary, and the Real—with the Symbolic acting in an uncanny relationship with the Real, especially attended to in the text published here, "In His Bold Gaze My Ruin Is Writ Large" (*Reader* text 12).

Following Lacan, Žižek asserts that there is an element of the human organism that remains other to the Symbolic order, an "alien" being that is the unconscious Real and depthless void consisting of anonymous, repetitious drives. Without an individual personality, or even a voice to own, Norman Bates is the quintessence of the disembodied drive, as revealed in *Psycho*'s last scene. However, the impersonal drives of the Real are not the only alternative to the constructed subjectivity governed by the Symbolic order. Žižek proposes that a key scene in *Psycho* points to the possibility of an irreducible enjoyment (jouissance) owing to a linkage, shaped in the form of a Moebius strip or band, between the two orders of the Symbolic and the Real. This scene is that of the murder of the detective Arbogast (and not, as might be expected, the infamous shower scene, even though it marks a crucial turning point in the film's narrative and temporality). Arbogast's murder is edited in such a way that the subjective gaze of the audience is led, initially, to identify with the inquisitive detective and, then, in a sudden cut to look at the scene from the outside perspective of a God's-eye view above the first floor landing. This apparently objective point of view is compromised by the entrance of the murderous "Thing," from the right below, which the audience is forced to "identify" with: an inhuman dimension (the Real) within ourselves. However, this scene has a further meaning for Žižek. The entrance of the murderous "Thing" exposes a blind spot—that of the unconscious Real—in the apparent schema of absolute knowledge represented by the view above. Therefore, Žižek argues, "*a certain radical ignorance must pertain to the status of God Himself* who clearly comes to epitomize a blind run of the symbolic machine . . . more precisely, [God] is *totally unable to understand us, living humans,* since His realm is that of the dead (i.e., since symbol is the murder of thing).'"

Insofar as God (alias the superego that governs the "symbol") inhabits the realm of the dead, and is utterly incapable of accounting for the unconscious drives (in the form of the murderer), this opens the way for a jouissance of the living body, for an enjoyment that proceeds "not only *outside his* knowledge—unbeknownst to him—but also *in his very ignorance*" (*Reader* text 12).

Movement, Time, and Societies of Control:
Lyotard; Deleuze; Rancière; Badiou

In his celebrated 1945 conference on *The Film and the New Psychology,* Merleau-Ponty posed a series of fundamental issues about cinema as a phenomenological, perceptual experience that he predicted would cast a legacy for "a certain way of being, a certain view of the world which belongs to a generation" (*Reader* text 4). Two of the philosophers of this generation who took up the mantle of Merleau-Ponty's project by developing his initial interest in the cinematic perceptive process were Lyotard and Deleuze. Whereas Lyotard turned primarily to experimental, underground cinema—a minoritarian cinema on the side of dissensus—for a phenomenology of cinematic movement as dissonant and excessive, resistant to codification ("Acinema," *Reader* text 7), Deleuze embarked upon a no less radical taxonomy of types of affectivity in respect to mainstream cinema.

Deleuze's point of departure for his writings on cinema is through Henri Bergson's phenomenology, which views every element in the universe as mutually interactive "images" and affects in continual interactive movement and change: what he terms "duration" (*durée*; *Reader* text 1). Eliding Western conceptions of space and measurement, Deleuze dismisses the common idea of film as a succession of images, whether still or otherwise, similar to the way Bergson opposed the conception of movement as a succession of separate elements. Deleuze proposes in "Cinema I: The Movement-Image" (*Reader* text 8) that classical cinema prior to the Second World War embodies a modern conception of movement "capable of thinking the production of the new."[40] Following Bergson's phenomenology, Deleuze conceives of modern cinema as an affective realm of universal variation without a center, in which all images act and react in relation to one another in a process of continuous relationality and temporal flux.

However, cinematic images are not entirely identical to the images of the phenomenal world; instead, cinema uses and adapts them as its plastic material, thereby creating its own "concepts"—affects—that are unique to cinema. In "Cinema I: The Movement-Image," Deleuze organizes these concepts into four types of temporal flux that operate as affects of bodies (perception-images), actions (the action-image), qualities (affection-image), and relations (mental- or relation-images). In the movement-image, time is conceived of in terms of an ever changing whole, an organic totality to which both the past and the future are connected. However, Deleuze argues that, despite its radical approach to movement and space, the movement-image remains organized by means of edited *linkages* (cuts, changes of camera angles, dissolves, fades, and so on) and units of time. Ultimately, therefore, time remains subordinated to movement in the cinema of the movement-image.

Deleuze observes that a sociopolitical and existential crisis occurred after the Second World War that fundamentally changed cinema, destroying its sensory-motor schema of organized succession. The aftermath of the war was a crucial turning point in modern consciousness, leading to a cinema in which time is no longer subordinate to movement (the time-image encompasses films from Italian neorealism through Yasujiro Ozu, Orson Welles, Michelangelo Antonioni, Alain Resnais, Chris Marker, Jean-Luc Godard, Jacques Rivette, and Jean-Marie Straub and Danièle Huillet). In this regard, Rancière offers a helpful explanation of the distinctions that Deleuze draws between the movement-image and the time-image as follows:

> The movement-image, the image organized according to the logic of sensory-motor schema, is conceived of as being but one element in a natural arrangement with other images within a logic of the set [*ensemble*] analogous to that of the finalized coordination of our perceptions and actions. The time-image is characterized by a rupture with this logic, by the appearance—in Rossellini—of pure optical and sound situations that are no longer transformed into incidents. From these pure optical and sound situations eventually emerges—in Welles—the crystal image, the image that no longer links up to another actual image, but only to its own virtual image.[41]

Once cinematic images ceased to be linked up by means of editing to successive units of movement in the manner of the movement-image, Deleuze proposes that they open up to time in a pure form of becoming. As with "Cinema I: The Movement-Image" the film directors discussed in "Cinema II: The Time-Image" (*Reader* text 9) exemplify different approaches to presenting time. In the work of these directors, space and movement are no longer predetermined or coherently organized: space has become "any-space-whatever." Furthermore, Deleuze observes that these films are composed of a series of edited "presents" as in, for instance, the opening sequence of Robert Bresson's *Au hasard Balthazar* (1966) or the concluding scenes of Antonioni's *The Eclipse* (1962). Deleuze argues that these "presents," formulated in terms of 1+,1+,1+, etc., form links only on condition that they are nonlinks: voids arising from, and reaching into, infinity. Additionally, Deleuze discusses the films of Hans Jürgen Syberberg, the Straubs, and Marguerite Duras as exemplifications of the time-image, for their disruption of the customary syncing of sound, including the voice, with the images on screen. The disjunction that these filmmakers introduce into this relationship of the audible and visible, Deleuze claims, completes a transformation of the elements (air, earth, water, fire) that cinematic montage began with the films of Abel Gance in France and Expressionist cinema in Germany.

Deleuze conjectures that cinema's invention of the time-image in the postwar period may still be relevant and affirmative for the electronic image today, noting how the cinema of Bresson's "automatism," the puppet and hypnotized characters of Eric Rohmer and Alain Robbe-Grillet and Resnais's "zombies" are already structured through a technics of information and data rather than a movement of energy and motivity oriented around a source such as the body. In Ozu's films, as well as films such as Michael Snow's *The Central Region* (1971), "Space muddles its directions, its orientations and loses all primacy of the vertical axis that could determine them," so that even the cinema screen hung vertically and viewed as a framed window into a pictorial space by an upright, seated audience is challenged as a convention. Deleuze argues that, effectively, in the cinema of Ozu and Snow the image is arranged across a flat screen that is seen as an opaque surface without depth (and, indeed, other types of frame were proposed by the cinema of the time-image such as Max Ophuls's mirror-frame (images cut into segments, as in some of the famous scenes of *Madame de . . .* [1953] and *Lola Montès* [1955]) and Hitchcock's idea of a screen surrounding the audience). Deleuze argues that in films such as *A Married Woman* (1964) and *Two or Three Things I Know About Her* (1967), Godard created a mise-en-scène that was akin to a system of informatics, the paradigm for which is not nature viewed pictorially in perspectival depth from a fixed position, but a network of information and incessant messages across the screen—multiple images cut or slid into other images that are not governed by units of succession (as in the movement-image) but by a continual exchange of undecidable contradictions and discontinuities. According to Deleuze, cinema anticipated and even participated in the creation of today's era of digital information, but he emphasizes the fact that this era is not defined by the development of new technologies per se but, echoing Benjamin, how such technologies are deployed and whether they are, "to the service of a powerful, obscure, condensed will to art" or put to use by reactionary forces of control. Deleuze weighs up these options when he says, "It is the time-image which calls on an original regime of images and signs, before electronics spoils it or, in contrast, relaunches it."

Both Rancière and Badiou have their differences with Deleuze's philosophy of cinema (*Reader* texts 15 and 16). Rancière is particularly skeptical, questioning Deleuze's account of history concerning his proposed transition from the movement-image to the time-image in the postwar period, and his conception of the image as part of a natural history of images that are autonomous, possessing the capacity to elide signification and overdetermined meanings.[42] What Rancière wishes to emphasize about film, in contrast to Deleuze, is that it is composed of a constant tension between classical narrative construction, ultimately derived from Aristotle's idea of "a story well told" (*muthos*), and its visual and sensate affects that have the potential to exceed signification (*opsis*). Of the latter tendency (opsis), Rancière cites examples such as the concluding scenes of descent and suicide in Roberto Rossellini's *Germany Year Zero* (1948) and Bresson's *Mouchette* (1967),[43] both of which, he claims, defy meaning and are, therefore, dissensual. Rancière's philosophy of cinema revolves around such moments as these in Rossellini's and Bresson's films—moments that he describes as "free-falls into the void"—that seem to defy all causal law constructed through the films' narratives (muthos), even though they remain dependent upon them for their affect. Here lies the irreducible disparity between the Aristotelian concepts of muthos (narrative and signification) and opsis (sensate experience) that Rancière wishes to affirm about cinema.

In Fritz Lang's *M* (1931), the scenes that fascinate Rancière are those in which the narrative is temporarily upheld by moments of flaneurism, but also, particularly, the trial scene toward the end of the film in which it is shown that both the murderer's and the witnesses' sense of self are not entirely based in preexisting categories of knowledge, as might be assumed from Kant's *Critique of Pure Reason* (*Reader* text 15). The conclusion to be gained from Rancière's reading of this scene is that, for him, cinema—the "old box of illusions" as he affectionately describes it—is a form of mimesis that has its own independent power to communicate and emotionally move the addressee even beyond ideology. Such dissensus, according to Rancière, requires that it works against the ordering of narratives that come under the aegis of consensual knowledge.

While Rancière recognizes that today's regime of control functions through a system of statistical power that constructs the subject in its own image of consumerist desires, nevertheless, he highlights the fact that this statistical "knowledge" is still a construct. In *While the City Sleeps,* Mobley, who personifies today's regime of power, adopts mimetically a knowledge that he does not actually possess. Rancière believes that this *performance* of knowledge always needs to be borne in mind when considering the status of today's transmissive methods of interpellation. In this regard, he believes it is important to recall Plato's critique of Homer in *The Republic* where he asks how the epic poet is supposed to "know" everything his characters—warriors and kings—know (since this is impossible, Plato feels entitled to consign Homer's mimetic art to the realm of simulacra). Rancière's hope is that this fable can still prove liberating for understanding that, ultimately, "knowledge" as an instrument of interpellation in today's data economy is a construct and a fabrication.

Badiou has a more qualified view of Deleuze's cinema project than Rancière, finding in it much of worth, even while he believes it has shortcomings. In his essay, "Cinema as Philosophical Experimentation" (2003; *Reader* text 16), Badiou upholds Deleuze's view that cinema and philosophy are fundamentally different praxes, "Cinema thinks with images, while philosophy thinks with concepts,"[44] and, like Deleuze, he proposes that a relationship between these two praxes can be affirmed which respects their differences. In order to think this relationship, Badiou introduces the notion of a "disjunctive synthesis" that recognizes the difference—Badiou calls it a "rupture"—between cinema and philosophy, but that also allows for a synthesis between these different praxes through a mutual sense of ontological transformation: "[Cinema] makes possible a transformation of the thinking of being and a fundamental transformation of philosophy."[45] Thus, Badiou observes that Deleuze's project consists of an ordering of cinema's images in terms of the movement-image and the time-image, and it is through this ordering that a new philosophical creation, "a new theory of the image," comes into existence, which, in turn, has the power to transform both philosophy and thought.

Ultimately, however, Badiou believes that there are limitations to Deleuze's philosophy of cinema, and this leads him to ask, "does cinema *really* have to be thought on the basis of the category of images?"[46] Underlying Badiou's recourse to this question is his belief that the advent of cinema is a transformative "event" that, as Benjamin also believed (*Reader* text 2), marks the possibility for technology to be put into the service of the masses, rather than vice versa. As such, cinema represents the unrepresentable—the freedom of the masses—as is the case with other momentous events in cultural and political history (the French Revolution of 1789 being, for Badiou, the paradigmatic event in this sense).

In keeping with Adorno and Horkheimer, Badiou remains aware that "cinema is *first and foremost* an industry" that both reinforces and reproduces the fantasies of the social imaginary. The consequence of this, Badiou says, is that cinema's audience only ever see what they hope to see, which are "disappointing things." Cinema, Badiou claims, consists of an oscillation between desire and disappointment that "can actually be called 'pornography.'" Cinema's Sisyphean task, therefore, is to resist the impurity of its means and thereby engage the audience in its own struggle against oppression. For Badiou, this struggle is the essence of cinema's potential, requiring a disjunctive mode of analysis for its representation that differs from Deleuze's ontological approach to cinema as an affective apparatus. Like Adorno, Stiegler, and others, Badiou believes that cinema is a problematic and regressive form of ideology, but he argues that it is also a site of continuing resistance that remains true to its evental status:

> At bottom, when we see a film we are seeing a fight: the struggle against the material's impurity. We don't see only the result, only the time-images or the movement-images; we see the battle, that artistic battle against impurity. And the battle is won at times and lost at others, even in the same film. A great film is one in which there are a lot of victories, only a few defeats for a lot of victories. That is why a great film always has something heroic about it. It is also why the relationship with cinema isn't one of contemplation but of participation, solidarity, admiration, or even jealousy, irritation, or hatred. Cinema's hand-to-hand combat amazes us. We take part in it; we assess the victories; we assess the defeats; we admire the creation of a few moments of purity. Those victorious moments are so extraordinary that they account for cinema's emotional power. There is an emotion of combat: all of a sudden the purity of an image seizes us and, similarly, so does the outcome of a battle. That is also why cinema is an art that makes you cry. You cry from joy; you cry from love, from fear, from rage; you cry on account of the victories and sometimes on account of the defeats. Something almost miraculous happens when cinema manages to extract a little bit of purity from all that is worst in the world.

* * *

Although Badiou and Deleuze are at variance over their understanding and treatment of cinema, both believe that philosophy learns from cinema and is inspired by it. Perhaps each philosopher in this book would agree with this; but, in relation to the deep anxiety among philosophers concerning capitalist hegemony and the "states of control" that Deleuze refers to predominating today, it is interesting, by way of conclusion, to read Kristeva's existential understanding of the consequences of this situation as explored in her essay "The Malady of Grief: Marguerite Duras" (1987; *Reader* text 10). Kristeva notes the discrepancy today that exists between the private and political domains. The latter was once, according to Hannah Arendt, "the field where human freedom unfurled," but now "the modern political domain is massively, in totalitarian fashion, social, leveling, exhausting." The effect of this, Kristeva argues, is to make the private domain a realm of suffering that is so entirely absorbing that it fills "the whole of the real . . . invalidating any other concern." With the private domain cut off from the political domain, the latter is rendered "unreal" from the perspective of the former, especially as the political has no power to remedy private suffering. By definition, psychosis cannot overcome the oppressive forces of the political. On the other hand, the private lies beyond the reach of the political; indeed, Kristeva argues that the outcrop of new variants of psychoses currently afflicting the social—depression, manic-depressive states, borderline states, false selves—defy representation and the symbolic order altogether. Therefore, Kristeva claims that Alain Resnais's film *Hiroshima mon amour* (1959), for which Marguerite Duras wrote the script, is an allegory of our times. The story of the film is about both love *and* its impossibility—an impossible love because the political domain has unleashed a malady of grief and death upon the world, which prohibits any romantic illusions about love as a conquering force, yet affirmatory because to love is to acknowledge and suffer difference. Under certain circumstances, the disjunctive combination of these two tendencies can provoke a jouissance of such intensity that it is inflammatory: *Hiroshima mon amour.*

Notes

1. The philosophers in the *Reader* refer principally to the classical canon of films: European, Hollywood, and Japanese cinema of the modern period. There are exceptions to this, such as Nancy, who has written about the films of Claire Denis and Abbas Kiorastami (*Reader* text 13). Also Žižek who embraces both the canon of modern films plus many recent movies, especially those produced in Hollywood (for example, *The Matrix* and the *Batman* trilogy).
2. Anton Kaes, *Shell Shock Cinema: Weimar Culture and the Wounds of War* (Princeton: Princeton University Press, 2009), p. 207.
3. Eugen Tannenbaum, "Der Grofsfilm," in *Der Film von Morgen*, ed. Hugo Zehder (Berlin: Kämmerer, 1923), pp. 63, 207.
4. Siegfried Kracauer, *The Mass Ornament: The Weimar Essays*, ed. and trans. Thomas Y. Levin (Cambridge, MA: Harvard University Press, 1995), p. 325.
5. Kracauer, p. 94.
6. Walter Benjamin, *Walter Benjamin: Selected Writings*, vol. 3: *1935–1938*, ed. Howard Eiland and Michael W. Jennings, trans. Edmund Jephcott, Howard Eiland, and others (Cambridge, MA: Belknap Press of Harvard University Press, 2006).
7. On the one hand, Kracauer thought that social change was imminent remarking that "walking in the streets of Berlin one is not seldom struck by the momentary insight that one day all this will suddenly burst apart" (Kracauer, *The Mass Ornament*, p. 327). On the other hand, Kracauer believed that cinema's uncanny sense of artifice, its two-dimensional representation of moving reality, could be ignored all too easily by its audiences. Thus, he urged film to "aim radically toward a kind of distraction that exposes disintegration instead of masking it." Adding, by way of conclusion, "It could be done in Berlin, home of the masses—who so easily allow themselves to be stupefied only because they are so close to the truth" (p. 328).
8. Ultimately, the idea of a universal engagement with the art work that is available to all commences with Kant's *Critique of Judgment* (1790). The German Romantic thinkers, especially Schiller in his *Letters upon the Aesthetic Education of Man* (1794), believed that art had the capacity to transform the social and that humankind is the material upon which the artist shapes and works. Thereafter, the idea of art as the

impetus for social change was adopted by Wagner and became a feature of many modernist philosophies of art—notably, that of the Bauhaus.

9. Theodor W. Adorno and Max Horkheimer, "The Concept of Enlightenment," in *Dialectic of Enlightenment*, trans. John Cumming (London: Verso, 1997), p. 3.

10. Adorno and Horkheimer, p. 3.

11. Famously, Kant described his project in the *Critique of Pure Reason* as a "Copernican revolution" involving a shift from the question "what must the mind be like in order to know?" to the question "what must objects be like in order to be known?" Ultimately, Kant's answer to this latter question was that objects are conformable to the categories of understanding that he established in the *Critique*.

12. These categories tend to assume questionable notions of unity, continuity, and coherence of representation.

13. Adorno and Horkheimer, *Dialectic of Enlightenment*, p. xvi.

14. Adorno and Horkheimer, p. xvi

15. Walter Benjamin, "On the Program of the Coming Philosophy" (1918), trans. Mark Ritter, in *Selected Writings*, vol. 1: *1913–1926*, ed. Marcus Bullock and Michael W. Jennings (Cambridge, MA: Belknap Press of Harvard University Press, 1997), p. 104.

16. In this regard, Benjamin may have been thinking specifically of the work of the Russian filmmaker Sergei Eisenstein, who often spoke of his use of montage in the 1920s as seeking to induce an affect of "shock" in the audience. Additionally, shock arises from an aesthetic sensitivity to perceiving reality in ways never experienced before by virtue of the originality of cinematic images transforming the world. This experience is what Benjamin calls in "The Work of Art . . ." "the optical unconscious."

17. This quotation appears in Benjamin's third version of "The Work of Art . . ." and is attributed to Georges Duhamel, *Scènes de la vie future* (Paris, 1930), p. 52, cf. Walter Benjamin, "The Work of Art in the Age of Mechanical Reproduction," in *Illuminations*, ed. Hannah Arendt, trans. Harry Zohn (London: Fontana/Collins, 1982), section 14, p. 240.

18. On March 18, 1936, Adorno wrote a letter from Oxford to Benjamin in Paris responding to the latter's request for his opinion about the second draft of "The Work of Art in the Age of Its Technological Reproducibility" that is republished here (*Reader* text 2). The letter highlights the differences between the two writers on cinema. Adorno criticizes Benjamin for not being sufficiently dialectical, sacrificing the political value of the autonomous, avant-garde work of art for the sake of film. As such, Adorno believes that Benjamin does not hold avant-garde art and popular culture (including cinema) in a comprehensive dialectical relation that would understand them as "torn halves of an integral freedom, to which, however, they do not add up." Whereas Benjamin envisaged political and affective potential in filmic montage and distraction, Adorno sees none. See Theodor W. Adorno and Walter Benjamin, *The Complete Correspondence, 1928–1940*, ed. Henri Lonitz, trans. Nicholas Walker (Cambridge: Polity, 1999), pp. 127–34. Adorno and Horkheimer reiterate this point in their essay "The Culture Industry: Enlightenment as Mass Deception" (*Reader* text 3), "[Films] are so designed that quickness, powers of observation, and experience are undeniably needed to apprehend them at all; yet sustained thought is out of the question if the spectator is not to miss the relentless rush of facts. Even though the effort required for his response is semi-automatic, no scope is left for the imagination."

19. "Postscript on the Societies of Control," *October* 59 (Winter 1992): 3–7, first published in *L'Autre*, no. 1 (May 1990). Deleuze notes that Foucault's idea of a disciplinary society organized through institutions (the family, school, factories, prisons, hospitals and

so on) is presently being replaced by a 'numerical language of control . . . made of codes that mark access to information, or reject it.'

20. Gilles Deleuze, *Cinema II: The Time-Image*, trans. Hugh Tomlinson and Robert Galeta (London: Athlone, 1989), p. 165.
21. Deleuze, p. 165.
22. A term Deleuze uses to indicate a form of affective sensibility.
23. Deleuze, *Cinema II: The Time-Image*, p. 164.
24. Deleuze, 164.
25. Alain Badiou, "Cinema as Philosophical Experimentation," in *Cinema*, trans. Susan Spitzer (Cambridge: Polity, 2013), p. 230.
26. Badiou, p. 230.
27. Bernard Stiegler, "Automatic Society: Londres, février 2015," *Journal of Visual Art Practice* 15, nos. 2–3 (2016): 194.
28. Stiegler, p. 194.
29. Theodor Adorno and Max Horkheimer, "The Culture Industry: Enlightenment as Mass Deception," in *Dialectic of Enlightenment*, trans. John Cumming (London: Verso, 1997), p. 134.
30. Deleuze, *Cinema II: The Time-Image*, p. 164.
31. Stiegler, "Automatic Society," p. 195.
32. Luce Irigaray, "This Sex Which Is Not One," in *This Sex Which Is Not One*, trans. Catherine Porter with Carolyn Burke (Ithaca, NY: Cornell University Press, 1985), p. 30.
33. Irigaray, p. 31.
34. Irigaray, p. 29.
35. Luce Irigaray, "The Poverty of Psychoanalysis," in *The Irigaray Reader*, ed. Margaret Whitford (Oxford: Blackwell, 1991), pp. 79–104.
36. See especially the chapters "Ugly Duckling Funny Butterfly: Bette Davis and *Now Voyager*" and "Stella's Taste: Reading *Stella* Dallas" in Cavell's *Contesting Tears: The Hollywood Melodrama of the Unknown Woman* (Chicago: University of Chicago Press, 1996), pp. 115–150 and 197–222, respectively.
37. Laura Mulvey, "Visual Pleasure and Narrative Cinema," *Screen* 16, no. 3 (1975): 6–18.
38. Kaja Silverman, *Flesh of My Flesh* (Stanford: Stanford University Press, 2009).
39. Cf. Kaja Silverman, *The Acoustic Mirror: The Female Voice in Psychoanalysis and Cinema* (Bloomington: Indiana University Press, 1988), p. x.
40. Gilles Deleuze, *Cinema I: The Movement-Image*, trans. Hugh Tomlinson and Barbara Habberjam (London: Athlone, 1986), p. 7.
41. Jacques Rancière, "From One Image to Another? Deleuze and the Ages of Cinema," in *Film Fables*, trans. Emiliano Battista (Oxford: Berg, 2006), p. 107.
42. Rancière, pp. 107–23.
43. Jacques Rancière, "Falling Bodies: Rossellini's Physics," in *Film Fables*, pp. 125–42; Rancière, "*Mouchette* and the Paradoxes of the Language of Images," in *The Intervals of Cinema* (London: Verso, 2014), pp. 41–67.
44. Badiou, "Cinema as Philosophical Experimentation," p. 223.
45. Badiou, p. 223.
46. Badiou, p. 223.

CHAPTER 1

CREATIVE EVOLUTION

HENRI BERGSON

The universe endures. *The more we study the nature of time, the more we shall comprehend that duration means invention, the creation of forms, the continual elaboration of the absolutely new.*

—*Creative Evolution* (1907)

Henri Bergson (1859–1941) was appointed chair of ancient philosophy at the Collège de France in 1900. In 1922 he became president of the International Commission for Intellectual Cooperation (a precursor of UNESCO) and was awarded the Nobel Prize in Literature in 1927. A visionary thinker, Bergson created an original account of the phenomenological, material world that confounded traditional ideas of space and time as well as long-established divisions between subject and object, mind and matter, and cause and effect.

As part of his phenomenology, Bergson developed radical accounts of both movement and time, which he thought were not upheld by cinema's approach to these two phenomena, as is evidenced in what he says about cinema in the accompanying text from *Creative Evolution* (1907). However, Bergson's position in the philosophy of cinema is assured not only because of this critique but owing to his philosophical influence upon Gilles Deleuze, whose two books on cinema, *Cinema I: The Movement-Image* and *Cinema II: The Time-Image* (*Reader* texts 8 and 9), were inspired by his work. (As Deleuze points out, Bergson's critique of cinema was based on early examples of film prior to cinema's expanded use of montage, which is essential for his own reading of its phenomenology).

Bergson's phenomenology conceives of matter as an indivisible whole composed of dynamic, interrelated, and mutually affective relations (for which Bergson used the comprehensive term *images*). Keith Ansell Pearson provides a vivid sketch of the ever changing affective universe Bergson envisioned,

> Everything that lives perceives, from simple beings that vibrate to complex beings that are able to contract trillions of vibrations and oscillations within a single perception. . . . Within the moving continuity of the real we can posit and locate the boundaries of bodies that exist in various degrees of individuation (. . . from the contractions of a simple protoplasm to living systems with highly developed nervous systems). All these bodies change "at every moment," resolving themselves into groups of qualities consisting of a succession of elementary movements. The stability of a body lies in its instability—it never ceases changing and it changes qualities without ceasing to be or become what it is . . . What is "real" are two things: the moving continuity of the whole and the continual change of form within a living body.[1]

Guided by this phenomenology of enduring and affective change, Bergson developed a radical conception of time that is continuous yet not organized according to the conventional, chronological terms of a past—present—future continuum. The thrust of Bergson's philosophy arose out of a fundamental critique of the tendency of Western philosophy and discourse to analyze both spatial movement and time by means of measurable units of numbers, successive progressions, and relationships of similarities or differences in kind. In place of methods of quantification and spatialization that support identitarian suppositions, Bergson outlined an entirely new way of thinking that embraced ideas of qualitative and ceaseless change as the conditions of both matter and time, for which he adopted the term *duration* (*durée*).

In the accompanying passages of writing from *Creative Evolution* (1907), Bergson proposes that physical and emotional states—"I am warm or cold, I am merry or sad, I work or do nothing"—shift constantly through time and are indivisible, since they partake in a ceaseless movement of qualitative changes. Relationships, Bergson argues, are not composed of individuated or separate identities, but of images in a state of perpetual change within themselves and between each other, as illustrated by his account of mixing a glass of water with sugar and waiting impatiently until the sugar dissolves. Writing about this "experiment," Ronald Bogue states,

> for Bergson there are ultimately no things in the universe but simply vibrations of a whole. The water, sugar, glass, and observer are all merely perturbations, movements, flows, each a different rhythm of an unfolding *durée*. The quality of the water obviously changes as the sugar dissolves, but the observer also changes, as does the glass (albeit it at a very slow pace). And there is no reason to restrict the number of changing elements to the water, sugar, glass, and observer.[2]

Bergson points out that "matter has a tendency to constitute isolable systems" and closed sets, but he emphasizes that this "is only a tendency," and even science recognizes that isolating systems from one another is only a provisional step; thus, to isolate artificially parts of the whole is to view erroneously the "whole" as if it, too, was a totality. As Bergson argues, the solar system is not a closed unit, "Our sun radiates heat and light beyond the farthest planet" reaching by a thread to the rest of the universe. This thread, Bergson acknowledges, "is doubtless very tenuous. Nevertheless, it is along this thread that is transmitted down to the smallest particle of the world in which we live the duration immanent to the whole of the universe." By this reasoning, Bergson holds that the universe is like a kaleidoscope in which there is no center since everything is bound together in mutually affective relations. The same holds true of all "bodies," including the brain and the nervous system, all of which exist in relation with the images of the material world.

The term *duration* (*durée*) in Bergson's philosophy has several connotations referring to the dynamic movement of the material world in an open, nondeterminable "Whole" and, in the same instance, to a conception of time that is enduring insofar as it passes and is not conformable even to retrospective analyses intent upon discovering fixed or stable points. For this reason, Bergson discounts the possibility of a historiography of the universe and of matter based upon mathematical, spatialized principles of time; thus, Bergson says, the experiment with the dissolving sugar in which the subject-object division is broken down is a "little fact big with meaning."

Memory, Bergson claims, constantly accrues experiences exponentially—"rolling upon itself, as a snowball on the snow"—and conserves everything that has ever occurred in the unconscious, "all that we have felt, thought and willed from our earliest infancy." Nevertheless, memory is not static, an inactive archive of recollections, rather it exists in conjunction with the present in a mutual state of transformation, with the consequence that the past cannot be repeated and that every moment is, and was, different and "unforeseeable" as future moments. Bergson states that the creative actualization of the past by the present produces "an original moment of a no less original history"—by which he implies that memory preserves the past but that, effectively, this past is "virtual," as selective aspects of the past are continually activated anew and recontextualized by the present; in other words, nothing is pregiven in a cause-effect relation of determinism. From this it follows that in Bergson's philosophy the present is not conditioned by a metaphysics of presence, but, rather, as Deleuze suggests in his books on cinema, by a twofold temporal process in which the virtual past is actualized in a present that opens toward the future. Memory—the past—is continually preserved *and* changed in the same instance by the contingent present and never remains the same. Just as the past is discontinuous, so time is nonchronological, while the future is both to come *and* in process of creation now. Bergson's reading of Zeno's fable of the flying arrow extends these ideas of duration in which he proposes that the arrow's flight is composed of a countless myriad of affects and indivisible movements, qualities and not quantities. There is no present point of the arrow in which it can be stabilized or understood as being at rest, a matter of extension and quantity and, therefore, divisible, since it is conditioned by the flux that is "movement." Consequentially, the temporal existence of the flying arrow is a present that is always already a contraction of past, present, and future times taken together. As Deleuze says about Bergson's conception of time, "'the only subjectivity is time, non-chronological time grasped in its foundation, and it is we who are internal to time, not the other way round. . . . Time is not the interior in us, but just the opposite, the interiority in which we are, in which we move, live and change.'"[3]

Bergson's conception of duration provides the context for his infamous criticism of cinema's representation of movement. Rightly, Bergson understood movement in film to be composed from sequences of individual frames that, classically, are projected at twenty-four frames a second (or eighteen, at the outset of cinema) so as to give the illusion of continuous movement. Bergson believed that, in breaking down movement into sequences of static movements and separate slices of time, the cinematographical method reiterated the error of spatializing movement into divisible parts. With respect to this point, Bergson gives the analogy of looking at a series of kaleidoscopic images and seeing them as individual, successive images without taking into account that the images are formed through (their) disruption. Thus, Bergson compares "*the mechanism of our ordinary knowledge*," based on mathematical quantification, and the cinematographical method of capturing movement—for instance, of "the marching past of a regiment"—via "a series of [static] snapshots."

It will be seen in "Cinema I: The Movement-Image" (*Reader* text 8) that Deleuze responds to Bergson's criticism of cinema suggesting that his philosophy of duration and phenomenological vitalism can be used against his critical judgment on cinema. And, as such, Deleuze embraces Bergson's phenomenology for his own purposes in his books on cinema (*Reader* texts 8 and 9).

Chapter I

The Evolution of Life-Mechanism and Teleology

The existence of which we are most assured and which we know best is unquestionably our own, for of every other object we have notions which may be considered external and superficial, whereas, of ourselves, our perception is internal and profound. What, then, do we find? In this privileged case, what is the precise meaning of the word "exist"?. . .

I find, first of all, that I pass from state to state. I am warm or cold, I am merry or sad, I work or I do nothing, I look at what is around me or I think of something else. Sensations, feelings, volitions, ideas—such are the changes into which my existence is divided and which color it in turns. I change, then, without ceasing. But this is not saying enough. Change is far more radical than we are at first inclined to suppose.

For I speak of each of my states as if it formed a block and were a separate whole. I say indeed that I change, but the change seems to me to reside in the passage from one state to the next: of each state, taken separately, I am apt to think that it remains the same during all the time that it prevails. Nevertheless, a slight effort of attention would reveal to me that there is no feeling, no idea, no volition which is not undergoing change every moment: if a mental state ceased to vary, its duration would cease to flow. Let us take the most stable of internal states, the visual perception of a motionless external object. The object may remain the same, I may look at it from the same side, at the same angle, in the same light; nevertheless the vision I now have of it differs from that which I have just had, even if only because the one is an instant older than the other. My memory is there, which conveys something of the past into the present. My mental state, as it advances on the road of time, is continually swelling with the duration which it accumulates: it goes on increasing—rolling upon itself, as a snowball on the snow. Still more is this the case with states more deeply internal, such as sensations, feelings, desires, etc., which do not correspond, like a simple visual perception, to an unvarying external object. But it is expedient to disregard this uninterrupted change, and to notice it only when it becomes sufficient to impress a new attitude on the body, a new direction on the attention. Then, and then only, we find that our state has changed. The truth is that we change without ceasing, and that the state itself is nothing but change.

This amounts to saying that there is no essential difference between passing from one state to another and persisting in the same state. If the state which "remains the same" is more varied than we think, on the other hand the passing from one state to another resembles, more than we imagine, a single state being prolonged; the transition is continuous. But, just because we close our eyes to the unceasing variation of every psychical state, we are obliged, when the change has become so considerable as to force itself on our attention, to speak as if a new state were placed alongside the previous one. Of this new state we assume that it remains unvarying in its turn, and so on endlessly. The apparent discontinuity of the psychical life is then due to our attention being fixed on it by a series of separate acts: actually there is only a gentle slope; but in following the broken line of our acts of attention, we think we perceive separate steps. True, our psychic life is full of the unforeseen. A thousand incidents arise, which seem to be cut off from those which precede them, and to be disconnected from those which follow. Discontinuous though they appear, however, in point of fact they stand out against the continuity of a background on which they are designed, and to which indeed they owe the intervals that separate them; they are the beats of the drum which break forth here and there in the symphony. Our attention fixes on them because they interest it more, but each of them is borne by the fluid mass of our whole psychical existence. Each is only the best illuminated point of a moving zone which comprises all that we feel or think or will—all, in short, that we are at any given moment. It is this entire zone which in reality makes up our state. Now, states thus defined cannot be regarded as distinct elements. They continue each other in an endless flow . . .

Duration is the continuous progress of the past which gnaws into the future and which swells as it advances. And as the past grows without ceasing, so also there is no limit to its preservation. Memory, as we have tried to prove,[4] is not a faculty of putting away recollections in a drawer, or of inscribing them in a register. There is no register, no drawer; there is not even, properly speaking, a faculty, for a faculty works intermittently, when it will or when it can, whilst the piling up of the past upon the past goes on without relaxation. In reality, the past is preserved by itself, automatically. In its entirety, probably, it follows us at every instant; all that we have felt, thought and willed from our earliest infancy is there, leaning over the present which is about to join it, pressing against the portals of consciousness that would fain leave it outside. The cerebral mechanism is arranged just so as to drive back into the unconscious almost the whole of this past, and to admit beyond the threshold only that which can cast light on the present situation or further the action now being prepared—in short, only that which can give *useful* work. At the most, a few superfluous recollections may succeed in smuggling themselves through the half-open door. These memories, messengers from the unconscious, remind us of what we are dragging behind us unawares. But, even though we may have no distinct idea of it, we feel vaguely that our past remains present to us. What are we, in fact, what is our *character*, if not the condensation of the history that we have lived from our birth—nay, even before our birth, since we bring with us prenatal dispositions? Doubtless we think with only a small part of our past, but it is with our entire past, including the original bent of our soul, that we desire, will and act. Our past, then, as a whole, is made manifest to us in its impulse; it is felt in the form of tendency, although a small part of it only is known in the form of idea.

From this survival of the past it follows that consciousness cannot go through the same state twice. The circumstances may still be the same, but they will act no longer on the same person, since they find him at a new moment of his history. Our personality, which is being built up each instant with its accumulated experience, changes without ceasing. By changing, it prevents any state, although superficially identical with another, from ever repeating it in its very depth. That is why our duration is irreversible. We could not live over again a single moment, for we should have to begin by effacing the memory of all that had followed. Even could we erase this memory from our intellect, we could not from our will.

Thus our personality shoots, grows and ripens without ceasing. Each of its moments is something new added to what was before. We may go further: it is not only something new, but something unforeseeable. Doubtless, my present state is explained by what was in me and by what was acting on me a moment ago. In analyzing it I should find no other elements. But even a superhuman intelligence would not have been able to foresee the simple indivisible form which gives to these purely abstract elements their concrete organization. For to foresee consists of projecting into the future what has been perceived in the past, or of imagining for a later time a new grouping, in a new order, of elements already perceived. But that which has never been perceived, and which is at the same time simple, is necessarily unforeseeable. Now such is the case with each of our states, regarded as a moment in a history that is gradually unfolding: it is simple, and it cannot have been already perceived, since it concentrates in its indivisibility all that has been perceived and what the present is adding to it besides. It is an original moment of a no less original history . . .

If I want to mix a glass of sugar and water, I must, willy nilly, wait until the sugar melts. This little fact is big with meaning. For here the time I have to wait is not that mathematical time which would apply equally well to the entire history of the material World, even if that history were spread out instantaneously in space. It coincides with my impatience, that is to say, with a certain portion of my own duration, which I cannot protract or contract as I like. It is no longer something *thought*, it is something *lived*. It is no longer a relation, it is an absolute. What else can this mean than that the glass of water, the sugar, and the process of the sugar's melting in the water are abstractions, and that the

Whole within which they have been cut out by my senses and understanding progresses, it may be in the manner of a consciousness?

Certainly, the operation by which science isolates and closes a system is not altogether artificial. If it had no objective foundation, we could not explain why it is clearly indicated in some cases and impossible in others. We shall see that matter has a tendency to constitute *isoloble* systems, that can be treated geometrically. In fact, we shall define matter by just this tendency. But it is only a tendency. Matter does not go to the end, and the isolation is never complete. If science does go to the end and isolate completely, it is for convenience of study; it is understood that the so-called isolated system remains subject to certain external influences. Science merely leaves these alone, either because it finds them slight enough to be negligible, or because it intends to take them into account later on. It is none the less true that these influences are so many threads which bind up the system to another more extensive, and to this a third which includes both, and so on to the system most objectively isolated and most independent of all, the solar system complete. But, even here, the isolation is not absolute. Our sun radiates heat and light beyond the farthest planet. And, on the other hand, it moves in a certain fixed direction, drawing with it the planets and their satellites. The thread attaching it to the rest of the universe is doubtless very tenuous. Nevertheless it is along this thread that is transmitted down to the smallest particle of the world in which we live the duration immanent to the whole of the universe.

The universe *endures*. The more we study the nature of time, the more we shall comprehend that duration means invention, the creation of forms, the continual elaboration of the absolutely new. The systems marked off by science *endure* only because they are bound up inseparably with the rest of the universe. It is true that in the universe itself two opposite movements are to be distinguished, as we shall see later on, "descent" and "ascent." The first only unwinds a roll ready prepared. In principle, it might be accomplished almost instantaneously, like releasing a spring. But the ascending movement, which corresponds to an inner work of ripening or creating, *endures* essentially, and imposes its rhythm on the first, which is inseparable from it.

There is no reason, therefore, why a duration, and so a form of existence like our own, should not be attributed to the systems that science isolates, provided such systems are reintegrated into the Whole. But they must be so reintegrated. The same is even more obviously true of the objects cut out by our perception. The distinct outlines which we see in an object, and which give it its individuality, are only the design of a certain kind of *influence* that we might exert on a certain point of space: it is the plan of our eventual actions that is sent back to our eyes, as though by a mirror, when we see the surfaces and edges of things. Suppress this action, and with it consequently those main directions which by perception are traced out for it in the entanglement of the real, and the individuality of the body is re-absorbed in the universal interaction which, without doubt, is reality itself . . .

Chapter IV

The Cinematographical Mechanism of Thought and the Mechanistic Illusion

Suppose we wish to portray on a screen a living picture, such as the marching past of a regiment. There is one way in which it might first occur to us to do it. That would be to cut out jointed figures representing the soldiers, to give to each of them the movement of marching, a movement varying from individual to individual although common to the human species, and to throw the whole on the screen. We should need to spend on this little game an enormous amount of work, and even then we should obtain but a very poor result: how could it, at its best, reproduce the suppleness and variety of life? Now, there is another way of proceeding, more easy and at the same time more effective. It is to take a series of snapshots of the passing regiment and to throw these instantaneous views on the screen, so that they replace each other very rapidly. This is what the cinematograph does. With photographs, each of which represents the regiment in a fixed attitude, it reconstitutes the mobility of the regiment marching. It is true that if we had to do with photographs alone, however much we might look at them, we should never see them animated: with immobility set beside immobility, even endlessly, we could never make movement. In order that the pictures may be animated, there must be movement somewhere. The movement does indeed exist here; it is in the apparatus. It is because the film of the cinematograph unrolls, bringing in turn the different photographs of the scene to continue each other, that each actor of the scene recovers his mobility; he strings all his successive attitudes on the invisible movement of the film. The process then consists in extracting from all the movements peculiar to all the figures an impersonal movement abstract and simple, *movement in general,* so to speak: we put this into the apparatus, and we reconstitute the individuality of each particular movement by combining this nameless movement with the personal attitudes. Such is the contrivance of the cinematograph. And such is also that of our knowledge. Instead of attaching ourselves to the inner becoming of things, we place ourselves outside them in order to recompose their becoming artificially. We take snapshots, as it were, of the passing reality, and, as these are characteristic of the reality, we have only to string them on a becoming, abstract, uniform and invisible, situated at the back of the apparatus of knowledge, in order to imitate what there is that is characteristic in this becoming itself. Perception, intellection, language so proceed in general. Whether we would think becoming, or express it, or even perceive it, we hardly do anything else than set going a kind of cinematograph inside us. We may therefore sum up what we have been saying in the conclusion that the *mechanism of our ordinary knowledge is of a cinematographical kind.*

Of the altogether practical character of this operation there is no possible doubt. Each of our acts aims at a certain insertion of our will into the reality. There is, between our body and other bodies, an arrangement like that of the pieces of glass that compose a kaleidoscopic picture. Our activity goes from an arrangement to a re-arrangement, each time no doubt giving the kaleidoscope a new shake, but not interesting itself in the shake, and seeing only the new picture. Our knowledge of the operation of nature must be exactly symmetrical, therefore, with the interest we take in our own operation. In this sense we may say, if we are not abusing this kind of illustration, that *the cinematographical character of our knowledge of things is due to the kaleidoscopic character of our adaptation to them.*

The cinematographical method is therefore the only practical method, since it consists in making the general character of knowledge form itself on that of action, while expecting that the detail of each act should depend in its turn on that of knowledge. In order that action may always be enlightened, intelligence must always be present in it; but intelligence, in order thus to accompany the progress of activity and ensure its direction, must begin by adopting its rhythm. Action is discontinuous, like every pulsation of life; discontinuous, therefore, is knowledge. The mechanism of the faculty of knowing has been constructed on this plan. Essentially practical, can it be of use, such as it is, for speculation? Let us try with it to follow reality in its windings, and see what will happen.

I take of the continuity of a particular becoming a series of views, which I connect together by "becoming in general." But of course I cannot stop there. What is not determinable is not representable: of "becoming in general" I have only a verbal knowledge. As the letter x designates a certain unknown quantity, whatever it may be, so my "becoming in general," always the same, symbolizes here a certain transition of which I have taken some snapshots; of the transition itself it teaches me nothing. Let me then concentrate myself wholly on the transition, and, between any two snapshots, endeavor to realize what is going on. As I apply the same method, I obtain the same result; a third view merely slips in between the two others. I may begin again as often as I will, I may set views alongside of views for ever, I shall obtain nothing else. The application of the cinematographical method therefore leads to a perpetual recommencement, during which the mind, never able to satisfy itself and never finding where to rest, persuades itself, no doubt, that it imitates by its instability the very movement of the real. But though, by straining itself to the point of giddiness, it may end by giving itself the illusion of mobility, its operation has not advanced it a step, since it remains as far as ever from its goal. In order to advance with the moving reality, you must replace yourself within it. Install yourself within change, and you will grasp at once both change itself and the successive states in which *it might* at any instant be immobilized. But with these successive states, perceived from without as real and no longer as potential immobilities, you will never reconstitute movement. Call them *qualities, forms, positions,* or *intentions,* as the case may be, multiply the number of them as you will, let the interval between two consecutive states be infinitely small: before the intervening movement you will always experience the disappointment of the child who tries by clapping his hands together to crush the smoke. The movement slips through the interval, because every attempt to reconstitute change out of states implies the absurd proposition, that movement is made of immobilities.

Philosophy perceived this as soon as it opened its eyes. The arguments of Zeno of Elea, although formulated with a very different intention, have no other meaning.

Take the flying arrow. At every moment, says Zeno, it is motionless, for it cannot have time to move, that is, to occupy at least two successive positions, unless at least two moments are allowed it. At a given moment, therefore, it is at rest at a given point. Motionless in each point of its course, it is motionless during all the time that it is moving.

Yes, if we suppose that the arrow can ever *be* in a point of its course. Yes again, if the arrow, which is moving, ever coincides with a position, which is motionless. But the arrow never *is* in any point of its course. The most we can say is that it might be there, in this sense, that it passes there and might stop there. It is true that if it did stop there, it would be at rest there, and at this point it is no longer movement that we should have to do with. The truth is that if the arrow leaves the point A to fall down at the point B, its movement AB is as simple, as indecomposable, in so far as it is movement, as the tension of the bow that shoots it. As the shrapnel, bursting before it falls to the ground, covers the explosive zone with an indivisible danger, so the arrow which goes from A to B displays with a single stroke, although over a certain extent of duration, its indivisible mobility. Suppose an elastic stretched from A to B, could you divide its extension? The course of the arrow is this very extension; it is equally simple and equally undivided. It is a single and unique bound. You fix a point C in the interval passed, and say that at a certain moment the arrow was in C. If it had been there, it would have been stopped there, and you would no longer have had a flight from A to B, but *two* flights, one from A to C and the other from C to B, with an interval of rest. A single movement is entirely, by the hypothesis, a movement between two stops; if there are intermediate stops, it is no longer a single movement. At bottom, the illusion arises from this, that the movement, *once effected,* has laid along its course a motionless trajectory on which we can count as many immobilities as we will. From this we conclude that the movement, *whilst being effected,* lays at each instant beneath it a position with which it coincides. We do not see that the trajectory is created in one stroke, although a certain time is required for it; and that though we can divide at will the trajectory once created, we cannot divide its creation, which is an act in progress and not a thing. To suppose that the moving body *is* at a point of its course is to cut the course in two by a snip of the scissors at this point, and to substitute two trajectories for the single trajectory which we were first considering. It is to distinguish two successive acts where, by the hypothesis, there is only one. In short, it is to attribute to the course itself of the arrow everything that can be said of the interval that the arrow has traversed, that is to say, to admit *a priori* the absurdity that movement coincides with immobility.

Notes

1. Keith Ansell Pearson, *Philosophy and the Adventure of the Virtual: Bergson and the Time of Life* (London: Routledge, 2002), pp. 50–51.
2. Ronald Bogue, *Deleuze on Cinema* (London: Routledge, 2003), p. 24. In *Cinema I: The Movement-Image,* Deleuze takes up the story of Bergson's experiment and expands upon its transformative meaning: "If I stir with the spoon, I speed up the movement, but I also change the whole, which now encompasses the spoon, and the accelerated movement continues to express the change of the whole." Gilles Deleuze, *Cinema I: The Movement-Image,* trans. Hugh Tomlinson and Barbara Habberjam (Minneapolis: University of Minnesota Press, 1986), p. 9.
3. Gilles Deleuze, *Cinema II: The Time Image,* trans. Hugh Tomlinson and Robert Galeta (London: Athlone, 1989), p. 82.
4. Henri Bergson, *Matière et mémoire* (Paris, 1896), chapters 2 and 3.

CHAPTER 2

THE WORK OF ART IN THE AGE OF ITS TECHNOLOGICAL REPRODUCIBILITY

WALTER BENJAMIN

Opposed equally to capitalist and fascist ideologies, Walter Benjamin (1892–1940) made a series of important contributions to debates in the 1930s about the work of art in relation to cinema and photography. Proposing that the ideas and concepts outlined in "The Work of Art in the Age of Its Technological Reproducibility" ("Das Kunstwerk im Zeitalter seiner technischen Reproduzierbarkeit") are "useful for the formulation of revolutionary demands in the politics of art," Benjamin's essay is addressed to the reactionary political situation in Europe of the mid-1930s. In particular, this concerned the rise of fascism and the permeation of social reality by technology, which was mobilized increasingly by capitalist economic forces for the purposes of war. In contrast to these developments, Benjamin sought freedom from the technological oppression of society not by rejecting technology per se but by achieving an "equilibrium" between technology and social organization (section 16). The possibility of realizing such an equilibrium depends upon the overthrow of the capitalist system of private property, but, in addition, Benjamin makes the case that certain technologies, both new and old, possess a capacity to establish the conditions through which social experience can be transformed into a newfound sense of freedom and enjoyment in play (*spiel*). A particular case in point is film: Benjamin proposes that film is second only to architecture in being a principal technology involved in the transformation of collective social experience although it is also in danger of being co-opted by ideology. The concept of "reproducibility" (otherwise referred to as "transmissibility") in Benjamin's terms refers to several interrelated elements: first, the industrial reproduction of images; second, the affirmation that meanings and values can change and that nothing is unique, original, or fixed in time; and, third, the conviction that the new forms of fragmentary affect imparted by cinematic montage is an aesthetic power of the present moment that reproduces the potentiality of the masses for freedom while resisting capture by fascist or bourgeois ideology.[1]

Benjamin's overarching dialectical argument in the essay is that since social reality is entirely coexistent with, and interpenetrated by, technology, this gives rise to the possibility that such reality can be freed from the oppressive uses of technology. In this respect, film has various roles to perform with respect to technology: it has the capacity to capitalize on the decay of the fetishism surrounding the work of art's aura and to liberate new forms of reception and expertise among the masses that counter ideological repression.

In section 1, Benjamin states that, like Marx, his intention is to understand the developmental tendencies of capitalism rather than predicting the utopian future of socialism. But, unlike Marx, Benjamin's focus is upon the sphere of culture rather than the economic "base" of society; indeed, contra Marx, Benjamin claims that the relationship between these two spheres is not simply one of reflection, whereby culture would be seen to mirror economic developments, but that this relationship is, in fact, more complex and asynchronic. Just as Marx provided a critique of economic concepts, supplementing them where necessary with new concepts, so Benjamin carries out a critique of what he believes are culturally "outmoded concepts," such as "creativity and genius, eternal value and mystery," while introducing new concepts appropriate to recent developmental tendencies in the social. In particular, these tendencies revolve around the expanded use of techniques of reproduction through the introduction in the nineteenth century of the media of photography and film. Acknowledging in sections 2 and 8 that the reproducibility of art works stretches back historically to Greek culture through techniques such as founding and stamping, Benjamin notes that because these methods were relatively limited in scope the Greeks tended to emphasize the uniqueness of art works, to which they attached values of originality and authenticity. In turn, these values supported a contemplative, cultic response to the work of art, casting it as the incarnation of eternal perfection and divinity. Benjamin argues that film does not strive for such perfection, but rather is assembled through montage from a number of takes so that, instead of being purportedly the manifestation of an eternal time, filmic time is a temporality composed of continual movement and transformation.

Paradoxically, the development of technical reproduction in the nineteenth century increased the authority of the "original" work of art rather than challenging it. Against such regressive effects, Benjamin proposes new possibilities of organizing "aesthetic" experience. For Benjamin, uniqueness per se does not exist, its mobilization in bourgeois culture is ideological, implying that the work of art exists outside of history. But, as Benjamin points out, works of art change through time in terms of their physical condition, ownership, and the use to which they are put. Benjamin believes that photographs support this last point by recontextualizing their subjects: Benjamin cites the examples of a photograph of a cathedral that "leaves its site to be received in the studio of a lover of art," the recording of "the choral work . . . enjoyed in a private room," and the case of close-up photography that alters preconceptions about the world (which elsewhere Benjamin describes as "the optical unconscious"; section 3). To a certain extent, bourgeois culture is able to incorporate the history pertaining to works of art within its ideology of authenticity so long as this history is seen in terms of preservation (this is the attitude of the nineteenth-century movement *l'art pour l'art*—art for art's sake; section 5), rather than the transformation of meaning and value. Benjamin, however, states that reproducibility is the essence of the work of art and one of its original possibilities. If such an attitude about the work of art's reproducibility were to be realized, this would mean the death of the fetishism of its aura, or, at least, its "decay," thus revolutionizing the function of art. Originally, aura is associated with cult value, ritual, and magic, exemplified by the prehistoric cave painting that was to be seen only by the spirits to whom they were dedicated as the powerful propitiators of nature (section 6). In addition, for Benjamin, aura is associated with the ideological notion of originality. However, Benjamin has somewhat contradictory attitudes about aura. Even in this essay, in which he critiques aura, on one occasion he equates aura with an experience of beauty (section 4) and, in other contexts, such as in the discussion of early portrait photography in "Little History of Photography," Benjamin uses the term *aura* to denote a vitalistic life force.

Attached to a work of art in the modern era, aura invites contemplation rather than political use, which Benjamin terms "exhibition value." The borders of such a work seem impermeable, as if fixed forever at a particular time and place (an idea that is underlined by the physical presence of an art work in a museum or household that is meant to be seen in one place at a particular time). Benjamin proposes that aura operates by definition at a removed distance; this is the point of the story told in section 4 about the contemplative experience of nature: "the unique semblance of distance no matter how close the object may be." Here Benjamin describes a dialectic of proximity and distance whereby the latter remains paramount, but he goes on to propose that this dialectic is reversed: the advent of the technology of industrial reproduction allowing the masses to seek proximity to the image so as to grasp the power of interactivity and dissemination with which it is now invested.

In section 3, Benjamin argues that "the technology of reproduction detaches the reproduced object from the sphere of tradition." Subsequently, he proposes that "in permitting the reproduction to reach the recipient in his or her own situation, it actualizes that which is reproduced." Benjamin's point is that the radical political dimension of reproducibility is realized in its reception and taken up by the masses. As he says, "Both processes" (meaning the processes of reproduction and effective political change) "are intimately related to the mass movements of our day" (section 3) and, later, at the beginning of section 18, "The masses are a matrix from which all customary behavior towards works of art is today emerging newborn." For Benjamin, "actualization" is part of "the desire of the present-day masses to 'get closer' to things, and their equally passionate concern for overcoming each thing's uniqueness by assimilating it as a reproduction" (section 4). (Another translation of this complex passage reads as, "To bring things spatially and humanly 'closer' is a no less passionate inclination of today's masses than is their tendency to overcome the uniqueness of every given event through the reception [Aufnahme] of its reproduction.")[2] A further passage in the essay where Benjamin uses the word Aufnahme is in section 11 where he states that

> for the first time—and this is the effect of film—the human being is placed in a position where he must operate with his whole living person, while foregoing its aura. For the aura is bound to his presence in the here and now. There is no facsimile of the aura. The aura surrounding Macbeth on the stage cannot be divorced from the aura which, for the living spectators, surrounds the actor who plays him. What distinguishes the shot (der Aufnahme) in the film studio, however, is that the camera is substituted for the audience.

Benjamin suggests that the reproducible nature of acting in film, and of performing in front of an apparatus rather than a live audience as in theater, far from being a form of alienation, in actual fact offers the actor the means for preserving a sense of humanity and for striking a blow of revenge on behalf of the masses "not only by asserting *his* humanity (or what appears to them as such) against the apparatus, but by placing that apparatus in the service of his triumph" (section 10). The context for this argument is Benjamin's assertion that film acting can be seen to consist of a series of "tests," not unlike those that workers are continually subject to for the purposes of assessing productivity. But in the case of the cinema actor the difference is that their performance, along with its meaning and contemporary significance as a test, is put on show while also being disseminated to millions. Composed from various camera angles, close-ups, and serial takes, film automatically engages the audience in multiple yet unconscious forms of such tests. Like the film actor, Benjamin believes that film audiences are becoming "experts" or "specialists" in understanding the fragmented, nonauratic ways technology constructs experience in modern society, the spirit of which is reflected in Chaplin's films, which prompt "a progressive attitude . . . characterized by an immediate, intimate fusion of pleasure—pleasure in seeing and experiencing—with an attitude of expert appraisal" (section 15). This figure of the "expert" viewer was modeled in Benjamin's mind upon the Russian Constructivist figure of the artist-engineer, a purported "expert" in modern forms of technological and aesthetic experience and new spatiotemporal relations.

The filmic apparatus takes up "the given" by dislocating and relocating its elements, recombining them into ensembles that have little to do with their initial state, a point that Benjamin elaborates in section 10 and the second part of section 11. Doing away with any notion of an original image, the film apparatus, by virtue of serial takes and editing, has the potential to create infinite possibilities of affects and meaning, challenging the very notion of a complete work. Such a radical potential for altering or switching meanings without reaching a limit can also be taken up by the audience—that is, "the masses" referred to at the beginning of section 12—who are in a position to take control of the actor's estrangement from himself. Benjamin, however, goes on to qualify this, pointing out that the potential power of cinema's audience cannot occur "until film has liberated itself from the fetters of capitalist exploitation."

Benjamin acknowledges in section 14 that the reproducibility apprehended by the masses in this process is necessarily both violent and fragmentary since it undermines any purported notion of ideological totality. He illustrates this idea by differentiating the traditional painter from the reproductive camera-man through a comparison of the practices of the magician (in other words, a witch doctor) and the surgeon. Whereas the magician "maintains the natural distance between himself and the person treated . . . the surgeon . . . diminishes the distance by penetrating the patient's body . . . unlike the magician (traces of whom are still found in the medical practitioner) the surgeon abstains at the decisive moment from confronting his patient person to person; instead he penetrates the patient by operating." Benjamin concludes from this comparison that the painter's image is a "total image," and, in other words, auratic, "whereas that of the cinematographer is piecemeal, its manifold parts being assembled according to a new law." In practice this "new law" is realized through the cutting of film in the editing process, a process that Benjamin claims is *"equipment-free"* (section 14). By this Benjamin does not mean that editing film is not a technological practice—as he readily acknowledges, film is *"the most intensive interpenetration of reality with equipment"*—rather, his point is that film is untrammeled by any duty toward an "original" image and can reproduce reality in any way that it wishes and desires. Hence, *"the presentation of reality in film is incomparably the more significant for people of today."*

In section 18 Benjamin explores the perception that the audience's reception of film is a way of "seeking distraction [*zerstreuung*] . . . a means of entertainment," as opposed to the art lover's aesthetic experience of the art work as "an object of devotion" that requires "concentration" and "contemplative immersion." Benjamin's use of the term *distraction* (*zerstreuung*) in the context of this essay is not the same as the common idea of it as a form of mindless consumerism, a diversion from the demands of work and the marketplace. Rather, for Benjamin, distraction is an experience that brings together the notions of (mass) movement with the dispersion of aura and, ultimately, the process of reproducibility. This is made clear in section 17 where Benjamin describes the scandalous effects of Dadaism as forms of "distraction [*Ablenkung*]" or "vehement distraction" that functioned in opposition to the type of contemplative immersion cultivated by the bourgeoisie with regard to their favored forms of art. For Benjamin, distraction is linked to the shock effect of both Dadaism and film, "the Dadaists turned the artwork into a missile. . . . *Film has freed the physical shock effect—which Dadaism had kept wrapped, as it were, inside the moral shock effect—from this wrapping.*" In his note 36 to this passage, Benjamin expands upon what he understands as the distracting shock effect of film upon its audience, which differs fundamentally from the affects of a painting. Montage—by which Benjamin seems to have in mind the montage effects of Russian filmmakers such as Sergei Eisenstein, with whom he was familiar—shocks (that is, distracts) the viewer to such an extent that it becomes impossible to put the experience of film into a representational form, with the consequence that the coordinates sustaining the ideology of the subject's identity are challenged. This is in contrast to "*the pronounced threat to life which people live today*" issuing from fascism's uses of technology. Fascism grants "expression to the masses—but on no account [grants] them rights" by altering or abolishing property relations (section 19). The means by which fascism grants "expression to the masses" is through images and representations of its own ideological making, whether this is "the dreamed of metallization of the human body" acclaimed by Marinetti (section 19) or images of "great ceremonial processions, giant rallies and mass sporting events . . . fed into the camera" (note 40); here Benjamin seems to have in mind images of fascist rallies and spectacles in the mold of the Nazi propagandist Leni Riefenstahl. Such images, Benjamin says, bring the masses "face to face with themselves" (note 40). This narcissistic affect of seeing and being seen, Benjamin believes, is fundamentally auratic, a means by which the masses are given an image (of themselves) and thereby constituted as subjects of ideology. Conversely, for Benjamin, to forego this reciprocity between subject and image is to interrupt the constitution of the auratic image. For Benjamin, Eugène Atget's photographs of Paris, emptied of any human presence, achieve such an interruption, which is their shock value. As such, they are like images of crime scenes, the traces of which Benjamin suggests transforms the viewer into the persona of a detective who, in the manner of an expert, fits together fragments of evidence to make meaning.

In section 7, Benjamin claims that prior to Atget the cultic value of photography was last seen in the portrait daguerreotypes of the second half of the nineteenth century, a point that Benjamin had explored previously in his essay "Little History of Photography."[3] Following the decay of aura represented by the daguerreotype, this magical affect of being seen, described by Karl Dauthendey, is finally extinguished with Atget's photographs of deserted Paris streets. As Benjamin says, the "political significance" of Atget's photographs lies in the fact that "they demand a specific kind of reception. Free-floating contemplation is no longer appropriate to them. This constitutes their hidden political significance. They unsettle the viewer; he feels challenged to find a particular way to approach them" (section 7) because the image on its own is insufficient in terms of reliable meaning.

If art were to be freed of its former ties to ritual, it can serve not so much as a master of nature as a master of technology, and, for Benjamin, this is of paramount importance since technology has become humankind's second nature. As such, this "second technology" has its origins in play, and its aim is to create an utopian interplay between nature and humanity. Left to the bourgeoisie and fascism, technology becomes an instrument of social repression and destruction, however in Benjamin's view, film can be an educative medium laying the ground for a newfound training in the art of playing, "*The function of film is to train human beings in the apperceptions and reactions needed to deal with a vast apparatus whose role in their lives is expanding almost daily*" (section 6). Given that revolutions are, by definition, an "innervation" of the collective body, a way of stimulating and changing its identity, thereby engendering new ways of "playing" (*das Spiel*), film has an avant-gardist role to help the individual grow accustomed to his new "scope for play, his field of action [*Spielraum*]" (note 15), thus inducing unprecedented experiences of space and time, which will bring with them the dissolution of previously valid experiences of identity and politics.

Unlike painting, which Benjamin believes is obsolete in an era of mass reproducibility, film therefore posits the possibility of a collective experience composed of a combination of both enjoyment and critical judgment, in the same way that architecture is responded to and critically adapted by its users. Indeed, Benjamin argues that film, like architecture, is composed from both optical and tactile affects. In film these tactile affects arise from the experience of shock that eschews contemplation and the development of habits to accommodate them (section 18 and note 36).

Benjamin is concerned that the destruction of existing patterns of spatiotemporal experience is more likely to be catastrophic rather than transformative, a point that is underlined in the essay's epilogue (section 19; entitled in the third version of the essay "The Aesthetics of War") where Benjamin foresees a self-destructive tendency for war within Germany, from which he concludes that this "destructiveness of war furnishes proof that society has not been mature enough to incorporate technology as its organ." Benjamin acknowledges that there is a "psychotic" aspect to film and that its visual affects are similar to hallucinations and dreams. In part, this is a consequence of "the exploded prison-world" and "the journeys of adventure" that film has both discovered and created through the uses of the close-up, slow motion, and camera edits that develop new forms of spatiotemporal experiences, composing what Benjamin terms "the optical unconscious" that underlies collective experience. However, given the existence of this "optical unconscious" within experience, Benjamin believes that film can be cathartic, a staging of psychosis whereby it functions as a form of inoculation against technology's potential destructiveness in the modern era. According to Benjamin, American slapstick comedies provide a cathartic release from the tensions generated by technology, while Disney films generate collective laughter: the sadomasochistic tendencies of Mickey Mouse and his friends are posited by Benjamin as heightened surrealistic effects drawn from the aggressive conflicts underlying modern society (section 16).[4]

✳ ✳ ✳

The true is what he can; the false is what he wants.

—Madame de Duras[5]

I

When Marx undertook his analysis of the capitalist mode of production, that mode was in its infancy.[6] Marx adopted an approach which gave his investigations prognostic value. Going back to the basic conditions of capitalist production, he presented them in a way which showed what could be expected of capitalism in the future. What could be expected, it emerged, was not only an increasingly harsh exploitation of the proletariat but, ultimately, the creation of conditions which would make it possible for capitalism to abolish itself.

Since the transformation of the superstructure proceeds far more slowly than that of the base, it has taken more than half a century for the change in the conditions of production to be manifested in all areas of culture. How this process has affected culture can only now be assessed, and these assessments must meet certain prognostic requirements. They do not, however, call for theses on the art of the proletariat after its seizure of power, and still less for any on the art of the classless society. They call for theses defining the tendencies of the development of art under the present conditions of production. The dialectic of these conditions of production is evident in the superstructure, no less than in the economy. Theses defining the developmental tendencies of art can therefore contribute to the political struggle in ways that it would be a mistake to underestimate. They neutralize a number of traditional concepts—such as creativity and genius, eternal value and mystery—which, used in an uncontrolled way (and controlling them is difficult today), allow factual material to be manipulated in the interests of fascism. *In what follows, the concepts which are introduced into the theory of art differ from those now current in that they are completely useless for the purposes of fascism. On the other hand, they are useful for the formulation of revolutionary demands in the politics of art [Kunstpolitik].*

II

In principle, the work of art has always been reproducible. Objects made by humans could always be copied by humans. Replicas were made by pupils in practicing for their craft, by masters in disseminating their works, and, finally, by third parties in pursuit of profit. But the technological reproduction of artworks is something new . . .

Around 1900, technological reproduction not only had reached a standard that permitted it to reproduce all known works of art, profoundly modifying their effect, but it also had captured a place of its own among the artistic processes. In gauging this standard, we would do well to study the impact which its two different manifestations—the reproduction of artworks and the art of film—are having on art in its traditional form.

Ill

In even the most perfect reproduction, *one* thing is lacking: the here and now of the work of art—its unique existence in a particular place. It is this unique existence—and nothing else—that bears the mark of the history to which the work has been subject. This history includes changes to the physical structure of the work over time, together with any changes in ownership. Traces of the former can be detected only by chemical or physical analyses (which cannot be performed on a reproduction), while changes of ownership are part of a tradition which can be traced only from the standpoint of the original in its present location.

The here and now of the original underlies the concept of its authenticity, and on the latter in turn is founded the idea of a tradition which has passed the object down as the same, identical thing to the present day. *The whole sphere of authenticity eludes technological—and of course not only technological— reproduction.* But whereas the authentic work retains its full authority in the face of a reproduction made by hand, which it generally brands a forgery, this is not the case with technological reproduction. The reason is twofold. First, technological reproduction is more independent of the original than is manual reproduction. For example, in photography it can bring out aspects of the original that are accessible only to the lens (which is adjustable and can easily change viewpoint) but not to the human eye; or it can use certain processes, such as enlargement or slow motion, to record images which escape natural optics altogether. This is the first reason. Second, technological reproduction can place the copy of the original in situations which the original itself cannot attain. Above all, it enables the original to meet the recipient halfway, whether in the form of a photograph or in that of a gramophone record. The cathedral leaves its site to be received in the studio of an art lover; the choral work performed in an auditorium or in the open air is enjoyed in a private room.

These changed circumstances may leave the artwork's other properties untouched, but they certainly devalue the here and now of the artwork. And although this can apply not only to art but (say) to a landscape moving past the spectator in a film, in the work of art this process touches on a highly sensitive core, more vulnerable than that of any natural object. That core is its authenticity. The authenticity of a thing is the quintessence of all that is transmissible in it from its origin on, ranging from its physical duration to the historical testimony relating to it. Since the historical testimony is founded on the physical duration, the former, too, is jeopardized by reproduction, in which the physical duration plays no part. And what is really jeopardized when the historical testimony is affected is the authority of the object, the weight it derives from tradition.

One might focus these aspects of the artwork in the concept of the aura, and go on to say: what withers in the age of the technological reproducibility of the work of art is the latter's aura. This process is symptomatic; its significance extends far beyond the realm of art. *It might be stated as a general formula that the technology of reproduction detaches the reproduced object from the sphere of tradition. By replicating the work many times over, it substitutes a mass existence for a unique existence. And in permitting the reproduction to reach the recipient in his or her own situation, it actualizes that which is reproduced.* These two processes lead to a massive upheaval in the domain of objects handed down from the past—a shattering of tradition which is the reverse side of the present crisis and renewal of humanity. Both processes are intimately related to the mass movements of our day. Their most powerful agent is film. The social significance of film, even—and especially—in its most positive form, is inconceivable without its destructive, cathartic side: the liquidation of the value of tradition in the cultural heritage. This phenomenon is most apparent in the great historical films. It is assimilating ever more advanced positions in its spread. When Abel Gance fervently proclaimed in 1927, "Shakespeare, Rembrandt, Beethoven will make films. . . . All legends, all mythologies, and all myths, all the founders of religions, indeed, all religions, . . . await their celluloid resurrection, and the heroes are pressing at the gates," he was inviting the reader, no doubt unawares, to witness a comprehensive liquidation.[7]

IV

Just as the entire mode of existence of human collectives changes over long historical periods, so too does their mode of perception. The way in which human perception is organized—the medium in which it occurs—is conditioned not only by nature but by history. The era of the migration of peoples, an era which saw the rise of the late-Roman art industry and the Vienna Genesis, developed not only an art different from that of antiquity but also a different perception. The scholars of the Viennese school Riegl and Wickhoff, resisting the weight of the classical tradition beneath which this art had been buried, were the first to think of using such art to draw conclusions about the organization of perception at the time the art was produced.[8] However far-reaching their insight, it was limited by the fact that these scholars were content to highlight the formal signature which characterized perception in late-Roman times. They did not attempt to show the social upheavals manifested in these changes in perception—and perhaps could not have hoped to do so at that time. Today, the conditions for an analogous insight are more favorable. And if changes in the medium of present-day perception can be understood as a decay of the aura, it is possible to demonstrate the social determinants of that decay.

What, then, is the aura? A strange tissue of space and time: the unique apparition of a distance, however near it may be.[9] To follow with the eye—while resting on a summer afternoon—a mountain range on the horizon or a branch that casts its shadow on the beholder is to breathe the aura of those mountains, of that branch. In the light of this description, we can readily grasp the social basis of the aura's present decay. It rests on two circumstances, both linked to the increasing emergence of the masses and the growing intensity of their movements. Namely: *the desire of the present-day masses to "get closer" to things, and their equally passionate concern for overcoming each thing's uniqueness [Überwindung des Einmaligen jeder Gegebenheit] by assimilating it as a reproduction.* Every day the urge grows stronger to get hold of an object at close range in an image [Bild], or, better, in a facsimile [Abbild], a reproduction. And the reproduction [Reproduktion], as offered by illustrated magazines and newsreels, differs unmistakably from the image. Uniqueness and permanence are as closely entwined in the latter as are transitoriness and repeatability in the former. The stripping of the veil from the object, the destruction of the aura, is the signature of a perception whose "sense for sameness in the world"[10] has so increased that, by means of reproduction, it extracts sameness even from what is unique. Thus is manifested in the field of perception what in the theoretical sphere is noticeable in the increasing significance of statistics. The alignment of reality with the masses and of the masses with reality is a process of immeasurable importance for both thinking and perception.

V

The uniqueness of the work of art is identical to its embeddedness in the context of tradition. Of course, this tradition itself is thoroughly alive and extremely changeable. An ancient statue of Venus, for instance, existed in a traditional context for the Greeks (who made it an object of worship) that was different from the context in which it existed for medieval clerics (who viewed it as a sinister idol). But what was equally evident to both was its uniqueness—that is, its aura. Originally, the embeddedness of an artwork in the context of tradition found expression in a cult. As we know, the earliest artworks originated in the service of rituals—first magical, then religious. And it is highly significant that the artwork's auratic mode of existence is never entirely severed from its ritual function. In other words: *the unique value of the "authentic" work of art always has its basis in ritual.* This ritualistic basis, however mediated it may be, is still recognizable as secularized ritual in even the most profane forms of the cult of beauty. The secular worship of beauty, which developed during the Renaissance and prevailed for three centuries, clearly displayed that ritualistic basis in its subsequent decline and in the first severe crisis which befell it. For when, with the advent of the first truly revolutionary means of reproduction (namely photography, which emerged at the same time as socialism), art felt the approach of that crisis which a century later has become unmistakable, it reacted with the doctrine of *l'art pour l'art*—that is, with a theology of art.[11] This in turn gave rise to a negative theology, in the form of an idea of "pure" art, which rejects not only any social function but any definition in terms of a representational content. (In poetry, Mallarmé was the first to adopt this standpoint.)[12]

No investigation of the work of art in the age of its technological reproducibility can overlook these connections. They lead to a crucial insight: for the first time in world history, technological reproducibility emancipates the work of art from its parasitic subservience to ritual. To an ever-increasing degree, the work reproduced becomes the reproduction of a work designed for reproducibility.[13] From a photographic plate, for example, one can make any number of prints; to ask for the "authentic" print makes no sense. *But as soon as the criterion of authenticity ceases to be applied to artistic production, the whole social function of art is revolutionized. Instead of being founded on ritual, it is based on a different practice: politics.*

VI

Art history might be seen as the working out of a tension between two polarities within the artwork itself, its course being determined by shifts in the balance between the two. These two poles are the artwork's cult value and its exhibition value.[14] Artistic production begins with figures in the service of magic. What is important for these figures is that they are present, not that they are seen. The elk depicted by Stone Age man on the walls of his cave is an instrument of magic, and is exhibited to others only coincidentally; what matters is that the spirits see it. Cult value as such even tends to keep the artwork out of sight: certain statues of gods are accessible only to the priest in the cella; certain images of the Madonna remain covered nearly all year round; certain sculptures on medieval cathedrals are not visible to the viewer at ground level. *With the emancipation of specific artistic practices from the service of ritual, the opportunities for exhibiting their products increase.* It is easier to exhibit a portrait bust that can be sent here and there than to exhibit the statue of a divinity that has a fixed place in the interior of a temple. A panel painting can be exhibited more easily than the mosaic or fresco which preceded it. And although a mass may have been no less suited to public presentation than a symphony, the symphony came into being at a time when the possibility of such presentation promised to be greater.

The scope for exhibiting the work of art has increased so enormously with the various methods of technologically reproducing it that, as happened in prehistoric times, a quantitative shift between the two poles of the artwork has led to a qualitative transformation in its nature. Just as the work of art in prehistoric times, through the exclusive emphasis placed on its cult value, became first and foremost an instrument of magic which only later came to be recognized as a work of art, so today, through the exclusive emphasis placed on its exhibition value, the work of art becomes a construct [*Gebilde*] with quite new functions. Among these, the one we are conscious of—the artistic function—may subsequently be seen as incidental. This much is certain: today, film is the most serviceable vehicle of this new understanding. Certain, as well, is the fact that the historical moment of this change in the function of art—a change which is most fully evident in the case of film—allows a direct comparison with the primeval era of art not only from a methodological but also from a material point of view.

Prehistoric art made use of certain fixed notations in the service of magical practice. In some cases, these notations probably comprised the actual performing of magical acts (the carving of an ancestral figure is itself such an act); in others, they gave instructions for such procedures (the ancestral figure demonstrates a ritual posture); and in still others, they provided objects for magical contemplation (contemplation of an ancestral figure strengthens the occult powers of the beholder). The subjects for these notations were humans and their environment, which were depicted according to the requirements of a society whose technology existed only in fusion with ritual. Compared to that of the machine age, of course, this technology was undeveloped. But from a dialectical standpoint, the disparity is unimportant. What matters is the way the orientation and aims of that technology differ from those of ours. Whereas the former made the maximum possible use of human beings, the latter reduces their use to the minimum. The achievements of the first technology might be said to culminate in human sacrifice; those of the second, in the remote-controlled aircraft which needs no human crew. The results of the first technology are valid once and for all (it deals with irreparable lapse or sacrificial death, which holds good for eternity). The results of the second are wholly provisional (it operates by means of experiments and endlessly varied test procedures). The origin of the second technology lies at the point where, by an unconscious ruse, human beings first began to distance themselves from nature. It lies, in other words, in play.

Seriousness and play, rigor and license, are mingled in every work of art, though in very different proportions. This implies that art is linked to both the second and the first technologies. It should be noted, however, that to describe the goal of the second technology as "mastery over nature" is highly questionable, since this implies viewing the second technology from the standpoint of the first. The first technology really sought to master nature, whereas the second aims rather at an interplay between nature and humanity. The primary social function of art today is to rehearse that interplay. This applies especially to film. *The function of film is to train human beings in the apperceptions and reactions needed to deal with a vast apparatus whose role in their lives is expanding almost daily.* Dealing with this apparatus also teaches them that technology will release them from their enslavement to the powers of the apparatus only when humanity's whole constitution has adapted itself to the new productive forces which the second technology has set free.[15]

VII

In photography, exhibition value begins to drive back cult value on all fronts. But cult value does not give way without resistance. It falls back to a last entrenchment: the human countenance. It is no accident that the portrait is central to early photography. In the cult of remembrance of dead or absent loved ones, the cult value of the image finds its last refuge. In the fleeting expression of a human face, the aura beckons from early photographs for the last time. This is what gives them their melancholy and incomparable beauty. But as the human being withdraws from the photographic image, exhibition value for the first time shows its superiority to cult value. To have given this development its local habitation constitutes the unique significance of Atget, who, around 1900, took photographs of deserted Paris streets.[16] It has justly been said that he photographed them like scenes of crimes. A crime scene, too, is deserted; it is photographed for the purpose of establishing evidence. With Atget, photographic records begin to be evidence in the historical trial [*Prozess*]. This constitutes their hidden political significance. They demand a specific kind of reception. Free-floating contemplation is no longer appropriate to them. They unsettle the viewer; he feels challenged to find a particular way to approach them. At the same time, illustrated magazines begin to put up signposts for him—whether these are right or wrong is irrelevant. For the first time, captions become obligatory. And it is clear that they have a character altogether different from the titles of paintings. The directives given by captions to those looking at images in illustrated magazines soon become even more precise and commanding in films, where the way each single image is understood seems prescribed by the sequence of all the preceding images.

VIII

The Greeks had only two ways of technologically reproducing works of art: casting and stamping. Bronzes, terra cottas, and coins were the only artworks they could produce in large numbers. All others were unique and could not be technologically reproduced. That is why they had to be made for all eternity. *The state of their technology compelled the Greeks to produce eternal values in their art.* To this they owe their preeminent position in art history—the standard for subsequent generations. Undoubtedly, our position lies at the opposite pole from that of the Greeks. Never before have artworks been technologically reproducible to such a degree and in such quantities as today. Film is the first art form whose artistic character is entirely determined by its reproducibility. It would be idle to compare this form in detail with Greek art. But on one precise point such a comparison would be revealing. For film has given crucial importance to a quality of the artwork which would have been the last to find approval among the Greeks, or which they would have dismissed as marginal. This quality is its capacity for improvement. The finished film is the exact antithesis of a work created at a single stroke. It is assembled from a very large number of images and image sequences that offer an array of choices to the editor; these images, moreover, can be improved in any desired way in the process leading from the initial take to the final cut. To produce *A Woman of Paris,* which is 3,000 meters long, Chaplin shot 125,000 meters of film.[17] *The film is therefore the artwork most capable of improvement. And this capability is linked to its radical renunciation of eternal value.* This is corroborated by the fact that for the Greeks, whose art depended on the production of eternal values, the pinnacle of all the arts was the form least capable of improvement—namely sculpture, whose products are literally all of a piece. In the age of the assembled [*montierbar*] artwork, the decline of sculpture is inevitable.

IX

The nineteenth-century dispute over the relative artistic merits of painting and photography seems misguided and confused today. But this does not diminish its importance, and may even underscore it. The dispute was in fact an expression of a world-historical upheaval whose true nature was concealed from both parties. Insofar as the age of technological reproducibility separated art from its basis in cult, all semblance of art's autonomy disappeared forever.[18] But the resulting change in the function of art lay beyond the horizon of the nineteenth century. And even the twentieth, which saw the development of film, was slow to perceive it.

Though commentators had earlier expended much fruitless ingenuity on the question of whether photography was an art—without asking the more fundamental question of whether the invention of photography had not transformed the entire character of art—film theorists quickly adopted the same ill-considered standpoint. But the difficulties which photography caused for traditional aesthetics were child's play compared to those presented by film. Hence the obtuse and hyperbolic character of early film theory. Abel Gance, for instance, compares film to hieroglyphs: "By a remarkable regression, we are transported back to the expressive level of the Egyptians.... Pictorial language has not matured, because our eyes are not yet adapted to it. There is not yet enough respect, not enough *cult,* for what it expresses."[19] Or, in the words of Severin-Mars: "What other art has been granted a dream . . . at once more poetic and more real? Seen in this light, film might represent an incomparable means of expression, and only the noblest minds should move within its atmosphere, in the most perfect and mysterious moments of their lives."[20] It is instructive to see how the desire to annex film to "art" impels these theoreticians to attribute elements of cult to film—with a striking lack of discretion. Yet when these speculations were published, works like *A Woman of Paris* and *The Gold Rush* had already appeared. This did not deter Abel Gance from making the comparison with hieroglyphs, while Severin-Mars speaks of film as one might speak of paintings by Fra Angelico.[21] It is revealing that even today especially reactionary authors look in the same direction for the significance of film—finding, if not actually a sacred significance, then at least a supernatural one. In connection with Max Reinhardt's film version of A Midsummer Night's Dream, Werfel comments that it was undoubtedly the sterile copying of the external world—with its streets, interiors, railway stations, restaurants, automobiles, and beaches—that had prevented film up to now from ascending to the realm of art. "Film has not yet realized its true purpose, its real possibilities. . . . These consist in its unique ability to use natural means to give incomparably convincing expression to the fairylike, the marvelous, the supernatural."[22]

X

To photograph a painting is one kind of reproduction, but to photograph an action performed in a film studio is another. In the first case, what is reproduced is a work of art, while the act of producing it is not. The cameraman's performance with the lens no more creates an artwork than a conductor's with the baton; at most, it creates an artistic performance. This is unlike the process in a film studio. Here, what is reproduced is not an artwork, and the act of reproducing it is no more such a work than in the first case. The work of art is produced only by means of montage. And each individual component of this montage is a reproduction of a process which neither is an artwork in itself nor gives rise to one through photography. What, then, are these processes reproduced in film, since they are certainly not works of art?

To answer this, we must start from the peculiar nature of the artistic performance of the film actor. He is distinguished from the stage actor in that his performance in its original form, from which the reproduction is made, is not carried out in front of a randomly composed audience but before a group of specialists—executive producer, director, cinematographer, sound recordist, lighting designer, and so on—who are in a position to intervene in his performance at any time. This aspect of filmmaking is highly significant in social terms. For the intervention in a performance by a body of experts is also characteristic of sporting performances and, in a wider sense, of all test performances. The entire process of film production is determined, in fact, by such intervention. As we know, many shots are filmed in a number of takes. A single cry for help, for example, can be recorded in several different versions. The editor then makes a selection from these; in a sense, he establishes one of them as the record. An action performed in the film studio therefore differs from the corresponding real action the way the competitive throwing of a discus in a sports arena would differ from the throwing of the same discus from the same spot in the same direction in order to kill someone. The first is a test performance, while the second is not.

The test performance of the film actor is, however, entirely unique in kind. In what does this performance consist? It consists in crossing a certain barrier which confines the social value of test performances within narrow limits. I am referring now not to a performance in the world of sports, but to a performance produced in a mechanized test. In a sense, the athlete is confronted only by natural tests. He measures himself against tasks set by nature, not by equipment—apart from exceptional cases like Nurmi, who was said to run against the clock.[23] Meanwhile the work process, especially since it has been standardized by the assembly line, daily generates countless mechanized tests. These tests are performed unawares, and those who fail are excluded from the work process. But they are also conducted openly, in agencies for testing professional aptitude. In both cases, the test subject faces the barrier mentioned above.

These tests, unlike those in the world of sports, are incapable of being publicly exhibited to the degree one would desire. And this is precisely where film comes into play. *Film makes test performances capable of being exhibited, by turning that ability itself into a test.* The film actor performs not in front of an audience but in front of an apparatus. The film director occupies exactly the same position as the examiner in an aptitude test. To perform in the glare of arc lamps while simultaneously meeting the demands of the microphone is a test performance of the highest order. To accomplish it is to preserve one's humanity in the face of the apparatus. Interest in this performance is widespread. For the majority of city dwellers, throughout the workday in offices and factories, have to relinquish their humanity in the face of an apparatus. In the evening these same masses fill the cinemas, to witness the film actor taking revenge on their behalf not only by asserting *his* humanity (or what appears to them as such) against the apparatus, but by placing that apparatus in the service of his triumph.

XI

In the case of film, the fact that the actor represents someone else before the audience matters much less than the fact that he represents himself before the apparatus. One of the first to sense this transformation of the actor by the test performance was Pirandello.[24] That his remarks on the subject in his novel *Sigira* [Shoot!] are confined to the negative aspects of this change, and to silent film only, does little to diminish their relevance. For in this respect, the sound film changed nothing essential. What matters is that the actor is performing for a piece of equipment—or, in the case of sound film, for two pieces of equipment. "The film actor," Pirandello writes, "feels as if exiled. Exiled not only from the stage but from his own person. With a vague unease, he senses an inexplicable void, stemming from the fact that his body has lost its substance, that he has been volatilized, stripped of his reality, his life, his voice, the noises he makes when moving about, and has been turned into a mute image that flickers for a moment on the screen, then vanishes into silence. . . . The little apparatus will play with his shadow before the audience, and he himself must be content to play before the apparatus."[25] The situation can also be characterized as follows: for the first time—and this is the effect of film—the human being is placed in a position where he must operate with his whole living person, while forgoing its aura. For the aura is bound to his presence in the here and now. There is no facsimile of the aura. The aura surrounding Macbeth on the stage cannot be divorced from the aura which, for the living spectators, surrounds the actor who plays him. What distinguishes the shot in the film studio, however, is that the camera is substituted for the audience. As a result, the aura surrounding the actor is dispelled—and, with it, the aura of the figure he portrays.

It is not surprising that it should be a dramatist such as Pirandello who, in reflecting on the special character of film acting, inadvertently touches on the crisis now affecting the theater. Indeed, nothing contrasts more starkly with a work of art completely subject to (or, like film, founded in) technological reproduction than a stage play. Any thorough consideration will confirm this. Expert observers have long recognized that, in film, "the best effects are almost always achieved by 'acting' as little as possible. . . . The development," according to Rudolf Arnheim, writing in 1932, has been toward "using the actor as one of the 'props,' chosen for his typicalness and . . . introduced in the proper context."[26] Closely bound up with this development is something else. *The stage actor identifies himself with a role. The film actor very often is denied this opportunity.* His performance is by no means a unified whole, but is assembled from many individual performances. Apart from incidental concerns about studio rental, availability of other actors, scenery, and so on, there are elementary necessities of the machinery that split the actor's performance into a series of episodes capable of being assembled. In particular, lighting and its installation require the representation of an action—which on the screen appears as a swift, unified sequence—to be filmed in a series of separate takes, which may be spread over hours in the studio. Not to mention the more obvious effects of montage. A leap from a window, for example, can be shot in the studio as a leap from a scaffold, while the ensuing fall may be filmed weeks later at an outdoor location. And far more paradoxical cases can easily be imagined. Let us assume that an actor is supposed to be startled by a knock at the door. If his reaction is not satisfactory, the director can resort to an expedient: he could have a shot fired without warning behind the actor's back on some other occasion when he happens to be in the studio. The actor's frightened reaction at that moment could be recorded and then edited into the film. Nothing shows more graphically that art has escaped the realm of "beautiful semblance," which for so long was regarded as the only sphere in which it could thrive.[27]

XII

The representation of human beings by means of an apparatus has made possible a highly productive use of the human being's self-alienation. The nature of this use can be grasped through the fact that the film actor's estrangement in the face of the apparatus, as Pirandello describes this experience, is basically of the same kind as the estrangement felt before one's appearance [*Erscheinung*] in a mirror—a favorite theme of the Romantics. But now the mirror image [*Bild*] has become detachable from the person mirrored, and is transportable. And where is it transported? To a site in front of the masses.[28] Naturally, the screen actor never for a moment ceases to be aware of this. While he stands before the apparatus, he knows that in the end he is confronting the masses. It is they who will control him. Those who are not visible, not present while he executes his performance, are precisely the ones who will control it. This invisibility heightens the authority of their control. It should not be forgotten, of course, that there can be no political advantage derived from this control until film has liberated itself from the fetters of capitalist exploitation. Film capital uses the revolutionary opportunities implied by this control for counterrevolutionary purposes. Not only does the cult of the movie star which it fosters preserve that magic of the personality which has long been no more than the putrid magic of its own commodity character, but its counterpart, the cult of the audience, reinforces the corruption by which fascism is seeking to supplant the class consciousness of the masses.[29]

XIII

It is inherent in the technology of film, as of sports, that everyone who witnesses these performances does so as a quasi-expert. Anyone who has listened to a group of newspaper boys leaning on their bicycles and discussing the outcome of a bicycle race will have an inkling of this. In the case of film, the newsreel demonstrates unequivocally that any individual can be in a position to be filmed. But that possibility is not enough. *Any person today can lay claim to being filmed.* This claim can best be clarified by considering the historical situation of literature today.

For centuries it was in the nature of literature that a small number of writers confronted many thousands of readers. This began to change toward the end of the past century. With the growth and extension of the press, which constantly made new political, religious, scientific, professional, and local journals available to readers, an increasing number of readers—in isolated cases, at first—turned into writers. It began with the space set aside for "letters to the editor" in the daily press, and has now reached a point where there is hardly a European engaged in the work process who could not, in principle, find an opportunity to publish somewhere or other an account of a work experience, a complaint, a report, or something of the kind. Thus, the distinction between author and public is about to lose its axiomatic character. The difference becomes functional; it may vary from case to case. At any moment, the reader is ready to become a writer. As an expert—which he has had to become in any case in a highly specialized work process, even if only in some minor capacity—the reader gains access to authorship. Work itself is given a voice. And the ability to describe a job in words now forms part of the expertise needed to carry it out. Literary competence is no longer founded on specialized higher education but on polytechnic training, and thus is common property.

All this can readily be applied to film, where shifts that in literature took place over centuries have occurred in a decade. In cinematic practice—above all, in Russia—this shift has already been partly realized. Some of the actors taking part in Russian films are not actors in our sense but people who portray *themselves*—and primarily in their own work process. In western Europe today, the capitalist exploitation of film obstructs the human being's legitimate claim to being reproduced. The claim is also obstructed, incidentally, by unemployment, which excludes large masses from production—the process in which their primary entitlement to be reproduced would lie. Under these circumstances, the film industry has an overriding interest in stimulating the involvement of the masses through illusionary displays and ambiguous speculations. To this end it has set in motion an immense publicity machine, in the service of which it has placed the careers and love lives of the stars; it has organized polls; it has held beauty contests. All this in order to distort and corrupt the original and justified interest of the masses in film—an interest in understanding themselves and therefore their class. Thus, the same is true of film capital in particular as of fascism in general: a compelling urge toward new social opportunities is being clandestinely exploited in the interests of a property-owning minority. For this reason alone, the expropriation of film capital is an urgent demand for the proletariat.

XIV

The shooting of a film, especially a sound film, offers a hitherto unimaginable spectacle. It presents a process in which it is impossible to assign to the spectator a single viewpoint which would exclude from his or her field of vision the equipment not directly involved in the action being filmed—the camera, the lighting units, the technical crew, and so forth (unless the alignment of the spectator's pupil coincided with that of the camera). This circumstance, more than any other, makes any resemblance between a scene in a film studio and one onstage superficial and irrelevant. In principle, the theater includes a position from which the action on the stage cannot easily be detected as an illusion. There is no such position where a film is being shot. The illusory nature of film is of the second degree; it is the result of editing. That is to say: *In the film studio the apparatus has penetrated so deeply into reality that a pure view of that reality, free of the foreign body of equipment, is the result of a special procedure— namely, the shooting by the specially adjusted photographic device and the assembly of that shot with others of the same kind.* The equipment-free aspect of reality has here become the height of artifice, and the vision of immediate reality the Blue Flower in the land of technology.[30]

This state of affairs, which contrasts so sharply with that which obtains in the theater, can be compared even more instructively to the situation in painting. Here we have to pose the question: How does the camera operator compare with the painter? In answer to this, it will be helpful to consider the concept of the operator as it is familiar to us from surgery. The surgeon represents the polar opposite of the magician. The attitude of the magician, who heals a sick person by a laying-on of hands, differs from that of the surgeon, who makes an intervention in the patient. The magician maintains the natural distance between himself and the person treated; more precisely, he reduces it slightly by laying on his hands, but increases it greatly by his authority. The surgeon does exactly the reverse: he greatly diminishes the distance from the patient by penetrating the patient's body, and increases it only slightly by the caution with which his hand moves among the organs. In short: unlike the magician (traces of whom are still found in the medical practitioner), the surgeon abstains at the decisive moment from confronting his patient person to person; instead, he penetrates the patient by operating.—Magician is to surgeon as painter is to cinematographer. The painter maintains in his work a natural distance from reality, whereas the cinematographer penetrates deeply into its tissue. The images obtained by each differ enormously. The painter's is a total image, whereas that of the cinematographer is piecemeal, its manifold parts being assembled according to a new law. *Hence, the presentation of reality in film is incomparably the more significant for people of today, since it provides the equipment-free aspect of reality they are entitled to demand from a work of art, and does so precisely on the basis of the most intensive interpenetration of reality with equipment.*

XV

The technological reproducibility of the artwork changes the relation of the masses to art. The extremely backward attitude toward a Picasso painting changes into a highly progressive reaction to a Chaplin film. The progressive attitude is characterized by an immediate, intimate fusion of pleasure—pleasure in seeing and experiencing—with an attitude of expert appraisal. Such a fusion is an important social index. As is clearly seen in the case of painting, the more reduced the social impact of an art form, the more widely criticism and enjoyment of it diverge in the public. The conventional is uncritically enjoyed, while the truly new is criticized with aversion. Not so in the cinema. The decisive reason for this is that nowhere more than in the cinema are the reactions of individuals, which together make up the massive reaction of the audience, determined by the imminent concentration of reactions into a mass. No sooner are these reactions manifest than they regulate one another. Again, the comparison with painting is fruitful. A painting has always exerted a claim to be viewed primarily by a single person or by a few. The simultaneous viewing of paintings by a large audience, as happens in the nineteenth century, is an early symptom of the crisis in painting, a crisis triggered not only by photography but, in a relatively independent way, by the artwork's claim to the attention of the masses.

Painting, by its nature, cannot provide an object of simultaneous collective reception, as architecture has always been able to do, as the epic poem could do at one time, and as film is able to do today. And although direct conclusions about the social role of painting cannot be drawn from this fact alone, it does have a strongly adverse effect whenever painting is led by special circumstances, as if against its nature, to confront the masses directly. In the churches and monasteries of the Middle Ages, and at the princely courts up to about the end of the eighteenth century, the collective reception of paintings took place not simultaneously but in a manifoldly graduated and hierarchically mediated way. If that has changed, the change testifies to the special conflict in which painting has become enmeshed by the technological reproducibility of the image. And while efforts have been made to present paintings to the masses in galleries and salons, this mode of reception gives the masses no means of organizing and regulating their response. Thus, the same public which reacts progressively to a slapstick comedy inevitably displays a backward attitude toward Surrealism.

XVI

The most important social function of film is to establish equilibrium between human beings and the apparatus. Film achieves this goal not only in terms of man's presentation of himself to the camera but also in terms of his representation of his environment by means of this apparatus. On the one hand, film furthers insight into the necessities governing our lives by its use of close-ups, by its accentuation of hidden details in familiar objects, and by its exploration of commonplace milieux through the ingenious guidance of the camera; on the other hand, it manages to assure us of a vast and unsuspected field of action [*Spielraum*].

Our bars and city streets, our offices and furnished rooms, our railroad stations and our factories seemed to close relentlessly around us. Then came film and exploded this prison-world with the dynamite of the split second, so that now we can set off calmly on journeys of adventure among its far-flung debris. With the close-up, space expands; with slow motion, movement is extended. And just as enlargement not merely clarifies what we see indistinctly "in any case," but brings to light entirely new structures of matter, slow motion not only reveals familiar aspects of movements, but discloses quite unknown aspects within them—aspects "which do not appear as the retarding of natural movements but have a curious gliding, floating character of their own."[31] Clearly, it is another nature which speaks to the camera as compared to the eye. "Other" above all in the sense that a space informed by human consciousness gives way to a space informed by the unconscious. Whereas it is a commonplace that, for example, we have some idea what is involved in the act of walking (if only in general terms), we have no idea at all what happens during the split second when a person actually takes a step. We are familiar with the movement of picking up a cigarette lighter or a spoon, but know almost nothing of what really goes on between hand and metal, and still less how this varies with different moods. This is where the camera comes into play, with all its resources for swooping and rising, disrupting and isolating, stretching or compressing a sequence, enlarging or reducing an object. It is through the camera that we first discover the optical unconscious, just as we discover the instinctual unconscious through psychoanalysis.

Moreover, these two types of unconscious are intimately linked. For in most cases the diverse aspects of reality captured by the film camera lie outside only the *normal* spectrum of sense impressions. Many of the deformations and stereotypes, transformations and catastrophes which can assail the optical world in films afflict the actual world in psychoses, hallucinations, and dreams. Thanks to the camera, therefore, the individual perceptions of the psychotic or the dreamer can be appropriated by collective perception. The ancient truth expressed by Heraclitus, that those who are awake have a world in common while each sleeper has a world of his own, has been invalidated by film—and less by depicting the dream world itself than by creating figures of collective dream, such as the globe-encircling Mickey Mouse.[32]

If one considers the dangerous tensions which technology and its consequences have engendered in the masses at large—tendencies which at critical stages take on a psychotic character—one also has to recognize that this same technologization [Technisierung] has created the possibility of psychic immunization against such mass psychoses. It does so by means of certain films in which the forced development of sadistic fantasies or masochistic delusions can prevent their natural and dangerous maturation in the masses. Collective laughter is one such preemptive and healing outbreak of mass psychosis. The countless grotesque events consumed in films are a graphic indication of the dangers threatening mankind from the repressions implicit in civilization. American slapstick comedies and Disney films trigger a therapeutic release of unconscious energies.[33] Their forerunner was the figure of the eccentric. He was the first to inhabit the new fields of action opened up by film—the first occupant of the newly built house. This is the context in which Chaplin takes on historical significance.

XVII

It has always been one of the primary tasks of art to create a demand whose hour of full satisfaction has not yet come.[34] The history of every art form has critical periods in which the particular form strains after effects which can be easily achieved only with a changed technical standard—that is to say, in a new art form. The excesses and crudities of art which thus result, particularly in periods of so-called decadence, actually emerge from the core of its richest historical energies. In recent years, Dadaism has amused itself with such barbarisms. Only now is its impulse recognizable: *Dadaism attempted to produce with the means of painting (or literature) the effects which the public today seeks in film.*

Every fundamentally new, pioneering creation of demand will overshoot its target. Dadaism did so to the extent that it sacrificed the market values so characteristic of film in favor of more significant aspirations—of which, to be sure, it was unaware in the form described here. The Dadaists attached much less importance to the commercial usefulness of their artworks than to the uselessness of those works as objects of contemplative immersion. They sought to achieve this uselessness not least by thorough degradation of their material. Their poems are "word-salad" containing obscene expressions and every imaginable kind of linguistic refuse. The same is true of their paintings, on which they mounted buttons or train tickets. What they achieved by such means was a ruthless annihilation of the aura in every object they produced, which they branded as a reproduction through the very means of its production. Before a painting by Arp or a poem by August Stramm, it is impossible to take time for concentration and evaluation, as one can before a painting by Derain or a poem by Rilke.[35] Contemplative immersion—which, as the bourgeoisie degenerated, became a breeding ground for asocial behavior—is here opposed by distraction [*Ablenkung*] as a variant of social behavior. Dadaist manifestations actually guaranteed a quite vehement distraction by making artworks the center of scandal. One requirement was paramount: to outrage the public.

From an alluring visual composition or an enchanting fabric of sound, the Dadaists turned the artwork into a missile. It jolted the viewer, taking on a tactile [*taktisch*] quality. It thereby fostered the demand for film, since the distracting element in film is also primarily tactile, being based on successive changes of scene and focus which have a percussive effect on the spectator.[36] *Film has freed the physical shock effect—which Dadaism had kept wrapped, as it were, inside the moral shock effect—from this wrapping.*

XVIII

The masses are a matrix from which all customary behavior toward works of art is today emerging newborn. Quantity has been transformed into quality: *the greatly increased mass of participants has produced a different kind of participation.* The fact that this new mode of participation first appeared in a disreputable form should not mislead the observer. The masses are criticized for seeking distraction [*Zerstreuung*] in the work of art, whereas the art lover supposedly approaches it with concentration. In the case of the masses, the artwork is seen as a means of entertainment; in the case of the art lover, it is considered an object of devotion.—This calls for closer examination.[37] Distraction and concentration form an antithesis, which may be formulated as follows. A person who concentrates before a work of art is absorbed by it; he enters into the work, just as, according to legend, a Chinese painter entered his completed painting while beholding it.[38] By contrast, the distracted masses absorb the work of art into themselves. Their waves lap around it; they encompass it with their tide. This is most obvious with regard to buildings. Architecture has always offered the prototype of an artwork that is received in a state of distraction and through the collective. The laws of architecture's reception are highly instructive.

Buildings have accompanied human existence since primeval times. Many art forms have come into being and passed away. Tragedy begins with the Greeks, is extinguished along with them, and is revived centuries later. The epic, which originates in the early days of peoples, dies out in Europe at the end of the Renaissance. Panel painting is a creation of the Middle Ages, and nothing guarantees its uninterrupted existence. But the human need for shelter is permanent. Architecture has never had fallow periods. Its history is longer than that of any other art, and its effect ought to be recognized in any attempt to account for the relationship of the masses to the work of art. Buildings are received in a twofold manner: by use and by perception. Or, better: tactilely and optically. Such reception cannot be understood in terms of the concentrated attention of a traveler before a famous building. On the tactile side, there is no counterpart to what contemplation is on the optical side. Tactile reception comes about not so much by way of attention as by way of habit. The latter largely determines even the optical reception of architecture, which spontaneously takes the form of casual noticing, rather than attentive observation. Under certain circumstances, this form of reception shaped by architecture acquires canonical value. *For the tasks which face the human apparatus of perception at historical turning points cannot be performed solely by optical means—that is, by way of contemplation. They are mastered gradually—taking their cue from tactile reception—through habit.*

Even the distracted person can form habits. What is more, the ability to master certain tasks in a state of distraction first proves that their performance has become habitual. The sort of distraction that is provided by art represents a covert measure of the extent to which it has become possible to perform new tasks of apperception. Since, moreover, individuals are tempted to evade such tasks, art will tackle the most difficult and most important tasks wherever it is able to mobilize the masses. It does so currently in film. *Reception in distraction—the sort of reception which is increasingly noticeable in all areas of art and is a symptom of profound changes in apperception—finds in film its true training ground.* Film, by virtue of its shock effects, is predisposed to this form of reception. In this respect, too, it proves to be the most important subject matter, at present, for the theory of perception which the Greeks called aesthetics.[39]

XIX

The increasing proletarianization of modern man and the increasing formation of masses are two sides of the same process. Fascism attempts to organize the newly proletarianized masses while leaving intact the property relations which they strive to abolish. It sees its salvation in granting expression to the masses—but on no account granting them rights.[40] The masses have a *right* to changed property relations; fascism seeks to give them *expression* in keeping these relations unchanged. *The logical outcome of fascism is an aestheticizing of political life.* With D'Annunzio, decadence made its entry into political life; with Marinetti, Futurism; and with Hitler, the Bohemian tradition of Schwabing.[41]

All efforts to aestheticize politics culminate in one point. That one point is war. War, and only war, makes it possible to set a goal for mass movements on the grandest scale while preserving traditional property relations. That is how the situation presents itself in political terms. In technological terms it can be formulated as follows: only war makes it possible to mobilize all of today's technological resources while maintaining property relations. It goes without saying that the fascist glorification of war does not make use of *these* arguments. Nevertheless, a glance at such glorification is instructive. In Marinetti's manifesto for the colonial war in Ethiopia, we read:

For twenty-seven years, we Futurists have rebelled against the idea that war is anti-aesthetic. . . . We therefore state: . . . War is beautiful because—thanks to its gas masks, its terrifying megaphones, its flame throwers, and light tanks—it establishes man's dominion over the subjugated machine. War is beautiful because it inaugurates the dreamed-of metallization of the human body. War is beautiful because it enriches a flowering meadow with the fiery orchids of machine-guns. War is beautiful because it combines gunfire, barrages, cease-fires, scents, and the fragrance of putrefaction into a symphony. War is beautiful because it creates new architectures, like those of armored tanks, geometric squadrons of aircraft, spirals of smoke from burning villages, and much more. . . . Poets and artists of Futurism, . . . remember these principles of an aesthetic of war, that they may illuminate . . . your struggles for a new poetry and a new sculpture![42]

This manifesto has the merit of clarity. The question it poses deserves to be taken up by the dialectician. To him, the aesthetic of modern warfare appears as follows: if the natural use of productive forces is impeded by the property system, then the increase in technological means, in speed, in sources of energy will press toward an unnatural use. This is found in war, and the destruction caused by war furnishes proof that society was not mature enough to make technology its organ, that technology was not sufficiently developed to master the elemental forces of society. The most horrifying features of imperialist war are determined by the discrepancy between the enormous means of production and their inadequate use in the process of production (in other words, by unemployment and the lack of markets). *Imperialist war is an uprising on the part of technology, which demands repayment in "human material" for the natural material society has denied it.* Instead of deploying power stations across the land, society deploys manpower in the form of armies. Instead of promoting air traffic, it promotes traffic in shells. And in gas warfare it has found a new means of abolishing the aura.

"Fiat ars—pereat mundus,"[43] says fascism, expecting from war, as Marinetti admits, the artistic gratification of a sense perception altered by technology. This is evidently the consummation of *l'art pour l'art.* Humankind, which once, in Homer, was an object of contemplation for the Olympian gods, has now become one for itself. Its self-alienation has reached the point where it can experience its own annihilation as a supreme aesthetic pleasure. *Such is the aestheticizing of politics, as practiced by fascism. Communism replies by politicizing art.*

Notes

Benjamin's essay underwent a number of drafts and revisions. The original version of the essay was entitled "Das Kunstwerk im Zeitalter seiner technischen Reproduzierbarkeit," which is translated by contemporary authors as "The Work of Art in the Age of Its Technological Reproducibility" or as "The Work of Art in the Time of Its Technological Reproducibility," the latter to emphasize the question of time and Benjamin's proposal of an alteration in its relation to space. This original version was written during the autumn and early winter of 1935 in the form of nineteen numbered and titled reflections, and to this day has not been published in English. The essay was published the following year in an abbreviated translation by Pierre Klossowski, having been modified on the recommendations of Max Horkheimer and the Institut für Sozialforschung, entitled, "L'œuvre d'art à l'époque de sa reproduction méchanisée"; this version was published in the institute's journal: *Zeitschrift für Sozialforschung* 5 (Paris: Félix Alcan, 1936), pp. 40–68. Meanwhile, Benjamin continued to work on the essay, incorporating suggestions made by Max Horkheimer and Theodor Adorno. Completed by the beginning of February 1936, this second version, reproduced here, is published in *Walter Benjamin: Selected Writings*, vol. 3: *1935–1938*, ed. Howard Eiland and Michael W. Jennings, trans. Edmund Jephcott and Harry Zohn (Cambridge, MA: Belknap Press of Harvard University Press, 2006). Soon after, Benjamin initiated a third rewrite, which went on until March or April 1939 and which deletes some sections of the first version while also changing a number of its formulations. This is the version reprinted in Theodor Adorno's 1955 edition of Benjamin's *Schriften* (*Gesammelte Schriften* 1.2 [Frankfurt: Suhrkamp, 1974], pp. 474 ff.) and is the version that has been known in the English-speaking world as "The Work of Art in the Age of Mechanical Reproduction" through Harry Zohn's translation in *Illuminations*, ed. Hannah Arendt (New York: Schocken, 1969), pp. 218–53, and republished in Walter Benjamin, *Selected Writings*, vol. 4: *1938–1940* (Cambridge, MA: Harvard University Press, 2006). Benjamin's redraftings reflect both his unfulfilled desire to get the essay published and his attempt to negotiate the differences of opinions raised and anticipated by the initial readers of his essay, which included Theodor W. Adorno, Bertolt Brecht, the scholar of Jewish mysticism Gersholm Scholem, and the Paris organization of communist writers.

1. In the past, readings of Benjamin's essay have tended to see it as an important forerunner of Pop Art, especially the work of Andy Warhol, with its use of mechanically produced repeated images. Certainly, Benjamin's essay is centrally concerned to overthrow the idea of the "original" work of art. More recently, however, there has been a reconsideration of Benjamin's essay, centered particularly upon the various meanings of the German word *reproduzierbarkeit*.

2. Samuel Weber, *Mass Mediauras: Form, Technics, Media*, ed. Alan Cholodenko (Stanford: Stanford University Press, 1996), p. 88.

3. In "Little History of Photography" Benjamin expands on this interpretation of the daguerreotype with particular reference to David Octavius Hill's photograph of *A Newhaven Fishwife* and Dauthendey's portrait of himself with his young wife. Dauthendey, himself, spoke of being "abashed" by the human presence in such images, believing "that the little tiny faces in the picture could see *us*, so powerfully was everyone affected by the unaccustomed clarity and the unaccustomed truth to nature of the first daguerreotypes." *Walter Benjamin, Selected Writings*, vol. 2, part 2: *1931–34*, ed. Michael W. Jennings, Howard Eiland, and Gary Smith (Cambridge, MA: Belknap Press of Harvard University Press, 1999), pp. 507–30.

4. For Theodor W. Adorno's letter of May 1936 in response to Walter Benjamin's essay, see Theodor W. Adorno and Walter Benjamin, *The Complete Correspondence, 1928–1940*, ed. Henri Lonitz, trans. Nicholas Walker (Cambridge: Polity, 1999), pp. 127–34. Additionally, see Theodor W. Adorno and Max Horkheimer, "The Culture Industry: Enlightenment as Mass Deception" (*Reader* text 3), which presents a diametrically opposed view about mass culture, critiquing Benjamin's arguments almost point by point.

5. Madame Claire de Duras, née Kersaint (1778–1828). Benjamin cites Madame de Duras in the original French.

6. Karl Marx (1818–1883), *Das Kapital,* 3 vols. (1867, 1885, 1895).
7. Abel Gance, "Le Temps de l'image est venu!" (It is time for the image!), in Léon Pierre-Quint, Germaine Dulac, Lionel Landry, and Abel Gance, *L'Art cinématographique* (Paris, 1927), 2:94–99.
8. Alois Riegl (1858–1905) was an Austrian art historian.
9. "Einmalige Erscheinung einer Ferne, so nah sie sein mag." At stake in Benjamin's formulation is an interweaving not just of time and space—*einmalige Erscheinung,* literally "one-time appearance"—but of far and near, *eine Ferne* suggesting both "a distance" in space or time and "something remote," however near it (the distance, or distant thing, that appears) may be.
10. Benjamin is quoting Johannes V. Jensen, *Exotische Novellen,* trans. Julia Koppel (Berlin: S. Fischer, 1919), pp. 41–42.
11. Applying Kant's idea of the pure and disinterested existence of the work of art, the French philosopher Victor Cousin made use of the phrase *l'art por art* (art for art's sake) in his 1818 lecture "Du Vrai, du beau, et du bien" (On the true, the beautiful, and the good). The idea was later given currency by writers such as Théophile Gautier, Edgar Allen Poe, and Charles Baudelaire.
12. Stéphane Mallarmé (1842–1898).
13. In film, the technological reproducibility of the product is not an externally imposed condition of its mass dissemination, as it is, say, in literature or painting. *The technological reproducibility of films is based directly on the technology of their production. This not only makes possible the mass dissemination of films in the most direct way, but actually enforces it.* It does so because the process of producing a film is so costly that an individual who could afford to buy a painting, for example, could not afford to buy a [master print of a] film. It was calculated in 1927 that, in order to make a profit, a major film needed to reach an audience of nine million. Of course, the advent of sound film [in that year] initially caused a movement in the opposite direction: its audience was restricted by language boundaries. And that coincided with the emphasis placed on national interests by fascism. But it is less important to note this setback (which, in any case, was mitigated by dubbing) than to observe its connection with fascism. The simultaneity of the two phenomena results from the economic crisis. The same disorders which led, in the world at large, to an attempt to maintain existing property relations by brute force induced film capital, under the threat of crisis, to speed up the development of sound film. Its introduction brought temporary relief, not only because sound film attracted the masses back into the cinema but also because it consolidated new capital from the electricity industry with that of film. Thus, considered from the outside, sound film promoted national interests, but, seen from the inside, it helped internationalize film production even more than before. [By "the economic crisis," Benjamin refers to the devastating consequences, in the United States and Europe, of the stock market crash of October 1929.—TRANS.]
14. This polarity cannot come into its own in the aesthetics of Idealism, which conceives of beauty as something fundamentally undivided (and thus excludes anything polarized). Nonetheless, in Hegel this polarity announces itself as clearly as possible within the limits of Idealism. We quote from his *Vorlesungen zur Philosophie der Geschichte* [Lectures on the philosophy of history]: "Images were known of old. In those early days piety required them for worship, but it could do without *beautiful* images. Such images might even be disturbing. In every beautiful image, there is also something external—although, insofar as the image is beautiful, its spirit still speaks to the human being. But religious worship, being no more than a spiritless torpor of the soul, is

directed at a *thing*. . . . Fine art arose . . . in the church . . . , though art has now gone beyond the ecclesiastical principle." Likewise, the following passage from the *Vorlesungen über die Ästhetik* [Lectures on aesthetics] indicates that Hegel sensed a problem here: "We are beyond the stage of venerating works of art as divine and as objects deserving our worship. Today the impression they produce is of a more reflective kind, and the emotions they arouse require a more stringent test."

15. The aim of revolutions is to accelerate this adaptation. Revolutions are innervations of the collective—or, more precisely, efforts at innervation on the part of the new, historically unique collective which has its organs in the new technology. This second technology is a system in which the mastering of elementary social forces is a precondition for playing [*das Spiel*] with natural forces. Just as a child who has learned to grasp stretches out its hand for the moon as it would for a ball, so humanity, in its efforts at innervation, sets its sights as much on currently utopian goals as on goals within reach. For in revolutions, it is not only the second technology which asserts its claims vis-à-vis society. Because this technology aims at liberating human beings from drudgery, the individual suddenly sees his scope for play, his field of action [*Spielraum*], immeasurably expanded. He does not yet know his way around this space. But already he registers his demands on it. For the more the collective makes the second technology its own, the more keenly individuals belonging to the collective feel how little they have received of what was due them under the dominion of the first technology. In other words, it is the individual liberated by the liquidation of the first technology who stakes his claim. No sooner has the second technology secured its initial revolutionary gains than vital questions affecting the individual—questions of love and death which had been buried by the first technology—once again press for solutions. Fourier's work is the first historical evidence of this demand. Charles Fourier (1772–1837), French social theorist and reformer.

16. Eugène Atget (1857–1927).

17. *A Woman of Paris* (1923)—which Benjamin refers to by its French title, *L'Opinion publique*—was written and directed by Charlie Chaplin.

18. On the nineteenth-century quarrel between painting and photography, see Benjamin, "Little History of Photography," 2.2:514–15, 526–27; and Benjamin, *The Arcades Project,* trans. Howard Eiland and Keven McLaughlin (Cambridge, MA: Harvard University Press, 1999), pp. 684–92.

19. Gance, "Le Temps de l'image est venu!" p. 101.

20. Séverin-Mars, cited in Gance, p. 100.

21. Charlie Chaplin wrote and directed *The Gold Rush* in 1925.

22. Franz Werfel, "Ein Sommernachtstraum: Ein Film von Shakespeare und Reinhardt," *Neues Wiener Journal,* cited in *Lu,* November 15, 1935.

23. Paavo Nurmi (1897–1973), a Finnish long-distance runner, was a winner at the Olympic Games in Antwerp (1920), Paris (1924), and Amsterdam (1928).

24. The Italian playwright and novelist Luigi Pirandello (1867–1936).

25. Luigi Pirandello, *Il turno* (The Turn), cited by Léon Pierre-Quint, "Signification du cinéma," *L'Art cinéematographique* 2:14–15.

26. Rudolf Arnheim, *Film als Kunst* (Berlin, 1932), pp. 176–77. In this context, certain apparently incidental details of film directing which diverge from practices on the stage take on added interest. For example, the attempt to let the actor perform without makeup, as in Dreyer's *Jeanne d'Arc.* Dreyer spent months seeking the forty actors who constitute the Inquisitors' tribunal. Searching for these actors was like hunting for rare props. Dreyer made every effort to avoid resemblances of age, build, and

physiognomy in the actors. See Maurice Schultz, "Le Maquillage" (Makeup), in *L'Art cinématographique* 6 (Paris, 1929): 65–66. If the actor thus becomes a prop, the prop, in its turn, not infrequently functions as actor. At any rate, it is not unusual for films to allocate a role to a prop. Rather than selecting examples at random from the infinite number available, let us take just one especially revealing case. A clock that is running will always be a disturbance on the stage, where it cannot be permitted its role of measuring time. Even in a naturalistic play, real-life time would conflict with theatrical time. In view of this, it is most revealing that film—where appropriate—can readily make use of time as measured by a clock. This feature, more than many others, makes it clear that—circumstances permitting—each and every prop in a film may perform decisive functions. From here it is but a step to Pudovkin's principle, which states that "to connect the performance of an actor with an object, and to build that performance around the object, . . . is always one of the most powerful methods of cinematic construction." V. I. Pudovkin, *Film Regie und Filmmanuskript* (Film direction and the film script) (Berlin, 1928), p. 126. Film is thus the first artistic medium which is able to show how matter plays havoc with human beings (*wie die Materie dem Menschen mitspielt*). It follows that films can be an excellent means of materialist exposition.

27. The significance of beautiful semblance (*schöner Schein*) is rooted in the age of auratic perception that is now coming to an end. The aesthetic theory of that era was most fully articulated by Hegel, for whom beauty is "the appearance [*Erscheinung*] of spirit in its immediate . . . sensuous form, created by the spirit as the form adequate to itself." Hegel, *Werke*, vol. 10, part 2 (Berlin, 1837), p. 121. Although this formulation has some derivative qualities, Hegel's statement that art strips away the "semblance and deception of this false, transient world" from the "true content of phenomena" (*Werke*, vol. 10, part 1, p. 13) already diverges from the traditional experiential basis (*Erfahrungsgrund*) of this doctrine. This ground of experience is the aura. By contrast, Goethe's work is still entirely imbued with beautiful semblance as an auratic reality. Mignon, Ottilie, and Helena partake of that reality. "The beautiful is neither the veil nor the veiled object but rather the object *in* its veil": this is the quintessence of Goethe's view of art, and that of antiquity. The decline of this view makes it doubly urgent that we look back at its origin. This lies in mimesis as the primal phenomenon of all artistic activity. The mime presents what he mimes merely as semblance (*Der Nachmachende macht, was er macht, nur scheinbar*). And the oldest form of imitation had only a single material to work with: the body of the mime himself. Dance and language, gestures of body and lips, are the earliest manifestations of mimesis.—The mime presents his subject as a semblance (*Der Nachmachende macht seine Sache scheinbar*). One could also say that he plays his subject. Thus we encounter the polarity informing mimesis. In mimesis, tightly interfolded like cotyledons, slumber the two aspects of art: semblance and play. Of course, this polarity can interest the dialectician only if it has a historical role. And that is, in fact, the case. This role is determined by the world-historical conflict between the first and second technologies. Semblance is the most abstract—but therefore the most ubiquitous—schema of all the magic procedures of the first technology, whereas play is the inexhaustible reservoir of all the experimenting procedures of the second. Neither the concept of semblance nor that of play is foreign to traditional aesthetics; and to the extent that the two concepts of cult value and exhibition value are latent in the other pair of concepts at issue here, they say nothing new. But this abruptly changes as soon as these latter concepts lose their indifference toward history. They then lead to a practical insight—namely, that what is lost in the

withering of semblance and the decay of the aura in works of art is matched by a huge gain in the scope for play (*Spiel-Raum*). This space for play is widest in film. In film, the element of semblance has been entirely displaced by the element of play. The positions which photography had occupied at the expense of cult value have thus been massively fortified. In film, the element of semblance has yielded its place to the element of play, which is allied to the second technology. Ramuz recently summed up this alliance in a formulation which, in the guise of a metaphor, gets to the heart of the matter. He says: "We are currently witnessing a fascinating process. The various sciences, which up to now have each operated alone in their special fields, are beginning to converge in their object and to be combined into a single science: chemistry, physics, and mechanics are becoming interlinked. It is as if we were eyewitnesses to the enormously accelerated completion of a jigsaw puzzle whose first pieces took several millennia to put in place, whereas the last, because of their contours, and to the astonishment of the spectators, are moving together of their own accord" (Charles Ferdinand Ramuz, "Paysan, nature" [Peasant, nature], *Mesure,* 4 [October 1935]). These words give ultimate expression to the dimension of play in the second technology, which reinforces that in art. [It should be kept in mind that *Schein* can mean "luster" and "appearance," as well as "semblance" or "illusion."—Trans.]

28. The change noted here in the mode of exhibition—a change brought about by reproduction technology—is also noticeable in politics. *The crisis of democracies can be understood as a crisis in the conditions governing the public presentation of politicians.* Democracies exhibit the politician directly, in person, before elected representatives. The parliament is his public. But innovations in recording equipment now enable the speaker to be heard by an unlimited number of people while he is speaking, and to be seen by an unlimited number shortly afterward. This means that priority is given to presenting the politician before the recording equipment. Parliaments are becoming depopulated at the same time as theaters. Radio and film are changing not only the function of the professional actor but, equally, the function of those who, like the politician, present themselves before these media. The direction of this change is the same for the film actor and the politician, regardless of their different tasks. It tends toward the exhibition of controllable, transferable skills under certain social conditions, just as sports first called for such exhibition under certain natural conditions. This results in a new form of selection—selection before an apparatus—from which the champion, the star, and the dictator emerge as victors.

29. It should be noted in passing that proletarian class consciousness, which is the most enlightened form of class consciousness, fundamentally transforms the structure of the proletarian masses. The class-conscious proletariat forms a compact mass only from the outside, in the minds of its oppressors. At the moment when it takes up its struggle for liberation, this apparently compact mass has actually already begun to loosen. It ceases to be governed by mere reactions; it makes the transition to action. The loosening of the proletarian masses is the work of solidarity. In the solidarity of the proletarian class struggle, the dead, undialectical opposition between individual and mass is abolished; for the comrade, it does not exist. Decisive as the masses are for the revolutionary leader, therefore, his great achievement lies not in drawing the masses after him, but in constantly incorporating himself into the masses, in order to be, for them, always one among hundreds of thousands. But the same class struggle which loosens the compact mass of the proletariat compresses that of the petty bourgeoisie. The mass as an impenetrable, compact entity, which Le Bon and others have made the subject of their "mass psychology," is that of the petty bourgeoisie. The petty

bourgeoisie is not a class; it is in fact only a mass. And the greater the pressure acting on it between the two antagonistic classes of the bourgeoisie and the proletariat, the more compact it becomes. In *this* mass the emotional element described in mass psychology is indeed a determining factor. But for that very reason this compact mass forms the antithesis of the proletarian cadre, which obeys a collective *ratio*. In the petty-bourgeois mass, the reactive moment described in mass psychology is indeed a determining factor. But precisely for that reason this compact mass with its unmediated reactions forms the antithesis of the proletarian cadre, whose actions are mediated by a task, however momentary. Demonstrations by the compact mass thus always have a panicked quality—whether they give vent to war fever, hatred of Jews, or the instinct for self-preservation. Once the distinction between the compact (that is, petty-bourgeois) mass and the class-conscious, proletarian mass has been clearly made, its operational significance is also clear. This distinction is nowhere more graphically illustrated than in the not uncommon cases when some outrage originally performed by the compact mass becomes, as a result of a revolutionary situation and perhaps within the space of seconds, the revolutionary action of a class. The special feature of such truly historic events is that a reaction by a compact mass sets off an internal upheaval which loosens its composition, enabling it to become aware of itself as an association of class-conscious cadres. Such concrete events contain in very abbreviated form what communist tacticians call "winning over the petty bourgeoisie." These tacticians have a further interest in clarifying this process. The ambiguous concept of the masses, and the indiscriminate references to their mood which are commonplace in the German revolutionary press, have undoubtedly fostered illusions which have had disastrous consequences for the German proletariat. Fascism, by contrast, has made excellent use of these laws—whether it understood them or not. It realizes that the more compact the masses it mobilizes, the better the chance that the counterrevolutionary instincts of the petty bourgeoisie will determine their reactions. The proletariat, on the other hand, is preparing for a society in which neither the objective nor the subjective conditions for the formation of masses will exist any longer.

30. Benjamin alludes here to *Heinrich von Ofterdingen,* an unfinished novel by Novalis first published in 1802 . . .

31. Arnheim, *Film als Kunst,* p. 138. [Benjamin's note. In English in Rudolf Arnheim, *Film as Art* (Berkeley: University of California Press, 1971), pp. 116–17].

32. Benjamin refers to Fragment 89 in the standard Diels-Kranz edition of the fragments of Heraclitus of Ephesus, the pre-Socratic philosopher of the sixth-fifth centuries BC. On Mickey Mouse, see the following note.

33. Of course, a comprehensive analysis of these films should not overlook their double meaning. It should start from the ambiguity of situations which have both a comic and a horrifying effect. As the reactions of children show, comedy and horror are closely related. In the face of certain situations, why shouldn't we be allowed to ask which reaction is the more human? Some recent Mickey Mouse films offer situations in which such a question seems justified. (Their gloomy and sinister fire-magic, made technically possible by color film, highlights a feature which up to now has been present only covertly, and shows how easily fascism takes over "revolutionary" innovations in this field too.) What is revealed in recent Disney films was latent in some of the earlier ones: the cozy acceptance of bestiality and violence as inevitable concomitants of existence. This renews an old tradition which is far from reassuring—the tradition inaugurated by the dancing hooligans to be found in depictions of medieval pogroms,

of whom the "riff-raff" in Grimm's fairy tale of that title are a pale, indistinct rear-guard.

34. "The artwork," writes André Breton, "has value only insofar as it is alive to reverberations of the future." And indeed every highly developed art form stands at the intersection of three lines of development. First, technology is working toward a particular form of art. Before film appeared, there were little books of photos that could be made to flit past the viewer under the pressure of the thumb, presenting a boxing match or a tennis match; then there were coin-operated peepboxes in bazaars, with image sequences kept in motion by the turning of a handle. Second, traditional art forms, at certain stages in their development, strain laboriously for effects which later are effortlessly achieved by new art forms. Before film became established, Dadaist performances sought to stir in their audiences reactions which Chaplin then elicited more naturally. Third, apparently insignificant social changes often foster a change in reception which benefits only the new art form. Before film had started to create its public, images (which were no longer motionless) were received by an assembled audience in the Kaiserpanorama. Here the audience faced a screen into which stereoscopes were fitted, one for each spectator. In front of these stereoscopes single images automatically appeared, remained briefly in view, and then gave way to others. Edison still had to work with similar means when he presented the first film strip—before the movie screen and projection were known; a small audience gazed into an apparatus in which a sequence of images was shown. Incidentally, the institution of the Kaiserpanorama very clearly manifests a dialectic of development. Shortly before film turned the viewing of images into a collective activity, image viewing by the individual, through the stereoscopes of these soon outmoded establishments, was briefly intensified, as it had been once before in the isolated contemplation of the divine image by the priest in the cella.

35. Hans Arp (1887–1966).

36. Let us compare the screen (*Leinwand*) on which a film unfolds with the canvas (*Leinwand*) of a painting. The image on the film screen changes, whereas the image on the canvas does not. The painting invites the viewer to contemplation; before it, he can give himself up to his train of associations. Before a film image, he cannot do so. No sooner has he seen it than it has already changed. It cannot be fixed on. The train of associations in the person contemplating it is immediately interrupted by new images. This constitutes the shock effect of film, which, like all shock effects, seeks to induce heightened attention. *Film is the art form corresponding to the pronounced threat to life in which people live today.* It corresponds to profound changes in the apparatus of apperception—changes that are experienced on the scale of private existence by each passerby in big-city traffic, and on the scale of world history by each fighter against the present social order. [Benjamin's note. A more literal translation of the last phrase before the sentence in italics is: "seeks to be buffered by intensified presence of mind [*Geistesgegenwart*]."—TRANS.]

37. Sections 17 and 18 of "The Work of Art in the Age of Its Technological Reproducibility" introduce the idea of a productive "reception in distraction" (*Rezeption in der Zerstreuung*), an idea indebted to the writings of Siegfried Kracauer and Louis Aragon. This positive idea of distraction—*Zerstreuung* also means "entertainment"—contrasts with the negative idea of distraction that Benjamin developed in such essays as "Theater and Radio" (1932) and "The Author as Producer" (1934); the latter idea is associated with the theory and practice of Bertolt Brecht's epic theater. See "Theory of Distraction" (1936). For these essays, see *Walter Benjamin: Selected Writings*, vol. 3: *1935–1938*.

38. Benjamin relates the legend of this Chinese painter in the earlier version of "The Mummerehlen," a section of *Berlin Childhood Around 1900*, trans. Howard Eiland, in *Walter Benjamin: Selected Writings*, vol. 3: *1935–1938*, ed. Howard Eiland and Michael W. Jennings, trans. Edmund Jephcott, Howard Eiland, and others (Cambridge, MA: Belknap Press of Harvard University Press, 2006).

39. The term *aesthetics* is a derivative of Greek *aisthētikos*, "of sense perception," from *aisthanesthai*, "to perceive."

40. A technological factor is important here, especially with regard to the newsreel, whose significance for propaganda purposes can hardly be overstated. *Mass reproduction is especially favored by the reproduction of the masses.* In great ceremonial processions, giant rallies and mass sporting events, and in war, all of which are now fed into the camera, the masses come face to face with themselves. This process, whose significance need not be emphasized, is closely bound up with the development of reproduction and recording technologies. In general, mass movements are more clearly apprehended by the camera than by the eye. A bird's-eye view best captures assemblies of hundreds of thousands. And even when this perspective is no less accessible to the human eye than to the camera, the image formed by the eye cannot be enlarged in the same way as a photograph. This is to say that mass movements, and above all war, are a form of human behavior especially suited to the camera.

41. Gabriele D'Annunzio (1863–1938), Italian writer, military hero, and political leader, was an ardent advocate of Italy's entry into World War I and, a few years later, an ardent Fascist. His life and his work are both characterized by superstition, amorality, and a lavish and vicious violence.

    Futurism was an artistic movement aiming to express the dynamic and violent quality of contemporary life, especially as embodied in the motion and force of modern machinery and modern warfare. It was founded by the Italian writer Emilio Filippo Tomaso Marinetti (1876–1944), whose "Manifeste de Futurisme" (Manifesto of futurism) was published in the Paris newspaper *Le Figaro* in 1909; his ideas had a powerful influence in Italy and Russia. After serving as an officer in World War I, he went on to join the Fascist Party in 1919. Among his other works are a volume of poems, *Guerra sola igiene del mundo* (War the only hygiene of the world; 1915), and a political essay, *Futurismo e fascismo* (1924), which argues that fascism is the natural extension of Futurism.

    Schwabing, a district of Munich, was much frequented by artists around the turn of the twentieth century; Hitler and other Nazi agitators met in certain of its restaurants and beer cellars and plotted the unsuccessful revolt against governmental authority known as the Beer Hall Putsch (1923).

42. Cited in *La Stampa Torino*. [The German editors of Benjamin's *Gesammelte Schriften* argue that this passage is more likely to have been excerpted from a French newspaper than from the Italian newspaper cited here.—TRANS.]

43. "Let art flourish—and the world pass away." This is a play on the motto of the sixteenth-century Holy Roman emperor Ferdinand I: "Fiat iustitia et pereat mundus" ("Let justice be done and the world pass away").

CHAPTER 3

THE CULTURE INDUSTRY

Enlightenment as Mass Deception

THEODOR W. ADORNO AND MAX HORKHEIMER

T heodor W. Adorno (1903–1969) and Max Horkheimer (1895–1973) were prominent Marxist philosophers affiliated to the Institute for Social Research at the University of Frankfurt—the so-called Frankfurt School—that had been founded by a wealthy, socialist-minded benefactor, Felix Weil, in 1923. Horkheimer became its director in 1930, helping move the school to New York in 1935 to protect its members from persecution by the Nazis. The purpose of the institute was to develop Marxist studies not just with respect to the economic sphere but also in regard to the issue of ideology as a force for precluding class consciousness and social revolution. Adorno's and Horkheimer's coauthored book *Dialectic of Enlightenment*, from which the accompanying text is taken,[1] mounts a scathing and critical analysis of the prescriptive methods by which the culture industry designs cultural and media products so as to suppress the masses and sustain the consumer market.

By the 1930s, with the rise of Stalin and the failure of the communist project in Russia, radical thinkers on the left in Europe, such as Adorno and Horkheimer, came to guard carefully against any envisaged idea of imminent social and political emancipation from the forces of tyranny. In addition, they argued that the unprecedented increase in the forces of production in modern times in the West had yielded an effect opposite from that anticipated by Marx. Rather than being an explosive force conductive to revolution as forecast by Marx, the expansion of technology in the service of capitalist industrial production had culminated in social and political repression on a scale never witnessed before. They believed that this acceleration of industrial forces along with concomitant levels of social repression was underpinned by the pervasive grip of ideology upon all forms of production and consumerism, including that of the cultural sphere. Adorno and Horkheimer, however, allowed for a certain autonomy from ideology with respect to some aspects of art while conceding that such art could only operate as a placeholder for the emancipation to come.

Adorno's and Horkheimer's essay on the culture industry—by which they mean industrially produced art such as cinema and radio, but also photography, television, and advertising—opens with the claim that despite the decline "of objectively established religion, the dissolution of the last remnants of precapitalism, together with technological and social differentiation or specialization," this has not resulted, as might be expected, in cultural chaos. Indeed, they say, never has culture been more unified or integrated: "culture now impresses the same stamp on everything. Films, radio and magazines make up a system which is uniform as a whole and in every part." Cultural production, they observe, is an integrated component of the capitalist economy, an industry that no longer has any pretense to art and which obeys the same rules of production as any other producer of commodities. Thus, they argue that what is called "culture" is, in fact, the general principle of an administrative mindset subsuming art into standardized products that are no more than "after-images of the work process itself." The irony is that, in selling "amusement" as a form of escapism for the consumer, the culture industry in actual fact supports "the prolongation of work": "[Amusement] is sought as an escape from the mechanized work process, and to recruit strength in order to be able to cope with it again."

Standardization, according to Adorno and Horkheimer, permeates every aspect of cultural production, all for the sole purpose of achieving maximum profitability. Adorno and Horkheimer believe that capitalism's ideological control of "individual consciousness" is total since "the man with leisure has to accept what the cultural manufacturer's offer him"; they see little or no room for independent interventions or private broadcasters, and no possibility for participation. Taste is either controlled by executives or already accounted for through the use of consumer research and statistics. Adorno and Horkheimer underline the point that standardization "is the result not of a law of movement in technology as such but of its function in today's economy."

For Adorno and Horkheimer, the calculation of the effects of commercial art forms and the standardization of its products that deny the audience its own reflective powers were shaped by an ideology of instrumental reason derived from the philosophies of positivism and the Enlightenment, especially the philosophy of Kant embodied in the *Critique of Pure Reason* (1781). Adorno and Horkheimer argue that the Enlightenment's faith in rationality as the chosen path leading toward humankind's emancipation was completely misplaced and, in fact, achieved the very opposite of what was promised. Far from obtaining social and political liberation, belief in rationality helped create the circumstances in which the ideologies of capitalism and fascism could flourish and, together, engender more absolute forms of social domination and repression than hitherto known in Western history.

In Adorno's and Horkheimer's view, Enlightenment rationality never escaped the problematic, identified by Kant, of what he called determinate judgment and reasoning. Utilized for the purposes of classification and explanation, this form of judgment subsumes the particular object or thing under a universal law, rule, or principle. Contrary to Kant's argument in the *Critique of Pure Reason,* Adorno and Horkheimer believe that to put the universal before the particular is to occlude particularity, replacing it with an ideological notion of identity, with the consequence that emphasis is placed upon what something represents and of what value it is. For Adorno and Horkheimer, the legacy of determinate reasoning found in the presuppositions of Enlightenment ideology has its counterpart in capitalism's system of exchange through the subsumption of commodities and labor power under a general system of monetary value. According to Adorno and Horkheimer, this rationalized system of production and exchange occludes the "sensuous particularity" of phenomena and objects, by which they mean something that is judged or thought in its own particularity without subsuming it under a pregiven universal system of value or exemplification. Capitalist exchange cannot allow for such particularity, and, indeed, its very possibility or existence, Adorno and Horkheimer believe, would undermine the entire capitalist system. Adorno and Horkheimer detect this subsumptive process at work in the fate of the detail in the work of art as it gets transposed from high art to the culture industry. In high art, especially in the period from Romanticism to Expressionism, the detail resisted assimilation into an ideal of the work of art's organic unity. Such was the role of color in painting at the expense of classical pictorial composition; similarly, dissonance in music or excessive psychological states in the novel opposed the false idea of the work of art's unity. All of this is done away with by the culture industry where the whole dominates over detail to such an extent that it no longer exists; everything either fits together perfectly, or, if dissonance is allowed, it is transformed into a technical effect and incorporated into the whole. In a similar manner of incorporation, the culture industry reconciles high and low, serious art and light entertainment for the purposes of consumerism; in this respect, Adorno and Horkheimer refer to the jazz musician Benny Goodman appearing with a Budapest string quartet and the musicians playing as uniformly and sweetly as bandleader Guy Lombardo.

The fate of detail in high art dovetails with Adorno's and Horkheimer's discussion of style. Capitalist "culture" as a "common denominator" functions as the general law or principle within which a genuine, individual style is subsumed into a safer, standardized version. The great artists of the past did not set out to achieve "a wholly flawless and perfect style," which is the dubious achievement of the culture industry "in the carefully contrived elegance of a film star, and even in the admirable expertise of a photograph of a peasant's squalid hut." In Adorno's and Horkheimer's argument, the artists of the past, as well as artists such as Arnold Schoenberg and Pablo Picasso, treat the attainment of a flawless and perfect style with suspicion; their dialectical struggle with, and refusal of, standardized ideas of unity and harmony *is* their style. While this means that they never entirely escape ideology, it keeps alive, albeit negatively, a relationship to the truth of class suffering and oppression, not by means of direct expression which, for Adorno and Horkheimer, is an impossible fantasy, but through the "force" of this dialectical struggle "without which life flows away unheard." The achievement of great art, then, for Adorno and Horkheimer, is to expose itself to failure, the failure to represent class struggle or shape the social itself ("lending new shape to the conventional social forms") for the sake of realizing a style that is contingent.

The culture industry provides amusement as a form of relief from work and labor—and, thus, ultimately, is inseparable from, and an extension of, work, "Amusement under late capitalism is the prolongation of work. It is sought as an escape from the mechanized work process, and to recruit strength in order to be able to cope with it again." And yet, in a further twist to their argument, Adorno and Horkheimer reveal that while "amusement" is sought as an escape from work, in fact, it reproduces the mechanization of work to such a degree that the experiences provided are "nothing but after-images of the work process itself." Even cartoons that "were once exponents of fantasy as opposed to rationalism" have degenerated into a reproduction of the cruelty and abjection of everyday life under capitalism, "Donald Duck in the cartoons and the unfortunate in real life get their thrashing so that the audience can learn to take their own punishment."

Whereas amusement is the prerogative of popular culture, high art—if it is worthy of the designation—forestalls such gratification and thereby attains an autonomy from capitalist and rationalist ideology. However, high art's autonomy, achieved for the sake of the lower classes, ends up excluding these very classes by reasserting the division between mental and manual labor. As such, high art has a "social bad conscience" that haunts it, of which it is constantly reminded by the popular success of mass art. For Adorno and Horkheimer this means that popular culture has a "legitimacy," or a role, reminding high art of its failure to achieve true universality. While both high art and popular culture are complicit in sustaining capitalist ideology, the division between the two spheres "does at least express the negativity of the culture which the different spheres constitute."

Adorno and Horkheimer argue that "the culture industry perpetually cheats its consumers of what it perpetually promises," especially concerning sexual pleasure and the meaning of love. Adorno and Horkheimer state that high art

was not sexual in the commercial sense of the term (it was "no sexual exhibition"). Rather, high art criticized sexual "deprivation"—that is, sexual
repression—"as negative," and, for these authors, this is a wholly different matter. They go on to say that high art refutes the promise of fulfillment through
sexuality that the culture industry trades upon yet endlessly defers: the culture
industry "only stimulates . . . unsublimated forepleasure . . . [but] indicate[s]
unmistakably that things can never go that far. . . . Love is downgraded to
romance." On the subject of love Adorno and Horkheimer quote the Latin
maxim *res severa verum gaudium,* from the Roman author Seneca, translated
as "a serious concern is true pleasure" or, alternatively, "true pleasure is a serious business"; for Adorno and Horkheimer, the culture industry denies the
depth and seriousness of this maxim as applied to the experience of love, and
even fears it, introducing a nervous laughter or humor in its stead that is the
mark of repression. This is why the culture industry is described contrarily as
"pornographic and prudish," whereas works of art are "ascetic" but "unashamed."
In the culture industry "jovial denial takes the place of the pain found in ecstasy
and in asceticism." Adopting a psychoanalytic interpretation, Adorno and
Horkheimer propose that such pain is also the truth of castration that the
culture industry tries to renounce through diversion, circumscribing the customer's desires and needs with its own and selling them as the only means of
fulfillment and escape. They see in the culture industry a type of deception,
epitomized by the daughter's abduction in the cartoon where the father aids
her escape by holding the ladder in the dark. Their interpretation of this joke is
that the paradise offered by the culture industry is, in fact, the same old everyday world. In no way, then, can the culture industry be understood to indulge
in Mark Twain's "happy nonsense," or a kind of pure clowning; art's disinter-
estedness gives way to a promotional purpose lurking behind every action and
every kiss.

* * *

The sociological theory that the loss of the support of objectively established
religion, the dissolution of the last remnants of precapitalism, together with
technological and social differentiation or specialization, have led to cultural
chaos is disproved every day; for culture now impresses the same stamp on
everything. Films, radio, and magazines make up a system which is uniform
as a whole and in every part. . . . Under monopoly all mass culture is identical,
and the lines of its artificial framework begin to show through. The people at
the top are no longer so interested in concealing monopoly: as its violence
becomes more open, so its power grows. Movies and radio need no longer pretend to be art. The truth that they are just business is made into an ideology in
order to justify the rubbish they deliberately produce. They call themselves

industries; and when their directors' incomes are published, any doubt about the social utility of the finished products is removed.

Interested parties explain the culture industry in technological terms. It is alleged that because millions participate in it, certain reproduction processes are necessary that inevitably require identical needs in innumerable places to be satisfied with identical goods. The technical contrast between the few production centers and the large number of widely dispersed consumption points is said to demand organization and planning by management. Furthermore, it is claimed that standards were based in the first place on consumers' needs, and for that reason were accepted with so little resistance. The result is the circle of manipulation and retroactive need in which the unity of the system grows ever stronger. No mention is made of the fact that the basis on which technology acquires power over society is the power of those whose economic hold over society is greatest. A technological rationale is the rationale of domination itself. It is the coercive nature of society alienated from itself. Automobiles, bombs, and movies keep the whole thing together until their leveling element shows its strength in the very wrong which it furthered. It has made the technology of the culture industry no more than the achievement of standardization and mass production, sacrificing whatever involved a distinction between the logic of the work and that of the social system. This is the result not of a law of movement in technology as such but of its function in today's economy. The need which might resist central control has already been suppressed by the control of the individual consciousness. The step from the telephone to the radio has clearly distinguished the roles. The former still allowed the subscriber to play the role of subject, and was liberal. The latter is democratic: it turns all participants into listeners and authoritatively subjects them to broadcast programs which are all exactly the same. No machinery of rejoinder has been devised, and private broadcasters are denied any freedom. They are confined to the apocryphal field of the "amateur," and also have to accept organization from above. But any trace of spontaneity from the public in official broadcasting is controlled and absorbed by talent scouts, studio competitions, and official programs of every kind selected by professionals. Talented performers belong to the industry long before it displays them; otherwise they would not be so eager to fit in. The attitude of the public, which ostensibly and actually favors the system of the culture industry, is a part of the system and not an excuse for it. If one branch of art follows the same formula as one with a very different medium and content; if the dramatic intrigue of broadcast soap operas becomes no more than useful material for showing how to master technical problems at both ends of the scale of musical experience—real jazz or a cheap imitation; or if a movement from a Beethoven symphony is crudely "adapted" for a film sound-track in the same way as a Tolstoy novel is garbled in a film script: then the claim that this is done to satisfy the spontaneous wishes of the public is no more than hot air.

We are closer to the facts if we explain these phenomena as inherent in the technical and personnel apparatus which, down to its last cog, itself forms part of the economic mechanism of selection. In addition there is the agreement—or at least the determination—of all executive authorities not to produce or sanction anything that in any way differs from their own rules, their own ideas about consumers, or above all themselves.

In our age the objective social tendency is incarnate in the hidden subjective purposes of company directors, the foremost among whom are in the most powerful sectors of industry—steel, petroleum, electricity, and chemicals. Culture monopolies are weak and dependent in comparison. They cannot afford to neglect their appeasement of the real holders of power if their sphere of activity in mass society (a sphere producing a specific type of commodity which anyhow is still too closely bound up with easygoing liberalism and Jewish intellectuals) is not to undergo a series of purges. The dependence of the most powerful broadcasting company on the electrical industry, or of the motion picture industry on the banks, is characteristic of the whole sphere, whose individual branches are themselves economically interwoven. All are in such close contact that the extreme concentration of mental forces allows demarcation lines between different firms and technical branches to be ignored. The ruthless unity in the culture industry is evidence of what will happen in politics. Marked differentiations such as those of A and B films, or of stories in magazines in different price ranges, depend not so much on subject matter as on classifying, organizing, and labeling consumers. Something is provided for all so that none may escape; the distinctions are emphasized and extended. The public is catered for with a hierarchical range of mass-produced products of varying quality, thus advancing the rule of complete quantification. Everybody must behave (as if spontaneously) in accordance with his previously determined and indexed level, and choose the category of mass product turned out for his type. Consumers appear as statistics on research organization charts, and are divided by income groups into red, green, and blue areas; the technique is that used for any type of propaganda.

How formalized the procedure is can be seen when the mechanically differentiated products prove to be all alike in the end. That the difference between the Chrysler range and General Motors products is basically illusory strikes every child with a keen interest in varieties. What connoisseurs discuss as good or bad points serve only to perpetuate the semblance of competition and range of choice. The same applies to the Warner Brothers and Metro-Goldwyn-Mayer productions. But even the differences between the more expensive and cheaper models put out by the same firm steadily diminish: for automobiles, there are such differences as the number of cylinders, cubic capacity, details of patented gadgets; and for films there are the number of stars, the extravagant use of technology, labor, and equipment, and the introduction of the latest psychological formulas. The universal criterion of merit is the amount of "conspicuous production," of blatant cash investment. The varying budgets in the culture industry do not bear the slightest relation to factual values, to the meaning of the products themselves. Even the technical media are relentlessly forced into uniformity. Television aims at a synthesis of radio and film, and is held up only because the interested parties have not yet reached agreement, but its consequences will be quite enormous and promise to intensify the impoverishment of aesthetic matter so drastically, that by tomorrow the thinly veiled identity of all industrial culture products can come triumphantly out into the open, derisively fulfilling the Wagnerian dream of the *Gesamtkunstwerk*—the fusion of all the arts in one work. The alliance of word, image, and music is all the more perfect than in *Tristan* because the sensuous elements which all approvingly reflect the surface of social reality are in principle embodied in the same technical process, the unity of which becomes its distinctive content. This process integrates all the elements of the production, from the novel (shaped with an eye to the film) to the last sound effect. It is the triumph of invested capital, whose title as absolute master is etched deep into the hearts of the dispossessed in the employment line; it is the meaningful content of every film, whatever plot the production team may have selected.

The man with leisure has to accept what the culture manufacturers offer him. Kant's formalism still expected a contribution from the individual, who was thought to relate the varied experiences of the senses to fundamental concepts; but industry robs the individual of his function. Its prime service to the customer is to do his schematizing for him, Kant said that there was a secret mechanism in the soul which prepared direct intuitions in such a way that they could be fitted into the system of pure reason. But today that secret has been deciphered. While the mechanism is to all appearances planned by those who serve up the data of experience, that is, by the culture industry, it is in fact forced upon the latter by the power of society, which remains irrational, however we may try to rationalize it; and this inescapable force is processed by commercial agencies so that they give an artificial impression of being in command. There is nothing left for the consumer to classify. Producers have done it for him. Art for the masses has destroyed the dream but still conforms to the tenets of that dreaming idealism which critical idealism balked at. Everything derives from consciousness: for Malebranche and Berkeley, from the consciousness of God; in mass art, from the consciousness of the production team. Not only are the hit songs, stars, and soap operas cyclically recurrent and rigidly invariable types, but the specific content of the entertainment itself is derived from them and only appears to change. The details are interchangeable. The short interval sequence which was effective in a hit song, the hero's momentary fall from grace (which he accepts as good sport), the rough treatment which the beloved gets from the male star, the latter's rugged defiance of the spoilt heiress, are, like all the other details, ready-made clichés to be slotted in any-where; they never do anything more than fulfill the purpose allotted them in the overall plan. Their whole *raison d'être* is to confirm it by being its constitu-ent parts. As soon as the film begins, it is quite clear how it will end, and who will be rewarded, punished, or forgotten. In light music, once the trained ear has heard the first notes of the hit song, it can guess what is coming and feel flattered when it does come. The average length of the short story has to be rigidly adhered to. Even gags, effects, and jokes are calculated like the setting in which they are placed. They are the responsibility of special experts and their narrow range makes it easy for them to be apportioned in the office. The development of the culture industry has led to the predominance of the effect, the obvious touch, and the technical detail over the work itself—which once expressed an idea, but was liquidated together with the idea. When the detail won its freedom, it became rebellious and, in the period from Romanticism to Expressionism, asserted itself as free expression, as a vehicle of protest against the organization. In music the single harmonic effect obliterated the awareness of form as a whole; in painting the individual color was stressed at the expense of pictorial composition; and in the novel psychology became more important than structure. The totality of the culture industry has put an end to this. Though concerned exclusively with effects, it crushes their insub-ordination and makes them subserve the formula, which replaces the work. The same fate is inflicted on whole and parts alike. The whole inevitably bears no relation to the details—just like the career of a successful man into which everything is made to fit as an illustration or a proof, whereas it is nothing more than the sum of all those idiotic events. The so-called dominant idea is like a file which ensures order but not coherence. The whole and the parts are alike; there is no antithesis and no connection. Their prearranged harmony is a mockery of what had to be striven after in the great bourgeois works of art. In Germany the graveyard stillness of the dictatorship already hung over the gayest films of the democratic era.

... Real life is becoming indistinguishable from the movies. The sound film, far surpassing the theater of illusion, leaves no room for imagination or reflec-tion on the part of the audience, who is unable to respond within the structure of the film, yet deviates from its precise detail without losing the thread of the story; hence the film forces its victims to equate it directly with reality. The stunting of the mass-media consumer's powers of imagination and spontane-ity does not have to be traced back to any psychological mechanisms; he must ascribe the loss of those attributes to the objective nature of the products them-selves, especially to the most characteristic of them, the sound film. They are so designed that quickness, powers of observation, and experience are unde-niably needed to apprehend them at all; yet sustained thought is out of the question if the spectator is not to miss the relentless rush of facts. Even though the effort required for his response is semi-automatic, no scope is left for the imagination. Those who are so absorbed by the world of the movie—by its images, gestures, and words—that they are unable to supply what really makes it a world, do not have to dwell on particular points of its mechanics during a screening. All the other films and products of the entertainment industry which they have seen have taught them what to expect; they react automatically. The might of industrial society is lodged in men's minds. The entertainments manufacturers know that their products will be consumed with alertness even when the customer is distraught, for each of them is a model of the huge economic machinery which has always sustained the masses, whether at work or at leisure—which is akin to work.

. . . The art historians and guardians of culture who complain of the extinction in the West of a basic style-determining power are wrong. The stereotyped appropriation of everything, even the inchoate, for the purposes of mechanical reproduction surpasses the rigor and general currency of any "real style," in the sense in which cultural *cognoscenti* celebrate the organic precapitalist past. No Palestrina could be more of a purist in eliminating every unprepared and unresolved discord than the jazz arranger in suppressing any development which does not conform to the jargon. When jazzing up Mozart he changes him not only when he is too serious or too difficult but when he harmonizes the melody in a different way, perhaps more simply, than is customary now. No medieval builder can have scrutinized the subjects for church windows and sculptures more suspiciously than the studio hierarchy scrutinizes a work by Balzac or Hugo before finally approving it. No medieval theologian could have determined the degree of the torment to be suffered by the damned in accordance with the *ordo* of divine love more meticulously than the producers of shoddy epics calculate the torture to be undergone by the hero or the exact point to which the leading lady's hemline shall be raised. The explicit and implicit, exoteric and esoteric catalog of the forbidden and tolerated is so extensive that it not only defines the area of freedom but is all-powerful inside it. Everything down to the last detail is shaped accordingly. Like its counterpart, avant-garde art, the entertainment industry determines its own language, down to its very syntax and vocabulary, by the use of anathema. The constant pressure to produce new effects (which must conform to the old pattern) serves merely as another rule to increase the power of the conventions when any single effect threatens to slip through the net. Every detail is so firmly stamped with sameness that nothing can appear which is not marked at birth, or does not meet with approval at first sight. And the star performers, whether they produce or reproduce, use this jargon as freely and fluently and with as much gusto as if it were the very language which it silenced long ago. Such is the ideal of what is natural in this field of activity, and its influence becomes all the more powerful, the more technique is perfected and diminishes the tension between the finished product and everyday life. The paradox of this routine, which is essentially travesty, can be detected and is often predominant in everything that the culture industry turns out. A jazz musician who is playing a piece of serious music, one of Beethoven's simplest minuets, syncopates it involuntarily and will smile superciliously when asked to follow the normal divisions of the beat. This is the "nature" which, complicated by the ever-present and extravagant demands of the specific medium, constitutes the new style and is a "system of non-culture, to which one might even concede a certain 'unity of style' if it really made any sense to speak of stylized barbarity."[2]

The universal imposition of this stylized mode can even go beyond what is quasi-officially sanctioned or forbidden; today a hit song is more readily forgiven for not observing the 32 beats or the compass of the ninth than for containing even the most clandestine melodic or harmonic detail which does not conform to the idiom. Whenever Orson Welles offends against the tricks of the trade, he is forgiven because his departures from the norm are regarded as calculated mutations which serve all the more strongly to confirm the validity of the system.

. . . In the culture industry the notion of genuine style is seen to be the aesthetic equivalent of domination. Style considered as mere aesthetic regularity is a romantic dream of the past. The unity of style not only of the Christian Middle Ages but of the Renaissance expresses in each case the different structure of social power, and not the obscure experience of the oppressed in which the general was enclosed. The great artists were never those who embodied a wholly flawless and perfect style, but those who used style as a way of hardening themselves against the chaotic expression of suffering, as a negative truth. The style of their works gave what was expressed that force without which life flows away unheard. Those very art forms which are known as classical, such as Mozart's music, contain objective trends which represent something different to the style which they incarnate. As late as Schönberg and Picasso, the great artists have retained a mistrust of style, and at crucial points have subordinated it to the logic of the matter. What Dadaists and Expressionists called the untruth of style as such triumphs today in the sung jargon of a crooner, in the carefully contrived elegance of a film star, and even in the admirable expertise of a photograph of a peasant's squalid hut. Style represents a promise in every work of art. That which is expressed is subsumed through style into the dominant forms of generality, into the language of music, painting, or words, in the hope that it will be reconciled thus with the idea of true generality. This promise held out by the work of art that it will create truth by lending new shape to the conventional social forms is as necessary as it is hypocritical. It unconditionally posits the real forms of life as it is by suggesting that fulfillment lies in their aesthetic derivatives. To this extent the claim of art is always ideology too. However, only in this confrontation with tradition of which style is the record can art express suffering. That factor in a work of art which enables it to transcend reality certainly cannot be detached from style; but it does not consist of the harmony actually realized, of any doubtful unity of form and content, within and without, of individual and society; it is to be found in those features in which discrepancy appears: in the necessary failure of the passionate striving for identity. Instead of exposing itself to this failure in which the style of the great work of art has always achieved self-negation, the inferior work has always relied on its similarity with others—on a surrogate identity.

In the culture industry this imitation finally becomes absolute. Having ceased to be anything but style, it reveals the latter's secret: obedience to the social hierarchy. Today aesthetic barbarity completes what has threatened the creations of the spirit since they were gathered together as culture and neutralized. To speak of culture was always contrary to culture. Culture as a common denominator already contains in embryo that schematization and process of cataloguing and classification which bring culture within the sphere of administration. And it is precisely the industrialized, the consequent, subsumption which entirely accords with this notion of culture. By subordinating in the same way and to the same end all areas of intellectual creation, by occupying men's senses from the time they leave the factory in the evening to the time they clock in again the next morning with matter that bears the impress of the labor process they themselves have to sustain throughout the day, this subsumption mockingly satisfies the concept of a unified culture which the philosophers of personality contrasted with mass culture.

. . . The consumers are the workers and employees, the farmers and lower middle class. Capitalist production so confines them, body and soul, that they fall helpless victims to what is offered them. As naturally as the ruled always took the morality imposed upon them more seriously than did the rulers themselves, the deceived masses are today captivated by the myth of success even more than the successful are. Immovably, they insist on the very ideology which enslaves them. The misplaced love of the common people for the wrong which is done them is a greater force than the cunning of the authorities. It is stronger even than the rigorism of the Hays Office,[3] just as in certain great times in history it has inflamed greater forces that were turned against it, namely, the terror of the tribunals. It calls for Mickey Rooney in preference to the tragic Garbo, for Donald Duck instead of Betty Boop.

. . . Amusement and all the elements of the culture industry existed long before the latter came into existence. Now they are taken over from above and brought up to date. The culture industry can pride itself on having energetically executed the previously clumsy transposition of art into the sphere of consumption, on making this a principle, on divesting amusement of its obtrusive naïvetés and improving the type of commodities. The more absolute it became, the more ruthless it was in forcing every outsider either into bankruptcy or into a syndicate, and became more refined and elevated—until it ended up as a synthesis of Beethoven and the Casino de Paris. It enjoys a double victory: the truth it extinguishes without it can reproduce at will as a lie within. "Light" art as such, distraction, is not a decadent form. Anyone who complains that it is a betrayal of the ideal of pure expression is under an illusion about society. The purity of bourgeois art, which hypostasized itself as a world of freedom in contrast to what was happening in the material world, was from the beginning bought with the exclusion of the lower classes—with whose cause, the real universality, art keeps faith precisely by its freedom from the ends of the false universality. Serious art has been withheld from those for whom the hardship and oppression of life make a mockery of seriousness, and who must be glad if they can use time not spent at the production line just to keep going. Light art has been the shadow of autonomous art. It is the social bad conscience of serious art. The truth which the latter necessarily lacked because of its social premises gives the other the semblance of legitimacy. The division itself is the truth: it does at least express the negativity of the culture which the different spheres constitute. Least of all can the antithesis be reconciled by absorbing light into serious art, or vice versa. But that is what the culture industry attempts.

The eccentricity of the circus, peepshow, and brothel is as embarrassing to it as that of Schönberg and Karl Kraus. And so the jazz musician Benny Goodman appears with the Budapest string quartet, more pedantic rhythmically than any philharmonic clarinettist, while the style of the Budapest players is as uniform and sugary as that of Guy Lombardo. But what is significant is not vulgarity, stupidity, and lack of polish. The culture industry did away with yesterday's rubbish by its own perfection, and by forbidding and domesticating the amateurish, although it constantly allows gross blunders without which the standard of the exalted style cannot be perceived. But what is new is that the irreconcilable elements of culture, art and distraction, are subordinated to one end and subsumed under one false formula: the totality of the culture industry. It consists of repetition. That its characteristic innovations are never anything more than improvements of mass reproduction is not external to the system. It is with good reason that the interest of innumerable consumers is directed to the technique, and not to the contents—which are stubbornly repeated, outworn, and by now half-discredited. The social power which the spectators worship shows itself more effectively in the omnipresence of the stereotype imposed by technical skill than in the stale ideologies for which the ephemeral contents stand in.

. . . Amusement under late capitalism is the prolongation of work. It is sought after as an escape from the mechanized work process, and to recruit strength in order to be able to cope with it again. But at the same time mechanization has such power over a man's leisure and happiness, and so profoundly determines the manufacture of amusement goods, that his experiences are inevitably afterimages of the work process itself.

. . . Cartoons were once exponents of fantasy as opposed to rationalism. They ensured that justice was done to the creatures and objects they electrified, by giving the maimed specimens a second life. All they do today is to confirm the victory of technological reason over truth. A few years ago they had a consistent plot which only broke up in the final moments in a crazy chase, and thus resembled the old slapstick comedy. Now, however, time relations have shifted. In the very first sequence a motive is stated so that in the course of the action destruction can get to work on it: with the audience in pursuit, the protagonist becomes the worthless object of general violence. The quantity of organized amusement changes into the quality of organized cruelty. The self-elected censors of the film industry (with whom it enjoys a close relationship) watch over the unfolding of the crime, which is as drawn-out as a hunt. Fun replaces the pleasure which the sight of an embrace would allegedly afford, and postpones satisfaction till the day of the pogrom. In so far as cartoons do any more than accustom the senses to the new tempo, they hammer into every brain the old lesson that continuous friction, the breaking down of all individual resistance, is the condition of life in this society. Donald Duck in the cartoons and the unfortunate in real life get their thrashing so that the audience can learn to take their own punishment.

The enjoyment of the violence suffered by the movie character turns into violence against the spectator, and distraction into exertion. Nothing that the experts have devised as a stimulant must escape the weary eye; no stupidity is allowed in the face of all the trickery; one has to follow everything and even display the smart responses shown and recommended in the film. This raises the question whether the culture industry fulfills the function of diverting minds which it boasts about so loudly. If most of the radio stations and movie theaters were closed down, the consumers would probably not lose so very much. To walk from the street into the movie theater is no longer to enter a world of dream; as soon as the very existence of these institutions no longer made it obligatory to use them, there would be no great urge to do so. Such closures would not be reactionary machine wrecking. The disappointment would be felt not so much by the enthusiasts as by the slow-witted, who are the ones who suffer for everything anyhow. In spite of the films which are intended to complete her integration, the housewife finds in the darkness of the movie theater a place of refuge where she can sit for a few hours with nobody watching, just as she used to look out of the window when there were still homes and rest in the evening. The unemployed in the great cities find coolness in summer and warmth in winter in these temperature-controlled locations. Otherwise, despite its size, this bloated pleasure apparatus adds no dignity to man's lives. The idea of "fully exploiting" available technical resources and the facilities for aesthetic mass consumption is part of the economic system which refuses to exploit resources to abolish hunger.

The culture industry perpetually cheats its consumers of what it perpetually promises. The promissory note which, with its plots and staging, it draws on pleasure is endlessly prolonged; the promise, which is actually all the spectacle consists of, is illusory: all it actually confirms is that the real point will never be reached, that the diner must be satisfied with the menu. In front of the appetite stimulated by all those brilliant names and images there is finally set no more than a commendation of the depressing everyday world it sought to escape. Of course works of art were not sexual exhibitions either. However, by representing deprivation as negative, they retracted, as it were, the prostitution of the impulse and rescued by mediation what was denied. The secret of aesthetic sublimation is its representation of fulfillment as a broken promise. The culture industry does not sublimate; it represses. By repeatedly exposing the objects of desire, breasts in a clinging sweater or the naked torso of the athletic hero, it only stimulates the unsublimated forepleasure which habitual deprivation has long since reduced to a masochistic semblance. There is no erotic situation which, while insinuating and exciting, does not fail to indicate unmistakably that things can never go that far. The Hays Office merely confirms the ritual of Tantalus that the culture industry has established anyway. Works of art are ascetic and unashamed; the culture industry is pornographic and prudish. Love is downgraded to romance. And, after the descent, much is permitted; even license as a marketable speciality has its quota bearing the trade description "daring." The mass production of the sexual automatically achieves its repression. Because of his ubiquity, the film star with whom one is meant to fall in love is from the outset a copy of himself. Every tenor voice comes to sound like a Caruso record, and the "natural" faces of Texas girls are like the successful models by whom Hollywood has typecast them. The mechanical reproduction of beauty, which reactionary cultural fanaticism wholeheartedly serves in its methodical idolization of individuality, leaves no room for that unconscious idolatry which was once essential to beauty. The triumph over beauty is celebrated by humor—the *Schadenfreude* that every successful deprivation calls forth. There is laughter because there is nothing to laugh at. Laughter, whether conciliatory or terrible, always occurs when some fear passes. It indicates liberation either from physical danger or from the grip of logic. Conciliatory laughter is heard as the echo of an escape from power; the wrong kind overcomes fear by capitulating to the forces which are to be feared. It is the echo of power as something inescapable. Fun is a medicinal bath. The pleasure industry never fails to prescribe it. It makes laughter the instrument of the fraud practised on happiness. Moments of happiness are without laughter; only operettas and films portray sex to the accompaniment of resounding laughter. But Baudelaire is as devoid of humour as Hölderlin. In the false society laughter is a disease which has attacked happiness and is drawing it into its worthless totality. To laugh at something is always to deride it, and the life which, according to Bergson, in laughter breaks through the barrier, is actually an invading barbaric life, self-assertion prepared to parade its liberation from any scruple when the social occasion arises. Such a laughing audience is a parody of humanity. Its members are monads, all dedicated to the pleasure of being ready for anything at the expense of everyone else. Their harmony is a caricature of solidarity. What is fiendish about this false laughter is that it is a compelling parody of the best, which is conciliatory. Delight is austere: *res severa verum gaudium.* The monastic theory that not asceticism but the sexual act denotes the renunciation of attainable bliss receives negative confirmation in the gravity of the lover who with foreboding commits his life to the fleeting moment. In the culture industry, jovial denial takes the place of the pain found in ecstasy and in asceticism. The supreme law is that they shall not satisfy their desires at any price; they must laugh and be content with laughter. In every product of the culture industry, the permanent denial imposed by civilization is once again unmistakably demonstrated and inflicted on its victims. To offer and to deprive them of something is one and the same. This is what happens in erotic films. Precisely because it must never take place, everything centers upon copulation. In films it is more strictly forbidden for an illegitimate relationship to be admitted without the parties being punished than for a millionaire's future son-in-law to be active in the labor movement. In contrast to the liberal era, industrialized as well as popular culture may wax indignant at capitalism, but it cannot renounce the threat of castration. This is fundamental. It outlasts the organized acceptance of the uniformed seen in the films which are produced to that end, and in reality. What is decisive today is no longer puritanism, although it still asserts itself in the form of women's organizations, but the necessity inherent in the system not to leave the customer alone, not for a moment to allow him any suspicion that resistance is possible. The principle dictates that he should be shown all his needs as capable of fulfillment, but that those needs should be so predetermined that he feels himself to be the eternal consumer, the object of the culture industry. Not only does it make him believe that the deception it practices is satisfaction, but it goes further and implies that, whatever the state of affairs, he must put up with what is offered. The escape from everyday drudgery which the whole culture industry promises may be compared to the daughter's abduction in the cartoon: the father is holding the ladder in the dark. The paradise offered by the culture industry is the same old drudgery. Both escape and elopement are predesigned to lead back to the starting point. Pleasure promotes the resignation which it ought to help to forget.

Amusement, if released from every restraint, would not only be the antithesis of art but its extreme role. The Mark Twain absurdity with which the American culture industry flirts at times might be a corrective of art. The more seriously the latter regards the incompatibility with life, the more it resembles the seriousness of life, its antithesis; the more effort it devotes to developing wholly from its own formal law, the more effort it demands from the intelligence to neutralize its burden. In some revue films, and especially in the grotesque and the funnies, the possibility of this negation does glimmer for a few moments. But of course it cannot happen. Pure amusement in its consequence, relaxed self-surrender to all kinds of associations and happy nonsense, is cut short by the amusement on the market: instead, it is interrupted by a surrogate overall meaning which the culture industry insists on giving to its products, and yet misuses as a mere pretext for bringing in the stars. Biographies and other simple stories patch the fragments of nonsense into an idiotic plot. We do not have the cap and bells of the jester but the bunch of keys of capitalist reason, which even screens the pleasure of achieving success. Every kiss in the revue film has to contribute to the career of the boxer, or some hit song expert or other whose rise to fame is being glorified. The deception is not that the culture industry supplies amusement but that it ruins the fun by allowing business considerations to involve it in the ideological clichés of a culture in the process of self-liquidation. Ethics and taste cut short unrestrained amusement as "naïve"—naïveté is thought to be as bad as intellectualism—and even restrict technical possibilities. The culture industry is corrupt; not because it is a sinful Babylon but because it is a cathedral dedicated to elevated pleasure. On all levels, from Hemingway to Emil Ludwig, from Mrs. Miniver to the Lone Ranger, from Toscanini to Guy Lombardo, there is untruth in the intellectual content taken ready-made from art and science. The culture industry does retain a trace of something better in those features which bring it close to the circus, in the self-justifying and nonsensical skill of riders, acrobats and clowns, in the "defense and justification of physical as against intellectual art."[4] But the refuges of a mindless artistry which represents what is human as opposed to the social mechanism are being relentlessly hunted down by a schematic reason which compels everything to prove its significance and effect. The consequence is that the nonsensical at the bottom disappears as utterly as the sense in works of art at the top.

Notes

1. Theodor Adorno's and Max Horkheimer's coauthored chapter "The Culture Industry: Enlightenment as Mass Deception" was published in their book *Dialectic of Enlightenment,* trans. John Cumming (London: Verso, 1997); it was originally titled "Philosophical Fragments" and is dated 1944.
2. Friedrich Nietzsche, *Unzeitgemässe Betrachtungen, Werke* (Leipzig, 1917), 1:187.
3. The Hays office controlled the moral guidelines that were applied to most U.S. motion pictures between 1930 and 1968.
4. Frank Wedekind, *Gesammelte Werke* (Munich, 1921), 9:426.

CHAPTER 4

THE FILM AND THE NEW PSYCHOLOGY

MAURICE MERLEAU-PONTY

M
aurice Merleau-Ponty (1908–1961) was a phenomenologist who taught at the École Normale Supérieure, the University of Lyon, and the Sorbonne. From 1952 until his death he held the chair of philosophy at the Collège de France. During the Second World War, Merleau-Ponty had been active in the French Resistance, and, following the conclusion of the war, he returned immediately to his nascent philosophical and journalistic career, establishing the directions of the phenomenological research that would occupy him for the rest of his life.

In a flurry of activity over the course of 1945, Merleau-Ponty graduated from the Sorbonne in Paris for his doctoral theses,[1] completed the essays "Cézanne's Doubt" and "The Film and the New Psychology" (the latter reprinted here),[2] and helped found the immensely influential journal *Les Temps Modernes* as member of an editorial committee that included Jean-Paul Sartre, Simone de Beauvoir, and Raymond Aron. Like Merleau-Ponty's other writings of this period, "The Film and the New Psychology" proposes a phenomenological account of experience, claiming that the human body makes sense of the world in ways that are prior to, and independent from, mental cognition and intentionality. According to Merleau-Ponty, classical psychology, exemplified by René Descartes's *Meditations on First Philosophy* (1641), assumed that the mind was responsible for organizing the data of sensation into a meaningful whole: "classical psychology made perception a real deciphering of sense data by the intelligence." However, as Merleau-Ponty writes in the *Phenomenology of Perception*, "There is . . . another subject beneath me, for whom a world exists before

I am here, and who marks out my place in it. This captive or natural spirit is my body." This body, as Merleau-Ponty says, is not "the instrument of my personal choices" that "fastens upon this or that world," but a "system of anonymous 'functions' which draw every particular focus into a general project."[3] Such "functions" of the body are attuned to movement, flux, spatial and physical differences prior to cognition that act in a broadly autonomous relationship to mental intentionality. Merleau-Ponty emphasizes in "The Film and the New Psychology" that perception, far from responding to stimuli in a chaotic fashion, in actual fact structures experience, organizing it into a "world." In this respect the body has an "intelligence" of its own.

Perception does not simply process the sense data of what is "out there" phenomenologically in the world and, furthermore, is irreducible merely to an assembly of bodily receptors and senses. This is why perception is capable, for instance, of composing an entire color field to which sensation can be partially blind, a point outlined in Merleau-Ponty's opening paragraph of the essay. While the mind organizes the world into a system of structures, so, too, does embodied perception. Indeed, Merleau-Ponty proposes that "our spontaneous way of seeing" and perceiving forms is primarily formed through "structure, grouping or configuration." As a way of underlining his point, Merleau-Ponty observes that there are habitual ways of grouping "the stars in the same constellations as the ancients" and of pairing together letters of the alphabet. This despite the fact that there could be other ways of organizing figure/ground relationships (as is the case with "a sick person contemplating the wallpaper in his room") and spatial experience ("for example, the space between the trees on the boulevard").

Merleau-Ponty acknowledges that there can be shifts in perception that are not necessarily logical. He gives the example of sitting in a stationary train yet believing that it is moving while another train pulls out beside it, and vice versa. Similarly, the position of "the steeple motionless against the sky with clouds" can be reversed so that the steeple appears to fall through space while the clouds and sky remain motionless. Such variations in the point of view underlines the fact that perception is a matter of embodiment, the body being anchored in a whole world of relations, "according to the way we settle ourselves in the world and the position our bodies assume in it."

Classical psychology proposed that the mind fills in the unseen elements in perception to create a sufficient sense of a visible world. Following this logic Merleau-Ponty says, "'I cannot see a cube, that is, a solid with six surfaces and twelve edges; all I ever see is a perspective figure of which the lateral surfaces are distorted and the back surface completely hidden. If I am able to speak of cubes, it is because my mind sets these appearances to rights and restores the hidden surface.'"

However, Merleau-Ponty wishes to confound this logic, pointing out in this example that the concealed surfaces of a cube and the objects behind our backs are not completed by the mind alone but by another means, "a commerce with the world and a presence with the world which is older than intelligence." What is older than mental intelligence is embodied perception, and this perception is intertwined with the world in an active relationship that is not regulated by a cognized representation of Euclidean space within which a cube appears in perspective by a viewing subject. Thus, Merleau-Ponty stresses that the mind does not organize the world and control appearances, "I do not think the world in the act of perception," rather "the world . . . organizes itself in front of me" in ways that are immediate: "I am at the cube itself in its manifestness through what I see. The objects behind my back . . . *count* for me."

In the absence of cognitive judgments about the world, perception requires a certain constancy of engagement with an object or situation in order to establish itself through its own phenomenological memory that is independent of the mind. This means that perception is not in every aspect an entirely open and receptive phenomenology with respect to sense data. Merleau-Ponty uses the example of several plates under varying lighting conditions with perception positing the plates as equivalent despite the differences in lighting levels. In contrast to this innate limitation in perception, Merleau-Ponty proposes that perception is polyvalent in terms of the relationship between the five senses that are capable of interacting "at once" synesthetically. Thus, colors can be perceived as sounds, or vice versa, or a color may be felt as a quality of material texture, or a sound or object can be experienced as a fragrance. In such a manner Cézanne "could see the velvetiness, the hardness, the softness, and even the odor of objects."

Merleau-Ponty claims that very little understanding of emotions or feelings can be gained through introspection: "If I try to study love or hate purely from inner observation, I will find very little to describe: a few pangs, a few heart-throbs—in short, trite agitations which do not reveal the essence of love or hate." Rather, moods and feelings are experienced through ways of behaving and are communicated in bodily gestures and expressive language—feelings are gauged *viscerally* through their outward expression in gestures, facial and bodily attitudes, not by treating such attitudes as signifiers *of* interior feelings, "Each time I find something worth saying [about feelings] it is . . . because I have succeeded in studying it as a way of behaving, as a modification of my relations with others and with the world." That it is no longer necessary to distinguish "between signs and their significance, between what is sensed and what is judged" has a particular significance for film since it does not render the thoughts of the characters directly, unlike in novels, but only their behavior towards each other. Merleau-Ponty advocates a form of filmmaking that can express through the actor's behavior feelings of "pleasure, grief, love and hate." In this context, he criticizes films such as Louis Daquin's *Premier de Cordée* (1943), a story about a young mountaineer's experience of vertigo, and André Malraux's *L'Espoir: Sierre de Teruel* (1945), a film about a Spanish Republican's resistance against Franco, which includes a scene of an air pilot emerging from his crashed airplane. Both films convey the experience of vertigo and dizziness through blurred images and steep camera angles; whereas Merleau-Ponty believes that their vertigo would have been conveyed more successfully through a visceral sense of the unsteadiness of the actor's gait that the audience could relate to.

Film, Merleau-Ponty claims, is composed of a series of *gestalts*, whereby the whole is greater than the sum of its parts (for Merleau-Ponty, perception operates in terms of wholes). This idea lies at the heart of Merleau-Ponty's claim for film as a work of art as well as its importance for phenomenology; film has the capacity to create affects that transcend its material substance and narrative content that audiences respond to at intuitive, phenomenological levels issuing in the body rather than cognition and understanding. Films are not representations but unmitigated experiences. A film such as *L'Étrange Sursis* (literally meaning "The strange suspended," but promoted as *On Borrowed Time*, 1939) is not reducible to "the idea that death is terrible only for the man who has not consented to it"; instead, what is of importance is the experience of the entire film as its meaning emerges through the rhythms of its editing, the combinations of sound, dialogue, and images over the time of the film's duration. In films, ideas are subservient to the ways in which they are manifested through "palpable symbols"; in this respect, Kant's aesthetics and, in particular, his prioritization in the *Critique of Judgment* (1790) of the faculty of imagination (sensibility) over the faculty of understanding and conceptualization is of importance (for further discussion of this point, see the introduction to the *Reader*).

The first gestalt that Merleau-Ponty calls attention to is the way in which films are constructed through the interaction between all of the film frames, rather than simply through a linear progression of the frames. To make his point, Merleau-Ponty refers to a short film, known as the *Kuleshov Effect* (1929), produced by the Russian and Soviet filmmakers Vsevolod Pudovkin (1893–1953) and Lev Kuleshov (1899–1970), in which the same shot of the Russian film star Ivan Mosjoukine's face is juxtaposed with other shots of a plate of soup, a girl in a coffin, and a woman on a divan. Asked to respond to the film, its original audience stated that Mosjoukine's face was different each time, displaying signs of hunger, grief, and desire in relation to the respective scenes. The experiment underlined the fact that film is experienced by the audience through combinations of images and scenes.

From a phenomenological point of view, Merleau-Ponty is interested in a proposal by the writer and filmmaker Roger Leenhardt (1903–1985), in an essay in the journal *Ésprit,* that the emotional effects of film require different temporal durations, "a short duration is suitable for an amused smile, one of intermediate length for an indifferent face, and an extended one for a sorrowful expression." Based on these observations, Merleau-Ponty concludes that "there really is, then, a cinematographic system of measurements with very precise and very imperious requirements," although he acknowledges that this system is yet to be consciously fully understood. More generally, Merleau-Ponty stresses the fact that film is a temporal medium and that a film's sense emerges, as in life, over time as well as spatially. Merleau-Ponty enjoys Leenhardt's citation of a scene from *Broadway Melody* (1929) in which one of the lead chorus girls (Queenie Mahoney) stops her act to argue with the director standing at the front of the audience while also having a running spat with a rival who is standing in the wings. This scene of Brechtian distantiation reveals not just the performative relationship required of the actors to their audience but, more important, the performative relationships—that have a "choreography" of their own in terms of gestures and expressive movements—between the actors, themselves, even when they are not actually acting. Mention of this musical leads Merleau-Ponty to the metric pacing of vision with sound, but also how the soundtracks of films form gestalts of their own through the syncopated use of noise and speech juxtaposed with measured intervals of silence, as well as by means of music that creates "a sonorous substance beneath the plastic substance of the image, [making] the internal rhythm of the scene physically palpable."

Film, Merleau-Ponty states by way of conclusion, does not follow philosophy, or vice versa, rather they are part of the same epistemology. In Merleau-Ponty's view, this explains and justifies a review of the film *Le Défunt Récalcitrant (Here Comes Mr. Jordan)* (1941) by the film critic Alexandre Astruc in Sartrean terms. The film's story tells of a boxer (Joe Pendleton, played by Robert Montgomery) who dies, but is granted by heaven the opportunity to fight for the world championship in another (dead) boxer's body (Murdoch). Despite the fact that Pendleton no longer knows himself, as he has become Murdoch, he and his former girlfriend (Betty Logan acted by Evelyn Keyes) have an intuitive sense of knowing each other. Using Sartrean terminology, Astruc believes that this film concerns the interrelationship between the *for itself* and *for others* or, as Merleau-Ponty puts it, "the mingling of consciousness with the world, its involvement in a body, and its coexistence with others." Such a phenomenology of visceral intuition, he proposes, is ripe for film to develop.

* * *

Classical psychology considers our visual field to be a sum or mosaic of sensations, each of which is strictly dependent on the local retinal stimulus which corresponds to it. The new psychology reveals, first of all, that such a parallelism between sensations and the nervous phenomenon conditioning them is unacceptable, even for our simplest and most immediate sensations. Our retina is far from homogeneous: certain parts, for example, are blind to blue or red, yet I do not see any discolored areas when looking at a blue or red surface. This is because, starting at the level of simply seeing colors, my perception is not limited to registering what the retinal stimuli prescribe but reorganizes these stimuli so as to re-establish the field's homogeneity. Broadly speaking, we should think of it not as a mosaic but as a system of configurations. Groups rather than juxtaposed elements are principal and primary in our perception. We group the stars into the same constellations as the ancients, yet it is *a priori* possible to draw the heavenly map many other ways. Given the series:

ab cd ef gh ij

we will always pair the dots according to the formula a-b, c-d, e-f, etc., although the grouping b-c, d-e, f-g, etc. is equally probable in principle. A sick person contemplating the wallpaper in his room will suddenly see it transformed if the pattern and figure become the ground while what is usually seen as ground becomes the figure. The idea we have of the world would be overturned if we could succeed in seeing the intervals between things (for example, the space between the trees on the boulevard) as *objects* and, inversely, if we saw the things themselves—the trees—as the ground. This is what happens in puzzles: we cannot see the rabbit or the hunter because the elements of these figures are dislocated and are integrated into other forms: for example, what is to be the rabbit's ear is still just the empty interval between two trees in the forest. The rabbit and the hunter become apparent through a new partition of the field, a new organization of the whole. Camouflage is the art of masking a form by blending its principal defining lines into other, more commanding forms.

The same type of analysis can be applied to hearing: it will simply be a matter of temporal forms rather than spatial ones. A melody, for example, is a figure of sound and does not mingle with the background noises (such as the siren one hears in the distance during a concert) which may accompany it. The melody is not a sum of notes, since each note only counts by virtue of the function it serves in the whole, which is why the melody does not perceptibly change when transposed, that is, when all its notes are changed while their interrelationships and the structure of the whole remain the same. On the other hand, just one single change in these interrelationships will be enough to modify the entire make-up of the melody. Such a perception of the whole is more natural and more primary than the perception of isolated elements: it has been seen from conditioned-reflex experiments, where, through the frequent association of a piece of meat with a light or a sound, dogs are trained to respond to that light or sound by salivating, that the training acquired in response to a certain series of notes is simultaneously acquired for any melody with the same structure. Therefore analytical perception, through which we arrive at absolute value of the separate elements, is a belated and rare attitude—that of the scientist who observes or of the philosopher who reflects. The perception of forms, understood very broadly as structure, grouping, or configuration should be considered our spontaneous way of seeing.

There is still another point on which modern psychology overthrows the prejudices of classical physiology and psychology. It is a commonplace to say that we have five senses, and it would seem, at first glance, that each of them is like a world out of touch with the others. The light or colors which act upon the eye do not affect the ears or the sense of touch. Nevertheless it has been known for a long time that certain blind people manage to represent the colors they cannot see by means of the sounds which they hear: for example, a blind man said that red ought to be something like a trumpet peal. For a long time it was thought that such phenomena were exceptional, whereas they are, in fact, general. For people under mescaline, sounds are regularly accompanied by spots of color whose hue, form, and vividness vary with the tonal quality, intensity, and pitch of the sounds. Even normal subjects speak of hot, cold, shrill, or hard colors, of sounds that are clear, sharp, brilliant, rough, or mellow, of soft noises and of penetrating fragrances. Cézanne said that one could see the velvetiness, the hardness, the softness, and even the odor of objects. My perception is therefore not a sum of visual, tactile, and audible givens: I perceive in a total way with my whole being; I grasp a unique structure of the thing, a unique way of being, which speaks to all my senses at once.

Naturally, classical psychology was well aware that relationships exist between the different parts of my visual field just as between the data of my different senses—but it held this unity to be a construction and referred it to intelligence and memory. In a famous passage from the *Méditations* Descartes wrote: I say that I see men going by in the street, but what exactly do I really see? All I see are hats and coats which might equally well be covering dolls that only move by springs, and if I say that I see men, it is because I apprehend "through an inspection of the mind what I thought I beheld with my eyes." I am convinced that objects continue to exist when I no longer see them (behind my back, for example). But it is obvious that, for classical thought, these invisible objects subsist for me only because my judgment keeps them present. Even the objects right in front of me are not truly seen but merely thought. Thus I cannot *see* a cube, that is, a solid with six surfaces and twelve edges; all I ever see is a perspective figure of which the lateral surfaces are distorted and the back surface completely hidden. If I am able to speak of cubes, it is because my mind sets these appearances to rights and restores the hidden surface. I cannot see a cube as its geometrical definition presents it: I can only think it. The perception of movement shows even more clearly the extent to which intelligence intervenes in what claims *to* be vision. When my train starts, after it has been standing in the station, I often "see" the train next to mine begin to move. Sensory data are therefore neutral in themselves and can be differently interpreted according to the hypothesis on which my mind comes to rest. Broadly speaking, classical psychology made perception a real deciphering of sense data by the intelligence, a beginning of science, as it were. I am given certain signs from which I must dig out the meaning; I am presented with a text which I must read or interpret. Even when it takes the unity of the perceptual field into account, classical psychology remains loyal to the notion of sensation which was the starting point of the analysis. Its original conception of visual data as a mosaic of sensations forces it to base the unity of the perceptual field on an operation of the intelligence. What does *gestalt* theory tell us on this point? By resolutely rejecting the notion of sensation it teaches us to stop distinguishing between signs and their significance, between what is sensed and what is judged. How could we define the exact color of an object without mentioning the substance of which it is made, without saying, of this blue rug, for example, that it is a "woolly blue?" Cézanne asked how one is to distinguish the color of things from their shape. It is impossible to understand perception as the imputation of a certain significance to certain sensible signs, since the most immediate sensible texture of these signs cannot be described without referring to the object they signify.

Our ability to recognize an object defined by certain constant properties despite changes of lighting stems, not from some process by which our intellect takes the nature of the incident light into account and deduces the object's real color from it, but from the fact that the light which dominates the environment acts as *lighting* and immediately assigns the object its true color. If we look at two plates under unequal lighting, they will appear equally white and unequally lighted as long as the beam of light from the window figures in our visual field. On the other hand, if we observe the same plates through a hole in a screen, one will immediately appear gray and the other white; and even if we *know* that it is nothing but an effect of the lighting, no intellectual analysis of the way they appear will make us see the true color of the two plates. When we turn on the lights at dusk, the electric light seems yellow at first but a moment later tends to lose all definite color; correlatively, the objects, whose color was at first perceptibly modified, resume an appearance comparable to the one they have during the day. Objects and lighting form a system which tends toward a certain constancy and a certain level of stability—not through the operation of intelligence but through the very configuration of the field. I do not think the world in the act of perception: it organizes itself in front of me. When I perceive a cube, it is not because my reason sets the perspectival appearances straight and thinks the geometrical definition of a cube with respect to them. I do not even notice the distortions of perspective, much less correct them; I am at the cube itself in its manifestness through what I see. The objects behind my back are likewise not represented to me by some operation of memory or judgment; they are present, they *count* for me, just as the ground which I do not see continues nonetheless to be present beneath the figure which partially hides it. Even the perception of movement, which at first seems to depend directly on the point of reference chosen by the intellect is in turn only one element in the global organization of the field. For, although it is true that, when either my train or the one next to it starts, first one, then the other may appear to be moving, one should note that the illusion is not arbitrary and that I cannot willfully induce it by the completely intellectual choice of a point of reference. If I am playing cards in my compartment, the other train will start moving; if, on the other hand, I am looking for someone in the adjacent train, then mine will begin to roll. In each instance the one which seems stationary is the one we have chosen as our abode and which, for the time being, is our environment. Movement and rest distribute themselves in our surroundings not according to the hypotheses which our intelligence is pleased to construct but according to the way we settle ourselves in the world and the position our bodies assume in it. Sometimes I see the steeple motionless against the sky with clouds floating above it, and sometimes the clouds appear still and the steeple falls through space. But here again the choice of the fixed point is not made by the intelligence: the looked-at object in which I anchor myself will always seem fixed, and I cannot take this meaning away from it except by looking elsewhere. Nor do I give it this meaning through thought. Perception is not a sort of beginning science, an elementary exercise of the intelligence; we must rediscover a commerce with the world and a presence to the world which is older than intelligence.

Finally, the new psychology also brings a new concept of the perception of others. Classical psychology unquestioningly accepted the distinction between inner observation, or introspection, and outer observation. "Psychic facts"— anger or fear, for example—could be directly known only from the inside and by the person experiencing them. It was thought to be self-evident that I can grasp only the corporal *signs* of anger or fear from the outside and that I have to resort to the anger or fear I know in myself through introspection in order to interpret these signs. Today's psychologists have made us notice that in reality introspection gives me almost nothing. If I try to study love or hate purely from inner observation, I will find very little to describe: a few pangs, a few heart-throbs—in short, trite agitations which do not reveal the essence of love or hate. Each time I find something worth saying, it is because I have not been satisfied to coincide with my feeling, because I have succeeded in studying it as a way of behaving, as a modification of my relations with others and with the world, because I have managed to think about it as I would think about the behavior of another person whom I happened to witness. In fact, young children understand gestures and facial expressions long before they can reproduce them on their own; the meaning must, so to speak, adhere to the behavior. We must reject that prejudice which makes "inner realities" out of love, hate, or anger, leaving them accessible to one single witness: the person who feels them. Anger, shame, hate, and love are not psychic facts hidden at the bottom of another's consciousness: they are types of behavior or styles of conduct which are visible from the outside. They exist *on* this face or *in* those gestures, not hidden behind them. Psychology did not begin to develop until the day it gave up the distinction between mind and body, when it abandoned the two correlative methods of interior observation and physiological psychology. We learned nothing about emotion as long as we limited ourselves to measuring the rate of respiration or heartbeat in an angry person, and we didn't learn anything more when we tried to express the qualitative and inexpressible nuances of lived anger. To create a psychology of anger is to try to ascertain the *meaning* of anger, to ask oneself how it functions in human life and what purpose it serves. So we find that emotion is, as Janet said, a disorganizing reaction which comes into play whenever we are stuck. On a deeper level, as Sartre has shown, we find that anger is a magical way of acting by which we afford ourselves a completely symbolic satisfaction in the imagination after renouncing effective action in the world, just as, in a conversation, a person who cannot convince his partner will start hurling insults at him which prove nothing or as a man who does not dare strike his opponent will shake his fist at him from a distance. Since emotion is not a psychic, internal fact but rather a variation in our relations with others and the world which is expressed in our bodily attitude, we cannot say that only the signs of love or anger are given to the outside observer and that we understand others indirectly by interpreting these signs: we have to say that others are directly manifest to us as behavior. Our behavioral science goes much farther than we think. When unbiased subjects are confronted with photographs of several faces, copies of several kinds of handwriting, and recordings of several voices and are asked to put together a face, a silhouette, a voice, and a handwriting, it has been shown that the elements are usually put together correctly or that, in any event, the correct matchings greatly outnumber the incorrect ones. Michelangelo's handwriting is attributed to Raphael in 36 cases, but in 221 instances it is correctly identified, which means that we recognize a certain common structure in each person's voice, face, gestures and bearing and that each person is nothing more nor less to us than this structure or way of being in the world. One can see how these remarks might be applied to the psychology of language: just as a man's body and "soul" are but two aspects of his way of being in the world, so the word and the thought it indicates should not be considered two externally related terms: the word bears its meaning in the same way that the body incarnates a manner of behavior.

The new psychology has, generally speaking, revealed man to us not as an understanding which constructs the world but as a being thrown into the world and attached to it by a natural bond. As a result it re-educates us in how to see this world which we touch at every point of our being, whereas classical psychology abandoned the lived world for the one which scientific intelligence succeeded in constructing.

* * *

If we now consider the film as a perceptual object, we can apply what we have just said about perception in general to the perception of a film. We will see that this point of view illuminates the nature and significance of the movies and that the new psychology leads us straight to the best observations of the aestheticians of the cinema.

Let us say right off that a film is not a sum total of images but a temporal *gestalt*. This is the moment to recall Pudovkin's famous experiment which clearly shows the melodic unity of films. One day Pudovkin took a close-up of Mosjoukin with a completely impassive expression and projected it after showing: first, a bowl of soup, then, a young woman lying dead in her coffin, and, last, a child playing with a teddy-bear. The first thing noticed was that Mosjoukin seemed to be looking at the bowl, the young woman, and the child, and next one noted that he was looking pensively at the dish, that he wore an expression of sorrow when looking at the woman, and that he had a glowing smile for the child. The audience was amazed at his variety of expression although the same shot had actually been used all three times and was, if anything, remarkably inexpressive. The meaning of a shot therefore depends on what precedes it in the movie, and this succession of scenes creates a new reality which is not merely the sum of its parts. In an excellent article in *Esprit*, R. Leenhardt added that one still has to bring in the time-factor for each shot: a short duration is suitable for an amused smile, one of intermediate length for an indifferent face, and an extended one for a sorrowful expression.[4] Leenhardt drew from this the following definition of cinematographic rhythm: "A certain order of shots and a certain duration for each of these shots or views, so that taken together they produce the desired impression with maximum effectiveness." There really is, then, a cinematographic system of measurements with very precise and very imperious requirements. "When you see a movie, try to guess the moment when a shot has given its all and must move on, end, be replaced either by changing the angle, the distance, or the field. You will get to know that constriction of the chest produced by an overlong shot which brakes the movement and that deliciously intimate acquiescence when a shot fades at the right moment." Since a film consists not only of montage (the selection of shots or views, their order and length) but also of cutting (the selection of scenes or sequences, and their order and length), it seems to be an extremely complex form inside of which a very great number of actions and reactions are taking place at every moment. The laws of this form, moreover, are yet to be discovered, having until now only been sensed by the flair or tact of the director, who handles cinematographic language as a man manipulates syntax: without explicitly thinking about it and without always being in a position to formulate the rules which he spontaneously obeys.

What we have just said about visual films also applies to sound movies, which are not a sum total of words or noises but are likewise a *gestalt*. A rhythm exists for sounds just as for images. There is a montage of noises and sounds, as Leenhardt's example of the old sound movie *Broadway Melody* shows. "Two actors are on stage. We are in the balcony listening to them speak their parts. Then immediately there is a close-up, whispering, and we are aware of something they are saying to each other under their breath. . . ." The expressive force of this montage lies in its ability to make us sense the coexistence, the simultaneity of lives in the same world, the actors as they are for us and for themselves, just as, previously, we saw Pudovkin's visual montage linking the man and his gaze to the sights which surround him. Just as a film is not merely a play photographed in motion and the choice and grouping of the shots constitutes an original means of expression for the motion picture, so, equally, the soundtrack is not a simple phonographic reproduction of noises and words but requires a certain internal organization which the film's creator must invent. The real ancestor of the movie soundtrack is not the phonograph but the radio play.

Nor is that all. We have been considering sight and sound by turns but in reality the way they are put together makes another new whole which cannot be reduced to its component parts. A sound movie is not a silent film embellished with words and sounds whose only function is to complete the cinematographic illusion. The bond between sound and image is much closer, and the image is transformed by the proximity of sound. This is readily apparent in the case of dubbed films, where thin people are made to speak with the voices of fat people, the young have the voices of the old, and tall people the voices of tiny ones—all of which is absurd if what we have said is true—namely, that voice profile, and character form an indivisible unit. And the union of sound and image occurs not only in each character but in the film as a whole. It is not by accident that characters are silent at one moment and speak at another. The alternation of words and silence is manipulated to create the most effective image. There are three sorts of dialogue, as Malraux said in *Verve* (1940).[5] First may be noted expository dialogue whose purpose is to make the circumstances of the dramatic action known. The novel and the film both avoid this sort of dialogue. Then there is *tonal* dialogue, which gives us each character's particular accent and which dominates, for example, in Proust where the characters are very hard to visualize but are admirably recognizable as soon as they start to talk. The extravagant or sparing use of words, their richness or emptiness, their precision or affectation reveal the essence of a character more surely than many descriptions. Tonal dialogue rarely occurs in movies, since the visible presence of the actor with his own particular manner of behaving rarely lends itself to it. Finally we have dramatic dialogue which presents the discussion and confrontation of the characters and which is the movies' principal form of dialogue. But it is far from continuous. One speaks ceaselessly in the theater but not in the film. "Directors of recent movies," said Malraux, "*break into* dialogue after long stretches of silence, just as a novelist breaks into dialogue after long narrative passages." Thus the distribution of silences and dialogue constitutes a metrics above and beyond the metrics of vision and sound, and the pattern of words and silence, more complex than the other two, superimposes its requirements upon them. To complete the analysis one would still have to study the role of music in this ensemble: let us only say that music should be incorporated into it, not juxtaposed to it. Music should not be used as a stopgap for sonic holes or as a completely exterior commentary on the sentiments or the scenes as so often happens in movies: the storm of wrath unleashes the storm of brass, or the music laboriously imitates a footstep or the sound of a coin falling to the ground. It should intervene to mark a change in a film's style: for example, the passage from an action scene to the "inside" of the character, to the recollection of earlier scenes, or to the description of a landscape. Generally speaking, it should accompany and help bring about a "rupture in the sensory balance," as Jaubert said.[6] Lastly, it must not be another means of expression juxtaposed to the visual expression. "By the use of strictly musical means (rhythm, form, instrumentation) and by a mysterious alchemy of correspondences which ought to be the very foundation of the film composer's profession, it should recreate a sonorous substance beneath the plastic substance of the image, should, finally, make the internal rhythm of the scene physically palpable without thereby striving to translate its sentimental, dramatic, or poetic content" (Jaubert). It is not the job of words in a movie to add ideas to the images, nor is it the job of music to add sentiments. The ensemble tells us something very precise which is neither a thought nor a reminder of sentiments we have felt in our own lives.

What, then, does the film *signify*: what does it mean? Each film tells a *story*: that is, it relates a certain number of events which involve certain characters and which could, it seems, also be told in prose, as, in effect, they are in the scenario on which the film is based. The talking film, frequently overwhelmed by dialogue, completes this illusion. Therefore motion pictures are often conceived as the visual and sonic representation, the closest possible reproduction of a drama which literature could evoke only in words and which the movie is lucky enough to be able to photograph. What supports this ambiguity is the fact that movies do have a basic realism: the actors should be natural, the set should be as realistic as possible; for "the power of reality released on the screen is such that the least stylization will cause it to go flat" (Leenhardt). That does not mean, however, that the movies are fated to let us see and hear what we would see and hear if we were present at the events being related; nor should films suggest some general view of life in the manner of an edifying tale. Aesthetics has already encountered this problem in connection with the novel or with poetry. A novel always has an idea that can be summed up in a few words, a scenario which a few lines can express. A poem always refers to things or ideas. And yet the function of the pure novel or pure poetry is not simply to tell us these facts. If it were, the poem could be exactly transposed into prose and the novel would lose nothing in summary. Ideas and facts are just the raw materials of art: the art of the novel lies in the choice of what one says and what one does not say, in the choice of perspectives (this chapter will be written from the point of view of this character, that chapter from another's point of view), in the varying tempo of the narrative; the essence of the art of poetry is not the didactic description of things or the exposition of ideas but the creation of a machine of language which almost without fail puts the reader in a certain poetic state. Movies, likewise, always have a story and often an idea (for example, in *l'Etrange sursis* the idea that death is terrible only for the man who has not consented to it), but the function of the film is not to make these facts or ideas known to us.

Kant's remark that, in knowledge imagination serves the understanding, whereas in art the understanding serves the imagination, is a profound one. In other words, ideas or prosaic facts are only there to give the creator an opportunity to seek out their palpable symbols and to trace their visible and sonorous monogram. The meaning of a film is incorporated into its rhythm just as the meaning of a gesture may immediately be read in that gesture: the film does not mean anything but itself. The idea is presented in a nascent state and emerges from the temporal structure of the film as it does from the coexistence of the parts of a painting. The joy of art lies in its showing how something takes on meaning—not by referring to already established and acquired ideas but by the temporal or spatial arrangement of elements. As we saw above, a movie has meaning in the same way that a thing does; neither of them speaks to an isolated understanding; rather, both appeal to our power tacitly to decipher the world or men and to coexist with them. It is true that in our ordinary lives we lose sight of this aesthetic value of the tiniest perceived thing. It is also true that the perceived form is never perfect in real life, that it always has blurs, smudges, and superfluous matter, as it were. Cinematographic drama is, so to speak, finer-grained than real-life dramas: it takes place in a world that is more exact than the real world. But in the last analysis perception permits us to understand the meaning of the cinema. A movie is not thought; it is perceived.

This is why the movies can be so gripping in their presentation of man: they do not give us his *thoughts*, as novels have done for so long, but his conduct or behavior. They directly present to us that special way of being in the world, of dealing with things and other people, which we can see in the sign language of gesture and gaze and which clearly defines each person we know. If a movie wants to show us someone who is dizzy, it should not attempt to portray the interior landscape of dizziness, as Daquin in *Premier de cordée* and Malraux in *Sierra de Terruel* wished to do. We will get a much better sense of dizziness if we see it from the outside, if we contemplate that unbalanced body contorted on a rock or that unsteady step trying to adapt itself to who knows what upheaval of space. For the movies as for modern psychology dizziness, pleasure, grief, love, and hate are ways of behaving.

* * *

This psychology shares with contemporary philosophies the common feature of presenting consciousness thrown into the world, subject to the gaze of others and learning from them what it is: it does not, in the manner of the classical philosophies, present mind *and* world, each particular consciousness *and* the others. Phenomenological or existential philosophy is largely an expression of surprise at this inherence of the self in the world and in others, a description of this paradox and permeation, and an attempt to make us *see* the bond between subject and world, between subject and others, rather than to *explain* it as the classical philosophies did by resorting to absolute spirit. Well, the movies are peculiarly suited to make manifest the union of mind and body, mind and world, and the expression of one in the other.

That is why it is not surprising that a critic should evoke philosophy in connection with a film. Astruc in his review of *Défunt récalcitrant* uses Sartrian terms to recount the film, in which a dead man lives after his body and is obliged to inhabit another. The man remains the same *for himself* but is different *for others*, and he cannot rest until through love a girl recognizes him despite his new exterior and the harmony between the *for itself* and the *for others* is re-established. The editors of *Le Canard enchaîné* are annoyed at this and would like to send Astruc back to his philosophical investigations. But the truth is that both parties are right: one because art is not meant to be a showcase for ideas, and the other because contemporary philosophy consists not in stringing concepts together but in describing the mingling of consciousness with the world, its involvement in a body, and its coexistence with others; and because this is movie material *par excellence.*

Finally, if we ask ourselves why it is precisely in the film era that this philosophy has developed, we obviously should not say that the movies grew out of the philosophy. Motion pictures are first and foremost a technical invention in which philosophy counts for nothing. But neither do we have the right to say that this philosophy has grown out of the cinema which it transposes to the level of ideas, for one can make bad movies; after the technical instrument has been invented, it must be taken up by an artistic will and, as it were, re-invented

before one can succeed in making real films. Therefore, if philosophy is in harmony with the cinema, if thought and technical effort are heading in the same
direction, it is because the philosopher and the moviemaker share a certain way
of being, a certain view of the world which belongs to a generation. It offers us
yet another chance to confirm that modes of thought correspond to technical
methods and that, to use Goethe's phrase, "What is inside is also outside."

Notes

1. Maurice Merleau-Ponty, *The Structure of Behaviour,* trans. Alden L. Fisher (Boston: Beacon, 1967); and *Phenomenology of Perception,* trans. Colin Smith (London: Routledge, 2006).
2. Originally delivered as a lecture on March 13, 1945, at l'Institut des Hautes Études Cinémato-graphiques.
3. Merleau-Ponty, *Phenomenology of Perception,* p. 296. Originally published in France in 1945.
4. Maurice Jaubert, *Ésprit* 44 (May 1936).
5. André Malraux, "Esquisse d'une psychologie du cinéma (Sketch for a Psychology of the Moving Pictures)," *Verve* 8 (1940).
6. Jaubert, *Esprit* 44 (May 1936); cf. also his article "Le Son au Cinéma," *Esprit* 43 (April 1936).

CHAPTER 5

ON CONTEMPORARY ALIENATION OR THE END OF THE PACT WITH THE DEVIL

JEAN BAUDRILLARD

Jean Baudrillard (1929–2007) studied with the Marxist urban theorist Henri Lefebvre and taught sociology at the Paris X, University Nanterre, from 1966 to 1987. Beginning with a critical approach toward capital and commodity logic in the 1970s, Baudrillard increasingly came to acknowledge the immense reach of capitalist ideology through technological mediatization supported by new technologies of mass distribution. Describing capital in the decades at the turn of the twentieth century, Baudrillard declared that "Commodity logic . . . today governs not only labor processes and material products, but the whole of culture, sexuality, and human relations, including even fantasies and individual drives."

Baudrillard argued that the totalizing extent of commodity logic under capital today meant that both classical and materialist conceptions of the social were outdated. These theories relied upon the assumption of a subject who possessed either a degree of agency or otherwise lacked such agency as a result of alienation and commodity fetishism. However, Baudrillard believed that the subject *no longer even exists*, owing to its implosion into a world "in which everything is *spectacularized* . . . evoked, provoked and orchestrated" by means of globalized media and transmission networks "into images, signs, consumable models." Baudrillard called this hyperreal world of images and signs "simulacra" following Plato's story about the Sophist philosopher whose identity, the classical philosopher claimed, was that of total dissimulation.[1]

Despite many commentaries on mass media, "On Contemporary Alienation or the End of the Pact with the Devil" (1970) is one of the few texts that

Baudrillard wrote that has an extended discussion of a film.[2] The essay begins with a comparison of the film *The Student of Prague* (the first version of which was made in 1913, although it is the second version of 1926 to which Baudrillard refers)[3] and a novella, *Peter Schlemihl's Miraculous Story* (1814), written originally in German by Adelbert von Chamisso (1781–1838). In *The Student of Prague* the main protagonist sells his mirror image to the devil "for a pile of gold" and, similarly, Peter Schlemihl sells his shadow to the devil for a limitless amount of money. Both stories are loosely based on the legend of Faust in which the eponymous protagonist is tempted by the devil and exchanges his soul for worldly knowledge and material pleasures. For Baudrillard, the devil in these fables can be read as the capitalist system of commodification, while the loss of the protagonists' likenesses (in other words, their very souls) to the devil represents the alienation and objectivization of labor power in the market place, "the image is not lost or abolished by chance: it is *sold*." Here, Baudrillard's ideas are informed by Marx's argument in the section on "The Fetishism of the Commodity," from the first volume of *Capital: A Critique of Political Economy* (1867), regarding "commodity logic and exchange value," in which the value of labor power is posited as subject to the dictates of the market based upon the competitive undercutting of commodity prices. This results in the alienation of labor: dispossessed by capitalism of self-determining powers of value, labor is either haunted by a distorted, ghostly image of its estranged self or, indeed, has no image at all. Both these scenarios are played out in *The Student of Prague*, and, according to Baudrillard, they can be taken as allegories of the alienated degradation of the subject under capitalism as envisaged by Marx, "I become another to myself; I am *alienated*."

However, Baudrillard suggests that, today, Marx's theory of alienation is no longer relevant for theorizing the subject under capital today. The marketing power of consumerism has become absolute, with the consequence that the metaphysical dichotomy of a *false* self alienated from an *authentic* self—the subjects of both *The Student of Prague* and *Peter Schlemihl's Miraculous Story*—are outdated allegories for contemporary purposes. Indeed, Baudrillard suggests that the social and economic circumstances today do not allow for the production of allegories or myths by which to narrativize, and thus offer a perspective, on these circumstances since the simulacral image has no vanishing points by which a viewer can be established. According to Baudrillard, with the advent of the consumer society there has been a rupture in the paradigmatic system of representation that dominated Western ideas since classical times. This system was based upon a dichotomy between, on the one hand, the idea of an originary model (the divine sphere of the gods, the Forms underlying the universe) and, on the other hand, in relation to this, a false copy of the model (the finite, corporeal realm of phenomenological life). Such a system allowed for the possibility of a representation in the form of a sign or an image of the originary model, and this is the conventional way by which Western ideas of representation are formulated and received. According to Baudrillard, even when Marx discusses the alienated subject of labor, or when *The Student of Prague* and *Peter Schlemihl's Miraculous Story* recount a story of the tragic loss of subjectivity, they posit an originary subject of that alienation or loss, "That part of us sold and forgotten is still us." Hence, it follows that, at the conclusion of *The Student of Prague,* the student has the possibility of regaining his own authentic sense of self, even if only momentarily prior to his death. Mortally wounded, the student peers into a shard of the shattered mirror and discovers "his normal likeness . . . restored to him." As Baudrillard says, "the faithfulness of that [mirror] reflection bears witness, to some degree, to a real reciprocity between the world and ourselves."

Baudrillard states that "alienation cannot be overcome: it is *the very structure of the bargain with the devil.* It is the very structure of the market society." But in today's consumer society, according to Baudrillard, there has been a fundamental shift in the nature of alienation such that there are no means by which to form a representation or an image of the subject, even an alienated one; the function of the mirror performed in *The Student of Prague* has become redundant. Therefore, both *The Student of Prague* and *Peter Schlemihl's Miraculous Story* are, in Baudrillard's opinion, outdated allegories that once were appropriate to Marx's understanding of the fate of labor in the era of industrial capitalism, but are no longer relevant to today's consumer society. To possess the means to produce a representation of alienation, and thereby gain a perspective upon this condition, requires a classical model of representation that establishes a reflective distance between the subject toward its other, whether this is its double, its image, or its shadow. But in the social now, Baudrillard claims, no such distance exists: the (alienated) subject is absorbed into the consumerist system itself, which is all encompassing and from which there are no vanishing points. All needs and desires in such a logic of universalized commodification are always already mediated through methods of anticipation and calculation that are filtered according to the dictates and predictions of the consumerist market. This leaves no space or distance by which to mirror or reflect the exploited subject, alienated or otherwise, since there is no subject as such: "In the generalized process of consumption, there is no longer any soul, no shadow, no double, and no image in the specular sense. There is no longer any contradiction within being, or any problematic of being and appearance. There is no longer anything but the transmission and reception of signs, and the individual being vanishes in this combinatory and calculus of signs."

What remains following the implosion of the subject and its alienated image are simulacra, images that cannot be conceived of in terms of either authenticity *or* falsity. Subjectivity, Baudrillard argues, is constructed as a simulation through signs that are circulated via capitalist modes of transmission.

In his book *Simulacra and Simulation*, Baudrillard claims that the effect on cinema of the implosion of the real under capital is the evacuation of felt history. Formerly, in cinema, as in Luchino Visconti's films—*Senso* (1954) and *The Leopard* (1963)—Baudrillard senses that "there is meaning, history, a sensual rhetoric, dead time, a passionate game, not only in the historical content, but in the mise-en-scène." However, in films such as *Chinatown* (1974), *Three Days of the Condor* (1975), *Barry Lyndon* (1975), *1900* (1976), and *All the President's Men* (1976), this felt sense of history no longer persists. Baudrillard observes that these films are made to high standards of technical quality, but that this serves only to create a sense of distance that, ultimately, leaves viewers with a feeling of indifference.[4]

* * *

The Student of Prague

The *Student of Prague* is an old silent film from the 1930s, an expressionist film of the German school.[5] It tells the story of a poor but ambitious student impatient for a more prosperous life. As he is taking part in a drinking bout in a cafe near Prague, a hunt is in progress all around in which that city's high society is finding what amusement it can. Someone rules over that society and is pulling the strings. He can be seen maneuvering the animals at will and regulating the movements of the hunters. And this man of relatively advanced years, with his top hat, gloves, knobbed stick, slight paunch and little turn-of-the-century goatee beard, looks like one of the hunters. He is the Devil. He contrives to have one of the women from the hunt lose her way. She meets the student—love at first sight! But the woman, being rich, is beyond his grasp. Returning home, the student broods on his ambition and dissatisfaction, which have now assumed a sexual dimension.

The Devil then appears in the student's seedy room, which contains only books and a life-size mirror. In exchange for his image in the mirror, he offers him a pile of gold. The deal is struck. The Devil peels the specular image from the mirror as though it were an etching or a sheet of carbon paper, rolls it up, puts it in his pocket, and leaves, in suitably obsequious and sardonic fashion. Here the film's real argument begins. Thanks to his money, the student enjoys success after success, avoiding, with cat-like tread, the mirrors with which the fashionable society in which he moves unfortunately surrounds itself. At the beginning, however, he retains his peace of mind; he is not greatly vexed at no longer seeing his own image. But then, one day, he sees his own flesh-and-blood image. This double, which now frequents the same circles and clearly takes an interest in him, follows him around and never lets him rest. It is, we surmise, his own image—the image he sold—which the Devil has revived and put back into circulation. As the good image it is, it remains attached to its model; but, as the bad image it has become, it now accompanies him not only when he chances to pass by mirrors, but in life itself, wherever he goes. He runs the risk of being compromised by it at any moment, if the two are seen together (a number of small incidents of this kind have already occurred). And if he flees society to avoid it, it takes his place and completes what he had begun, distorting his actions to the point of rendering them criminal. One day when he has provoked a duel, but has resolved to make his excuses on the dueling ground, he arrives at the appointed place at dawn. But he is too late: his double has passed that way before him and the opponent is already dead. The student hides. His image continues to hound him, as though to be avenged for having been sold. He sees the image everywhere. It appears to him behind tombs, or at the edge of the cemetery. He is no longer able to have any social life; his existence is impossible. In this despairing state, he rejects even a sincere offer of love and, to put an end to all his troubles, settles on the plan of killing his own image.

One day, the image pursues him into his room. In the course of a violent scene between the two, it happens to pass in front of the mirror from which it came. At the memory of this initial scene, nostalgia for his image, mingled with fury at what he is enduring on its account, pushes the student to the brink. He fires at it. Naturally, the mirror is smashed and the double, become again the phantasm it once was, vanishes into thin air. But at the same moment, the student slumps to the ground; it is *he* who is dying. For, by killing his image, he is killing himself, since, without his noticing it, the image has become living and real in his stead. In his death throes, however, he grasps at one of the fragments of the mirror scattered about the floor and realizes that *he can see himself again.* He loses his body, but, by paying that price, his *normal* likeness is restored to him just before he dies.

The mirror image here symbolically represents the meaning of our acts. These build up around us a world that is *in our image.* The transparency of our relation to the world is expressed rather well by the individual's unimpaired relation to his image in a mirror: the faithfulness of that reflection bears witness, to some degree, to a real reciprocity between the world and ourselves. Symbolically, then, if that image should be missing, it is the sign that the world is becoming opaque, that our acts are getting out of our control and, at that point, we have no perspective on ourselves. Without that guarantee, no identity is possible any longer: I become another to myself; I am *alienated.*

This is the first element, then, which the film presents. But it is not content merely to tell a general tale. It immediately supplies the concrete meaning of the situation. The image is not lost or abolished by chance: it is *sold.* It falls into the commodity sphere, we might say, and this is indeed the sense of *concrete, social* alienation. At the same time, the fact that the Devil can pocket this image as an object is also the fantastic illustration of the real process of commodity fetishism: from the moment they are produced, our works and our acts fall out of our grasp and are objectivized; they fall, literally, into the Devil's hands. Thus, in Chamisso's *Peter Schlemihl* the shadow too is separated from the person maleficently and becomes a pure thing, an article of apparel one might leave at home if one were not careful and which could get stuck to the ground if there were too sharp a frost. Schlemihl, who has lost his shadow, fancies he might have one drawn for him by a painter—one which will follow him about. And Egyptian legends say that one should not walk too close to water, since crocodiles have a taste for passing shadows. The plots of the two tales are equivalent: whether we are speaking of image or shadow, it is in each case the transparency of our relation to ourselves and to the world that is shattered, and life then loses its meaning. But there is one thing in the fables of *Schlemihl* and *The Student of Prague* that is superior to many other pacts with the Devil: the fact that they put Gold, and Gold alone—that is to say, commodity logic and exchange-value—at the center of alienation.

The two fables do, however, proceed in quite different ways after that, with the logic of the Schlemihl story—in which Chamisso does not carry through the consequences of the shadow being transformed into an object—lacking rigor. Chamisso fills out his tale with fantastical, comic episodes, like the chase over the "sunlit sandy plain" after a wandering, masterless shadow, which might be his, or when the Devil gives him back his shadow to try out again for a few hours. But Schlemihl does not suffer directly from his alienated shadow; he suffers only the social reprobation which attaches to the absence of a shadow. Once it has escaped, it does not turn against him to become the instrument which destroys his very being. Schlemihl is condemned to solitude, but *he remains the same.* Neither his consciousness nor his life is taken from him, only life in society. Hence the final compromise, in which he stoically rejects the second bargain proposed by the Devil, which would give him back his shadow in exchange for his soul. Thus, *he loses his shadow, but he saves his soul.*

The Student of Prague follows a much tighter logic. As soon as he has sold his image or, in other words, has sold a part of himself, the student is hounded to *his death* by it in real life. This translates the unvarnished truth of the process of alienation: nothing of what is alienated runs off into some neutral circuit, into an "external world" over against which we might be said to remain free—suffering, with each dispossession, only a loss in our *having,* but always retaining possession of ourselves in our "private" sphere and ultimately remaining intact in our *being.* This is the reassuring fiction of the "inner self" or "heart of hearts" [*for intérieur*], where the soul is free of the world. Alienation goes much deeper than that. There is a part of us which gets away from us in this process, but we do not get away from it. The object (the soul, the shadow, the product of our labor become object) *takes its revenge.* All we are dispossessed of remains attached to us, but negatively. In other words, it *haunts* us. That part of us sold and forgotten is still us, or rather it is a caricature of us, the ghost, the *specter* which follows us; it is our continuation and takes its revenge.

We encounter the troubling atmosphere of this inversion of subject and object, this sorcery of the otherness of the same, in the most everyday expressions: "He followed him about like a shadow." And also in our cult of the dead—a propitiating of a part of us which is alienated once and for all, and from which, as a consequence, we can expect only ill. Now, there is a part of ourselves by which, *when living,* we are collectively haunted: social labor power, which, once sold, returns, through the whole social cycle of the commodity, to dispossess us of the meaning of labor itself; labor power which has become—by a social, not a diabolical, operation, of course—the materialized obstacle to the fruits of our labors. It is all this which is symbolized in *The Student of Prague* by the sudden emergence, live and hostile, of the image, and by the long suicide (for such we must call it) which that image imposes on the one who sold it.

What is crucial here, and is dramatically demonstrated to us, is that the alienated human being is not merely a being diminished and impoverished but left intact in its essence: it is a being turned inside out, changed into something evil, into its own enemy, set against itself. This is, on another level, the process Freud describes in repression: the repressed returning through the agency of repression itself. It is the body of Christ on the cross changing into a woman to obsess the monk who has taken a vow of chastity. In alienation, it is the human being's objectivized life-forces which at any moment change *into him to his cost,* and thus drive him to his death.

In the end, Schlemihl gives relative meaning to his life and dies a natural death, like a solitary American industrialist, in a charitable institution he himself founded in the days when he was wealthy. He saved his soul by rejecting the second bargain. This division of the action flows necessarily from the ambiguity of the initial idea and, as a result, the fable entirely loses its rigor.

In *The Student of Prague,* there is no second bargain. The student dies inexorably from the *logical* consequences of the first. This means that, for Chamisso, it is possible to sell one's shadow—that is to say, to be alienated in all respects of one's behavior—and *still to save one's soul.* Alienation leads only to a conflict in social *appearances,* and, that being the case, Schlemihl can very easily overcome it *abstractly* in solitude, whereas *The Student of Prague* develops the *objective* logic of alienation in all its rigor and shows that *there is no way out but death.* Every ideal solution for overcoming alienation is cut off. Alienation cannot be overcome: it is *the very structure of the bargain with the Devil.* It is the very structure of market society.

The End of Transcendence

The Student of Prague is a remarkable illustration of the processes of alienation, that is to say, of the generalized pattern of individual and social life governed by commodity logic. Moreover, since the early Middle Ages, the Pact with the Devil has been the central myth of a society engaged in the historical and technical process of the domination of Nature, that process being always simultaneously a process of the taming of sexuality. Among the forces of evil, indexed to the Devil, the Western "Sorcerer's Apprentice" has served constantly to thematize the immense guilt attaching to the puritanical, Promethean enterprise of Progress, of sublimation and labor, of rationality and efficiency. That is why this medieval theme of the re-emergence of the repressed—of being haunted by the repressed and selling one's soul (the "pact" reflecting the irruption of market processes into early bourgeois society)—was revived by the romantics in the very earliest years of the "industrial age." Since then, the theme has continued to run (parallel to the myth of the "miracle of technology") beneath the myth of the *inevitability of technology.* All our current science fiction is steeped in it, as is the whole of everyday mythology, from the peril of the atomic catastrophe (the technological suicide of civilization) to the theme, played out in a thousand variations, of the fatal gap between technical Progress and human social morality.

We may, therefore, suggest that the age of consumption, being the historical culmination of the whole process of accelerated productivity under the sign of capital, is also the age of radical alienation. Commodity logic has become generalized and today governs not only labor processes and material products, but the whole of culture, sexuality, and human relations, including even fantasies and individual drives. Everything is taken over by that logic, not only in the sense that all functions and needs are objectivized and manipulated in terms of profit, but in the deeper sense in which everything is *spectacularized* or, in other words, evoked, provoked and orchestrated into images, signs, consumable models.

But the question then is: in so far as it revolves around *the alterity of the self-same* (that is to say, around an alienated, abducted, essence of man), can this schema (or this concept) of alienation still be operative in a context in which the individual is no longer ever confronted with his own split image? The myth of the Pact and the Sorcerer's Apprentice is still a *demiurgic myth,* the myth of the Market, Gold and Production, the transcendent objective of which turns around against human beings themselves. By contrast, consumption is not Promethean; it is hedonistic and regressive. Its process is no longer one of labor and self-surpassing, but *a process of absorption of signs and absorption by signs.* It is, therefore, characterized, as Marcuse says, by the *end of transcendence.* In the generalized process of consumption, there is no longer any soul, no shadow, no double, and no image in the specular sense. There is no longer any contradiction within being, or any problematic of being and appearance. There is no longer anything but the transmission and reception of signs, and the individual being vanishes in this combinatory and calculus of signs. Consumer man never comes face to face with his own needs, any more than with the specific product of his labor; nor is he ever confronted with his own image: *he is Immanent in the signs he arranges.* There is no transcendence any more, no finality, no objective: what characterizes this society is the absence of "reflection," of a perspective on itself. There is, therefore, no *maleficent agency* either, like that of the Devil, with whom one could enter into a Faustian pact to gain wealth and glory, since one is given these things by a *beneficent,* maternal *ambience*—the affluent society itself. Or, alternatively, we must suppose that it is society as a whole, as a *société anonyme,* as a thing of "limited liability," which has struck a contract with the Devil, has bartered all transcendence and finality for affluence, and is now haunted by an absence of ends.

In the specific mode of consumption, there is no transcendence anymore, *not even the fetishistic transcendence of the commodity.* There is now only immanence in the order of signs. Just as there is no agonizing ontological struggle, but a logical relation between the signifier and the signified, so there is no longer an ontological struggle between the being and its double (its shadow, its soul, its ideal), whether divine or diabolic; there is logical calculation of signs and absorption into the system of signs. There is no longer any mirror or looking-glass in the modern order in which the human being would be confronted with his image for better or for worse; there is only the *shop-window*—the site of consumption, in which the individual no longer produces his own reflection, but is absorbed in the contemplation of multiple signs/objects, is absorbed into the order of signifiers of social status, etc. He is not reflected in that order, but absorbed and abolished. *The subject of consumption is the order of signs.* Whether we define this latter structurally, as the instance of a code, or empirically as the generalized ambience of objects, the involvement of the subject is no longer, at any event, that of an "alienated" essence in the philosophical, Marxist sense of the term. It is not that of an essence which is dispossessed, taken over by some alienating agency and become foreign to itself. For there is no longer, properly speaking, any "selfsame," any "subject itself," or, therefore, any "alterity of the selfsame," and therefore no alienation in the strict sense. The situation is rather like that of the child kissing his image in the mirror before going to bed: he doesn't entirely mistake the image for himself, since he has already "recognized" it. Nor is it an alien double in which he is reflected: he *plays* with it, *somewhere between sameness and otherness.* So it is with the consumer: he "plays out" his personalization between one term and another, one sign and another. Between signs there is no contradiction, just as there is no exclusive opposition between the child and his image: there is collusion and ordered involvement. The consumer defines himself by his choice within a "game" played between different models or, in other words, by his combinatorial involvement in that game. It is in this sense that consumption is ludic and that *the ludic dimension of consumption has gradually supplanted the tragic dimension of identity.*

Notes

1. See Plato, *The Sophist* (ca. 360 BC). A paradox ensues from Plato's condemnation of the Sophist as someone convincingly posing as a philosopher. The question arises, how could Plato tell that the Sophist was an inauthentic philosopher if his pose is so convincing? This is a paradox that Baudrillard embraces in his understanding of the term *simulacral*. For further discussion of this paradox, see Gilles Deleuze, "Plato and the Simulacrum," *October* 27 (Winter 1983): 45–46, although it should be pointed out that Deleuze's approach to thinking the simulacrum is different and ultimately less ambivalent than that of Baudrillard.
2. Originally published as the conclusion to Jean Baudrillard, *The Consumer Society: Myths and Structures* (London: Sage, 1998); *La Société de consommation: Ses mythes, ses structures* (Denoël, 1970).
3. *Sometimes considered to be the first feature-length horror film, The Student of Prague (1913) is loosely based on Edgar Allan Poe's short story "William Wilson" (1839), a poem by Alfred de Musset, and Faust.* It was released in Germany in 1913, directed by Stellan Rye and Paul Wegener and written by Hans Heinz Ewers. Baudrillard's analysis is drawn from a second version of the film, of 1926, directed by Henrik Galeen.
4. Jean Baudrillard, *Simulacra and Simulations,* trans. Sheila Faria Glaser (Ann Arbor: University of Michigan Press, 1994), pp. 43–48.
5. There have been at least three versions of this film. From what he says, Baudrillard is clearly not referring to the first of these (directed by Stellan Rye and Paul Wegener, 1913), and it seems most likely that he is familiar with the 1926 film by the Dutch-born writer-director Henrik Galeen (who was also involved in the earlier production). A further German version was made in 1935 by the Chicago-born director Arthur Robison.

CHAPTER 6

THE LOOKING GLASS, FROM
THE OTHER SIDE

LUCE IRIGARAY

Luce Irigaray (b. 1940) came to prominence in France as one of the principal writers who responded to Hélène Cixous's appeal in 1976 for "Woman to write her self" and to participate in a new language, a language of *l'écriture feminine*.[1] Writing in "1,000 tongues,"[2] *l'écriture feminine* aimed to affirm woman by developing a new radicalism opposed to patriarchy that differed from the approach of the previous generation of feminist thinkers. In the opinion of Irigaray and her contemporaries, gaining access to political rights and economic opportunities as the way forward for women to achieve liberation—as proposed by Simone de Beauvoir in her landmark book *The Second Sex* (1949)—was not sufficiently far-reaching. Instead, they believed that a radical rethinking of established metaphysical notions of identity and representation was required since only this approach was capable of striking at the fundamental premises of the patriarchal ideology to which they were opposed. Irigaray published two landmark works in the 1970's dedicated to this theme: *Speculum of the Other Woman* (1974) and *This Sex Which Is Not One* (1977).[3]

One of Irigaray's few writings about film, "The Looking Glass, from the Other Side" forms the opening text of the collection of writings that make up *This Sex Which Is Not One*,[4] a reading of Swiss director Michel Soutter's film *The Surveyors* (*Les Arpenteurs*, 1972). The essay exemplifies the lyrical, and, at times, parodic, style that Irigaray developed during the 1970s as a strategy for opening up a space for an-other voice, that "other" being woman's libidinal desire.[5] The title of the book from which the essay is taken, *This Sex Which Is*

Not One, is indicative of Irigaray's feminist stance regarding woman (referred to as *This Sex*), which is rooted in a critique of patriarchy and its conception of identity as formed by means of a metaphysical, structural opposition between the One and its lack.

Metaphysics, a term coined by Aristotle, is a tradition of thought that, according to continental philosophers and feminist thinkers, dominates Western systems of conceptualization and underlies its ideas of identity and representation. As a binary system of conceptualization, metaphysics revolves around a dominating ideal of unity and transcendent presence: One. Historically, such an ideal has been represented in European culture by the figures of the monotheistic God and, subsequently, the Cartesian subject I of consciousness, emblematized by the maxim "I think therefore I am." In the 1970s, metaphysical ideals were challenged in relation to the traditions of logocentrism that prioritizes speech over writing (the former purportedly a direct form of communication) and patriarchy to which attributes of mastery, consciousness, and control are associated with respect to the male subject. In patriarchal ideology, woman is conceived of as lacking these masculine attributes and only acquires an identity by default as the negative to the positive that is the male subject. Rather than conceiving of identity in such metaphysical terms, Irigaray dissolves them altogether and subsequently conceives of the notion of woman as a radical absence of identity—zero rather than One—for which there is no definition.[6]

In her essay "This Sex Which Is Not One," Irigaray claims that woman's "sexuality . . . is plural," and, since "her genitals are formed of two lips in continuous contact . . . that caress each other," this sexuality is, first and foremost, autoerotic and situated in the unconscious, "before there is any way to distinguish activity from passivity."[7] It is by virtue of these factors, which are essentially beyond patriarchal forms of identification structured in terms of the One and its lack, that Irigaray affirms woman's libidinal desire as the key subject that requires new forms of thinking through writing. "The Looking Glass, from the Other Side" can be seen as a response to this call in its attempt to figure oman "from the other side" of patriarchal and male forms of projection by interpreting Soutter's film as an updating of Lewis Carroll's fable of *Alice in Wonderland* (1865) in terms of Irigaray's feminism.

In Soutter's film, patriarchal masculinity is metaphorized through the idea of surveying and calculation (*"measured, bounded, triangulated"*) to which Alice, initially, as a schoolmistress bearing her father's name, Taillefer, is subjected, *"Listen to them all talking . . . according to their needs and desires."* However, as Irigaray says, Alice's eyes are not just blue but the color of blood, and the film is a journey toward a libidinal pleasure of her own that moves, first, out of the shadow of Eugene while avoiding Lucien's advances and then toward a discovery of herself, initially through her relationship to Leon but with the enigma of her double (Ann) preceding her quest and upon whom, in the first instance, she attempts to model herself, only to reach a limit with respect to this. Finally, Irigaray claims that Alice, "she," does not exist as such within the patriarchal regime, *"'she' never has a proper name . . . 'Alice' underground."* The scenes and positions of the characters are formed in a series of "duplicating, doubling, dividing: of sequences, images, utterances, 'subjects'": Leon falls in love with Alice, but withdraws into an anxiety about the law; Lucien desires and envies Alice, on whom he is fixated (*"That unseen glass whose existence punctures his gaze"*); and yet he, too, momentarily gets caught up in the confusion of a *"whirling"* dance. And throughout the film there is the imminent possibility, for Alice, and even the other characters, of an-other way of seeing and, more broadly, an-other form of experience, *"But everything is forgotten: 'the measuring instruments,' the 'coat,' the 'case,' and especially the 'glasses.' 'How can anyone live without all that?"*

The sequences of Soutter's film are described in a chronological, descriptive manner by Irigaray (the film's narrative set up is summarized in a brief footnote toward the end of the essay), but the text also opens up to reflection and thought in the spaces between the characters, isolating each of them in their moments of pause, waiting, or perplexity, and revealing, often despite themselves, their inconsistencies or capacities for transformation. Grammatically, in Irigaray's writing, the characters are not always tied to the subject positions of the first person *I* or the third person *he* or *she:* sometimes an inner monologue takes precedence, or the subject is designated in the second person as *you.* In this way, the text inhabits the inner personalities of the characters tracing their thoughts, while also evaluating them in terms of their propensity to hold on to some form of property (*"a hiding-place,"* for instance) and propriety (*"What are we to think of a lawyer who gets his feet dirty?"*) or, alternatively to give themselves over to a libidinal pleasure, or *jouissance,* even if this is not actually made visible within the film's plot and sequences, as such. In other words, a key aspect that seems to appeal to Irigaray about *The Surveyors,* and what prompts her performative writing, is that in the film woman is conceived of as a becoming, rather than an ontological essence, that elides both the masculine gaze (symbolized by the glasses and the trope of surveillance) and even (the film's) narrative.

* * *

. . . she suddenly began again. "Then it really has *happened, after all! And now, who am I? I will remember, if I can! I'm determined to do it!" But being determined didn't help her much, and all she could say, after a great deal of puzzling, was: "L, I* know *it begins with L."*

—Through the Looking-Glass

Alice's eyes are blue. And red. *She opened them while going through the mirror. Except for that, she still seems to be exempt from violence. She lives alone, in her house. She prefers it that way, her mother says. She only goes out to play her role as mistress. Schoolmistress, naturally. Where unalterable facts are written down whatever the weather. In white and black, or black and white, depending on whether they're put on the blackboard or in the notebook. Without color changes, in any case. Those are saved for the times when Alice is alone.* Behind the screen of representation. *In the house or garden.*

* * *

But just when it's time for the story to begin, begin again, "it's autumn." That moment when things are still not completely congealed, dead. It ought to be seized so that something can happen. But everything is forgotten: the "measuring instruments," the "coat," the "case," and especially the "glasses." "How can anyone live without all that?" Up to now, that's what has controlled the limits of properties, *distinguished outside from inside, differentiated what was looked on with approval from what wasn't. Made it possible to appreciate, to recognize the value of everything. To fit in with it, as needed.*

There they are, all lost, without their familiar reference points. What's the difference between a friend and no friend? A virgin and a whore? Your wife and the woman you love? The one you desire and the one you make love with? One woman and another woman? The one who owns the house and the one who uses it for her pleasure, the one you meet there for pleasure? In which house and with which woman does—did-—will love happen? And when is it time for love, anyway? Time for work? How can the stakes in love and work be sorted out? Does "surveying" have anything to do with desire, or not? Can pleasure be measured, bounded, triangulated, or not? Besides, "it's autumn," the colors are changing. Turning red. Though not for long.

* * *

No doubt this is the moment Alice ought to seize. Now is the time for her to come on stage herself. With her violet, violated eyes. Blue and red. *Eyes that recognize the right side, the wrong side, and the other side: the blur of deformation; the black or white of a loss of identity. Eyes always expecting appearances to alter, expecting that one will turn into the other, is already the other. But Alice is at school. She'll come back for tea, which she always takes by herself. At least that's what her mother claims. And she's the only one who seems to know who Alice is.*

* * *

So at four o'clock sharp, the surveyor goes into her house. And since a surveyor needs a pretext to go into someone's house, especially a lady's, he's carrying a basket of vegetables. From Lucien. Penetrating into "her" place under cover of somebody else's name, clothes, love. For the time being, *that doesn't seem to bother him. He opens the door, she's making a phone call. To her fiancé. Once again he slips in between them, the two of them. Into the breach that's bringing a woman and a man closer together, today at four o'clock. Since the relationship between Lucien and Alice lies in the zone of the "not yet." Or "never." Past and future both seem subject to quite a few risks, "That's what love is, maybe?" And his intervention cuts back across some other in-betweens: mother-Alice, Lucien-Gladys, Alice-her friend ("She already has a friend, one's enough"), tall-short (surveyors). To mention only what we've already seen.*

Does his intervention succeed? Or does he begin to harbor a vague suspicion that she is not simply herself? He looks for a light. To hide his confusion, fill in the ambiguity. Distract her by smoking. She doesn't see the lighter, even though it's right in front of her; instead she calls him into the first bedroom where there must be a light. His familiarity with the house dispels the anxiety. He goes upstairs. She invites him to enjoy her, as he likes. They separate in the garden. One of them has forgotten "her" glasses by the telephone, the other "his" cap on the bed. The "light" has changed places.

* * *

He goes back to the place where he works. She disappears into nature. Is it Saturday or Sunday? Is it time for surveying or love? He's confused. There's only one thing to do: pick a fight with a "cop." The desire is compelling enough to make him leave at once.

* * *

No more about cops, at least for the time being. He finds himself (they find each other) near the garden. A man in love and a man in love with a woman who lives in the house. The first asks the second, or rather the second asks the first, if he can go (back) and see the woman he loves. He is beginning to be frightened, and begs to be allowed . . . Afterward.

Good (common or proper) sense—any sense of propriety or property—escapes Lucien. He gives things out, sets them in motion, without counting. Cap, vegetables, consent. Are they his? Do they belong to the others? To his wife? To somebody else's? As for what is his, it comes back to him in the dance. Which does not prevent him from allowing others to take it. Elsewhere.

So he comes (back) in. It's teatime. She . . . She? She who? Who's she? She (is) an other . . . looking for a light. Where's a light? Upstairs, in the bedroom, the surveyor, the tall one, points out cheerfully. Pleased at last to come across a specific, unquestionable, verifiable fact. Pleased that he can prove it (himself) using a + b, *or* 1 + 1, *that is, an element that repeats itself, one that stays the same and yet produces a displacement in the sum; pleased that it's a matter of a series, of a sequence. In short, of a story. Might as well say it's true. That he had already been there. That he . . . ? That she? Was? Wasn't? She.*

For the vegetables no longer prove anything. "I must have eaten them." "I" who? Only the "light" is left. But it isn't there to shore up the argument. And even if it were, no trace of what has happened would remain. As for attesting that the light has moved from here to there, or stating that its current whereabouts are known, or naming Alice's room as the only place it can be found, these are all just claims that depend on "magic."

Alice has never liked occultism. Not that the implausible surprises her. She knows more than anyone about fabulous, fantastic, unbelievable things . . . But she's always seen what she talks about. She's observed all the marvels first-hand. She's been "in wonderland." She hasn't simply imagined, "intuited." Induced, perhaps? Moreover, from a distance. And across partitions? Going through the looking-glass, that's something else again.

Besides, there are no traces of such an adventure in that gentleman's eyes. It's a matter of nuances. So it's urgent for him to get out of the house at once. He won't? Then she's the one who'll leave, who'll desert it. The out-of-doors *is an extraordinary refuge. Especially in this season, with all its colors. He too goes into the garden. Right up close. So one no longer has the right to be alone? Where is one to go? If the house and garden are open to all comers. Omniscient surveyors, for example. It's imperative to hurry and invent a retreat they can't get to. Curl up somewhere protected from their scheming eyes, from their inquiries. From their penetration.* Where?

Lucien knows how to wait, even for quite a long time. His patience holds out indefinitely, at the edge of the vegetable garden. Installed outside the property, he peels. *Preferably beet stalks, which make little girls grow up. And lead them imperceptibly to marriage. From a long way off, very carefully, he's preparing a future. Improbable. That's not the only thing he's peeling. Perhaps that accounts for his arrival.* Empty-handed. *He doesn't even take the path, like everyone else. He comes across the grass.* Always a little unseemly.

Alice smiles. Lucien smiles. They smile at each other, complicitously. They are playing. *She makes him a gift of the cap. "What will Gladys say?" That he has accepted a gift from Alice? That she has offered him that cap? A "dragonfly" whose furtive flight volatizes the giver's identity in the present moment. Who deserves more gratitude, the woman who* duplicates *the possibility of sexual pleasure or the woman who offers it a first time? And if one goes back and forth between them, how can one keep on telling them apart? How can one know where one is, where one stands? The confusion suits Lucien. He's delighted. Since this is the way things are, since everyone is giving up being simply "myself," tearing down the fences of "mine," "yours," "his," "hers," he sheds all restraint. For although he looked as if he didn't care about anything, as if his prodigality were boundless, he was holding onto a little place for himself. A hiding-place, to be precise. A refuge, still private. For the day when everything goes wrong for everyone. For the time when troubles are too hard to bear. For a "rainy day." He's going to share that ultimate possession, that shred of property, with Alice. He's going to dissipate its private character. He takes her to a sort of cave. A concealed, hidden, protected place. A bit dark. Is this what Alice was trying to find? What he's looking for himself? And, since they've gotten to the point of telling secrets, they whisper in each other's ear. Just for fun, not to say anything. But Lucien realizes that the cap has been forgotten on the "bed." That detail disturbs his stability. Leads him to act hastily. In an echo effect, he'll slip up again. Very softly, whispering, in confidential tones, he nevertheless imposes what is.*

Is? For him? For another? And who is he, to expose this way what might be? Alice is paralyzed. Closed up. Frozen.

* * *

Since we've reached the point where we expound upon everyone's right to pleasure, let's go on to the lawyer's office. The meeting will take place outside. Inside, "the woman eavesdrops," he says.

"I've made love with a girl, in a girl's house. What am I in for?"

"Nothing." This outstrips anything one might imagine. All that for nothing. For free. Not even the shadow of a danger. Or penalty, or debt, or loss. Who can keep on surveying in the midst of such excesses? Yet there has to be a sequel. To the story.

Let's go on. "So I've slept with a lady I don't know, in the house of another lady I don't know. What am I in for?"

"Four years."

"Why?"

"Breaking and entering, cruelty. Two plus two make four, $2 \times 2 = 4$, $2^2 = 4$. Four years."

"How can I get off?"

"That depends on the two of them. Separately and together. First you have to identify these two non-units. Then go on to their relationships."

"I've identified one of them. The one to whom the coefficient 'house' can be assigned."

"Well?"

"I can't supply any other details, she's banned me from her property."

"That's too bad. And the other one? The vagabond, the wanderer: the mobile unit?"

"She's disappeared into nature."

"So . . ."

"Can you help me find her again?"

"My wife will be furious. I'll get dirty."

"I'll take you. I'll get you there. I'm the one who'll carry the load; I'll do the dirty work."

"O.K."

But where in nature? It's huge. Here? There? You have to stop somewhere. And if you put his feet on the ground a bit too abruptly, of course he'll realize that he's covered with mud. Which was absolutely not supposed to happen. "What will my wife say?" What are we to think of a lawyer who gets his feet dirty? And who, after all, forbids dirtiness? The lawyer, or his wife? Why once again transfer to the other one the charge one refuses to address to one's own account? Because it might look a little disgusting. The gentleman's unattractive side. The one who claims he's a gentleman.

Even though the surveyor came to get (back) on the right side of the law, he is revolted. If the numerical assessment gives him "four years," he sets the lawyer's worth at "zero." He's going to have to start over again from that point.

* * *

Lucien has gone back to Gladys's house. He's sighing. Again. Too much precision makes him sad. Lost. Indefinitely, he contemplates the representation of the scene, behind a windowpane. That unseen glass whose existence punctures his gaze. Rivets it, holds it fast. Gladys closes the door of the house. Lucien speaks. Finally. "The scum, they've made love together." "Who's made love, Lucien? Who's one? Who's the other? And is she really the one you want her to be? The one you'd want?" The ladies blur together, virgin and/or whore. One blends into the other, imperceptibly. Confusion again becomes legitimate. The looking glass dissolves, already broken. Where are we? How far along? Everything is whirling. Everyone is dancing.

* * *

Let's have some music, then, to accompany the rhythm, to carry it along. The orchestra is about to play. Somewhere else, of course. You've begun to notice that it is always in/on another stage that things are brought to their conclusion. That the manifestation of things is saturated to the point where it exceeds plain evidence and certainty. Present visibility of the event. Incessant transferral: the complement of what is fomenting here moves over there—where? Moves from now to afterward—after the fact? From one to the other—who? And vice versa. Duplicating, doubling, dividing: of sequences, images, utterances, "subjects." Representation by the other of the projects of the one. Which he/she brings to *light by displacing them.* Irreducible expropriation of desire occasioned by its impression in/on the other. *Matrix and support of the possibility of its repetition and reproduction. Same, and other.*

* * *

The duet being (re)produced at the moment has Alice's mother and her fiancé as interpreters. The instruments—let us be clear—are cellos. For the first time the third party, one of the third parties, is a member of the party. Alice. Off to one side, in a corner of the room—a third bedroom—she seems to be listening, or looking. But is she really there? Or is she at least half absent? Also observing what is going to happen. What has already happened. Inside and outside. Without presuming to know what might define either once and for all. Difference always in displacement. If "she" is dreaming, "I" must leave? The session continues. Someone has disappeared. Someone else is going to fill in for this missing subject. It's enough—just barely—to wait.

* * *

He reopens the door of the house. Listens, looks. But his role is really to intervene. To subvert all the couples, by "stepping between." "Houses, people, feelings." In order to sort them out, possibly to reconcile them. After he has passed through, the surface has lost its other side. Perhaps its under side as well. But "how can anyone live without that?" With a single side, a single face, a single sense. On a single plane. Always on the same side of the looking glass. What is cut *cuts each one from its own other, which suddenly starts to look like any other. Oddly unknown. Adverse, ill-omened. Frigidly other.*

"How can anyone live with that?" "She's been cruel to me for five years!" "Just look at him: he always has a sinister look about him!" But when Eugene is imitating the cat whose tail has been cut off, when he unburdens himself, on the surveyor's person, of the only instrument whose intromission she allows into her house, he is fierce. And if she sighs, frets, weeps, you'll understand that she's not always cheerful. Moreover, just try to advise the one to leave since he is being made to suffer; he'll leave his tool behind so he'll be sure to have to come back. Tell the other that she doesn't love him, not any longer: she'll laugh. Even if she's sad. And yet you were there—perhaps just for an instant— with eyes that know how to look, at least at a certain aspect of the situation: they can't find each other this time, they can no longer get back together. It's better for them to separate. At least for today. Anyway, they've never been united. Each one has been putting up with the other's other. While waiting.

* * *

Alice is alone. With the surveyor, the tall one. The one who made love with the one who took over her house. It even happened on her bed. She knows, now. He too has begun to understand the misunderstanding in the meantime. "Do you regret that mistake?" "No." "Do you want us to clear up the confusion?" " . . . ?" "Would you like to?" " . . . . . ?" How can they be differentiated in a single attribution?

How can I be distinguished from her? Only if I keep on pushing through to the other side, if I'm always beyond, *because on this side of the screen of their projections, on this* plane *of their representations, I can't live. I'm stuck, paralyzed by all those images, words, fantasies.* Frozen. Transfixed, *including by their admiration, their praises, what they call their "love." Listen to them all talking about Alice: my mother, Eugene, Lucien, Gladys . . . You've heard them dividing me up, in their own best interests. So either I don't have any "self" or else I have a multitude of "selves" appropriated by them, for them, according to their needs or desires. Yet this last one isn't saying what he wants—of me. I'm completely lost. In fact, I've always been lost, but I didn't feel it before. I was busy conforming to their wishes. But I was more than half absent. I was on the other side. Well, I can say this much about my identity: I have my father's name, Taillefer. I've always lived in this house. First with my father and my mother. He's dead now. Since then, I've lived here alone. My mother lives next door. And then? . . .*

"What did she do next?" *She is not I. But I'd like to be "she" for you. Taking a detour by way of her, perhaps I'll discover at last what "I" could be.* "What did she do??" " *She went upstairs to look for a light. She called me.*" "What's your name?" "Leon . . ." *So I go up, since that's the way she's acted. The only thing I do differently—on purpose? by mistake?—is that I call his name from a different bedroom. The second. He arrives, but it's the first room that he wants to go into. Is he mistaken again? Has he never been mistaken? For there to be a mistake, one of them has to be "she," the other not. Is it possible to tell who is "she," or not? What's important, no doubt, is that the scene is repeated. Almost the same way. From that point on, "she" is unique. However the situation may be re-dressed.*

"What do I do now?" "I don't know." *Alice was all alone when she was elsewhere. When she saw all sorts of wonders. While she was coming and going from one side to the other. On this side, she is only acquainted with contrived points of reference, artificial constraints. Those of school, in a way: nursery school, grade school. And there, in front of him, she doesn't feel she is mistress. But he doesn't know that. Either. He takes off his coat, as she had done. And then? . . .*

"First do I take off what I have on top, then underneath? Or the other way around? Do I go from outside to inside? Or vice versa?" " . . . ?" *And because she has always been secretive, she has always hidden everything, and because in this hiding place no one has discovered her, she thinks it will suffice simply to turn everything inside out. To expose herself in her nakedness so that she can be looked at, touched, taken, by someone, by him.*

"Do you like me?" Does he know? What does that mean? How can the source of pleasure be named? Why part with it for her? *And who, what is that "she" who is asking him,* scarcely a subject himself, *to assign her certain attributes, to grant her some distinctive characteristics? Apparently surveying isn't much use in love. At least not for loving her. How can anyone measure or define,* in truth, *what is kept* behind the plane of projections? *What goes beyond those/its limits? Still* proper *ones. No doubt he can take pleasure in what is produced there, in the person presented or represented. But how can he go beyond that horizon? How can he desire if he can't fix his line of sight? If he can't take aim at the other side of the looking glass?*

Outside, Alice, it's nighttime. You can't see a thing. You can't even walk straight, you can't stay upright, in the total darkness. You lose your balance. No more aplomb. At best, you're swaying. "Someone's limping outside. I'll go see."

✳ ✳ ✳

The story *is coming to its end. Turning, and returning, in a closed space,* an enclosure *that is not to be violated, at least not while the story unfolds: the space of a few private properties. We are not going to cross a certain boundary line, we are not going above a certain peak. That would have forced us to find another style, a different procedure, for afterward. We would have needed,* at least, two genres. *And more. To bring them into articulation. Into conjunction. But at what moment? In what place? And won't this second one be just the* other side *of the first? Perhaps more often its complement. A more or less adequate complement, more or less apt to be joined by a copulative. We've never been dealing with more than one, after all. A unity divided in halves. More, or less. Identifiable, or not. Whose possibilities of pleasure have not even been exhausted. There are still remainders. Left* behind. *For another time.*

Because we're approaching the borders of its field, of its present frame, however, the affair is growing acrimonious. Subsequent events attest to an increasing exacerbation. But we can't be sure that it won't all end up in a sort of regression. With all parties retreating to their positions.

✳ ✳ ✳

Since day has dawned, the surveyor, the tall one, *thinks it's fitting to take certain measures. Even if it's finally Sunday. Not daring to act alone, he phones the* short one *and asks him to go look for his coat, which he didn't forget at Alice's. To find out where things stand. To explain. To calculate the risks. Of an indictment . . . He takes him in his car up to the gate of the house. He's to wait for him in the bar, where he's meeting Lucien. Things are going rather badly between them. They've reached the point of insulting each other:* "asshole" *on the part of you know who,* "rude" coming from the more timid one, who gets himself roundly scolded just the same for this insignificant outburst: It's because Leon doesn't joke around with rules; they're so necessary in his work. Alice doesn't have the coat, but she'll keep it. Because she wants to see him again. "Why do you want to?" "I just do." "Why?" "To live on the right side." But you can't understand what it's all about. You don't see anything at all. Or hardly anything. Well, it so happens that he has just noticed a detail that's crucial if we're to look the facts straight in the face: the glasses Ann forgot (?) by the telephone. She tries them on. Smiles. "How can anyone live without these?" They absolutely have to be given back to Leon, to whom they don't belong. Because everyone—and especially Leon and Alice—ought to wear them when something really important happens. It would help them straighten out the situation, or the opposite. Then they could throw them away. That's undoubtedly what Ann did. Little Max hands Ann's glasses over to Leon, while Alice is phoning her to tell her to come get them at her house, because she's afraid she'll break them: all glass is fragile in her hands. Leon uncovers the riddle of Ann's disappearance. She couldn't live without that. He goes to the police station and confesses everything. As for the policeman, he doesn't understand a thing. Again, it's a question of optics. He doesn't see any reason for severity, doesn't see the cause for guilt, a fortiori doesn't see the possibility of reparations. But he's ready to turn his job over to a specialist. So Leon is not allowed to clear himself. Increasingly overwhelmed, he goes back to her house, the house belonging to one of them, whom he now appoints as his judge. Ann got there on her bicycle before he did.

* * *

Still looking for her, Alice gets Ann to tell how it happened. She reassures her, of course, that it was the same for her. And to prove (to herself) that she is really "her," Alice gets ahead of Ann in telling the rest of the story. She tells what happens when everything is already over. What happened to her the next day, which for her hasn't come yet. She says that love is fine once, but you mustn't ever start over again. Says that he may well be rather tiresome with his tendency to repeat everything.

Who spoke? In whose name? Filling in for her, it's not certain that she isn't trying also to replace her. To be even more (than) "she." Hence the postscript that she adds to what was said to have taken place: "He even wants to have a baby with me." Then they fall silent, differently confused.

* * *

That's the moment when the surveyor, of course, is going to intervene. But how can he tell them apart? Who is she? And she? Since they are not the sum of two units, where can one pass between them?

They get up, both of them, to answer him. But Ann can do it better. She's the one who'll tell him what they think. They? Or she? Which We? "One, or the other, or both of us, or neither." "It's you!" "It's I " She's right there in front of me, as if nothing had ever happened. So I've invented everything that was supposed to have happened to her? Everything she was? "I don't want to see you again." That's too much. Just when she is finally present again, when that seeing-again could finally be confirmed, perhaps, by recognition, she claims to disappear then and there. "And Alice?" "Not her either." Neither one nor the other. Neither one of the two. Nor the two, either, together or separately. How can she/they be allowed to escape that way? Behind. The door of the house, for example. "You cunt(s), you'll see me again, you'll hear from me. I'll come back with big machines and I'll knock everything down, I'll flatten everything, I'll destroy it all. The house, the garden. Everything."

* * *

Alice blinks her eyes. Slowly, several times. No doubt she's going to close them again. Reverse them. But before her eyelids close, you'll have time to see that her eyes were red.

* * *

And since it can't be simply a matter, here, of Michel Soutter's film,8 nor simply of something else—except that "she" never has a "proper" name, that "she" is at best "from wonderland," even if she has no right to a public existence except in the protective custody of the name of Mister X—then, so that she may be taken, or left, unnamed, forgotten without even having been identified "i"—who?—will remain uncapitalized. Let's say:
    "Alice" underground

Notes

1. Hélène Cixous, "The Laugh of the Medusa," trans. Keith Cohen and Paula Cohen, *Signs* 1, no. 4 (Summer 1976): 875–93.
2. "She lets the other language speak—the language of 1,000 tongues which knows neither enclosure nor death." Cixous, p. 889.
3. It was owing to Irigaray's feminist critique, in *Speculum of the Other Woman*, of the traditions of European philosophy and Freudian psychoanalysis that she lost her job as a lecturer at the University of Paris at Vincennes and was expelled from the École Freudienne de Paris, of which Jacques Lacan was director.
4. This essay was originally published as "Le miroir, de l'autre côté," *Critique*, no. 309 (February 1973).
5. Irigaray's recent style of writing has become more direct, and her latest feminism is explored through the subject of the earth, see, for instance, her book coauthored with

Michael Marder, *Through Vegetal Being: Two Philosophical Perspectives* (New York: Columbia University Press, 2016).

6. In effect, Irigaray follows the same philosophical and deconstructive moves of patriarchy that Nietzsche makes with respect to metaphysics in the passage of writing entitled, "How the 'True World' Finally Became a Fable: The History of an Error," in *Twilight of the Idols* (1888). For a discussion of this passage of writing, see Christopher Kul-Want, ed., *Philosophers on Art from Kant to the Postmodernists* (New York: Columbia University Press, 2010), pp. 2–4 and 60–64.

7. Luce Irigaray, *This Sex Which Is Not One*, trans. Catherine Porter with Carolyn Burke (Ithaca, NY: Cornell University Press, 1985), p. 24.

8. *The Surveyors.* The story goes like this: Alice lives alone in her childhood home, after her father's death. Her mother lives next door. Lucien and Gladys live in the same small village. There is also Ann, about whom we know nothing except that she makes love. And Eugene, Alice's friend, who only plays the cello. A highway is to cut through the village. So two surveyors arrive—Leon and Max. But surveying means "striding back and forth between houses, people, and feelings."

CHAPTER 7

ACINEMA

JEAN-FRANÇOIS LYOTARD

Jean-François Lyotard (1924–1998) was professor of philosophy at the University of Vincennes in Saint Denis from 1974 to 1987, after which he became professor emeritus at the university and held numerous international posts in the U.S., Canada, Brazil, Denmark, and Germany. Lyotard became globally famous following the publication of his book *The Postmodern Condition: A Report on Knowledge* (1984), in which he defined the postmodern epoch of the late twentieth century as consisting of an "incredulity toward metanarratives," meaning the existence of a fundamental skepticism toward totalizing ideas of truth and belief in sociopolitical progress whether this ideology is capitalist or Marxist driven.[1] Prior to this in the 1970s, and inspired by Freud's often repeated dictum that in the unconscious "'No,' does not exist," Lyotard reevaluated Marx's analysis of capital through a notion of the unconscious as a site of unrestrained and exorbitant desire. In this essay on *Acinema* (1978)—meaning a neutral or nondefinable cinema—Lyotard takes up these arguments, which he had advanced in his book *Libidinal Economy*,[2] to develop a reading of cinematography (literally meaning the inscription of movement) in terms of an economy of libidinal desire that constantly exceeds preconceived notions of self-same identity.

In *Acinema*, Lyotard argues that it is fundamentally important to mount a critical reevaluation of film in terms of its approach to the issue of movement, an analysis that should take precedence over consideration of cinema as part of the entertainment industry. Lyotard suggests that cinematography is based upon a judgment of what is an appropriate form of movement that includes the ordering and selection of "the film shot . . . the spatio-temporal synthesis of the narration (*découpage*)," as opposed to forms of movement that are deemed to be inappropriate or aberrant and that therefore require editing out from the film. Lyotard argues that discontinuous or dissonant forms of movement are not always necessarily eliminated from films, but rather they are often incorporated and utilized within the overall filmic aesthetic: "Thus all sorts of gaps, jolts, postponements, losses and confusion can occur, but they no longer act as real diversions or wasteful drifts; when the final count is made they turn out to be nothing but beneficial detours." Applying this argument to the Hollywood film *Joe*,[3] Lyotard proposes that the use of montage and of arrested movement in some of the film's violent scenes are not for their own affective sake but rather for the purpose of the narrative order. Lyotard's point is not to advocate a cinema consisting entirely of unregulated forms of movement ("like Debuffet demanded an *art brut*"), but to propose that it is this foregoing cinematographic economy of subsumption and incorporation that is, itself, exploitative, "a plus or minus on the ledger book . . . is *valuable* because it *returns* to something else, because it is thus potential return and profit."

Lyotard states that "cinematic movements generally follow the figure of return, that is, the repetition and propagation of sameness." As Lyotard indicates, this exploitative idea of cinematic movement adheres to the ideological systems that Marx, Freud, and Nietzsche recognized, in their different ways, as fundamental to the perpetuation of Western, metaphysical values and assumptions of unitary identity. Thus, for Marx, capitalism is an economy that converts labor as well as material resources, inventions, and technologies into its own system for the purposes of profit, thereby extending the capitalist system, itself; in short, this is what Lyotard refers to as "the cyclical organization of capital." In *Beyond the Pleasure Principle* (1920),[4] Freud argues that the psyche is governed by an economy based upon the repetition of the pleasure principle; this is the continuous regulation of all unbounded, excessive and so-called unpleasurable feelings within a principle of containment, thereby reducing these feelings to the level of an indifferent "pleasure" that avoids confrontation with the conflicts inherent within the reality principle. Nietzsche's concept of the eternal return of the same is analogous both to Marx's analysis of capitalism and Freud's understanding of the repressive economy of the psyche, but this time it is directed toward the way in which, historically, Western political and philosophical ideologies have inhibited divergent libidinal drives so as to pursue a self-sustaining control over life's vital, creative forces.

Following these three thinkers' conceptions of the cyclical and incorporative economy by which repression is perpetuated, Lyotard concludes that the ordering and "directing" of a film (and, correspondingly, reality, too) "eliminates *all impulsional movement, real or unreal, which will not lend itself to reduplication,* all movement which would escape identification, recognition and the mnesic fixation" (*mnesic* meaning pertaining to memory). In other words, film eliminates all types of movement that cannot be incorporated into an economy that perpetuates the self-same, preconceived orders of identity. Lyotard observes that this economy relies upon an a priori concept of identity in the same way that was posited by Marx (concerning capitalism's pursuit of gain and profit), Freud (regarding the regulative order of the pleasure principle), and Nietzsche (about the construction of metaphysical ideals). Lacan, too, perpetuated this idea in his essay "The Mirror Stage as Formative of the Function of the I as Revealed in Psychoanalytic Experience" (1949), arguing that the self is built upon an ideal, imaginary imago.[5]

However, Lyotard points out that both Freud and Nietzsche develop an alternative form of movement of return that is not subordinate to an endless cycle of the repetition of the same incorporative and repressive movement (this accords with Lyotard's ideas of a libidinal or desiring economy). These thinkers' ideas of an-other (eternal) return, Lyotard suggests, are not forms of repetition, as such, rather they conceive of the return in this context as systemically repeated challenges to thought itself, "To the point that . . . the concept." In other words, for Freud and Nietzsche, the return is a "difference" that cannot be contained within a preexisting system or ideology. Lyotard pursues these ideas advocating a "savage," visceral cinema, an experimental cinema (rather than mainstream) that accepts "what is fortuitous, dirty, confused, unsteady, unclear, poorly framed, overexposed": a cinema that affirms intensity, impulsional movement and the misspending of energies for the sake of agitation and emotional turmoil, rather than for the purpose of stabilization. Lyotard proposes that there are two forms of movement or e-motion that affirm this excess, the first ("immobility") is exemplified by the tableau vivant as represented in the art and writings of Pierre Klossowski, while the second ("excessive movement") is lyrical abstract art (in this context Lyotard references variously the art of Gianfranco Baruchello, Pol Bury, Viking Eggeling, Jackson Pollock, Hans Richter, and Mark Rothko).

With respect to the first form of movement, Lyotard references Klossowski's story *La Monnaie Vivante* (1970), which means "Living currency," the title of which is significant in the context of Lyotard's aim to affirm a libidinal economy rather than the repressive economies of capital, self, and metaphysics as analyzed by Marx, Freud, and Nietzsche, respectively. In Klossowski, the posed, statuesque model serves to *represent* an unobtainable ideal of fantasy, a master signifier or unity to which the client's patriarchal identity is attached, "Thus representation is essential to this phantasmatic: that is, it is essential that the spectator be offered instances of identification, recognizable forms, all in all, matter for the memory." However, in this scenario, the masochistic client does not use the model to perpetuate his own a priori identity, rather the client is aroused by the enforced law of physical distance between himself and the model, a law that he himself has agreed to so as to transgress its coldness by turning it into a means for prolonged sexual pleasure.

This perverse combination of prolonged excitement and suffering, of pleasure and pain, reaches such a degree that the client loses himself in a "motion which in going beyond the point of no return spills the libidinal forces outside the whole, at the expense of the whole (at the price of the ruin and disintegration of this whole)," this whole being the subject/object, client/model distinction instituted by paternal authority governing the principles of representation and identification. "We must sense the price, beyond price, as Klossowski admirably explains, that the organic body, the pretended unity of the pretended subject, must pay so that the pleasure will burst forth in its irreversible sterility" (sterility because this perverse excess has no purpose, procreative or otherwise). Furthermore, Lyotard argues that such an economy of dissipation is not based upon a corresponding exchange, no balancing of the books is sought to offset the subject's loss (minus) with a corresponding return and input (plus), "Thus, if he is assuredly an artist by producing a simulacrum, he is one most of all because this simulacrum is not an object of worth valued for another object . . . as a composite of decompositions." In other words, the client transgresses his identity governed by patriarchal law and perpetuated in memory ("mnesiac fixation"), dissipating it in sexual intensity and through submission to the power of the feminine, "it is at the price, we repeat, of going beyond this [matter for the memory] and disfiguring the order of propagation that the intense emotion is felt." Thus, in Klossowski's art it is necessary to hold the support (the page/the law) of representation in place, preserving it all the better to transgress its usual purpose through establishing a libidinal relation to the model that is inscribed onto the supporting page.

However, in lyrical abstract painting the support (the canvas) itself becomes the object of libidinal desire insofar as it is inseparable from the agitated surface composed of infinite shifts and changes in color, line, and form. Thus, both the support and the image coalesce together in boundless agitations and dissolutions, "the flesh posing itself" as an affect of transfixion that is discernible to perception through the eye-cortex alone. Similarly, in abstract forms of cinema—Lyotard may be thinking here of structural filmmakers such as Michael Snow and Hollis Frampton—the film strip and the film screen become libidinal movements of the flesh-images. In such art there is no representation of a master signifier, model, or whole serving as a means of transgression. Rather the client/spectator's pleasure, itself, becomes transfixed by the libidinal enjoyment (*jouissance*) and experience of the agitations and pulsations of the support as images: "the whole body is neutralized in a tension blocking all escape of drives from passages other than those necessary to the detection of very fine differences."

In both cases, of the tableau vivant and lyrical abstraction, pleasure is derived in the loss of the subject's ideal of unified identity that, in any case, is a fantasy and therefore "nothing"; nevertheless, a certain specter of unity, Lyotard posits at the end of his essay, is a requisite upon which the "extreme intensities" of the eternal return of difference depend, "founded on at least this empty permanence, on the phantom of the organic body." But this requisite phantom, Lyotard conjectures, is not necessarily comparable to the phantasmatic lack or "nothing" that exists between the subject and the ideal upon which capitalism is founded and by means of which desire is exploited.

✳ ✳ ✳

The Nihilism of Convened, Conventional Movements

Cinematography is the inscription of movement, a writing with movement, a writing with movements—all kinds of movements: for example, in the film shot, those of the actors and other moving objects, those of lights, colors, frame, and lens; in the film sequence, all these again plus the cuts and splices of editing; for the film as a whole, those of the final script and the spatiotemporal synthesis of the narration (*découpage*). And over or through all these movements are those of the sound and words coming together with them.

Thus there is a crowd (nonetheless a countable crowd) of elements in motion, a throng of possible moving bodies that are candidates for inscription on film. Learning the techniques of filmmaking involves knowing how to eliminate a large number of these possible movements. It seems that image, sequence, and film must be constituted at the price of these exclusions.

Here arise two questions that are really quite naive considering the deliberations of contemporary cine-critics: *which* movements and moving bodies are these? Why is it necessary to select, sort out, and exclude them?

If no movements are picked out, we will accept what is fortuitous, dirty, confused, unsteady, unclear, poorly framed, overexposed. . . . For example, suppose you are working on a shot in video, a shot, say, of a gorgeous head of hair à la Renoir; upon viewing it you find that something has come undone: all of a sudden, swamps, outlines of incongruous islands and cliff edges appear, lurching forth before your startled eyes. A scene from elsewhere, representing nothing identifiable, has been added, a scene not related to the logic of your shot, an undecidable scene, worthless even as an insertion because it will not be repeated and taken up again later. So you cut it out.

We are not demanding a raw cinema, like Dubuffet demanded an *art brut*. We are hardly about to form a club dedicated to the saving of rushes and the rehabilitation of clipped footage. And yet . . . We observe that if the mistake is eliminated it is because of its incongruity, and in order to protect the order of the whole (shot and/or sequence and/or film) while banning the intensity it carries. And the order of the whole has its sole object in the functioning of the cinema: that there be order in the movements, that the movements be made in order, that they make order. Writing with movements—cinematography—is thus conceived and practiced as an incessant organizing of movements following the rules of representation for spatial localization, those of narration for the instantiation of language, and those of the form "film music" for the soundtrack. The so-called impression of reality is a real oppression of orders.

This oppression consists of the enforcement of a nihilism of movements. No movement, arising from any field, is given to the eye-ear of the spectator for what it is: a simple *sterile difference* in an audiovisual field. Instead, every movement put forward *sends back* to something else, is inscribed as a plus or minus on the ledger book that is the film, *is valuable* because it *returns* to something else, because it is thus potential return and profit. The only genuine movement with which the cinema is written is that of value. The law of value (in so-called political economy) states that the *object*, in this case the movement, is valuable only insofar as it is exchangeable against other objects and in terms of equal quantities of a definable unity (for example, in quantities of money). Therefore, to be valuable the object must move: proceed from other objects ("production" in the narrow sense) and disappear, but on the condition that its disappearance *makes room for still other objects* (consumption). Such a process is not sterile, but productive; it is production in the widest sense.

Pyrotechnics

Let us be certain to distinguish this process from sterile motion. A match once struck is consumed. If you use the match to light the gas that heats the water for the coffee which keeps you alert on your way to work, the consumption is not sterile, for it is a movement belonging to the circuit of capital: merchandise-match → merchandise-labor power → money-wages → merchandise-match. But when a child strikes the match-head *to see* what happens—just for the fun of it—he enjoys the movement itself, the changing colors, the light flashing at the height of the blaze, the death of the tiny piece of wood, the hissing of the tiny flame. He enjoys these sterile differences leading nowhere, these uncompensated losses; what the physicist calls the dissipation of energy.

Intense enjoyment and sexual pleasure (*la jouissance*), insofar as they give rise to perversion and not solely to propagation, are distinguished by this sterility. At the end of *Beyond the Pleasure Principle*, Freud cites them as an example of the combination of the life and death instincts. But he is thinking of pleasure obtained through the channels of "normal" genital sexuality: all jouissance, including that giving rise to a hysterical attack or contrariwise, to a perverse scenario, contains the lethal component, but normal pleasure hides it in a movement of return, genital sexuality. Normal genital sexuality leads to childbirth, and the child is the *return* of, or on, its movement. But the motion of pleasure as such, split from the motion of the propagation of the species, would be (whether genital or sexual or neither) that motion which in going beyond the point of no return spills the libidinal forces outside the whole, at the expense of the whole (at the price of the ruin and disintegration of this whole).

In lighting the match the child enjoys this diversion *(détournement,* a word dear to Klossowski) that misspends energy. He produces, in his own movement, a simulacrum of pleasure in its so-called death-instinct component. Thus if he is assuredly an artist by producing a simulacrum, he is one most of all because this simulacrum is not an object of worth valued for another object. It is not composed with these other objects, compensated for by them, enclosed in a whole ordered by constitutive laws (in a structured group, for example). On the contrary, it is essential that the entire erotic force invested in the simulacrum be promoted, raised, displayed, and burned in vain. It is thus that Adorno said the only truly great art is the making of fireworks: pyrotechnics would simulate perfectly the sterile consumption of energies in jouissance. Joyce grants this privileged position to fireworks in the beach sequence in *Ulysses.* A simulacrum, understood in the sense Klossowski gives it, should not be conceived primarily as belonging to the category of representation, like the representations that imitate pleasure; rather, it is to be conceived as a kinetic problematic, as the paradoxical product of the disorder of the drives, as a composite of decompositions.

The discussion of cinema and representational-narrative art in general begins at this point. Two directions are open to the conception (and production) of an object, and in particular, a cinematographic object, conforming to the pyrotechnical imperative. These two seemingly contradictory currents appear to be those attracting whatever is intense in painting today. It is possible that they are also at work in the truly active forms of experimental and underground cinema.

These two poles are immobility and excessive movement. In letting itself be drawn toward these antipodes, the cinema insensibly ceases to be an ordering force; it produces true, that is, vain, simulacra, blissful intensities, instead of productive/consumable objects.

The Movement of Return

Let us back up a bit. What do these movements of return or returned movements have to do with the representational and narrative form of the commercial cinema? We emphasize just how wretched it is to answer this question in terms of a simple superstructural function of an industry, the cinema, the products of which, films, would lull the public consciousness by means of doses of ideology. If film direction is a directing and ordering of movements it is not so by being propaganda (benefiting the bourgeoisie, some would say, and the bureaucracy, others would add), but by being a propagation. Just as the libido must renounce its perverse overflow to propagate the species through a normal genital sexuality allowing the constitution of a "sexual body" having that sole end, so the film produced by an artist working in capitalist industry (and all known industry is now capitalist) springs from the effort to eliminate aberrant movements, useless expenditures, differences of pure consumption. This film is composed like a unified and propagating body, a fecund and assembled whole transmitting instead of losing what it carries. The diegesis locks together the synthesis of movements in the temporal order; perspectivist representation does so in the spatial order.

Now, what are these syntheses but the arranging of the cinematographic material following the figure of *return?* We are not only speaking of the requirement of profitability imposed upon the artist by the producer, but also of the formal requirements that the artist weighs upon his material. All so-called good form implies the return of sameness, the folding back of diversity upon an identical unity. In painting this may be a plastic rhyme or an equilibrium of colors; in music, the resolution of dissonance by the dominant chord; in architecture, a proportion. Repetition, the principle of not only the metric but even of the rhythmic, if taken in the narrow sense as the repetition of the same (same color, line, angle, chord), is the work of Eros and Apollo disciplining the movements, limiting them to the norms of tolerance characteristic of the system or whole in consideration.

It was an error to accredit Freud with the discovery of the very motion of the drives. Because Freud, in *Beyond the Pleasure Principle,* takes great care to dissociate the repetition of the same, which signals the regime of the life instincts, from the repetition of the other, which can only be other to the first-named repetition. These death drives are just outside the regime delimited by the body or whole considered, and therefore it is impossible to discern *what* is returning, when returning with these drives is the intensity of extreme jouissance and danger that they carry. To the point that it must be asked if indeed any repetition is involved at all, if on the contrary something different returns at each instance, if the *eternal return* of these sterile explosions of libidinal discharge should not be conceived in a wholly different time-space than that of the repetition of the same, as their impossible copresence. Assuredly we find here the insufficience of *thought,* which must necessarily pass through that sameness which is the concept.

Cinematic movements generally follow the figure of return, that is, of the repetition and propagation of sameness. The scenario or plot, an intrigue and its solution, achieves the same resolution of dissonance as the sonata form in music; its movement of return organizes the affective charges linked to the filmic "signifieds," both connotative and denotative, as Metz would say. In this regard all endings are happy endings, just by being endings, for even if a film finishes with a murder, this too can serve as a final resolution of dissonance. The affective charges carried by every type of cinematographic and filmic "signifier" (lens, framing, cuts, lighting, shooting, etc.) are submitted to the same law of a return of the same after a semblance of difference; a difference that is nothing, in fact, but a detour.

The Instance of Identification

This rule, where it applies, operates principally, we have said, in the form of exclusions and effacements. The exclusion of certain movements is such that the professional filmmakers are not even aware of them; effacements, on the other hand, cannot fail to be noticed by them because a large part of their activity consists of them. Now these effacements and exclusions form the very operation of film directing. In eliminating, before and/or after the shooting, any extreme glare, for example, the director and cameraman condemn the image of film to the sacred task of making itself recognizable to the eye. The image must cast the object or set of objects as the double of a situation that from then on will be supposed real. The image is representational because recognizable, because it addresses itself to the eye's *memory*, to fixed references or identification, references known, but in the sense of "well-known," that is, familiar and established. These references are identity measuring the returning and return of movements. They form the instance or group of instances connecting and making them take the form of cycles. Thus all sorts of gaps, jolts, postponements, losses, and confusions can occur, but they no longer act as real diversions or wasteful drifts; when the final count is made, they turn out to be nothing but beneficial detours. It is precisely through the return to the ends of identification that cinematographic form, understood as the synthesis of good movement, is articulated following the cyclical organization of capital.

One example chosen from among thousands: in *Joe* (a film built entirely upon the impression of reality) the movement is drastically altered twice: the first time when the father beats to death the hippie who lives with his daughter; the second when, "mopping up" a hippie commune, he unwittingly guns down his own daughter. This last sequence ends with a freeze-frame shot of the bust and face of the daughter, who is struck down in full movement. In the first murder, we see a hail of fists falling upon the face of the defenseless hippie, who quickly loses consciousness. These two effects, the one an immobilization, the other an excess of mobility, are obtained by waiving the rules of representation, which demand real motion recorded and projected at twenty-four frames per second. As a result we could expect a strong affective charge to accompany them, since this greater or lesser perversion of the realistic rhythm responds to the organic rhythm of the intense emotions evoked. And it is indeed produced, but to the benefit, nevertheless, of the filmic totality, and thus, all told, to the benefit of order; both arrhythmies are produced not in some aberrant fashion but at the culminating points in the tragedy of the impossible father/daughter incest underlying the scenario. So while they may upset representational order, clouding for a few seconds the celluloid's necessary transparency (which is that order's condition), these two affective charges do not fail to suit the narrative order. On the contrary, they mark it with a beautiful melodic curve, the first accelerated murder finding its resolution in the second immobilized murder.

Thus, the memory to which films address themselves is *nothing* in itself, just as capital is nothing but an instance of capitalization; it is an instance, a set of empty instances that in no way operate through their content; *good* form, *good* lighting, *good* editing, *good* sound mixing are not good because they conform to perceptual or social reality, but because they are a priori scenographic *operators* that, on the contrary, determine the objects to be recorded on the screen and in "reality."

Directing: Putting in and Out of Scene

Film direction is not an artistic activity; it is a general process touching all fields of activity, a profoundly unconscious process of separation, exclusion, and effacement. In other words, direction is simultaneously executed on two planes, with this being its most enigmatic aspect. On the one hand, this task consists of separating reality on one side and a play space on the other (a "real" or an "unreal"—that which is in the camera's lens): to direct is to institute this limit, this frame, to circumscribe the region of deresponsibility at the heart of a whole that, *ideo facto*, is posed as responsible (we will call it *nature*, for example, or *society* or *final instance*). Thus is established between the two regions a relation of representation or doubling accompanied necessarily by a relative devaluation of the scene's realities, now only representative of the realities of reality. But, on the other hand, and inseparably, in order for the function of representation to be fulfilled, the activity of directing (a placing in and out of scene, as we have just said) must also be an activity that unifies all the movements, those on *both sides* of the frame's limit, imposing here *and* there, in "reality" just as in the real (*reel*), the *same norms,* the same ordering of all drives, excluding obliterating, effacing them *no less off* the scene than on. The references imposed on the filmic object are imposed just as necessarily on all objects outside the film. Direction first divides—along the axis of representation—and due to the theatrical limit—a reality and its double, and this disjunction constitutes an obvious repression. But also, beyond this representational disjunction and in a "pre-theatrical" economic order, it eliminates *all impulsional movement, real or unreal, that will not lend itself to reduplication,* all movement that would escape identification, recognition, and the mnesic fixation. Considered from the angle of this primordial function of an exclusion spreading to the exterior as well as to the interior of the cinematographic playground, film direction acts always as a factor of *libidinal normalization,* and does so independently of all "content," be it as "violent" as might seem. This normalization consists of the exclusion from the scene of whatever cannot be folded back upon the body of the film, and outside the scene, upon the social body.

The *film,* strange formation reputed to be normal, is no more normal than the *society* or the *organism.* All these so-called objects are the result of the imposition and hope for an accomplished totality. They are supposed to realize the reasonable goal par excellence, the subordination of all partial drives, all sterile and divergent movements to the unity of an organic body. The film is the organic body of cinematographic movements. It is the *ecclesia* of images: just as politics is that of the partial social organs. This is why direction, a technique of exclusions and effacements, a political activity par excellence, and political activity, which is direction *par excellence,* are the religion of the modern irreligion, the ecclesiastic of the secular. The central problem for both is not the representational arrangement and its accompanying question, that of knowing how and what to represent and the definition of good or true representation; the fundamental problem is the exclusion and foreclosure of all that is judged unrepresentable because nonrecurrent.

Thus film acts as the orthopedic mirror analyzed by Lacan in 1949 as constitutive of the imaginary subject of *object a;* that we are dealing with the social body in no way alters its function. But the real problem, missed by Lacan due to his Hegelianism, is to know why the drives spread about the polymorphous body *must have* an object where they can unite. That the imperative of unification is given as hypothesis in a philosophy of "consciousness" is betrayed by the very term *consciousness,* but for a "thought" of the unconscious (of which the form related most to pyrotechnics would be the economy sketched here and there in Freud's writings) the question of the production of unity, even an imaginary unity, can no longer fail to be posed in all its opacity. We will no longer have to pretend to understand how the subject's unity is constituted from his image in the mirror. We will have to ask ourselves how and why the *specular wall* in general, and thus the cinema screen in particular, can become a privileged place for the libidinal cathexis; why and how the drives come to take their place on the film (*pellicule,* or *petite peau*), opposing it to themselves as the place of their inscription, and what is more, as the support that the filmic operation in all its aspects will efface. A libidinal economy of the cinema should theoretically construct the operators that exclude aberrations from the social and organic bodies and channel the drives into this apparatus. It is not clear that narcissism or masochism are the proper operators: they carry a tone of subjectivity (of the theory of self) that is probably still much too strong.

The Tableau Vivant

The acinema, we have said, would be situated at the two poles of the cinema taken as a writing of movements: thus, extreme immobilization and extreme mobilization. It is only for *thought* that these two modes are incompatible. In a libidinal economy they are, on the contrary, necessarily associated; stupefaction, terror, anger, hate, pleasure—all the intensities—are always displacements in place. We should read the term *emotion* as a *motion* moving toward its own exhaustion, an immobilizing motion, an immobilized mobilization. The representational arts offer two symmetrical examples of these intensities, one where immobility appears: the tableau vivant; another where agitation appears: lyric abstraction.

Presently there exists in Sweden an institution called the *posering*, a name derived from the *pose* solicited by portrait photographers: young girls rent their services to these special houses, services that consist of assuming, clothed or unclothed, the poses desired by the client. It is against the rules of these houses (which are not houses of prostitution) for the clients to touch the models in any way. We would say that this institution is made to order for the phantasmatic of Klossowski, knowing as we do the importance he accords to the tableau vivant as the near perfect simulacrum of fantasy in all its paradoxical intensity. But it must be seen how the paradox is distributed in this case: the immobilization seems to touch only the erotic object while the subject is found overtaken by the liveliest agitation.

But things are probably not as simple as they might seem. Rather, we must understand this arrangement as a demarcation on both sides, that of model and client, of the regions of extreme erotic intensification, a demarcation performed by one of them, the client whose integrity reputedly remains intact. We see the proximity such a formulation has to the Sadean problematic of jouissance. We must note, given what concerns us here, that the tableau vivant in general, if it holds a certain libidinal potential, does so because it brings the theatrical and economic orders into communication; because it uses "whole persons" as detached erotic regions to which the spectator's impulses are connected. (We must be suspicious of summing this up too quickly as a simple voyeurism.) We must sense the price, beyond price, as Klossowski admirably explains, that the organic body, the pretended unity of the pretended subject, must pay so that the pleasure will burst forth in its irreversible sterility. This is the same price

that the cinema should pay if it goes to the first of its extremes, immobilization: because this latter (which is not simple immobility) means that it would
be necessary to endlessly undo the conventional syntheses that normally all cinematographic movements proliferate. Instead of good, unifying, and reasonable forms proposed for identification, the image would give rise to the most
intense agitation through its fascinating paralysis. We could already find many
underground and experimental films illustrating this direction of immobilization. Here we should begin the discussion of a matter of singular importance:
if you read Sade or Klossowski, the paradox of immobilization is seen to be
clearly distributed along the representational axis. The object, the victim, the
prostitute, takes the pose, offering his or her self as a detached region, but *at
the same time giving way and humiliating this whole person.* The allusion to this
latter is an indispensable factor in the intensification, since it indicates the inestimable price of diverting the drives in order to achieve perverse pleasure.
Thus representation is essential to this phantasmatic; that is, it is essential that
the spectator be offered instances of identification, recognizable forms, all in
all, matter for the memory: for it is at the price, we repeat, of going beyond this
and disfiguring the order of propagation that the intense emotion is felt. It follows that the simulacrum's support, be it in the writer's descriptive syntax, the
film of Pierre Zucca whose photographs illustrate (?) Klossowski's *La Monnaie
Vivante,* the paper on which Klossowski himself sketches—it follows that
the support itself must not submit to any noticeable perversion in order that the
perversion attack only what is supported, the representation of the victim:
the support is held in insensibility or unconsciousness. From here springs
Klossowski's active militancy in favor of representational plastics and his
anathema for abstract painting.

Abstraction

But what occurs if, on the contrary, it is the support itself that is touched by
perverse hands? Then the film, movements, lightings, and focus refuse to produce the recognizable image of a victim or immobile model, taking on themselves the price of agitation and libidinal expense and leaving it no longer to
the fantasized body. All lyric abstraction in painting maintains such a shift. It
implies a polarization no longer toward the immobility of the model but toward
the mobility of the support. This mobility is quite the contrary of cinematographic movement; it arises from any process that undoes the beautiful forms
suggested by this latter, from any process that to a greater or lesser degree
works on and distorts these forms. It blocks the synthesis of identification and
thwarts the mnesic instances. It can thus go far toward achieving an *ataxy* of

the iconic constituents, but this is still to be understood as a mobilization of the support. This way of frustrating the beautiful movement *by means of the support* must not be confused with that working through a paralyzing attack on the victim who serves as motif. The model is no longer needed, for the relation to the body of the client-spectator is completely displaced.

How is jouissance instantiated by a large canvas by Pollock or Rothko or by a study by Richter, Baruchello, or Eggeling? If there is no longer a reference to the loss of the unified body due to the model's immobilization and its diversion to the ends of partial discharge, just how inestimable must be the disposition the client-spectator can have; the represented ceases to be the libidinal object while the screen itself, in all its most formal aspects, takes its place. The film strip is no longer abolished (made transparent) for the benefit of this or that flesh, for it offers itself as the flesh posing itself. But from what unified body is it torn so that the spectator may enjoy, so that it seems to him to be beyond all price? Before the minute thrills that hem the contact regions adjoining the chromatic sands of a Rothko canvas, or before the almost imperceptible movements of the little objects or organs of Pol Bury, it is at the price of renouncing his own bodily totality and the synthesis of movements making it exist that the spectator experiences intense pleasure: these objects demand the paralysis not of the object-model but of the "subject"-client, the decomposition of his own organism. The channels of passage and libidinal discharge are restricted to very small partial regions (eye-cortex), and almost the whole body is neutralized in a tension blocking all escape of drives from passages other than those necessary to the detection of very fine differences. It is the same, although following other modalities, with the effects of the excess of movement in Pollock's paintings or with Thompson's manipulation of the lens. Abstract cinema, like abstract painting, in rendering the support opaque reverses the arrangement, making the client a victim. It is the same again, though differently, in the almost imperceptible movements of the Noh theater.

The question, which must be recognized as being crucial to our time because it is that of the staging of scene and society, follows: is it necessary for the victim to be in the scene for the pleasure to be intense? If the victim is the client, if in the scene is only film screen, canvas, the support, do we lose to this arrangement all the intensity of the sterile discharge? And if so, must we then renounce the hope of finishing with the illusion, not only the cinematographic illusion but also the social and political illusions? Are they not really illusions then? Or is believing so the illusion? Must the return of extreme intensities be founded on at least this empty permanence, on the phantom of the organic body or subject which is the proper noun, and at the same time that they cannot really accomplish this unity? This foundation, this love, how does it differ from that anchorage in nothing which founds capital?

Translated by Paisley N. Livingston

Notes

These reflections would not have been possible without the practical and theoretical work accomplished for several years by and with Dominique Avron, Claudine Eizykman, and Guy Fihman.

1. See Jean-François Lyotard, *The Postmodern Condition: A Report on Knowledge*, trans. Régis Durand (Manchester: Manchester University Press, 1986), p. xxiv. Lyotard's book was written in the context of the demise of the Soviet influence in Eastern Europe and the exponential growth of multinational corporate capitalism. Lyotard brought a reading of Kant's notion of the sublime (the experience of being overwhelmed, succeeded by an experience of pleasurable *jouissance*) to explore the aesthetic possibilities of the postmodern condition.

2. Jean-François Lyotard, *Libidinal Economy*, trans. Iain Hamilton Grant (Bloomington: Indiana University Press, 1993). First published in France in 1974, *Économie libidinale* (Paris: Minuit, 1974).

3. *Joe* (1970), a Hollywood drama film about the conflictual relationship of a father and daughter and the father's murder of a hippie commune, including his daughter. Directed by John G. Avildsen.

4. Sigmund Freud, *The Standard Edition of the Complete Psychological Works of Sigmund Freud*, ed. James Strachey (London: Hogarth and the Institute of Psychoanalysis, 1981), 18:3–64.

5. Jacques Lacan, *Écrits: The First Complete Edition in English*, trans. Bruce Fink (New York: Norton, 2006), pp. 75–81.

CHAPTER 8

CINEMA I

The Movement-Image

GILLES DELEUZE

A major figure of continental philosophy in the latter part of the twentieth century, Gilles Deleuze (1925–1995) was professor of philosophy at the University of Vincennes in Saint-Denis between 1969 and 1987. Deleuze's innovative approach in his studies of the antirationalist philosophers Benedict de Spinoza, David Hume, Friedrich Nietzsche, and Henri Bergson reflected his own commitment to a definition of philosophy as an art "that involves 'creating concepts.'"[1] Wary of the legacy of metaphysics informing Western structures of thinking, Deleuze was openly critical of Hegelian dialectics as well as Freudian and Lacanian psychoanalysis, all of which he believed conceived of desire in terms of a lack based upon illusory ideals, rather than as forms of becoming. In contrast to these theories, and drawing inspiration from Spinoza on affect (in Latin, *affectus*),[2] Deleuze elaborated a philosophy concerned with nonrepresentational qualities and modes of experience comprised of what he described as "intensities, experiences, experiments"[3]—the initial outcome of which was the landmark book of schizoid flow *Anti-Oedipus: Capitalism and Schizophrenia* (1972), coauthored with the antipsychiatry writer Félix Guattari.[4] With his two major books on cinema, *Cinema I: The Movement-Image* (1983) and *Cinema II: The Time-Image* (1985), Deleuze provided an exhaustive taxonomy of cinema's invention of its own unique forms and affects during the period from the 1920s to the 1980s. Of fundamental importance to this project is an understanding of cinema's development as it decenters space to the point that a direct expression of time is produced.

In French the titles of Deleuze's works on cinema—*L'Image-Mouvement* and *L'Image-Temps*—emphasize the primacy of the image as expounded by Henri Bergson, whose philosophy informs Deleuze's two books. In *Matter and Memory* (1896) and *Creative Evolution* (1907), Bergson conceived of the universe ("the whole") as a fluid process of infinite variation and change, for which he used the term *duration* (*durée*). For Bergson, everything that exists participates in a fluid and moving continuity of becomings and mutually interactive affects and sensations (*Reader* text 1). In order to describe these affects in as impersonal and nonrepresentational terms as possible Bergson used the words *impressions* or *images*.

In his book *Philosophy and the Adventure of the Virtual: Bergson and the Time of Life*, Keith Ansell Pearson suggests that socially engrained habits of understanding and rationalization have tended "to solidify the fluid continuity of the real or the open whole into discontinuous or discrete images . . . turn[ing] away from the movement of life or becom[ing] interested only in the unmoveable part and plan of the movement rather than the movement itself."[5]

However, while habitual forms of understanding disavow the movement of bodies and the whole, Deleuze believes that cinema bears a relationship to Bergson's philosophy, producing moving images in reciprocal forms of interaction and affect. Deleuze's project in both *Cinema I: The Movement-Image* and *Cinema II: The Time-Image* is to provide a taxonomy of cinematic images in terms of the structure of their fluxual interactions. For this purpose Deleuze developed concepts that are specific to cinema, although he claims that they "can be only formed philosophically."[6] In forming this taxonomy, Deleuze puts forward a history of cinema divided between the periods of the movement-image, from the beginnings of cinema to the Second World War, and, thereafter, the time-image of modern cinema.

Primarily, in these extracts from *Cinema I: The Movement-Image*, Deleuze discusses the different uses of montage in the early cinema of the American school (Griffith), the Soviet school (Eisenstein), the prewar French school, and German Expressionism, as well as three types of image structures in cinema: the perception-image, the affection-image, and the action-image. Deleuze's book concludes with a discussion of the mental image in connection with Hitchcock's films that signal the end of the movement-image and the final disruption of spatiotemporal relations by which duration is subordinated to linked forms of movement and continuity.

In the postwar period (although it is anticipated before then), cinema, Deleuze argues, undergoes a crisis in terms of its "sensory-motor schema" involving the way in which characters react to situations that produce the story; in particular, spatial coordinates are disrupted and the films' protagonists experience different kinds of alienation, "characters no longer 'know' how to react to situations that are beyond them, too awful, or too beautiful, or insoluble."[7]

More important, cinema no longer utilizes edited shots that are composed in terms of linkages and an overall sense of unity and totality (even if this is in terms of change). This means that time is no longer related to spatialized forms of movement and therefore subordinated to it, thus allowing time to be presented directly. Such is the cinema of *The Time-Image*.

In both *Cinema I: The Movement-Image* and *Cinema II: The Time-Image*, the focus of attention is upon the films' means of expression—formal devices and affects—that Deleuze argues *are* the very things that cinema expresses. As Deleuze says of Griffith's use of montage, "It is wrong to criticize it as being subordinate to the narration; it is the reverse, for the narrativity flows from this conception of montage." This comment applies to Deleuze's whole approach to cinema; story and plot are shaped by, and integral to, the affects that are the subject of his taxonomy. In both his books on cinema, Deleuze considers these affects across the entire oeuvre of a director or school of film.

From Chapter 3, Montage

Deleuze's initial consideration in *Cinema I: The Movement-Image* is montage. For Deleuze, montage is not simply the technical configuration of edited shots composing the film, but rather the underlying method composing the film that shapes its development. In the movement-image this development is always structured as an organic totality with an inferred temporality of an open past and open future. As such, film is largely seen in terms of "continuities" along a spatially conceived trajectory of time that inhibits a direct sense of time (see *Reader* text 1 on this problem of conceptions of space dominating time). In early cinema, montage determines the film insofar as it is considered as a changing whole composed through the relation of its parts. Griffith's approach to film as a temporal medium was in the form of an organic unity shaped like a spiral that is open at one end toward an infinite past and, at the other end, toward an infinite future. Within this overall compositional shape, Griffith's films were composed from binary oppositions or "duels," with "the image of one part succeeding another according to a rhythm" of evolutionary convergence, as in *Intolerance* (1916). While Eisenstein considered time in similar terms as Griffith, as an organic unity shaped in the form of a spiral, he structured his films dialectically, rather than in terms of convergences, with the montage of images embodying ideas of radical change, revolutionary leaps, and universal, cosmic becomings (a "general line" of revolution that leaps from the old to the new). The French school was preoccupied with accelerated and decelerated forms of movement, which, in Gance's epic, three-screen film *Napoléon*, achieved a remarkable sense of liquid, measureless movement. By dissolving movement in this way, the French school gained a sense of time, in the form of past and future, occurring simultaneously, thus placing the openness of the past in a constant exchange with an open future (a "simultaneism" that Deleuze says also fascinated the painter Robert Delaunay). In films such as Murnau's *Faust* (1926) and Pabst's *Pandora's Box* (1929), German Expressionism developed a sense of movement as an infinitely rising point that Deleuze characterizes as the tip of a pyramid. This rising point is juxtaposed to an infinitely shrinking, contracted point that results in the base of the pyramid shearing away from the tip. German Expressionism's obsession with black (negation = 0) as the condition of the fall of light expressed a nonorganic sense of being, a primordial horror arising from a lack of reciprocity between nature and the subject. For Deleuze, the films of the French school and German Expressionism correspond to Kant's two conceptions of the sublime as outlined in the *Critique of Judgment*: the mathematical sublime and the dynamic sublime, respectively. The experience of the sublime presented in these schools of film exceeds the subject's categories of understanding and comprehension. However, in the French school this affirms the flow of experience, including that of historical experience; while in German Expressionism the effect of the movement of the base from the tip of the pyramid is to detach the past from the future.

From Chapter 5, The Perception-Image

3 Toward a Gaseous Perception

The perception-image affirms perception beyond conventional space-time coordinates, and reaches its most radical expression in Dziga Vertov's *Man with a Movie Camera* (1929), a film that Deleuze likens to the ephemerality of a gas in dissolution unbounded by the contours of an impermeable body. Deleuze's analysis of Vertov's films is influenced, in part, by the filmmaker's own writings, which saw the Russian Revolution of 1917 not just as the destruction of capitalist institutions but also as the end of an anthropocentric conception of "man" and his "world." The concept of the cine-eye, or kino-eye, that Deleuze refers to as a "non-human eye," was first announced by Vertov in a 1923 manifesto, "I am kino-eye, I am a mechanical eye. I, a machine, show you the world as only I can see it. . . . Freed from the rule of sixteen–seventeen frames per second, free of the limits of time and space. I put together any given points in the universe, no matter where I've recorded them. My path leads to the creation of a fresh perception of the world. I decipher in a new way a world unknown to you."[8]

Later, in an essay of 1929, Vertov expanded upon what he meant by such a machinic idea of the eye,

Kino-eye = kino-seeing (I see through the camera) + kino-writing (I write on film with the camera) = kino-organisation (I edit). . . . Kino-eye means the conquest of space, the visual linkage of people throughout the entire world based on the continuous exchange of visible fact. . . . Kino-eye is the possibility of seeing life processes in any temporal order or at any speed. . . . Kino-eye uses every possible means in montage, comparing and linking all points of the universe in any temporal order, breaking, when necessary, all the laws and conventions of film construction.[9]

The "I see," therefore, is no longer under the direction of a subject conceived in terms of a form of perception limited by the human body; Rather the kino-eye is a machinic eye capable of showing what is beyond that which is immediately visible to a single person. As Deleuze says, "This is not a human eye," since such an eye is restricted by "its relative immobility." Rather, as Deleuze observes, Vertov's montage is "the pure vision of a non-human eye" that has the capacity to overcome perception as governed by conventional notions of both space and time.

While *Man with a Movie Camera* puts together episodic elements of Moscow's city life, Deleuze claims that, effectively, it couples together any point of the universe whatsoever, in any temporal order. Furthermore, Deleuze states that "what montage does . . . is to carry perception into matter, so that any point whatsoever in space perceives all the points on which it acts, or which act on it, however far these actions and reactions extend." In other words, the effect of Vertov's style of montage, involving "slow or high speed shots, superimposition, fragmentation, deceleration, micro-shooting," is to break open the limits of the human body,[10] dissolving perception (the kino-eye) directly into things—that is, into matter. With this dissolution, there is no center or privileged image, rather any given image and movement or point in space is linked to all other images, movements, and points in space on which they act affectively, and vice versa, all the way to infinity: "It is the eye of matter, the eye in matter, not subject to time, which has 'conquered' time, which reaches the 'negative of time,' and which knows no other whole than the material universe and its extension."

The velocity of motion in Vertov's *Man with a Movie Camera* does not operate at a fixed rate. The film encompasses many kinds of motion, sometimes slow, even still, at other times rapid; in between these rates, there are sequences of various degrees of acceleration and deceleration. All these different velocities of montaged film are what Deleuze refers to as "the interval." According to Deleuze, in Vertov this interval blurs and overrides the sense of a gap or a delay between a received and an executed movement, an action and a reaction that, since Aristotle, have governed conventional philosophies of movement and linear progression. On the contrary, Deleuze says that in Vertov there is no "distancing between two consecutive images but, on the contrary, a correlation of two images that are distant (and incommensurable from the viewpoint of our human perception)." Rather than an action leading to a reaction, there are a multiplicity of simultaneous affective movements without origin or end. This was Vertov's revolutionary contribution to Soviet revolutionary communism in which even his film's intertitles formed a part since they were conceived as images enunciated by an anonymous voice-off.

From Chapter 7, The Affection-Image: Qualities, Powers, Any-Space-Whatevers

1 The Complex Entity or the Expressed

In the glossary to *Cinema I: The Movement-Image*, Deleuze defines the affection-image as "that which occupies the gap between an action and a reaction, that which absorbs an external action and reacts on the inside."[11] Deleuze believes that this type of image has two kinds of expression in cinema: first, there is the close-up, which is associated largely with the face, and, second, there are the qualities and powers of the "any-space-whatever." In relation to the first type of expression, Deleuze claims that Dreyer's *Passion of Arc* (1928) is, "the affective film *par excellence*." While the film refers to a specific historical situation and time, that of Joan of Arc's trial and execution in Rouen in 1431, nevertheless, Deleuze argues that the film essentially is not a narrative of these events and nor is it simply composed of a series of (aggressive) actions and (victimized) reactions between the opposed protagonists, namely Joan and her judges. Dreyer's film exemplifies Deleuze's claim that the affection-image internalizes incoming perception—in this case, Joan's inward torment—but she fails to translate these successively into external bodily motor actions. Instead, the motor tendencies turn inward onto "a sensitive nerve . . . an immobilised plate of nerve"[12] that is composed of the series of micro-movements of Joan's face, conveying her torment and ecstasy, the qualities of which are achieved "through the differentiation of [the face's] own material parts and its capacity to make their relations vary: parts which are hard and tender, shadowy and illuminated, dull and shiny, smooth and grainy, jagged and curved."[13] These contrasting qualities constitute Joan's passion as it "appears in the 'ecstatic' mode and passes through the face, its exhaustion, its turning away, its encounter with the limit."

Such an intensive expression of the experience of Joan of Arc's passion is ultimately irreducible to the spatiotemporal circumstances of her trial, even though they constrain her person, "this mystery of the present . . . is the difference between the trial and the Passion, which are nevertheless inseparable." Composed largely of a series of flowing close-ups, Joan's face becomes virtually the entire image, with little sense of bodily movement or extension. This concentration on the face, along with a reduced sense of bodily motility, has the effect of subverting any grounding forms of spatiality in favor of an indeterminate temporality composed of qualities that are irreducible to a consciousness, since these are "what is new in experience, what is fresh, fleeting and nevertheless eternal . . . because they have no relations to an ego."[14]

Deleuze observes that while a film such as Dreyer's *Passion of Joan of Arc* "extracts the face (or its equivalent) from all spatio-temporal co-ordinates," this affect can be conveyed also by spaces glimpsed behind the face, "a scrap of sky, countryside or background" composed either in flattened perspective or in depth. This observation leads Deleuze to propose that the affection-image may not require supporting close-ups of the face at all. Such is the case with Robert Bresson's film *The Trial of Joan of Arc* (1962). Whereas Dreyer utilizes close-ups of faces to release the potentialities of the intensive image, Bresson impregnates space itself with these potentialities by isolating parts of the body, particularly hands, legs, and feet, rather than faces. To characterize Bresson's sense of fragmented, groundless space, Deleuze borrows the term *any-space-whatever* (Deleuze credits Pascal Augé with this term, but probably means the film and video artist Pascal Auger). Space lacks homogeneity; linkages are made by means of a "haptic" montage that connects spaces blindly. (Ultimately, this means that Bresson's films belong to the regime of the time-image rather than that of the movement-image).

From Chapter 9, The Action-Image: The Large Form

1 From Situation to Action: Secondness"

The third primary movement-image of Deleuze's schema is the action-image that is epitomized by the realist films of classical Hollywood cinema. The qualities and affects that concern Deleuze in *Cinema I: The Movement-Image* are not displayed in the action-image through the creation of "any-space-whatever," as in Bresson's films, but rather are actualized directly in determinate, geographical, historical, and social space-times. The dramatic development of such films are structured either in a large or small form, expressed in the acronyms SAS' and ASA.' Both forms underline the fact that the action-image, like the other forms of the movement-image, develops in terms of an organic and open whole within a time continuum of an open past and open future. The large form typically opens with, or develops, an initial dramatic situation composed of conflicting forces (S), which eventually prompts the hero or heroine into taking responsive action (A) to right a wrong or resolve a problem that, by the end of the film, produces a modified or new situation (S'). In discussing the action-image, Deleuze uses a number of theoretical terms: *encompasser,* *milieu,* and *situation.* The milieu is the determining relations among the group (the film's protagonists) that can be either a fixed group—for example, the folk of a town beset by outlaws (*The Man Who Shot Liberty Valence* [1962]) or a family in conflict (*Red River* [1948])—or it can be a makeshift group: for example, the groups thrown together in Anthony Mann's westerns such as *Bend of the River* (1952) and *The Naked Spur* (1953). Speaking of John Ford's movies, Deleuze says that his "originality lies in the fact that only the encompasser gives measure to movement, or the organic rhythm." By *encompasser,* Deleuze refers to the wider context of the film that introduces and encompasses forms of becoming: the wind of hardship but also change in Sjöström's *The Wind* (1928) or the sky and the river in Ford's *The Big Sky* (1952) that, together, give a sense of fluidity to the whole as the pioneers seek to create new forms of exchange with the native Americans. Both the encompasser and milieu expand and contract through the film like a form of respiration and breath. Since the milieu in the great westerns is riven by duels and dualities—in other words, differences and conflicts (for example, the law of the gun versus the law book in *The Man Who Shot Liberty Valence*)—the initial situation is put under pressure, and this eventually leads to the action of the hero or heroine to change the situation so as to create a different situation. The action-image, therefore, is composed of the interactions and relations among the milieu within which the principal protagonist acts to transform the milieu, by means of which he or she is also transformed.

Films of this type, Deleuze says, are organized as an organic unity in terms of two inverse spiral movements shaped in the form of an hourglass or egg timer. One of these spirals "incurves" on the hero or heroine and leads toward decisive action, while the other moves outward from the action, opening onto a new temporal situation. These spiraling movements are not simply smooth and continuous, since the hero's or heroine's action, prompted by the conflicts of the milieu, arises only gradually, often in fits and starts that are contiguous with the contractions and expansions of the encompasser. The consequence of this is that the action frequently does not occur until toward the end of the film. As Deleuze observes, "On the one hand the situation must permeate the character deeply and continuously, and on the other hand the character who is thus permeated must burst into action, at discontinuous intervals."[15] An essential aspect of the action-image, therefore, is the temporal interval or gap between the cause of the action arising through the milieu, and the action itself, that allows time for affect (the hero or heroine's qualities) to become embodied in action.

In *The Man Who Shot Liberty Valence,* the initial situation (S) facing Rance Stoddard (James Stewart) is the fear felt by the township toward Liberty Valence and his gang, who are hired guns for the big cattle ranchers in the territory.

Eventually, Stoddard's refusal to be cowed, his stubbornness, leads him to confront Valence in a duel (A), and, with the gangster's death, an altered situation (S') transpires, paving the way for Stoddard to marry and rise to become a senator. Typically, westerns exemplify the large form of the action-image (SAS'), but Deleuze also identifies this form with the film noirs of Howard Hawks and John Huston, in the psychosocial dramas of King Vidor as well as with the historical films of Griffith and DeMille. However, certain film noirs, such as Hawks's *The Big Sleep* (1946), Deleuze proposes, are structured in terms of the small form (ASA'), as are many comedies where the action moves to a partially disclosed situation that requires a further action to resolve it.

From Chapter 12, Crisis of Action-Image: Peirce's "Thirdness" and Mental Relations

Deleuze's discussion of Hitchcock's films revolve around his theory of the mental-image, otherwise known as the relation-image, which encompasses a series of concepts and terms: *postulate, sets of relations, thirdness*. Thirdness is a further level to the action-image on top of what was its primary feature, namely, affects embodied in actions. With Hitchcock, a level of interpretation, a type of in-built reflexive commentary on the action, is introduced during, and as part of, the very passage of SAS' in the film that maintains an openness to the whole.

Deleuze declares that in Hitchcock's films "what counts is not the author of the action, what Hitchcock calls with scorn the *whodunit*, but neither is it the action itself: it is the set of relations within which the action and its author are held." For Deleuze, Hitchcock's films are not simply detective films dependent upon solving a mystery or uncovering the author of a crime. Such solutions and discoveries are part of Hitchcock's film narratives, but often the audience are made aware of the perpetrator or perpetrators of the crime long before the detectives discover it themselves, as in *Rope* (1948), *Dial M for Murder* (1954), and *Vertigo* (1958). This consciousness of whodunit by the audience is partly the reason why Deleuze suggests that Hitchcock's films incorporate the audience in a manner never experienced before: "In the history of cinema, Hitchcock appears as the one who no longer conceives of the constitution of a film as a function of two terms, the director and the film to be made, but as a function of three, the director, the film, and the public which must enter into the film." Furthermore, Deleuze believes that Hitchcock's films exceed the detective genre because "the criminal has always committed his crime *for* another," either on behalf of another (*Strangers on a Train* (1951) or in relation to another, thereby transferring what would be a criminal action governed by a purpose in conventional films to an act of exchange that exceeds a definitive purpose (what

Deleuze refers to as "the gift"): in *Dial M for Murder,* Captain Lesgate, aka Swann, is co-opted into carrying out the murder planned by Tony Wendice; in *Stage Fright* (1950), Jonathan Cooper embroils Eve Gill in his murderous passion; in *I Confess* (1953), Father Logan, the Catholic priest, maintains a silence about his knowledge of the murderer, Otto Keller (O. E. Hasse); and, in *Psycho* (1960), Norman Bates murders Marion Crane in the guise of his mother. These third parties to murder, or attempted murder, act as pivotal points around which sets of relations develop between different protagonists. As such, these "characters and actions become specular, quasi-meditative—processed for their spectrality to create suspense or unease."[16]

Deleuze positions Hitchcock at the conclusion of the tradition of the movement-image and as a director who anticipated the advent of the time-image in cinema, particularly in his later films. In this respect it is significant, Deleuze says, that James Stewart's characters in both *Rear Window* (1954) and *Vertigo* (1958) are afflicted with a certain immobility; in *Vertigo*, Scottie suffers from agoraphobia, while in *Rear Window* L.B. is wheelchair bound. Effectively, Stewart's immobility begins to counter the idea in the tradition of the movement-image of succession as integral to time within an open whole. A further feature of Hitchcock's film *Family Plot* (1976) that Deleuze observes is a concern with clairvoyance—which, for him, is significant in relation to his ideas about thought. However, in the cinema of the time-image, thought no longer thinks the whole, as it did in the cinema of the movement-image, because the idea of an organic unity composed of an open past and open future comes to an end.

✳ ✳ ✳

From Chapter 3, Montage

1 The Third Level: The Whole, the Composition of Movement-Images, and the Indirect Image of Time

Griffith conceived of the composition of movement-images as an organization, an organism, a great organic unity. This was his discovery. The organism is, firstly, unity in diversity, that is, a set of differentiated parts; there are men and women, rich and poor, town and country, North and South, interiors and exteriors, etc. These parts are taken in binary relationships which constitute a *parallel alternate montage*, the image of one part succeeding another according to a rhythm . . . The parts must necessarily act and react on each other in order to show how they simultaneously enter into conflict and threaten the unity of the organic set, and how they overcome the conflict or restore the unity. From some parts actions arise which oppose good and bad, but from other parts convergent actions arise which come to the aid of the good: through all these actions the form of a duel develops and passes through different stages. Indeed, it is in the nature of the organic set that it should continually be threatened: the accusation raised against the Negroes in *Birth of a Nation* is that of a wanting to shatter the newly won unity of the United States by using the South's defeat to their own advantage. . . . American montage is organico-active. It is wrong to criticize it as being subordinate to the narration; it is the reverse, for the narrativity flows from this conception of montage. In *Intolerance*, Griffith discovers that the organic representation can be immense, encompassing not merely families and a society, but different epochs and civilizations. The parts thrown together by parallel montage are the civilizations themselves. The relative dimensions which are interchanged range from the king's city to the capitalist's office. And the convergent actions are not just the duels proper to each civilization—the chariot race in the Babylonian episode, the race between the car and the train in the modern episode—but the two races themselves converge through the centuries in an accelerated montage which superimposes Babylon and America. Never again will such organic unity be achieved by means of rhythm, from parts which are so different and actions which are so distant.

2 The Soviet School

The dialectical assemblage, involves not only the organic—that is, genesis and growth—but also the *pathetic* or the "development." The pathetic should not be confused with the organic. The point is that from one point to another on the spiral one can extend vectors which are like the strings of a bow, or the spans of the twist of a spiral. It is no longer a case of the formation and progression of the oppositions themselves, following the twists of the spiral, but of the transition from one opposite to the other, or rather into the other, along the spans: the leap into the opposite. There is not simply the opposition of earth and water, of the one and the many; there is the transition of the one into the other, and the sudden upsurge of the other out of the one. There is not simply the organic unity of opposites, but the pathetic passage of the opposite into its contrary. There is not simply an organic link between two instants, but a pathetic jump, in which the second instant gains a new power, since the first has passed into it. From sadness to anger, from doubt to certainty, from resignation to revolt . . . The pathetic, for its part, involves these two aspects: it is simultaneously the transition from one term to another, from one quality which is born from the transition which has been accomplished. It is both "compression" and "explosion."[17] *The General Line* divides its spiral into two opposed parts, "the Old" and "the New," and reproduces its division, redistributes its oppositions on one side and the other: this is the organic. But in the famous scene of the creamer, we witness the transition from one moment to the other, from suspicion and hope to triumph, from the empty tube to the first drop, a transition which accelerates as the new quality, the triumphant drop, approaches; this is the pathetic, the jump or qualitative leap. The organic was the bow, the collection of bows; but the pathetic is both the string and the arrow, the change in quality and the sudden upsurge of the new quality, its squaring, its raising to the power two . . .

It is at once the dawn of consciousness and consciousness attained, revolutionary consciousness attained, at least to a certain degree: which may be the very limited degree of Ivan, or the merely anticipatory degree of *Battleship Potemkin*, or the culminating degree of *October*. If the pathetic is development, it is because it is the development of consciousness itself: it is the leap of the organic which produces an external consciousness of society and its history, of the social organism from one moment to the next. And there are yet other leaps—in variable relationships with those of consciousness—all expressing new dimensions, formal and absolute changes, raisings to yet higher powers. It is the leap into color, like the red flag of *Battleship Potemkin*, or Ivan's red banquet . . . the qualitative leap can attain formal or absolute changes which already constitute powers to the "nth degree": the stream of milk in *The General Line* gives way to jets of water (passage to scintillation), then to a firework (passage to color) and finally to zigzags of figures (passage from the visible to the legible) . . . The jets of water and fire raise the drop of milk to a properly cosmic dimension. And it is consciousness which becomes cosmic at the same time as it becomes revolutionary—having reunited in a final leap of pathos the whole of the organic in itself—earth, air, fire and water . . . In Eisenstein the dialectical conception of the organism and of montage combines the ever open-spiral and the perpetually leaping instant.

3 The Prewar French School

In the prewar French school (whose recognized leader, in certain respects, was Gance) we also witness a break with the principle of organic composition. . . . These directors were primarily interested in the *quantity of movement* and in the metrical relations which allow us to define it. . . . Take, for example, a number of scenes which have become part of the anthology of French cinema: Epstein's traveling fair (*Coeur fidèle*), L'Herbier's ball (*El Dorado*), Grémillon's farandoles (from *Maldone* onwards). In a group dance, there is certainly an organic composition of the dancers and a dialectical composition of their movements, not merely fast and slow, but also linear and circular, etc. But, even while recognizing these movements, one can extract or abstract from them a single body which might be "the" dancer, the single body of all these dancers, and a single movement which might be "the" fandango of L'Herbier, the movement of all fandangos made visible . . .

Depending on the variations of the present or the contractions and dilations of the interval, one might say that a very slow movement realizes the greatest possible quantity of movement, just as much as a very fast movement does in another case: if Gance's *La Roue* was a model of increasingly fast movement, with accelerated montage, then Epstein's *The Fall of the House of Usher* remains the masterpiece of a slow motion which nevertheless constitutes the maximum of movement in a form which is infinitely drawn out . . .

A famous case is accelerated montage as it appears in [Gance's] *La Roue* and again in *Napoleon*. But absolute movement is defined by a quite different figure, which Gance calls "simultaneous horizontal montage" and which finds its two principal forms in *Napoleon*: on the one hand, the invention of the triple screen and polyvision; on the other hand the original use of superimpressions. By superimposing a very large number of superimpressions (sixteen at times), by introducing little temporal shifts between them, and by adding some and removing others, Gance is perfectly aware that the spectator will not see what is superimposed: the imagination is, as it were, surpassed, saturated, quickly reaching its limit . . .

In short, with Gance the French school invents a cinema of the sublime . . . What appeared in this way with the French school was a new way of conceiving the two signs of time: the interval has become the variable and successive numerical unit, which enters into metrical relationships with the other factors, in each case defining the greatest relative quantity of movement in the content and for the imagination; the whole has become simultaneous, the measureless, the immense, which reduces imagination to impotence and confronts it with its own limit, giving birth in the spirit to the pure thought of a quantity of absolute movement which expresses its whole history or change, its universe. This is exactly Kant's mathematical sublime.

4 German Expressionism

The French school could be contrasted point by point with German Expressionism. The reply to "more movement!" is "more light!" Movement is unleashed but to serve the light, to make it scintillate, to form or dismember stars, multiply reflections, leave brilliant trails, as in the great music-hall scene in Dupont's *Vaudeville*, or in the dream of Murnau's *The Last Laugh* . . .

Light's role, effectively, is to develop a relationship with black as negation = 0, as a function of which it is defined as intensity, as intensive quantity. Here the instant appeared (contrary to the extensive unit and part) as that which apprehends the luminous magnitude or degree in relation to black. That is why intensive movement is inseparable from a fall, even a virtual one, which only expresses this distance of the degree of light from zero. Only the idea of the fall measures the degree to which the intensive quantity *rises* and, even in its greatest glory, natural light falls and continues to fall. Therefore, the idea of fall must also necessarily be actualized, and become a real or material fall in individual beings. Light only has one ideal fall, but daylight has a real fall: such is the adventure of the individual soul, caught up in a black hole, of which Expressionism was to give us some dizzy examples (Marguerite's fall in Murnau's *Faust*, that of the hero of *The Last Laugh*, devoured by the black hole of the washrooms in the grand hotel, or that of Pabst's *Lulu*) . . .

In all this, Expressionism was breaking with the principle of organic composition introduced by Griffith and taken up by most of the Soviet dialecticians. But it made this rupture in a completely different way from the French school. It does not invoke the clear mechanics of the quantity of movement in the solid or the fluid but a dark, swampy life into which everything plunges, whether chopped up by shadows or plunged into mists. The non-organic life of things, a frightful life, which is oblivious to the wisdom and limits of the organism, is the first principle of Expressionism . . . Thus automata, robots and puppets are no longer mechanisms which validate or "major" [*majorent*] a quantity of movement, but somnambulists, zombies or golems who express the intensity of this non-organic life: not simply Wegener's *The Golem*, but also the Gothic horror film of around 1930, for example Whale's *Frankenstein* and *The Bride of Frankenstein* and Halpérin's *White Zombie* . . .

The infinite had not ceased to work in the finite, which reinstates it in this still sensible form. Sprit had not left Nature, it animates all non-organic life, but it can only discover and rediscover itself as the spirit of evil which burns Nature in its entirety. It is the flaming circle of the invocation of the demon in Wegener's *The Golem* or Murnau's *Faust*. It is Faust's funeral pyre. It is the "phosphorescent demon head with sad and empty eyes" in Wegener. It is the blazing head of Mabuse and of Mephisto. These are the moments of the sublime, the rediscovery of the infinite in the spirit of evil: in Murnau, in particular, *Nosferatu* . . . bursts forth from an even more direct bottomlessness, giving him an aura of omnipotence which goes beyond his two-dimensional form . . .

This new sublime is not that of the French school. Kant distinguished two kinds of Sublime, mathematical and dynamic, the immense and the powerful, the measureless and formless. . . . In the dynamic sublime, it is intensity which is raised to such a power that it dazzles or annihilates our organic being, strikes terror into it, but arouses a thinking faculty by which we feel superior to that which annihilates us, to discover in us a supra-organic spirit which dominates the whole inorganic life of things: then we lose our fear, knowing that our spiritual "destination" is truly invincible . . . the whole is on high,[18] and is identical to the summit of a pyramid which, in rising up, constantly pushes down its base.

The whole has become the truly infinite intensification which is extracted from all the degrees, which has passed through the fire, but only to break its sensible attachments to the material, the organic, and the human, to detach itself from all states of the past, and this to discover the spiritual abstract Form of the future (Hans Richter's *Rhythms*).

From Chapter 5, The Perception-Image

3 Toward a Gaseous Perception

In the "cine-eye," Vertov was aiming to attain or regain the system of universal variation, in itself. All the images vary as a function of each other, on all their facets and in all their parts. Vertov himself defined the cine-eye: it is that which "couples together any point whatsoever of the universe in any temporal order whatsoever."[19] Everything is at the service of variation and interaction: slow or high speed shots, superimposition, fragmentation, deceleration [*démultiplication*], micro-shooting [*micro-prise de vue*]. This is not a human eye—even an improved one . . . the cinema is not simply the camera: it is montage. And if from the point of view of the human eye, montage is undoubtedly a construction, from the point of view of another eye, it ceases to be one; it is the pure vision of a non-human eye, of an eye which would be in things. Universal variation, universal interaction *(modulation)* . . . What montage does, according to Vertov, is to carry perception into things, to put perception into matter, so that any point whatsoever in space itself perceives all the points on which it acts, or which act on it, however far these actions and reactions extend. This is the definition of objectivity, "to see without boundaries or distances" . . . Vertov's non-human eye, the cine-eye, is not the eye of a fly or of an eagle, the eye of another animal . . . it is the eye of matter, the eye in matter, not subject to time, which has "conquered" time, which reaches the "negative of time," and which knows no other whole than the material universe and its extension . . . It is, first, a machine assemblage of movement-images. We have seen that the gap, the interval between two movements sketches out an empty place which prefigures the human subject in so far as he appropriates perception to himself. But, for Vertov, the most important thing was to restore the intervals to matter. This is the meaning of montage, and of the "theory of intervals," which is more profound than that of movement. . . . The originality of the Vertovian theory of the interval is that it no longer marks a gap which is carved out, a distancing between two consecutive images but, on the contrary, a correlation of two images which are distant (and incommensurable from the viewpoint of our human perception). And, on the other hand, the cinema could not run in this way from one end of the universe to the other without having at its disposal an agent which was capable of making all the parts converge: what Vertov took from the spirit—that is, the power of a whole which is constantly becoming—now passes into the correlate of matter, of its variations and interaction . . .

In the final analysis, we would have to speak of a perception which was no longer liquid but gaseous. For, if we start out from a solid state, where molecules are not free to move about (molar or human perception), we move next to a liquid state, where the molecules move about and merge into one another, but we finally reach a gaseous state, defined by the free movement of each molecule. According to Vertov, it is perhaps necessary to move beyond flowing to that stage: the particle of matter or gaseous perception.

From Chapter 7, The Affection-Image: Qualities, Powers, Any-Space-Whatevers

1 The Complex Entity or the Expressed

In the affective film *par excellence,* Dreyer's *Passion of Joan of Arc,* there is a whole historical state of things, social roles and individual or collective characters, real connections between them—Joan, the bishop, the Englishman, the judges, the kingdom, the people: in short, the trial. But there is something else, which is not exactly eternal or suprahistorical: it is what Peguy called "internal." It is like two presents which ceaselessly intersect, one of which is endlessly arriving and the other is already established. Peguy also said that one goes the whole length of the historical event, but that one ascends inside the other event: the first has long been embodied, but the second continues to express itself and is even still looking for an expression. It is the same event, but one part of it is profoundly realized in a state of things, whilst the other is all the more irreducible to all realization. This mystery of the present . . . is the difference between the trial and the Passion, which are nevertheless inseparable. Active causes are determined in the state of things: but the event itself, the affective, the effect, goes beyond its own causes, and only refers to other effects, whilst the causes for their part fall aside. It is the anger *of* the bishop and the martyrdom *of* Joan; but, all that will be preserved from the roles and situations will be what is needed for the affect to be extracted and to carry out its conjunctions—this "power" of anger or of ruse, this "quality" of victim or of martyrdom. To extract the Passion from the trial, to extract from the event this inexhaustible and brilliant part which goes beyond its own actualization, "the completion which is never completed." The affect is like the expressed of the state of things, but this expressed does not refer to the state of things, it only refers to the faces which express it and, coming together or separating, give it its proper moving context. Made up of short close-ups, the film took upon itself that part of the event which does not allow itself to be actualized in a determinate milieu.

The perfect fit between the technical means and this end is also important. Affective framing proceeds by *cutting close-ups* [*gros plans coupants*]. Sometimes howling lips or toothless sneers are cut into the mass of the face. Sometimes the frame cuts a face horizontally, vertically or aslant, obliquely. And movements are cut in their course, the continuity shots systematically false, as if it was necessary to break over-real or over-logical connections. Also, Joan's face is often pushed back to the lower part of the image, so that the close-up carries with it a fragment of white decor, an empty zone, a space of sky from which she draws an inspiration. It is an extraordinary document on the turning toward and turning away of faces. . . . Dreyer avoids the shot-reverse shot [*champ-contrechamp*] procedure which would maintain a real relation between each face and the other, and would still be part of an action-image. He prefers to isolate each face in a close-up which is only partly filled, so that the position to the right or to the left directly induces a virtual conjunction which no longer needs to pass through the real connection between the people.

2 The Spiritual Affect and Space in Bresson

Although the close-up extracts the face (or its equivalent) from all spatio-temporal co-ordinates, it can carry with it its own space-time—a scrap of vision, sky, countryside or background. Sometimes it is depth of field which gives the close-up a behind. Sometimes, on the contrary, it is the negation of perspective and of depth which assimilates the medium shot to a close-up. But, if the affect obtains a space for itself in this way, why could it not do so even without the face, and independently of the close-up, independently of all reference to the close-up?

Take, for example, Bresson's *The Trial of Joan of Arc*. . . . The film is primarily made up of medium shots, shots and reverse-shots; and Joan is perceived at her trial rather than in her Passion, as a prisoner who resists rather than as victim and martyr.[20] Whilst it is certainly true that this expressed trial is not to be confused with the historical trial, it is itself Passion—in Bresson as much as in Dreyer—and enters into a virtual conjunction with that of Christ. But, in Dreyer, the Passion appeared in the "ecstatic" mode and passed through the face, its exhaustion, its turning away, its encounter with the limit. Whilst, in Bresson it is in itself "trial" [*procès*] that is *halt* [*station*], step and advance (*Diary of a Country Priest* highlights this aspect of stations on a pathway to the Cross). It is the construction of a space, fragment by fragment, a space of tactile value, where the hand ends up by assuming the directing function which returns to it in *Pickpocket,* dethroning the face. The law of this space is "fragmentation."[21]

Tables and doors are not given whole. Joan's room and the courtroom, the death cell, are not presented to us in long shots but successively apprehended from continuity shots which make them a reality which is closed each time, but to infinity. Hence the special role of deframings. The external world itself therefore seems to be a cell, like the aquarium-forest of *Lancelot du Lac*. It is as if the mind collides with each part as if it were a closed angle, but enjoying a manual freedom in the linking of the parts. Indeed, the linking of neighbouring areas can be done in many different ways and depends on new conditions of speed and of movement, on rhythmic values which are opposed to all prior determination—"A new dependence. . . ." Longchamp and the Gare de Lyon in *Pickpocket* are vast fragmented spaces, transformed through rhythmic continuity shots which correspond to the affects of the thief. Ruin and salvation are played on an amorphous table whose successive parts await the connection which they lack from our gestures, or rather from the mind. Space itself has left behind its own co-ordinates and its metric relations. It is a tactile space. In this way Bresson can achieve a result which in Dreyer was only indirect. The spiritual affect is no longer expressed by a face, and space no longer needs to be subjected or assimilated to a close-up, treated as a close-up. The affect is now directly presented in medium shot, in a space which is capable of corresponding to it. And the famous treatment of voices by Bresson, white voices, not only marks an upsurge of free indirect discourse in every expression, but also a potentialization of what happens and is expressed—an equivalence of space and the affect expressed as pure potentiality.

Space is no longer a particular determined space, it has become *any-space-whatever* [*espace quelconque*], to use Pascal Augé's term. Certainly, Bresson does not invent any-space-whatevers (although he constructs them on his own account and in his own way). . . . Any-space-whatever is not an abstract universal, in all times, in all places. It is a perfectly singular space, which has merely lost its homogeneity, that is, the principle of its metric relations or the connection of its own parts, so that the linkages can be made in an infinite number of ways. It is a space of virtual conjunction, grasped as pure locus of the possible.

From Chapter 9, The Action-Image: The Large Form

1 From Situation to Action: "Secondness"

We are approaching a domain which is easier to define: derived milieus assert their independence and start to become valid for themselves. Qualities and powers are no longer displayed in any-space-whatevers, no longer inhabit originary worlds, but are actualized directly in determinate, geographical, historical and social space-times. Affects and impulses now only appear as embodied in behavior, in the form of emotions or passions which order and disorder it. This is Realism. . . . It can include the fantastic, the extraordinary, the heroic and above all melodrama. It can include exaggeration and lack of moderation, as long as these are of its own type. What constitutes realism is simply this: milieus and modes of behavior, milieus which actualize and modes of behavior which embody. The action-image is the relation between the two and all the varieties of this relation. It is this model which produced the universal triumph of the American cinema, to the point of acting as a passport for foreign directors who contributed to its formation . . .

The situation, and the character or the action, are like two terms which are simultaneously correlative and antagonistic. The action in itself is a duel of forces, a series of duels: duel with the milieu, with the others, with itself. Finally, the new situation which emerges from the action forms a couple with the initial situation. This is the set [*ensemble*] of the action-image, or at least its first form. It constitutes the organic representation, which seems to be endowed with breath or respiration. For it expands toward the milieu and contracts from the action. More precisely, it expands or contracts on either side, according to the states of the situation and the demands of the action.

In the set nevertheless it can be said that there are, as it were, two inverse spirals, of which one narrows toward action and the other broadens toward the new situation: a form like an hour-glass, or an egg-timer, which includes both space and time. This organic and spiral representation has, as its formula, SAS' (from the situation to the transformed situation via the intermediary of the action). . . . Take for example Sjöström's *The Wind* (his first American film). The wind never stops blowing across the plain. It is almost an originary naturalist world, or even an Expressionist any-space-whatever, the space of the wind as affect. But there is also a whole state of things which actualizes this power, combines it with that of the prairie, in a determinate space, Arizona: a realist milieu. A girl from the South arrives in this country, which she is not used to, and finds herself caught in a series of duels, a physical duel with the milieu, a psychological duel with the hostile family which takes her in, a sentimental duel with the rough cowboy who is in love with her, a bodily duel with the cattle dealer who tries to rape her. Having killed the dealer, she tries desperately to bury him in the sand, but the wind uncovers the corpse each time. This is the moment at which the milieu throws down the strongest challenge to her, and where she reaches the essence [*fond*] of the duel. Reconciliation then begins: with the cowboy who understands and helps her, with the wind, whose power she comprehends as she feels a new mode of being growing within her. . . .

The Western . . . is solidly anchored in a milieu. . . . Here, the principal quality of the image is breath, respiration. It not only inspires the hero, but brings things together in a whole of organic representation and contracts or expands depending on the circumstances. . . . The ultimate encompasser is the sky and its pulsations, not only in Ford, but also in Hawks who makes one of the characters in *Big Sky* say: it is a big country, the only thing that is bigger is the sky.... Encompassed by the sky, the milieu in turn encompasses the collectivity. It is as representative of the collectivity that the hero becomes capable of an action which makes him equal to the milieu and re-establishes its accidentally or periodically endangered order: mediations of the community and of the *land* are necessary in order to form a leader and render an individual capable of such a great action.[22] We recognize the world of Ford, with the intense collective moments (marriage, festival, dances and songs), the constant presence of the land and the immanence of the sky ... The outside encompasses the inside, both communicate, and we advance by passing from the one to the other in both directions, as in the images of *Stagecoach* where the diligence inside alternates with the diligence seen from the outside. One can go from a known to an unknown point, the promised land, as in *Wagonmaster:* the essential point remains the encompasser, which includes both and which expands as one advances painfully and contracts when one stops and rests. Ford's originality lies in the fact that only the encompasser gives measure to movement, or the organic rhythm. It is thus the melting pot of minorities, that is, what brings them together, what reveals their correspondences even when they appear to be opposed, what already shows the fusion between them necessary for the birth of a nation: for example, the three groups of persecuted people who meet in *Wagonmaster*—the Mormons, the travelling players and the Indians.

... In Ford, the hero is not content to re-establish the episodically threatened order. The organization of the film, the organic representation, is not a circle, but a spiral where the situation of arrival differs from the situation of departure: SAS'. It is an ethical rather than an epic form. In *The Man Who Shot Liberty Valance,* the bandit is killed and order re-established: but the cowboy who has killed him allows us to think that it is the future senator, thus accepting the transformation of the law which ceases to be the tacit epic law of the West in order to become the written or novelistic law of industrial civilization. Similarly, in *Two Rode Together,* where this time the sheriff gives up his job and refuses to accept the evolution of the small town.[23] In both cases Ford invents an interesting procedure, which is the modified image: an image is shown twice, but the second time, it is modified or completed in such a way as to make us feel the difference between S and S'. In *Liberty Valance,* the end shows the true death of the bandit and the cowboy who shoots, whilst we had previously seen the truncated image which the official version would stick to (it is the future senator who killed the bandit). In *Two Rode Together,* we are shown the same silhouette of the sheriff in the same posture, but it is no longer the same sheriff. It is true that between the two, between S and S', there is a lot of ambiguity and hypocrisy. The hero of *Liberty Valance* is bent on cleansing himself of the crime in order to become a respectable senator, whilst the journalists are bent on leaving him his legend, without which he would be nothing. And as Roy has shown, *Two Rode Together* has as its subject the spiral of money which, from the start, undermines the community and goes on to enlarge its empire.

But one might say that, in both cases, what counts for Ford is that the community can develop certain illusions about itself. This would be the great difference between healthy and pathogenic milieus . . . One cannot, therefore, criticize the American dream for being only a dream: this is what it wants to be, drawing all its power from the fact that it is a dream. For Ford, as for Vidor, society changes, and does not stop changing, but its changes take place in an Encompasser which covers them and blesses them with a healthy illusion as continuity of the nation.

From Chapter 12, The Crisis of the Action-Image

1 Peirce's "Thirdness" and Mental Relations

It was also Hitchcock's task to introduce the mental image into the cinema and to make it the completion of the cinema, the perfection of all the other images. As Rohmer and Chabrol say of *Dial M for Murder,* "the whole aim of the film is only the exposition of a reasoning, and nevertheless the attention never wanders."[24] And this does not merely come at the end, it starts from the beginning: with its famous false flash-back, *Stage Fright* begins with an interpretation, which is presented as a memory of recent events, or even a perception. In Hitchcock, actions, affections, perceptions, all is interpretation, from beginning to end.[25] *The Rope* is made up of a single shot in so far as the images are only the winding paths of a single reasoning process. The reason for this is simple: in Hitchcock's films an action, once it is given (in present, future or past), is literally surrounded by a set of relations, which vary its subject, nature, aim, etc. What matters is not who did the action—what Hitchcock calls with contempt the *whodunit*—but neither is it the action itself: it is the set of relations in which the action and the one who did it are caught . . .

Hitchcock will, therefore, borrow a particularly striking action of the type "killing," "stealing" from the detective or the spy film. As it is engaged in a set of relations that the characters do not know (but that the spectator already knows or will discover before them), it only appears to be a duel which governs all action: it is already something else, since the relation constitutes the thirdness which elevates it to the state of mental image . . . the criminal has always done his crime *for* another, the true criminal has done his crime for the innocent man who, whether we like it or not, is innocent no longer. In short, the crime is inseparable from the operation by which the criminal has "exchanged" his crime, as in *Strangers on a Train,* or even "given" and "delivered up" his crime to the innocent, as in *I Confess*. One does not commit a crime in Hitchcock, one delivers it up, one gives it or one exchanges it. . . . The relation (the exchange, the gift, the rendering . . .) does not simply surround action, it penetrates it in advance and in all its parts, and transforms it into a necessarily symbolic act. . . . The characters can act, perceive, experience, but they cannot testify to the relations which determine them. These are merely the movements of the camera, and their movements toward the camera. . . . It is the camera, and not a dialogue, which *explains* why the hero of *Rear Window* has a broken leg (photos of the racing car, in his room, broken camera). It is the camera in *Sabotage* which means that the woman, the man and the knife do not simply enter into a succession of pairs, but into a true relation (thirdness) which makes the woman deliver up her crime to the man.[26] In Hitchcock there is never duel or double: even in *Shadow of a Doubt*, the two Charlies, the uncle and the niece, the assassin and the girl, both appeal to the same state of the world which, for the one, justifies his crimes, and, for the other, cannot be justified in producing such a criminal.[27] And, in the history of the cinema Hitchcock appears as one who no longer conceives of the constitution of a film as a function of two terms—the director and the film to be made—but as a function of three: the director, the film and the public which must come into the film, or whose reactions must form an integrating part of the film (this is the explicit sense of suspense, since the spectator is the first to "know" the relations).[28]

. . . Hitchcock . . . begins from relations, the mental image, from what he calls the postulate. It is from this basic postulate that the film is developed with a mathematical or absolute necessity, despite the improbabilities of the plot and the action. Now, if one begins from relations, what happens, by virtue of their very exteriority? It may be that the relation vanishes, suddenly disappears, without the characters changing, but leaving them in the void: the comedy *Mr. and Mrs. Smith* belongs to Hitchcock's oeuvre, precisely because the couple learn all of a sudden that, their marriage not being legal, they have never been married. It may be, on the contrary, that the relation proliferates and multiplies itself, according to the terms in view and the apparent thirds which arise to join up with it, subdividing it or orientating it in a new direction (*The Trouble with Harry*). Finally, it may be that the relation itself passes through variations, depending on variables which carry it out, and entailing changes in one or more characters. In this sense Hitchcock's characters are certainly not intellectuals, but have feelings that can be called intellectual feelings, rather than affects, in that they are modeled on a varied play of experienced conjunctions; because . . . although . . . since . . . if . . . even if . . . (*Secret Agent, Notorious, Suspicion*). In all these cases the relation introduces an essential instability between the characters, the roles, the actions, the set [*décor*]. The model of this instability will be that of the guilty and the innocent. But, also, the autonomous life of the relation will make it tend toward a kind of equilibrium, even though it may be devastated, desperate or even monstrous. The innocent-guilty equilibrium, the restitution to each of his role, the retribution upon each for his action, will be achieved, but at the price of a limit which risks corroding and even effacing the whole like the indifferent face of the wife who has gone crazy in *The Wrong Man*.[29] It is in this respect that Hitchcock is a tragic director: in his work the shot, as always in the cinema, has two faces, the one turned toward the characters, the objects and the actions in movement, the other turned toward a whole which changes progressively as the film goes on. But, in Hitchcock, the whole which changes is the evolution of relations, which move from the disequilibrium that they introduce between characters to the terrible equilibrium that they attain in themselves . . .

Including the spectator in the film, and the film in the mental image, Hitchcock brings the cinema to completion. However, some of Hitchcock's finest films give us a glimpse of a fundamental question. *Vertigo* communicates a genuine image to us; and, certainly, what is vertiginous, is, in the heroine's heart, the relation of the Same with the Same which passes through all the variations of its relations with others (the dead woman, the husband, the inspector). But we cannot forget the other, more ordinary, vertigo—that of the inspector who is incapable of climbing the bell-tower staircase, living in a strange state of contemplation which is communicated to the whole film and which is rare in Hitchcock. And in *Family Plot* the discovery of relations refers, even if jokingly, to a clairvoyant function. In a still more direct way the hero of *Rear Window* has access to the mental image, not simply because he is a photographer, but because he is in a state of immobility: he is reduced as it were to a pure optical situation. If one of Hitchcock's innovations was to implicate the spectator in the film, did not the characters themselves have to be capable—in a more or less obvious manner—of being assimilated to spectators? But then it may be that one consequence appears inevitable: the mental image would then be less a bringing to completion of the action-image, and of the other images, than a re-examination of their nature and status, moreover, the whole movement-image which would be re-examined through the rupture of the sensory-motor links in a particular character. What Hitchcock had wanted to avoid, a crisis of the traditional image of the cinema, would nevertheless happen in his wake, and in part as a result of his innovations.

Notes

1. Gilles Deleuze and Félix Guattari, *What Is Philosophy?*, trans. Hugh Tomlinson and Graham Burchell (New York: Columbia University Press, 1994), p. 5.
2. See books 2 and 3 of Spinoza's *Ethics* (1664–1665), trans. Robert Hurley (London: Penguin, 1996).

3. Gilles Deleuze, *Negotiations, 1972–1990*, trans. Martin Joughin (New York: Columbia University Press, 1995), p. 6.

4. A number of Deleuze's books were written in association with Félix Guattari, including *Anti-Oedipus: Capitalism and Schizophrenia* (1972), its follow-up, *A Thousand Plateaus: Capitalism and Schizophrenia* (1980), and *Kafka: Toward a Minor Literature* (1975).

5. Keith Ansell Pearson, *Philosophy and the Adventure of the Virtual: Bergson and the Time of Life* (London: Routledge, 2002), p. 51.

6. Deleuze, *Negotiations*, p. 58. On this subject of inventing concepts, Deleuze said, "I put forward almost raw concepts . . . while others work with more mediations. I've never worried about going beyond metaphysics or the death of philosophy, and I have never made a big thing about giving up Totality, Unity, the Subject. I've never renounced a kind of empiricism, which sets out to present concepts directly. I haven't approached things through linguistics or psychoanalysis, through science or even through history, because I think philosophy has the raw materials that allows it to enter into more fundamental external relations with these other disciplines" (pp. 88–89).

7. Deleuze, *Negotiations*, p. 59.

8. Dziga Vertov, "Kinoks: A Revolution," in *Kino-Eye: The Writings of Dzigo Vertov*, ed. with an introduction by Annette Michelson, trans. Kevin O'Brien (Berkeley: University of California Press, 1984), pp. 17–18.

9. Dziga Vertov, "From Kino-Eye to Radio-Eye," in *Kino-Eye*, pp. 87–88.

10. Gilles Deleuze, *Cinema I: The Movement-Image*, trans. Hugh Tomlinson and Barbara Habberjam (Minneapolis: University of Minnesota Press, 1986), p. 80.

11. Deleuze, p. 217.

12. Deleuze, p. 87.

13. Deleuze, p. 103.

14. Deleuze, p. 98.

15. Deleuze, p. 155.

16. John Mullarkey and Gilles Deleuze, *Film, Theory, and Philosophy: The Key Thinkers*, ed. Felicity Coleman (Durham: Acumen, 2009), p. 183.

17. Sergei Eisenstein, *Mémoires*, vol. 1 (Paris: Boutique 10/18, 1978), pp. 283–84.

18. Immanuel Kant, *Critique of Judgment*, trans. Werner S. Pluhar (Indianapolis: Hackett, 1987), paras 26–28.

19. Dziga Vertov, *Articles, journaux, projets* (Paris: Union générale d'editions, 1972), pp. 126–27.

20. Cf. the articles by Jean Semolué and Michel Estève in *Jeanne d'Arc à l'ecran: Etudes cinématographiques*, Procès de Jeanne d'Arc, 18–19, 1962.

21. Robert Bresson, *Notes on Cinematography*, trans. Jonathan Griffin (New York: Urizen, 19771977), p. 46: "ON FRAGMENTATION: This is indispensable if one does not want to fall into REPRESENTATION. To see beings and things in their separate parts. To isolate these parts. Render them independent in order to give them a new dependence."

22. English in the original.

23. A scrupulous analysis of *Two Rode Together* can be found in Jean Roy, *Pour John Ford* (Paris: Éditions du Cerf, 1976.). He emphasizes the "spiral" character of the film, and shows that this form of the spiral is common in Ford (p. 120). See also his excellent analysis of *Wagonmaster*, pp. 56–59.

24. Éric Rohmer and Claude Chabrol, *Hitchcock* (Paris: Éditions Universitaires, 1957), p. 124.

25. Cf. Jean Narboni, "Visages d'Hitchcock," in François Truffaut, *Le Cinéma selon Hitchcock* (Paris: Robert Laffont, 1966).

26. On these two examples, cf. Truffaut, *Le Cinéma selon Hitchcock*, pp. 165 and 79–82. And p. 15: "Hitchcock is the only film-maker to be able to film and to make perceptible to us the thoughts of one or several characters without the help of dialogue."

27. Rohmer and Chabrol, *Hitchcock*, pp. 76–78, in this respect complete the work of Truffaut, who had only emphasized the importance of the figure 2 in *Shadow of a Doubt*. They show that, even there, there is a relation of exchange.

28. Truffaut, *Le Cinéma selon Hitchcock*, p. 14: "The art of creating suspense is at the same time that of putting the public in the know by making it participate in the film. In the sphere of the spectacle, making a film is no longer a game played by two (the director and his film) but by three (the director and his film and the public)." Jean Douchet in particular has emphasized this inclusion of the spectator in the film in his *Alfred Hitchcock* (Paris: Éditions de l'Herne, 1967). And Douchet often discovers a ternary structure in the very content of Hitchcock's films (p. 49): for example, with *North by Northwest*, 1, 2, 3 in such conditions that the first is himself, 1 (the head of the FBI), the second, 2 (the couple), and the third, 3 (the trio of spies). This is completely in line with Peirce's thirdness.

29. This is why one finds commentaries both on an "essential instability of the image" in Hitchcock (Bazin) and on "a strange equilibrium," as a limit, "and which defines the constitutive defect" of human nature (Rohmer and Chabrol, *Hitchcock*, p. 117).

CHAPTER 9

CINEMA II

The Time-Image

GILLES DELEUZE

*Time is out of joint: Hamlet's words signify that time is no longer subor-
dinated to movement, but rather movement to time . . . The movement-
image of the so-called classical cinema gave way, in the post-war period,
to a direct time-image.*[1]

*We no longer believe in a whole as interiority of thought—even an open
one; we believe in a force from the outside which hollows itself out, grabs
us and attracts the inside. We no longer believe in an association of
images—even crossing voids; we believe in breaks which take on an absolute value and subordinate all association.*[2]

With Hitchcock's later films, such as *Rear Window* and *Vertigo*, affect (Stewart's immobility) begins to exceed the linkage of images so that eventually with the full-blown cinema
of the time-image sequences of images operate as if added to one another irra-
tionally: 1+ 1+ 1+, etc. However radical the cinema of the movement-image, it is
still characterized by linked-up images. The film's cuts—edited cuts, changes
of camera angle, dissolves, fades, and so on—are, for Deleuze, lacunae or voids
and, as such, irreducible to understanding. Deleuze argues that these cuts in
the movement-image are repressed, that is to say "rationalized," and made to
act as linkages for the purposes of continuity, used to associate images together

and, thereby, offer a sense of the whole, "rational cuts always determine commensurable relations between series of images, and thereby constitute the whole rhythmic system and harmony of classical cinema, at the same time as they integrate associated images in an always open totality."[3]

In this scenario time is expressed indirectly through various forms of change and becoming. But for time to be expressed directly, it is necessary that the film's cuts become "irrational" so that their inherent lacunae can be affirmed. Thus, the "irrational cut" in the time-image,

> is no longer a lacuna that the associated images would be assumed to cross; the images are certainly not abandoned to chance, but there are only relinkages subject to the cut, instead of cuts subject to the linkage. . . . Ultimately, there are no longer any rational cuts, but only irrational ones. There is thus no longer association through metaphor or metonymy, but relinkage on the literal image; there is no longer linkage of associated images, but only relinkages of independent images. Instead of one image after the other, there is one image *plus* another, and each shot is deframed in relation to the framing of the following shot.[4]

"Irrational cuts" rather than "rational cuts" that imply a continual process of broken "relinkages" rather than "linkages." As Deleuze says of Godard, one of the proponents of the cinema of the time-image, "It is the method of BETWEEN, 'between two images' which does away with all cinema of the One. It is the method of AND, 'this and then that,' which does away with all the cinema of Being = is. Between two actions, between two affections, between two perceptions, between two visual images, between two sound images, between the sound and the visual: make the indiscernible, that is the frontier, visible (*Six fois deux*)."[5]

The "frontier" that Deleuze refers to is infinity (that is, time). *Cinema II: The Time-Image* (1985) outlines the ways in which the work of the film directors of the "modern school" are "hollowed out" by time; succession, associations, development still persist but, ultimately, there is a blind force that undermines the very idea of a whole. Thus, it will be seen that the method by which this is achieved by different postwar directors operates variously through feedback loops, or in the form of divisible crystals of time, or across inexplicable differences between points of the present, or through sheets of virtual atemporalities that may be either separate or contiguous.

From Chapter 1, Beyond the Movement-Image

Deleuze characterizes the essence of Antonioni's films as "Eros sick." He compares the director's work to Nietzsche's "symptomatologist method," a reference to his evaluation of the vitality of a culture in terms of its libidinal and psychic desire for change and becoming, a desire that Nietzsche christened "the will to power." Haunted by the ghost of an absent figure, a former lover, a vanished or dead woman—*Story of a Love Affair* (1950), *The Outcry* (1957), *The Adventure* (1960), *Identification of a Woman* (1982)—the desperately aimless protagonists of Antonioni's films possess little capacity to change their lives. This haunting absence is transposed into the gaze of the camera that seems to watch the protagonists' doomed struggles to find love. Deleuze cites the lift scene in *Story of a Love Affair* that exemplifies this state of affairs. The eponymous story is of an adulterous couple, Paola and Guido, both of whom are haunted by the death of a mutual friend in an elevator shaft fall some years previously (it turns out that Paola and Guido did not act to prevent their friend's death). In this particular scene, the couple ducks into a hotel lobby and mounts the stairs to escape being seen by Paola's jealous husband. Significantly enough, given what happened in the past, the camera pans across the hotel's elevator shaft, so that the shaft remains in the foreground throughout the scene, until finally the scene closes with a view of the shaft's vertiginous depth. Spatially and emotionally, the couple is lost in a "disconnected space" that Deleuze defines as the first type of the "any-space-whatever" (as seen in Bresson's films discussed earlier). The second type of the "any-space-whatever"—"empty or deserted space"—predominates in *The Adventure* and in many of the films from *The Eclipse* (1962) onward. In these films the empty gaze of the camera sets the tone for the profound melancholy that grips the protagonists and places them in crisis. However much the protagonists attempt to communicate with each other and establish a sense of mutuality, they are continually blocked in their attempts to achieve this. As such, these films are "subject to rapid breaks, interpolations, and infinitesimal injections of a-temporality" (see, particularly, the final scenes of *The Eclipse* set in the brave new world of Rome's suburbs as well as the lift scene in *Story of a Love Affair* to which Deleuze refers). The imaginary realm of the missing person's/camera's empty gaze circumscribes all the protagonists to the point that they themselves are another facet of this shadowy emptiness, "The imaginary gaze makes the real something imaginary at the same time as it in turn becomes real and gives us back some reality. It is like a circuit which exchanges, corrects, selects and sends us off again."

From Chapter 5, Peaks of Present and Sheets of Past . . .

Deleuze analyses the relationship between the actual and virtual initially by mapping the temporalities of the present and the past/future onto these respective terms. However, in Deleuze's thinking the actual is the present and the virtual is synonymous with the past, encompassing all that has occurred as well as the infinite possibilities of what might have occurred and might be taken up in the future. For Deleuze, the past is not fixed in memory or time; quite the opposite: the past is open to change and becoming. As Deleuze points out the actual present is composed of two aspects: the present "itself," but also the virtual past/future that encompasses even the present "itself." Indeed, Deleuze argues that the present requires this virtuality so that it can become past.

The past's openness to change and its infinite possibilities is taken up by Deleuze in connection with Alain Resnais's *Last Year at Marienbad* (1961), which was scripted by Alain Robbe-Grillet. Deleuze argues that such infinite possibilities for the registers of present and past are explored in conflicting ways by Resnais's and Robbe-Grillet's different contributions to the film, which are reflected in the diverging desires of the principle characters. On the one hand, Resnais constructs an "architecture of time," an archaeological topology consisting of multiple possible layers or "sheets" of past times and events, to which X (the man) refers in an attempt to "envelop" A (the woman). As Deleuze says of Resnais's ideas on this subject of memory, "In Resnais, there are no more flashbacks, but rather feedbacks and failed feedbacks."[6] On the other hand, Robbe-Grillet is concerned with the idea of a "perpetual present," or peaks of the present, composed of multiple points of deactualized presents (since the present is never at one with itself, owing to the fact that it is always double, both actual and virtual). Robbe-Grillet's concerns eschew Resnais's interest in notions of dreams, fantasies, and hallucinations that are the stuff of memory insofar as it also involves forgetting as much as remembering (what Deleuze terms "the imaginary"). Robbe-Grillet's idea of multiple points of the present infuses the film with an immobility that, nevertheless, offers opportunities for A to jump "from one bloc to another, continually crossing an abyss between two points, two simultaneous presents," and hence avoid X's persistent attempts to envelop her in his desires for time to change. In connection with the "crystal" structure (as Deleuze calls it) of *Last Year at Marienbad*, a structure of division that has the capacity to create an exchange between the actual and the virtual, Deleuze states,

> For the time-image to be born . . . the actual image must enter into relation with its *own* virtual image, as such; from the outset pure description must divide in two "repeat itself, take itself up again, fork, contradict, itself." An image which is double-sided, mutual, both actual and virtual, must be constituted. We are no longer in the situation of a relationship between the actual and other virtual images, recollections or dreams, which thus become actual in turn; this is still a mode of linkage. We are in the situation of an actual image and its own virtual image, to the extent that there is no longer any linkage of the real with the imaginary, but *indiscernibility of the two*, a perpetual exchange.[7]

In other words, the present and the past and, by implication, the future become indiscernible. Since the present can contain its past, rather than falling into it, this allows A to escape X's own desire for time to change, because the past is already a part of her. Thus, Deleuze's concept of "the crystal image" of time is as a multifaceted crystal that simultaneously contains the past, present, and future, to the point where they are indiscernible as different facets of these temporalities come to light.

From Chapter 6, The Powers of the False

In this section, Deleuze offers a reading of "the powers of the false," drawing together Orson Welles's films with Nietzsche's philosophy "beyond good and evil." Arguing that Welles's films are engaged in a deconstruction of the metaphysical relationship between truth and falsity, reality and appearances, and, ultimately, good and evil, Deleuze refers to the section in Nietzsche's *Twilight of the Idols* (1889) entitled "The History of an Error: How the True World Finally Became a Fable." This passage concludes, "with the real world we have also abolished the apparent world." Deleuze believes that this conclusion delivers the final blow to the hierarchically constructed oppositions of the Western tradition of metaphysics sustained from Plato onward. The logic that Nietzsche pursues in "The History of an Error" undoes the traditional Western metaphysical valuation in which truth was prized over falsity, reality over appearances (a devaluation that also implicated illusion, artifice, and images), and moral good over evil. The particular metaphysical reasoning that is at work in this tradition is that truth, reality, and the good are conceived of as fixed and unchanging essences that exist as moral ideals; compared to these ideals, falsity, appearances, and evil are found to be wanting—they are *lacking* in truth, *lacking* any element of reality, *lacking* in goodness. But Nietzsche rejects fixed, essentialist ideals of truth, reality, and the good and, in an initial deconstructive step, abolishes them as philosophical irrelevances. Thereafter, Nietzsche asks what are the consequences of this step? Notions of falsity, appearances, and evil remain, but they are no longer situated within a metaphysical dyad in which they are contrasted negatively to their respective ideals. Rather, as they are *all* that remain, they possess the same status that truth, reality, and the good formerly held, and, in effect, no difference can be discerned between these oppositions. This is what lies behind Deleuze's interest in Welles's problematization of the question of judgment. Rather than metaphysical oppositions constructing symbolic and moral valuations, Deleuze, following Nietzsche, proposes that what are in play in a revalued world are *forces*: active and reactive forces, "There remain bodies, which are forces, nothing but forces." Active forces affirm life in all its potential becomings (these forces are of the kind that Nietzsche explores in his concept of the "will to power as art"). On the other hand, reactive forces strive for fixity and are resistant to change, often harboring a "ressentiment"—that is, a desire for revenge against the forces of life; hence, the desire to judge others, and even life, as morally deficient or evil. Ultimately, Quinlan in Welles's *Touch of Evil* (1958) is an example of a reactive force, for although he is an immense character both physically and personally, nevertheless, he clings desperately to power (his planting of false evidence eventually costs him his life). Deleuze also cites Vargas, the upright cop opposed to Quinlan, as an example of a reactive force, since he is obsessed with the law, justice, and the truth, the consequence of which nearly costs him his marriage. Shakespeare's Othello (Welles's film *Othello* was released in 1951) is a reactive force seeking the truth "out of jealousy, or, worse, out of revenge for being black." Othello, of course, in the end loses everything, and, while a reactive force can often exercise considerable strength and power, it is often characterized by a self-destructive tendency: hence, the story of the frog stung by a scorpion that it carries over the river in *Mr. Arkadin* (1955), to which Deleuze relates not only the characters of Arkadin himself but also Bannister in *The Lady from Shanghai* (1947), Iago in *Othello,* as well as Quinlan. While Iago may differ significantly from *Othello*—the former harbors a perverse ressentiment toward life and the latter, initially, seeks higher values of affirmation—they are both, ultimately, forces of a reactive nihilism, two sides of the same coin that no longer transform themselves. On the other hand, Welles developed characters exemplifying an active force in life's becoming, such as Falstaff (*Falstaff: Chimes at Midnight* [1965]) and *Don Quixote* (in an unfinished film begun in 1957), both of whom, Deleuze says, possess a sense of abundant life and vivacity, "an artistic will or 'virtue which gives,' the creation of new possibilities, in the outpouring becoming."[8]

Deleuze suggests that the consequence of the multiple movements of active and reactive forces in a perpetual process of affirmative becoming and exhaustion is the loss of a center of gravity. This is reflected particularly in the "jumble of vanishing centers" in the opening sequence of *Touch of Evil*. With this loss, movement gives way to time; composed of a series of recollections, films such as *Citizen Kane* (1941) and *Mr. Arkadin* undermine the idea of a fixed point in time in which a secret or a mystery can be discovered, for instance, the "mystery" of the word *Rosebud* in *Citizen Kane*: as one of the journalists at the end of the film says, "I don't think any word can explain a man's life." Clearly, this understanding runs counter to a psychoanalytic interpretation of the film. Rather, Deleuze's reading draws upon the fact that the life of Charles Kane in the film is recalled in flashback through the contingent memories of his various friends and colleagues. In *The Trial* (1962), Deleuze states, "*Nothing is decidable any more,*"[9] and yet, in this bottomless sense of time, different sheets of time can be also contiguous with each other. This is the meaning, for Deleuze, of Welles's frequent use of depth of field in deep focus, a cinematic technique in which objects in the foreground and deep background are all in focus; for instance, the scene of the parents' boarding house at the beginning of *Citizen Kane* and the kitchen scene in *The Magnificent Ambersons* (1942). However far apart the sheets of time are from one another, there remains the possibility that they can be reordered into a different sequence so that an altered past offers the chance for an altered present that would break open the terrible stagnancy that besets many of Welles's characters.

From Chapter 7, Thought and Cinema

In the cinema of the movement-image there existed a capacity to think the whole (not just the whole of the film but also the whole of time as an open past with an open future). However, in the cinema of the time-image the whole, as such, no longer exists. What results from the inexistence of the whole that no longer can be thought are certain paradoxes with respect to thought. Maurice Blanchot outlines these paradoxes, which Deleuze subsequently applies to cinema, "the presence of an unthinkable in thought, which would be both its source and barrier . . . the presence to infinity of another thinker in the thinker, who shatters every monologue of a thinking self."[10] Deleuze emphasizes that the cinema of the time-image does not make the matter of thinking transparent and graspable within a conceivable whole, "the cinematographic image . . . carries out a *suspension of the world* or affects the visible with a *disturbance*, which far from making thought visible, as Eisenstein wanted, are on the contrary directed to what does not let itself be thought in thought, and equally to what does not let itself be seen in vision."[11] Deleuze goes on to link these ideas to his foregoing discussion of "the power of the false" with respect to Nietzsche in terms of a revaluation of the metaphysical dyad of truth and appearances. The issue of "disturbance" can be seen at work in modern cinema's break with the action-image through the use of various strategies of alienation and disruption, along with many other formal affects in Godard's films, that are often foregrounded in the films of the *Nouvelle Vague*, especially those of Godard (such as the frequent introduction of burlesque, a desynchronization between image and sound, and the use of jump cuts that create, Deleuze asserts, "false continuities").

Deleuze observes that the basis for Godard's films are often different types of genre: he cites the musical comedy (*Une Femme est une femme* [1961]), the comic strip (*Made in USA* [1966]), and the war movie (*Les Carabiniers* [1963]), to which could be added many different aspects of American film noir (gangster movie, crime thriller, lovers on the run, conspiracy plot) that inform films such as *Vivre sa vie* (1962), *Bande à part* (1964), *Le Petit soldat* (1960), and *Pierrot le fou* (1965). Usually, there are several, if not more, genres referenced in Godard's films, and, together, Deleuze says, these shape their form into a composition of series not unlike a musical score, albeit a score that is composed of repetitions and not necessarily linked in terms of continuities. Thus, the genres referenced in the various sequences of Godard's films are no longer dominant as shaping forms but rather constitute "the limit of images." Ultimately, this is because many of Godard's films continually play upon an interchange between the love story and the virtual, with the effect that the actual, as such, is almost entirely superseded by *desire*. What is at stake, for instance, in *Une Femme est une femme* is Angela's desire and the virtual choices before her for pursuing this. In the story of the film, Angela wants to choose the right man with whom to lead her life and have a child. The "great square pillar in the middle of the bedroom and the patch of white wall between two doors" in Angela's apartment are cuts forming compositional discontinuities, which Deleuze says represent "the virtualities of the heroine"—that is, the cuts and jumps between possible choices virtualized in sheets of time that compose her desire. Genre in this film, for instance, the dance and striptease sequences, are moments in Angela's pursuit of her desire, staged enactments of this desire as much as, if not more than, scenes of seduction and masculine voyeuristic pleasure. This is what Deleuze means when he says, "It is characteristic of cinema . . . to 'do' cinema, to do dance, to do novel, to do theatre." Godard's films, like Hitchcock's films before him, are "reflective"; whereas Hitchcock's films displaced plot into the milieu of the characters, so the characters in Godard's films embody in their singular ways their own questions that emerge to counter any purported continuity to the whole. Sometimes, Deleuze, says, the characters require "interceders" to aid them in this quest to think the unthinkable, like the discussion in the café between Nana and the philosopher Brice Perain in *Vivre sa vie*. Deleuze observes that Godard's use of color can function as a category. Here Deleuze has in mind Kant's notion of the categories as expounded in the *Critique of Pure Reason*. Color in Godard functions not so much as a category of understanding, as in Kant, but rather as a primordial quality that can substitute metonymically for the identity of a place, an encounter, or an event. Such are the colors blue, green, and gray characterizing Lausanne in Godard's *Letter to Freddy Buache* (1982). Another example is the color green in *La Chinoise* (1967), which acts as a counterpoint to the primary colors red, blue, and yellow embellished around the Parisian apartment where the young group struggle to forge a new language. The green of the countryside, and of the silent majorities living in the suburbs, seen through the window of the train, absorbs Veronique's communist/terrorist aspirations (red, blue, and yellow) as she expresses them to Francis Jeanson.[12]

From Chapter 10, Conclusions

Deleuze recognizes that, with the advent of the digital image, along with new networks of distribution and screening, "cinema" may be something that seems outdated, an art form that has become redundant. But, for Deleuze, "cinema" is not about whether the medium is analogical or digital. Rather, the essential issue at stake is time and the legacy of the cinema for the time-image that affirmed time unconditionally by virtue of the inexistence of a whole and the overcoming of linked-up space. Like the cinema of the time-image, digital images, Deleuze says, operate in any-space-whatever without an inside or outside or in terms of a whole, "They are the object of a perpetual reorganization, in which a new image can arise from any point whatever of the preceding image." These affects were already anticipated in the cinema of the time-image and, so too, the spectral quality of the automaton-like personae of the digital world, in relation to which Deleuze cites as precedents the protagonists in the films of Bresson, Rohmer, and Resnais, all of whom are conditioned by the irreducible temporalities of "the powers of the false."

Nevertheless, Deleuze implicitly acknowledges that a new epoch of images is, indeed, in the process of development. Whether this production will be subordinated to the interests of "business," "pornography," and the dictates of a persistent "Hitlerism" depends, Deleuze, says, on whether an "original will to art" can emerge to counter these traits, in the same way as such a will emerged to create the event that was the time-image. Deleuze affirms that such a will is required if the exploitative misuses of technology are to be defeated.

* * *

From Chapter 1, Beyond the Movement-Image

In Antonioni, from his first great work, *Story of a Love Affair,* the police investigation, instead of proceeding by flashback, transforms the actions into optical and sound descriptions, whilst the tale itself is transformed into actions which are dislocated in time (the episode where the maid talks while repeating her tired gestures, or the famous scene with the lifts).[13] And Antonioni's art will continue to evolve in two directions: an astonishing development of the idle periods of everyday banality; then, starting with *The Eclipse,* a treatment of limit-situations which pushes them to the point of dehumanized landscapes, of emptied spaces that might be seen as having absorbed characters and actions, retaining only a geophysical description, an abstract inventory of them . . .

The optical and sound situations of neo-realism contrast with the strong sensory-motor situations of traditional realism. The space of a sensory-motor situation is a setting which is already specified and presupposes an action which discloses it, or prompts a reaction which adapts to or modifies it. But a purely optical or sound situation becomes established in what we might call "any-space-whatever," whether disconnected, or emptied (we find the passage from one to the other in *The Eclipse,* where the disconnected bits of space lived by the heroine—stock exchange, Africa, air terminal—are reunited at the end in an empty space which blends into the white surface). In neo-realism, the sensory-motor connections are now valid only by virtue of the upsets that affect, loosen, unbalance, or uncouple them: the crisis of the action-image. . . .

Antonioni's aesthetic visions are inseparable from an objective critique (we are sick with Eros, because Eros is himself objectively sick: what has love become that a man or a woman should emerge from it so disabled, pitiful and suffering, and act and react as badly at the beginning as at the end, in a corrupt society?) . . .

The distinctions, on one hand between the banal and the extreme, and on the other between the subjective and the objective, have some value, but only relatively. They are valid for an image or a sequence, but not for the whole. They are still valid in relation to the action-image, which they bring into question, but already they are no longer wholly valid in relation to the new image that is coming into being. They mark poles between which there is continual passage. In fact, the most banal or everyday situations release accumulated "dead forces" equal to the life force of a limit-situation (thus, in De Sica's *Umberto D,* the sequence where the old man examines himself and thinks he has fever). In addition, the idle periods in Antonioni do not merely show banalities of daily life, they reap the consequences or the effect of a remarkable event which is reported only through itself without being explained (the break-up of a couple, the sudden disappearance of a woman . . .). The method of report in Antonioni always has this function of bringing idle periods and empty spaces together: drawing all the consequences from a decisive past experience, once it is done and everything has been said. "When everything has been said, when the main scene seems over, there is what comes afterwards . . ."[14]

As for the distinction between subjective and objective, it also tends to lose its importance, to the extent that the optical situation or visual description replaces the motor action. We run in fact into a principle of indeterminability, of indiscernibility: we no longer know what is imaginary or real, physical or mental, in the situation, not because they are confused, but because we do not have to know and there is no longer even a place from which to ask. It is as if the real and the imaginary were running after each other, as if each was being reflected in the other, around a point of indiscernibility.

. . . In Antonioni, it is as if the most objective images are not formed without becoming mental, and going into a strange, invisible subjectivity. It is not merely that the method of report has to be applied to feelings as they exist in a society, and to draw from them such consequences as are internally developed in characters: Eros sick is a story of feelings which go from the objective to the subjective, and are internalized in everyone. In this respect, Antonioni is much closer to Nietzsche than to Marx; he is the only contemporary author to have taken up the Nietzschean project of a real critique of morality, and this thanks to a "symptomatologist" method. But, from yet another point of view, it is noticeable that Antonioni's objective images, which impersonally follow a becoming, that is, a development of consequences in a story [*récit*], none the less are subject to rapid breaks, interpolations and "infinitesimal injections of a-temporality": for example, the lift scene in *Story of a Love Affair*. We are returned once more to the first form of the any-space-whatever: disconnected space. The connection of the parts of space is not given, because it can come about only from the subjective point of view of a character who is, nevertheless, absent, or has even disappeared, not simply out of frame, but passed into the void. In *The Outcry*, Irma is not only the obsessive, subjective thought of the hero who runs away to forget, but the imaginary gaze under which this flight takes place and connects its own segments: a gaze which becomes real again at the moment of death. And, above all in *The Adventure*, the vanished woman causes an indeterminable gaze to weigh on the couple—which gives them the continual feeling of being spied on, and which explains the lack of co-ordination of their objective movements, when they flee whilst pretending to look for her. Again in *Identification of a Woman*, the whole quest or investigation takes place under the presumed gaze of the departed woman, concerning whom we will not know, in the marvelous images at the end, whether or not she has seen the hero curled up in the lift cage. The imaginary gaze makes the real something imaginary, at the same time as it in turn becomes real and gives us back some reality. It is like a circuit which exchanges, corrects, selects and sends us off again. From *The Eclipse* onward, the any-space-whatever had achieved a second form: empty or deserted space. What happened is that, from one result to the next, the characters were objectively emptied: they are suffering less from the absence of another than from their absence from themselves (for example, *The Passenger*). Hence, this space refers back again to the lost gaze of the being who is absent from the world as much as from himself.

From Chapter 5, Peaks of Present and Sheets of Past . . .

The crystal reveals a direct time-image, and no longer an indirect image of time deriving from movement. It does not abstract time; it does better: it reverses its subordination in relation to movement. The crystal is like a *ratio cognoscendi* of time, while time, conversely, is *ratio essendi*.[15] What the crystal reveals or makes visible is the hidden ground of time, that is, its differentiation into two flows, that of presents which pass and that of pasts which are preserved. Time simultaneously makes the present pass and preserves the past in itself. There are, therefore, already, two possible time-images, one grounded in the past, the other in the present. Each is complex and is valid for time as a whole . . .

Still more instructive is the confrontation between Robbe-Grillet and Resnais in *Last Year in Marienbad.* What seems extraordinary in this collaboration is that two authors (for Robbe-Grillet was not just scriptwriter) produced so coherent a work while approaching it in such different and almost opposite ways. They perhaps reveal in this way the truth about all real collaboration, where the work is not simply understood but constructed according to quite different creative procedures which marry to make a success that is repeatable but each time unique. This confrontation between Resnais and Robbe-Grillet is complex, blurred by their extremely amicable statements, and may be considered on three different levels. First, there is a level of "modern" cinema, marked by the crises of the action-image. *Last Year . . .* was itself an important point in this crisis: the failure of sensory-motor models, the wandering of characters, the rise of clichés and postcards were a constant inspiration in Robbe-Grillet's work. And in his work the bonds of the captive woman do not just have erotic and sadistic value, they are the simplest way to stop the movement.[16] But in Resnais too, wanderings, immobilizings, petrifications and repetitions are constant evidence of a general dissolution of the action-image. The second level is that of the real and the imaginary: it has been noted that, for Resnais, there is always something real which persists, and notably spatio-temporal co-ordinates maintaining their reality, even though they come into conflict with the imaginary. It is in this way that Resnais maintains that something actually did happen "Last Year . . . ," and, in his subsequent films, establishes a topography and a chronology which are all the more rigorous because what happens in them is imaginary or mental.[17] While in Robbe-Grillet everything happens "in the head" of the characters, or, better, of the viewer himself. Yet this difference exhibited by Robbe-Grillet is hardly the point. Nothing happens in the viewer's head which does not derive from the character of the image. . . . In the image, a distinction is always made between the real and the imaginary, the objective and the subjective, the physical and the mental, and the actual and the virtual, but that this distinction becomes reversible, and in that sense indiscernible. *Distinct and yet indiscernible*—these are the characteristics of the imaginary and the real in each of the two authors. So that the difference between the two can only appear in other ways. It would present itself rather in the manner identified by Mireille Latil: large continuums of real and imaginary in Resnais, in contrast to Robbe-Grillet's discontinuous blocs or "shocks." But this new criterion seems incapable of development at the level of the imaginary-real pair; a third level must necessarily intervene—this is time.[18]

Robbe-Grillet himself suggests that the difference between himself and Resnais must ultimately be sought at the level of time. The dissolution of the action-image, and the indiscernibility which results, sometimes take place in favor of an "architecture of time" (this would be the case with Resnais), sometimes in favor of a "perpetual present" cut off from its temporality, that is, of a structure stripped of time (the case of Robbe-Grillet himself).[19] Nevertheless, here again we should not rush into thinking that a perpetual present implies less time-image than an eternal past. The present belongs no less to time than the pure past. The difference is thus in the nature of the time-image, which is plastic in one case and architectural in the other. For Resnais conceived *Last Year . . .* like his other films, in the form of sheets or regions of past, while Robbe-Grillet sees time in the form of points of present. If *Last Year . . .* could be divided, the man X might be said to be closer to Resnais, and the woman A closer to Robbe-Grillet. The man basically tries to envelop the woman with con-tinuous sheets of which the present is the narrowest, like the advance of a wave, whilst the woman, at times wary, at times stiff, at times almost convinced, jumps from one bloc to another, continually crossing an abyss between two points, two simultaneous presents. In any event, the two authors . . . are no lon-ger in the domain of the real and the imaginary but in time, in the even more alarming domain of the true and the false. Of course the real and the imagi-nary continue their circuit, but only as the base of a higher figure. This is no longer, or no longer only, the *indiscernible becoming* of distinct images; it is *undecidable alternatives* between circles of past, *inextricable differences* between peaks of present. With Resnais and Robbe-Grillet, an understanding occurs, all the stronger for being based on two opposed conceptions of time which crashed into each other. The coexistence of sheets of virtual past, and the simul-taneity of peaks of deactualized present, are the two direct signs of time itself.

From Chapter 6, The Powers of the False

There is a Nietzscheanism in Welles, as if Welles were retracing the main points of Nietzsche's critique of truth: the "true world" does not exist, and, if it did, would be inaccessible, impossible to describe, and, if it could be described, would be useless, superfluous. The true world implies a "truthful man," a man who wants the truth, but such a man has strange motives, as if he were hiding another man in him, a revenge: Othello wants the truth, but out of jealousy, or, worse, out of revenge for being black, and Vargas, the epitome of the truthful man, for a long time seems indifferent to the fate of his wife, engrossed in the archives in amassing proofs against his enemy. The truthful man in the end wants nothing other than to judge life; he holds up a superior value, the good, in the name of which he will be able to judge, he is craving to judge, he sees in life an evil, a fault which is to be atoned for: the moral origin of the notion of truth. In the Nietzschean fashion, Welles has constantly battled against the system of judgment: there is no value superior to life, life is not to be judged or justified, it is innocent, it has "the innocence of becoming" beyond good and evil . . .[20]

In Welles, the system of judgment becomes definitively impossible, even and especially for the viewer. The ransacking of the judge's office in *The Lady from Shanghai,* and especially the infinite sham of judgment in *The Trial,* will be evidence of this new impossibility. Welles constantly constructs characters who are unjudicable and who have not to be judged, who evade any possible judgment. If the ideal of truth crumbles, the relations of appearance will no longer be sufficient to maintain the possibility of judgment. In Nietzsche's phrase, "with the real world we have also abolished the apparent world."[21]

What remains? There remain bodies, which are forces, nothing but forces. But force no longer refers to a center, any more than it confronts a setting or obstacles. It only confronts other forces, it refers to other forces, that it affects or that affect it. Power (what Nietzsche calls "will to power" and Welles, "character") is this power to affect and be affected, this relation between one force and others. This power is always fulfilled, and this relation is necessarily carried out, even if in a variable manner according to the forces which are present.[22] We already sense that short, cut-up and piecemeal montage, and the long sequence shot serve the same purpose. The one presents bodies in a successive way, each of which exercises its force or experiences that of another: "each shot shows a blow, a counter-blow, a blow received, a blow struck."[23] The other presents in a simultaneous way a relation of forces in its variability, in its instability, its proliferation of centers and multiplication of vectors (the scene of the questioning in *Touch of Evil*).[24] In both cases, there is the shock of forces, in the image or of the images between themselves. Sometimes a short montage reproduces a sequence shot, through cutting, as in the battle in *Chimes at Midnight,* or a sequence shot produces a short montage, through constant reframing, as in *Touch of Evil* . . .

Is this to say that, in life, everything is a matter of forces? Yes, if it is understood that the relation of forces is not quantitative, but necessarily implies certain "qualities." There are forces which are now able to respond to others only in a single, uniform and invariable way: the scorpion in *Mr. Arkadin* knows only how to sting, and stings the frog that carries him over the water, even if it means death by drowning. Variability thus survives in the relation of forces, since the scorpion's sting turns against itself, when it is directed in this case at the frog. None the less, the scorpion is the type of a force which no longer knows how to metamorphose itself according to the variations of what it can affect and what it can be affected by. Bannister is a big scorpion who knows only how to sting. Arkadin knows only how to kill, and Quinlan how to fix the evidence. This is a type of exhausted force, even when it has remained quantitatively very large, and it can only destroy and kill, before destroying itself, and perhaps in order to kill itself. It is here that it rediscovers a center, but one which coincides with death. No matter how large it is, it is exhausted because it no longer knows how to transform itself. It is thus descending, decadent and degenerate: it represents impotence in bodies, that is, that precise point where the "will to power" is nothing but a will-to-dominate, a being for death, which thirsts for its own death, as long as it can pass through that of others. Welles multiplies the list of these all-powerful impotents: Bannister and his artificial limbs, Quinlan and his cane; Arkadin and his helplessness when he no longer has an aeroplane; Iago, the impotent *par excellence*.[25] These are men of revenge: not in the same way, however, as the truthful man who claimed to judge life in the name of higher values. They, on the contrary, take themselves to be *higher men*, these are higher men who claim to judge life by their own standards, by their own authority. But is this not the same spirit of revenge in two forms: Vargas, the truthful man who invokes the laws for judging, but also his double, Quinlan, who gives himself the right to judge without law; Othello, the man of duty and virtue, but also his double, Iago, who takes revenge by nature and perversion? . . .

The so-called higher men are base or bad. But the good has only one name; it is "generosity," and this is the trait by which Welles defines his favorite character, Falstaff; it is also the trait which we suppose is dominant in Don Quixote's eternal project. If becoming is the power of the false, then the good, the generous, the noble is what raises the false to the nth power or the will to power to the level of artistic becoming. Falstaff and Don Quixote may appear to be braggarts or to be pitiful, history having passed them by; they are experts in metamorphoses of life; they oppose becoming to history. Incommensurable to any judgment, they have the innocence of becoming.[26] . . . What Welles sees in Falstaff and Don Quixote is the "goodness" of life in itself, a strange goodness which carries the living being to creation. It is in this sense that we can talk about an authentic or a spontaneous Nietzscheanism in Welles.

. . . In becoming, the earth has lost all center, not only in itself, but in that it no longer has a center around which to turn. Bodies no longer have centers except that of their death when they are exhausted and return to the earth to dissolve there. Force no longer has a center precisely because it is inseparable from its relation to other forces: so . . . short shots constantly topple to right and left and the sequence shot likewise throws up a jumble of vanishing centers (the opening of *Touch of Evil*). . . . And this is what we have been trying to say from the beginning of this study: a cinematographic mutation occurs when aberrations of movement take on their independence; that is, when the moving bodies and movements lose their invariants. There then occurs a reversal where movement ceases to demand the true and where time ceases to be subordinate to movement: both at once. *Movement which is fundamentally decentered becomes false movement, and time which is fundamentally liberated becomes power of the false which is now brought into effect in false movement* (Arkadin always already there). Welles seems to be the first to have opened this breach, where neo-realism and the new wave were to be introduced with completely different methods. Welles, through his conception of bodies, forces and movement, constructs a world which has lost all motor center or "configuration"; the earth.

Nevertheless we have seen that Welles's cinema kept some essential centers (and it is on this very point that Resnais parts company from Welles). But what we have to evaluate here is the radical change to which Welles subjected the very notion of center . . . the different witnesses to the past in *Mr. Arkadin* could be considered as a series of projections of Arkadin himself, who is simultaneously what is projected on to each plane and the commanding point of view according to which we pass from one projection to the next; similarly in *The Trial* all the characters, policemen, colleagues, student, concierge, lawyer, little girls, painter and priest, constitute the projective series of a single instance which does not exist outside its metamorphoses. But, from the other aspect, the sequence shot with depth of field powerfully emphasizes volumes and reliefs, the bands of shadow from which bodies emerge and into which they return, oppositions and combinations of light and dark, violent stripes which affect bodies when they are in a see-through space (*The Lady from Shanghai, The Trial*; a whole neo-expressionism which has rid itself both of its moral assumptions and the ideal of the true).[27]

From Chapter 7, Thought and Cinema

Godard has used every method of free indirect vision. Not that he has limited himself to borrowing and renewing; on the contrary, he created the original method which allowed him to make a new synthesis, and in so doing to identify himself with modern cinema. If we are looking for the most general formula for the series in Godard, we should call every sequence of images *in so far as it is reflected in a genre* a series. An entire film may correspond to a dominant genre, as *Une femme est une femme* does to musical comedy, or *Made in USA* does to the strip cartoon. But even in this case the film moves through sub-genres, and the general rule is that there are several genres, hence several series. The passage from one genre to the next day may be through straight discontinuity, or equally in an imperceptible and continuous manner with "intercalary genres," or again through recurrence or feedback,[28] with electronic procedures (new possibilities are opening everywhere for montage). This reflective status of genre has important consequences: instead of genre subsuming images which naturally belong to it, it constitutes the limit of images which do not belong to it but are reflected in it.[29] Amengual rightly pointed this out for *Une femme est une femme*: whilst dance, in a classical musical comedy, informs all the images, even preparatory or intercalary ones, it arises here, in contrast, as a "moment" in the behavior of the heroes, as the limit toward which a sequence of images is moving, a limit which will be realized only by forming another sequence moving toward another limit.[30] This is the case of dance not only in *Une femme* . . . , but in the café scene in *Bande à part*, or that of the pinewood in *Pierrot le fou,* a passage from the wander-genre to the ballad-genre.[31] These are three great moments in Godard's work. Losing its capacities for subsuming or constituting in favor of a free power of reflection, genre may be said to be all the purer for marking the direction of pre-existing images, more than the character of the present images (Amengual shows that the scenery of *Une femme . . .* , the great square pillar in the middle of the bedroom and the patch of white wall between two doors, contributes all the more to dance in that it "demolishes what is danced," in a kind of pure and empty reflection which gives the virtual a specific reality: the virtualities of the heroine).

Categories, then, are never final answers but categories of problems which introduce reflection into the image itself. They are problematic or propositional functions. Henceforth, the question for each of Godard's films is: What performs the function of categories or of reflexive genres? In the simplest case, it can be aesthetic genres, the epic, theater, the novel, dance, cinema itself. It is characteristic of cinema to reflect itself, and reflect the other genres, without the visual images referring to a pre-established dance, novel, theater, or film, but themselves setting out to "do" cinema, to do dance, to do novel, to do theater, throughout a series, for an episode . . . The categories of genres can also be psychic faculties (imagination, memory, forgetting . . .). But sometimes the category or genre assumes much more unusual aspects, for example in the well-known interventions of reflexive types, that is, original individuals who exhibit for what it is, in its singularity, the limit toward which a given series of visual images was moving and would move in the future: these are thinkers, like Jean-Pierre Melville in *Breathless,* Brice Parain in *Vivre sa vie,* Jeanson in *La Chinoise;* they are burlesque like Devos or the queen of the Lebanon in *Pierrot le fou;* they are examples like the extras in *Two or Three Things I Know About Her* (my name is this, I do this, I like that . . .). They are all interceders who function as a category, by giving it a complete individuation: the most moving example is perhaps the intervention of Brice Parain, who exhibits and individuates the category of language, as the limit toward which the heroine was moving, with all her energy, through the series of images (the problem of Nana).

In short, the categories can be words, things, acts, people. *Les carabiniers* is not another film *about* war, to glorify or attack it. It films the categories of war, which is something quite different. Now, as Godard says, these can be specific things, armies of sea, earth and air, or "specific ideas," occupation, countryside, resistance, or "specific feelings," violence, rout, absence of passion, derision, disorder, surprise, void, or "specific phenomena," noise, silence . . . It will be noted that colors themselves can fulfill the function of categories. Not only do they affect things and people, and even written words; but they form categories in themselves: red is one in *Weekend.* If Godard is a great colorist, it is because he uses colors as great, individuated genres in which the image is reflected. This is Godard's consistent method in the films in color (unless there is rather reflection in music, or in both at once). The *Letter to Freddy Buache* releases the chromatic procedure in the pure state: there is the high and the low, the blue, celestial Lausanne, and the green, terrestrial and aquatic Lausanne. Two curves or peripheries, and, between the two, there is grey, the center, the straight lines. The colors have become almost mathematical categories in which the town reflects its images and makes a problem out of them. Three series, three states of matter, the problem of Lausanne. All the technical aspects of the film, its high-angle shots, low-angle shots, halts on the image, are at the service of this reflection. He will be criticized for not having fulfilled the brief of a film "about" Lausanne: this is because he has inverted the relation between Lausanne and the colors; he has made Lausanne pass into the colors as on a table of categories which was, however, applicable only to Lausanne. This is definitely constructivism: he has reconstructed Lausanne with colors, the discourse of Lausanne, its indirect vision.

Cinema ceases to be narrative, but it is with Godard that it becomes the most "novelesque." As *Pierrot le fou* puts it, "Next chapter. Despair. Next chapter. Freedom. Bitterness." Bakhtin defined the novel, in contrast to the epic or tragedy, as no longer having the collective or distributive unity through which the characters still spoke one and the same language. On the contrary, the novel necessarily borrows sometimes the everyday anonymous language, sometimes the language of a class, a group, a profession, sometimes the particular language of a character. To the extent that the characters, classes and genres form the free indirect discourse of the author, as much as the author forms their free indirect vision (what they see, what they know or do not know). Or rather the characters express themselves freely in the author's discourse-vision, and the author, indirectly, in that of the characters. In short, it is reflection in genres, anonymous or personified, which constitutes the novel, its "plurilingualism," its speech and its vision. Godard gives cinema the particular powers of the novel. He provides himself with the reflexive types as so many interceders through whom I is always another. It is a broken line, a zigzag line, which brings together the author, his characters and the world, and which passes between them. Thus modern cinema develops new relations with thought from three points of view: the obliteration of a whole or of a totalization of images, in favor of an outside which is inserted between them; the erasure of the internal monologue as whole of the film, in favor of a free indirect discourse and vision; the erasure of the unity of man and the world, in favor of a break which now leaves us with only a belief in this world.

From Chapter 10, Conclusions

The electronic image, that is, the tele and video image, the numerical image coming into being, either had to transform cinema or to replace it, to mark its death. We do not claim to be producing an analysis of the new images, which would be beyond our aims, but only to indicate certain effects whose relation to the cinematographic image remains to be determined.[32] The new images no longer have any outside (out-of-field), any more than they are internalized in a whole; rather, they have a right side and a reverse, reversible and non-superimposable, like a power to turn back on themselves. They are the object of a perpetual reorganization, in which a new image can arise from any point whatever of the preceding image. The organization of space here loses its privileged directions, and first of all the privilege of the vertical which the position of the screen still displays, in favor of an omni-directional space which constantly varies its angles and co-ordinates, to exchange the vertical and the horizontal. And the screen itself, even if it keeps a vertical position by convention, no longer seems to refer to the human posture, like a window or a painting, but rather constitutes a table of information, an opaque surface on which are inscribed "data," information replacing nature, and the brain-city, the third eye, replacing the eyes of nature. Finally, sound achieving an autonomy which increasingly lends it the status of image, the two images, sound and visual, enter into complex relations with neither subordination nor commensurability, and reach a common limit in so far as each reaches its own limit. In all these senses, the new spiritual automatism in turn refers to new psychological automata.

But we are all the time circling the question: cerebral creation or deficiency of the cerebellum? The new automatism is worthless in itself if it is not put in the service of a powerful, obscure, condensed will to art, aspiring to deploy itself through involuntary movements which none the less do not restrict it. An original will to art has already been defined by us in the change affecting the intelligible content of cinema itself: the substitution of the time-image for the movement-image. So that electronic images will have to be based on still another will to art, or on as yet unknown aspects of the time-image. The artist is always in the situation of saying simultaneously: I claim new methods, and I am afraid that the new methods may invalidate all will to art, or make it into a business, a pornography, a Hitlerism . . .[33] What is important is the cinematographic image was already achieving effects which were not like those of electronics, but which had autonomous anticipatory functions in the time-image as will to art. Thus Bresson's cinema had no need of computing or cybernetic machines, yet the "model" is a modern psychological automaton, because it is defined in relation to the speech-act, and no longer, as before, by motor action (Bresson was constantly thinking about automatism). Similarly, Rohmer's puppet characters, Robbe-Grillet's hypnotized ones, and Resnais' zombies are defined in terms of speech or information, not of energy or motivity. In Resnais there are no more flashbacks, which, however, need no special machinery (except in the deliberately rudimentary case of *Je t'aime, je t'aime*). In Ozu, it is the daring of the continuity shots at 180° that is enough to assemble an image "end to end with its obverse," and to make "the shot turn round."[34] Space muddles its directions, its orientations, and loses all primacy of the vertical axis that could determine them, as in Snow's *The Central Region*, using only a single camera and a rotary machine obeying electronic sounds. And the vertical of the screen now has only a conventional meaning when it ceases to make us see a world in movement, when it tends to become an opaque surface which receives, in order to disorder, and on which characters, objects and words are inscribes as "data." The readability of the image makes it as independent of the vertical human position as a newspaper can be. Bazin's alternative, either the screen acts as a frame of painting or as a mask (window), was never sufficient; for there was also the frame-mirror in the style of Ophüls, the wallpaper frame in the style of Hitchcock. But, when the frame or the screen functions as instrument panel, printing or computing table, the image is constantly being cut into another image, being printed through a visible mesh, sliding over other images in an "incessant stream of messages," and the shot itself is less like an eye than an overloaded brain endlessly absorbing information: it is the brain information, brain-city couple which replaces that of eye-Nature.[35] Godard will move in this direction (*A Married Woman, Two or Three Things I Know About Her*), even before starting to use video methods. And, in the Straubs, and in Marguerite Duras, in Syberberg, the sound framing, the disjunction of the sound image and the visual image, use cinematographic methods, or simple video methods, instead of calling on new technologies. The reasons are not simply economic. The fact is that the new spiritual automatism and the new psychological automata depend on an aesthetic before depending on technology. It is the time-image which calls on an original regime of images and signs, before electronics spoils it or, in contrast, relaunches it.

Notes

1. Gilles Deleuze, "Preface to the English Edition," in *Cinema II: The Time-Image*, trans. Hugh Tomlinson and Robert Galeta (London: Athlone, 1989).
2. Deleuze, *Cinema II: The Time-Image*, p. 212.
3. Deleuze, p. 213.
4. Deleuze, pp. 213–14.
5. Deleuze, p. 180.
6. Deleuze, p. 266.
7. Deleuze, p. 273.
8. Deleuze, p. 141.
9. Deleuze, p. 114.
10. Deleuze, p. 168.
11. Deleuze, p. 168.
12. Cf. Jacques Rancière, "The Red of *La Chinoise*: Godard's Politics," in *Film Fables*, trans. Emiliano Battista (New York: Berg, 2006), pp. 143–53.

13. Cf. the commentary by Nöel Burch, *Praxis du cinéma* (Paris: Gallimard, 1969), pp. 112–18.

14. Antonioni, *Cinéma 58* (September 1958). And Pierre Leprohon's formulation, *Michelangelo Antonioni* (Paris: Seghers, 1961), p. 76: "The story can only be read in filigree, through images which are consequences and no longer act."

15. Translators note: the *ratio cognoscendi* of a thing is its being in the mode of being known; the *ratio essendi* of a thing is its essence or "formal reason."

16. "The sadistic characteristics in my novels are always of a special sort in that they attempt to immobilize something which is moving"; in *Trans-Europe Express,* the young woman never stops moving in every direction: "Him, he is there, he is watching me, and I think that you can feel arising in him the desire to stop that." It is thus a transformation from a motor-situation to a purely optical situation. The passage is quoted by André Gardies, *Alain Robbe-Grillet* (Paris: Seghers, 1972), p. 74.

17. Mireille Latil-Le Dantec, "Notes sur la fiction et l'imaginaire chez Resnais et Robbe-Grillet," *Études cinématographiques,* nos. 100–3, *Alain Resnais and Alain Robbe-Grillet, evolution d'une écriture,* ed. Michel Estève, p. 126. On a chronology of Marienbad, cf. *Cahiers du cinema,* nos. 123 and 125.

18. Many commentators see this necessity of going beyond the level of the real and the imaginary: beginning with the adherents of a language-based semiology who find in Robbe-Grillet a key example; cf. Dominique Chateau and François Jost, *Nouveau cinema, nouvelle sémiologie* (Paris: Éditions de Minuit, 1979); and André Gardies, *Le cinéma de Robbe-Grillet* (Paris: Albatros, 1983). But, for them, the third level is that of the "signifier," whilst our enquiry concerns the time-image and its a-signifying power.

19. This is the difference suggested by Robbe-Grillet between Proust and Faulkner (*Snapshots, or Towards a New Novel*). And, in the chapter "Time and Description," he says that the new novel and modern cinema are very little concerned with time; he criticizes Resnais for being too interested in memory and forgetting.

20. In most interviews with Welles, the critique of the notion of truth comes back to the impossibility of judging man and life. Cf. Jean Gili, "Orson Welles ou le refus de juger," *Études cinématographiques, Orson Welles,* no. 13 (Spring 1963).

21. Friedrich Nietzsche, *Twilight of the Idols,* trans. R. J. Hollingdale (Harmondsworth: Penguin, 1968), p. 41.—Trans.

22. On body-forces, cf. Petr Kral, "Le film comme labyrinthe," *Positif,* no. 256 (June 1982); and Jean Narboni, "Un cinéma en plongée," *Orson Welles,* ed. Alain Bergala and Jean Narboni, special issue of *Cahiers du cinéma* (Paris: Éditions de l'Etoile, 1982). Narboni compares "character" according to Welles and the Nietzschean will to power.

23. Interview by Juan Cobos and Miguel Rubio with Orson Welles on Falstaff, *Cahiers du cinéma,* no. 179 (June 1966): 42: about the battle in *Falstaff.* Similarly the cut-up montage of the characters in *The Lady from Shanghai* is suggestive for Didier Goldschmidt: the shots do not link up, "they rush at each other, the series of cross-cuttings in extreme close-up, especially of O'Hara and Grisby, tip the weight of the image from left to right; movements are brusquely interrupted; everything contributes to the freeing of an *energy* which conditions an almost exclusively plastic perception of the film." Didier Goldschmidt, "La dame de Shanghai," *Cinématographe,* no. 75 (February 1982): 64.

24. Cf. Robin Wood's detailed analyses of *Touch of Evil,* "Welles, Shakespeare et Webster (*Le Soif du mal*)," *Positif,* no. 167 (March 1975): Vargas and Quinlan, "each of the two men dominates the frame in turn, or both occupy the image in an ephemeral and precarious equilibrium."

25. On the "impotence" of Welles's characters, as the "price to pay for exercising the power of voice and script," cf. Michel Chion, "Orson Welles Speaking," *Cahiers du cinéma, Orson Welles,* no. 12 (1982): 93. Similarly, Iago's assumed sexual impotence is not a motive or explanation but refers at a deeper level to a certain state or quality of life. Richard Marienstras, "Orson Welles interprète et continuateur de Shakespeare," *Positif,* no. 167 (March 1975): 37.
26. Welles makes some lyrical declarations about Falstaff's vital goodness: "He is goodness; he is the character in whom I believe the most . . . his goodness is like the bread and the wine." Interview, *Cahiers du cinéma,* p. 41; and also Marienstras, "Orson Welles," p. 43.
27. Charles Tesson (*Cahiers du cinéma*) analyzes depth of field as a factor of disequilibrium, "off-balance": it is as if a scorpion were filmed head on, "the important thing is not in front but at the back," to the extent that the image must "topple over towards a pure clairvoyance." There is an effect of toppling over in the sequence shot as well as in short montage.
28. Georges Bouligand, *Le déclin des absolus mathématico-logiques* (Paris: Société d'édition d'enseignement supérieur, 1949).
29. On Godard's graphic forms, cf. Jacques Fieschi, "Words in Images," *Cinématographe,* no. 21 (October 1976): "In the great silent mystery, the phrase in the intertitle arrived to secure the sense. In Godard, this written sense is brought into question and inflected with a new interference."
30. Cf. Jean-Claude Bonnet, "Le petit théâtre de Jean-Luc Godard," *Cinématographe,* no. 41 (November 1978). It is not a question in Godard's case of introducing a play or rehearsals into a film (Rivette); for him theater is inseparable from an improvisation, a "spontaneous *mise-en-scène*" or a "theatricalization of the everyday." Similarly for dance, cf. the . . . remarks of Amengual: "There, dance is only accident, or, if you like, only a moment in the heroes' behavior . . . [Cukor's] *Girls* dance for the viewer. Angelo, Emile and Alfred dance for themselves, the time needed for their plots . . . While the rhythm of dance aims to set up an imaginary temporality on the stage, Godard's cutting never for a moment removes the characters from a concrete time. Hence the constantly derisory aspect of their agitation." Barthélemy Amengual, "Jean-Luc Godard et la remise en cause de notre civilisation de l'image," *Études cinématographiques, Jean-Luc Godard,* no. 27 (1967): 117–18.
31. Jean-Luc Godard, "Feu sur *Les Carabiniers,*" *Cahiers du cinéma,* no. 146 (August 1963).
32. On not only the technical but phenomenological differences between the types of image, the reader is particularly referred to the studies of Jean-Paul Fargier in *Cahiers du cinéma* and of Dominique Belloir in the special number, "Video Art Explorations." In an article in *Revue d'aesthétique* ("Image puissance image," no. 7, 1984), Edmond Couchot defines certain characteristics of numerical or digital images, which he calls "immedia," because there is no longer a medium properly speaking. The fundamental idea is that, already in television, there is no space or image either, but only electronic lines: "the fundamental concept in television is time." Nam June Paik, interview with Fragier, *Cahiers di cinéma,* no. 299 (April 1979).
33. Sometimes an artist, becoming aware of the death of the will to art in a particular medium, confronts the "challenge" by a use which is apparently destructive of that medium: one might thus believe in negative goals in art, but it is rather a question of making up lost time, of converting a hostile area to art, with a certain violence, and of turning means against themselves, cf. in regard to television, Wolf Vostell's

attitude as analyzed by Fargier. "The Great Trauma," *Cahiers du cinéma*, no. 332 (February 1982).

34. Noël Burch, *Pour un observateur lointain* (Paris: Gallimard), p. 185.

35. Leo Steinberg ("Other Criteria," lecture at the Museum of Modern Art, New York, 1968) was already refusing to define modern painting by the conquest of pure optical space, and isolated two characteristics which, according to him, were complementary: the loss of reference to the vertical human carriage, and the treatment of the painting as a surface of information; for instance, Mondrian, when he metamorphoses the sea and sky more or less into signs, but above all with reference to Rauschenberg. "The painted surface no longer presents an analogy with a natural visual experience, but becomes related to operational processes. . . . The plane of Rauschenberg's painting is the equivalent of consciousness plunged into the city's brain." In the case of cinema, even for Snow who offers himself a "fragment of nature in the wild state," nature and the machine "inter-represent themselves": to the extent that visual determinations are information data "caught in the machine's operations and passage": "This is a film as concept where the eye has reached the point of not seeing." Marie-Christine Questerbert, "Michael Snow's *The Central Region*," *Cahiers du cinéma*, no. 296 (January 1979): 36–37.

CHAPTER 10

THE MALADY OF GRIEF

Duras

JULIA KRISTEVA

J ulia Kristeva is a former member of *Tel Quel*, a radical literary group in France of the 1960s and 1970s, and an advocate of *l'écriture feminine*. which was also espoused by her contemporaries Hélene Cixous and Luce Irigaray (see *Reader* text 6). While Kristeva's work is wide-ranging, it is unified by a psychoanalytic and phenomenological interest in emotive affects that defy representation in terms of a definable object support-ing the constitution of the subject I. In this regard, Kristeva has explored exam-ples of semiotic *jouissance* in literature and art that rupture signification and,[1] additionally, has coupled together subjective experiences of abjection and revul-sion with jouissance.[2] Such jouissance in these contexts is violent and painful, and yet, part of the violence of this experience, its excess, is that it is also joyful and ecstatic. Jouissance, therefore, according to Kristeva, cannot be defined since, as an affective experience, it challenges and exceeds the boundaries lying between an interiority guaranteeing the subject I and the formless "outside" that threatens its dissolution. In the accompanying essay about Marguerite Duras's script for the film *Hiroshima Mon Amour* (directed by Alain Resnais and released in 1959), Kristeva reevaluates Freud's ideas about melancholia and the death drive to discover a jouissance that the founder of psychoanalysis prompted in his work but tended largely to overlook. "Psychosis, depression, manic-depressive states, borderline states, false selves": these are the psychic disor-ders Kristeva cites as rising in prevalence today that prompt her inquiry into the history of an art shaped by traumatic melancholia in her book *Black Sun: Depression and Melancholia* (1987). Alongside the work of Gérard de Nerval,

Dostoyevsky, and Hans Holbein, Kristeva devotes a chapter to the writings of Marguerite Duras: "The Malady of Grief: Duras." Besides writing novels and plays, Duras wrote nineteen film scripts, of which perhaps the most famous is that for *Hiroshima mon amour*. Kristeva's discussion of this script is set against the historical background of the two world wars of the twentieth century that fundamentally transformed human consciousness, a consequence of which was the knowledge that "we now know not only that we are mortal . . . we also know that we can inflict death upon ourselves." This awareness, Kristeva claims, has overturned not only the postwar subject's psyche, afflicting it with an omnipresent sense of melancholia, but also the very terms of representation that once supported the subject's sense of symbolic belonging and agency: "As if overtaxed or destroyed by too powerful a breaker, our symbolic means find themselves hollowed out, nearly wiped out, paralyzed." Kristeva's foregoing statement expands on an earlier passage in *Black Sun* in which she challenges Freud's often repeated dictum that "'No' does not exist in the unconscious." In Freud's view, death is fundamentally unrepresentable in consciousness owing to the subject's innate narcissism. However, Kristeva modifies Freud's argument by asserting that death is "imprinted" in the unconscious, "by spacings, blanks, discontinuities, or destruction of representation. Consequently, death reveals itself as such to the imaginative ability of the self."[3] In depressive melancholia, a deathlike pall is drawn over the subject with the consequence that even the emotion of love is gripped by a force of compulsive and unshakable nihilism. In *Hiroshima mon amour*, Elle (played by Emmanuelle Riva) continues to love her dead lover, a Nazi soldier, with a melancholic passion, "His being dead does not keep her from desiring him." Nor does she give up on this passion as she encounters another lover in Hiroshima—a Japanese architect (Eija Okada)— who merges in her mind with the memory of the dead German soldier, her former lover. She is drawn to the architect since he is "marked by death because he necessarily bears the moral scars of the atomic bomb of which his countrymen were the first victims." Hence, Duras equates Hiroshima, the city that suffered the first atomic explosion, with Riva's passionate and intense love, a love that, paradoxically, is composed of melancholia and the death drive: *Hiroshima mon amour*.

Kristeva is uncertain whether love is capable today of triumphing over humankind's tendency for self-destruction—"Love stronger than death? Perhaps."—and she stresses the fact that this tendency, which will not go away following the human waste of Hiroshima and the world wars, means that politics is no longer a matter of freedom "as it was for Hannah Arendt, the field where human freedom is unfurled. The modern world, the world of world wars, the Third world, the underground world of death that acts upon us, do not have the civilized splendor of the Greek city state." As a result, politics has become severed from personal life and private experience, and these are mutually incompatible. While the public domain bears the "responsibility for having triggered the malady of death," personal existence cannot help but reflect this malady, although such an extreme sense of anguish, and even madness, may achieve through its very excess of selfhood a kind of "free individuation": *Hiroshima mon amour*. This is the affirmation that Kristeva perceives is wagered by the apparent nihilism of Marguerite Duras's work.

* * *

The Blank Rhetoric of the Apocalypse

We, as civilizations, we now know not only that we are mortal, as Paul Valéry, asserted after the war of 1914;[4] we also know that we can inflict death upon ourselves. Auschwitz and Hiroshima have revealed that the "malady of death" as Marguerite Duras might say, informs our most concealed inner recesses. If military and economic realms, as well as political and social bonds, are governed by passion for death, the latter has been revealed to rule even the once noble kingdom of the spirit. A tremendous crisis of thought and speech, a crisis of representation, has indeed emerged; one may look for analogues in past centuries (the fall of the Roman empire and the dawning of Christianity, the years of devastating medieval plagues and wars) or for its causes in economic, political, and juridical bankruptcies. Nonetheless, never has the power of destructive forces appeared as unquestionable and unavoidable as now, within and without society and the individual The despoliation of nature, lives, and property is accompanied by an upsurge, or simply a more obvious display, of disorders whose diagnoses are being refined by psychiatry—psychosis, depression, manic-depressive states, borderline states, false selves, etc. . . .

If it is still possible to speak of "nothing" when attempting to chart the minute meanderings of psychic grief and death, are we still in the presence of nothing when confronting the gas chambers, the atomic bomb, or the gulag? Neither the spectacular aspect of death's eruption in the universe of the Second World War nor the falling apart of conscious identity and rational behavior ending in institutional aspects of psychosis, often equally spectacular, are at stake. What those monstrous and painful sights do damage to are our systems of perception and representation. As if overtaxed or destroyed by too powerful a breaker, our symbolic means find themselves hollowed out, nearly wiped out, paralyzed. On the edge of silence the word "nothing" emerges, a discreet defense in the face of so much disorder, both internal and external, incommensurable. Never has a cataclysm been more apocalyptically outrageous; never has its representation been assumed by so few symbolic means.

Within some religious movements there was a feeling that in the presence of so much horror silence alone was appropriate; death should be removed from living speech and be called to mind only in indirect fashion in the rifts and unspoken bits of a concern bordering on contrition. A fascination with Judaism—one would rather not call it a flirtation—was conspicuous along those lines, revealing the guilt of an entire generation of intellectuals in the presence of antisemitism and the collaboration [with the Germans] that existed during the early years of the war.

A new rhetoric of apocalypse (etymologically, *apocalypso* means demonstration, dis-covering through sight, and contrasts with *aletheia*, the philosophical disclosure of truth) seemed necessary for a vision of this nevertheless monstrous nothing to emerge—a monstrosity that blinds and compels one to be silent. Such a new apocalyptic rhetoric was carried out in two seemingly opposite, extreme fashions that complement each other: a wealth of images and a holding back of words.

On the one hand, the art of imagery excels in the raw display of monstrosity. Films remain the supreme art of the apocalypse, no matter what the refinements, because the image has such an ability to "have us walk into fear," as Augustine had already seen.[5] On the other hand, verbal and pictorial arts have turned to the "uneasy, infinite quest of [their] source."[6] Beginning with Heidegger and Blanchot respectively evoking Hölderlin and Mallarmé, and including the Surrealists, commentators have noticed that poets—doubtless diminished in the modern world by the ascendancy of politics—turn back to language, which is their own mansion, and they unfold its resources rather than tackle innocently the representation of an external object. Melancholia becomes the secret mainspring of a new rhetoric: what is involved this time is to follow ill-being step by step, almost in clinical fashion, without ever getting the better of it.

Within this image/words dichotomy, it falls to films to spread out the coarseness of horror or the external outlines of pleasure, while literature becomes internalized and withdraws from the world in the wake of the crisis in thought . . .

Hiroshima of Love

Because of what took place in history, there can be no artifice involving Hiroshima. Neither tragical nor pacifist artifice facing the atomic explosion, nor rhetorical artifice facing the mutilation of feelings. "All one can do is to speak of the impossibility of speaking of Hiroshima. The knowledge of Hiroshima is something that must be set down, a priori, as being an exemplary delusion of the mind."[7] Hiroshima itself, and not its repercussions, is the sacrilege, the death-bearing event. The text sets out to "be done with description of horror through horror, for that has been done by the Japanese themselves" and to "have the horror rise from its ashes by having it inscribed into a love that will inevitably be distinctive and 'wonder-filling.'"[8] The nuclear explosion therefore permeates love itself, and its devastating violence makes love both impossible and gorgeously erotic, condemned and magically alluring—as is the nurse, portrayed by Emmanuelle Riva, at one of the high points of passion. The text and the film open not with the image of the nuclear mushroom as initially planned, but with parts of clasping bodies belonging to a couple of lovers who might be a couple of dying people. "In their place and stead mutilated bodies are seen—at the level of the head and hips—moving—preys either to love or to the pangs of death—successively covered with ashes, dew, atomic death—and the sweat of love fulfilled."[9] Love stronger than death? Perhaps. "Always their personal history, brief as it might be, will prevail over Hiroshima." But perhaps not. For, if He comes from Hiroshima, She comes from Nevers where "she has been mad with meanness." Her first lover was German, he was killed during the Liberation, her hair was shorn. A first love destroyed by the "utterness and dreadfulness of stupidity." On the other hand, the horror of Hiroshima somehow liberated her from her French tragedy. The recourse to the atomic weapon seems to prove that horror is not limited to one side; it knows neither place nor party but can rage absolutely. Such a transcendence of horror frees the loving woman of mistaken guilt. The young woman henceforth wanders with her "purposeless love" all the way to Hiroshima. Beyond their wedding, which they term a happy one, the new love of the two protagonists—although powerful and strikingly authentic—will also be "strangled": sheltering a disaster on either side, Nevers here, Hiroshima there. However intense it may be in its unnameable silence, love is henceforth in suspense, pulverized, atomized.

To love, from her point of view, is to love a dead person. The body of her new lover merges with the corpse of her first love, which she had covered with her own body, a day and a night, and whose blood she savored. Furthermore, passion is intensified by a taste for the impossible forced on her by the Japanese lover. In spite of his "international" appearance and Western face as per the scriptwriter's directions, he remains if not exotic at least other, from an other world, a beyond, to the extent of merging with the image of the German who was loved and who died in Nevers. But the very dynamic Japanese engineer is also marked by death because he necessarily bears the moral scars of the atomic death of which his countrymen were the first victims.

A love crippled by death or a love of death? A love that was made impossible or a necrophilic passion for death? *My love is a Hiroshima,* or else, *I love Hiroshima for its suffering is my Eros? Hiroshima mon amour* preserves that ambiguity, which is, perhaps, the postwar version of love. Unless that historical version of love reveals the profound ambiguity of love with respect to death, the death-bearing halo of all passion . . . "His being dead does not keep her from desiring him. She can no longer help herself wanting him, dead as he might be. Her body is drained, breathless. Her mouth is moist. Her posture is that of a desiring woman, shameless to the point of crudeness. More shameless than anywhere else. Disgusting. She desires a dead man."[10] "The purpose of love is to die more comfortably into life."[11]

The implosion of love into death and of death into love reaches its highest expression in the unbearable grief of madness. "They pretended I was dead . . . I went mad. With meanness. I would spit, so I was told, in my mother's face."[12] Such a madness, bruised and deadly, might be no more than the absorption, on Her part, of His death. "One might think her dead, so fully is she dying of his own death."[13] The identification of the protagonists with each other as they fuse their borders, their words, their being, is a standing metaphor with Duras. While she does not die as he does, while she outlasts their dead love, she nevertheless becomes *like* a dead woman—severed from others and from time, she has the endless, animal stare of cats, she is mad—"Having died of love in Nevers." "I couldn't manage to find the slightest difference between that dead body and mine. . . . Between that body and mine I could find only similarities . . . such that I could scream, do you understand?"[14] Frequent, even permanent, identification with the object of mourning is nonetheless absolute and inescapable. Because of that very fact, mourning becomes impossible and changes the heroine into a crypt inhabited by a living corpse . . .

Private and Public

Duras' entire work is perhaps contained in the 1960 text that sets the plot of Resnais' film in the year 1957, fourteen years after the atomic explosion. Everything is there—suffering, death, love, and their explosive mixture within a woman's mad melancholia; but above all the combination of sociohistorical *realism* adumbrated in *Un Barrage contre le Pacifique* (1950; *The Sea Wall*, 1986), which resurfaced in *L'Amant*, with the *X-ray of depression* that was inaugurated in *Moderato cantabile* (1958; Eng. tr. 1960) and would become the favorite ground, the exclusive area of the subsequent intimist texts.

While history is unobtrusive and later disappears, it is here cause and setting. This drama of love and madness appears to be independent of the political drama as the power of passion outstrips political events, atrocious as they may be. What is more, this mad, impossible love seems to triumph over the events—if one may speak of triumph when eroticized suffering or love in suspense hold sway.

Nevertheless, Duras' melancholia is *also* like an explosion in history. Private suffering absorbs political horror into the subject's psychic microcosm. The French woman in Hiroshima might have come out of Stendhal; perhaps she is even eternal and yet she nonetheless exists because of the war, the Nazis, the bomb . . .

Because of its integration into private life, however, political life loses the autonomy that our consciousness persists in setting aside for it, religiously. The different participants in the global conflict do not disappear, for all that, through a global condemnation that would amount to a remission of the crime in the name of love. The young German is an enemy, the Resistance's severity has its logic, and nothing is said that could justify the Japanese intervention on the side of the Nazis any more than the violence of the belated American counter-attack. Political events having been acknowledged by an implicit political consciousness that belongs to the left (the Japanese man should unquestionably appear as a leftist), the aesthetic stake just the same remains that of love and death. It therefore sets public events in the light of madness.

Today's milestone is human madness. Politics is part of it, particularly in its lethal outbursts. Politics is not, as it was for Hannah Arendt, the field where human freedom is unfurled. The modern world, the world of world wars, the Third World, the underground world of death that acts upon us, do not have the civilized splendor of the Greek city state. The modern political domain is massively, in totalitarian fashion, social, leveling, exhausting. Hence madness is a space of antisocial, apolitical, and paradoxically free individuation. Confronting it, political events, outrageous and monstrous as they might be—the Nazi invasion, the atomic explosion—are assimilated to the extent of being measured only by the human suffering they cause. Up to a point, considering moral suffering, there is no common ground between a shorn lover in France and a Japanese woman scorched by the atom. In the view of an ethic and an aesthetic concerned with suffering, the mocked private domain gains a solemn dignity that depreciates the public domain while allocating to history the imposing responsibility for having triggered the malady of death. As a result, public life becomes seriously severed from reality whereas private life, on the other hand, is emphasized to the point of filling the whole of the real and invalidating any other concern. The new world, necessarily political, is unreal. We are living the reality of a new suffering world.

Starting with that imperative of fundamental uneasiness, the various political commitments appear identical and disclose their strategies for flight and mendacious weakness: "Collaborators, the Fernandezes. And myself, two years after the war, a member of the communist party. An absolute, final equivalence. It's the same thing, the same call for help, the same judgment deficiency, let's say the same superstition, which consists in believing there is a political solution to a personal problem."[15]

One might, on that basis, defer the examination of political matters and scrutinize only the spectrum of suffering. We are survivors, living dead, corpses on furlough, sheltering personal Hiroshimas in the bosom of our private worlds.

It is possible to imagine a form of art that, while acknowledging the weight of contemporary suffering, would drown suffering in the conquerors' triumph, or in metaphysical sarcasms and enthusiasms, or yet in the fondness of erotic pleasure. Is it not also true, is it not especially true, that contemporary man succeeds, better than ever, in defeating the grave, that life prevails in the experience of the living, and that, from a military and political standpoint, the destructive forces of the Second World War appear to have been arrested? Duras chooses or yields to the appeal of another path—the conniving, voluptuous, bewitching contemplation of death within us, of the wound's constancy.

Notes

1. Julia Kristeva, *Desire in Language: A Semiotic Approach to Literature and Art*, ed. Leon S. Roudiez (Oxford: Basil Blackwell, 1987). The work of James Joyce is seminal to this book, as is the art of Giotto in Padua and Bellini's paintings of the Madonna and Child.

2. Julia Kristeva, *Powers of Horror: An Essay on Abjection*, trans. Leon S. Roudiez (New York: Columbia University Press, 1982).

3. Julia Kristeva, *Black Sun: Depression and Melancholia* (New York: Columbia University Press, 1989 [1987]), p. 138.

4. Paul Valéry, "La Crise de l'esprit," in *Variété, Oeuvres*, Bibliothèque de la Pléiade (Paris: Gallimard, 1957), 1:988.

5. "Even though man worries to no avail, nevertheless he proceeds within the image." Augustine, "Images," in *On the Trinity*, 14.4.6.

6. See Maurice Blanchot, "Où va la literature?" in *Le Livre à venir* (Paris: Gallimard, 1959), p. 289.

7. Marguerite Duras, *Hiroshima mon amour*, synopsis (Paris: Gallimard, 1960), p. 10.

8. Duras, p. 11.

9. Duras, pp. 9–10.

10. Duras, pp. 136–37.

11. Duras, p. 132.

12. Duras, p. 149.

13. Duras, p. 125.

14. Duras, p. 100.

15. Duras, *L'Amant*, p. 85. (Betty Fernandez was a Nazi collaborator who is referred to in Duras's novel *L'Amant* (*The Lover*). In real life Betty Fernandez was married to the author Ramon Fernandez, also a collaborator, both of whom were personal friends of Duras. Kristeva's purpose in quoting Duras about her relationship to the Fernandez couple underlines the strained, incompatible relation between the personal and the political realms. In the case of the Fernandez couple and Duras, both continued to believe—however erroneously—that political solutions could remedy personal suffering.—ED.

CHAPTER 11

NOTES ON GESTURE

GIORGIO AGAMBEN

G iorgio Agamben (b. 1942) is the Baruch Spinoza Chair at the European Graduate School, a professor of aesthetics at the University of Verona, Italy, and teaches philosophy at the Collège International de Philosophie in Paris and at the University of Macerata in Italy. Agamben has come to prominence over recent years for his political work on totalitarian policies of exclusion in Western democracies that breach citizens' rights by means of antiterrorism legislation.[1] Alongside this work, Agamben seeks to develop a philosophy that is both politically and ethically motivated by positing the irreducibility of language to a signifying purpose that thereby elides the objectification of the other. The accompanying essay, "Notes on Gesture" (1992), develops the German theater practitioner Bertolt Brecht's notion of *gestus,* a term that refers to the movements and postures of the body, both physiological and expressive.

So-called pathological movements of the body, "tics, spasmodic jerks, and mannerisms—a proliferation that cannot be defined in any way other than as a generalized catastrophe of the sphere of gestures" (section 1), formed the basis for new research and classification at the end of the nineteenth century by physicians and neurologists such as Gilles de la Tourette (1857–1904) and Jean-Martin Charcot (1825–1893), both of whom worked as clinicians at the Salpêtrière Hospital outside Paris. Their research decomposed movement into a series of broken-down instants of movement that assisted in its objectivization. Agamben observes that for nearly a century after 1885 such disorders of movement "ceased to be recorded," and he likes to imagine that so-called pathological movements of the body were not viewed as strange or "abnormal" during the intervening period between the late nineteenth century and Oliver Sacks's observation of three examples of Tourettism in New York in 1971. This fondly imagined scenario, he says, is supported by looking at the jerky physical movements evidenced in the early cinema of directors such as Étienne-Jules Marey and the Lumière brothers. In the early modern period, a last-ditch attempt was made by the *Jugendstil* movement, silent movies, and other art forms to create gestural affects irreducible to preconceived forms of understanding; this was in the face of a recognition that bodily movements and affects were increasingly incorporated into ideological notions of directed, purposive actions. In contrast to this, the bourgeoisie, in its anxiety over an assumed anarchy of gestures, sought explanations for them in "psychology": the belief that there is a causal and symptomatic relationship between gestures and the individual's psyche, an idea that had already been anticipated in the work of Charcot and, later, Freud (see sections 1 and 2).

For Agamben, there is always an antinomy at stake in the image, an idea that he derives most immediately from the philosophy of Walter Benjamin. On the one hand, there is the fetishized, auratic image in which the subject seeks solace in the image's possible decipherment and meaning by unearthing its past genealogy: "the *imago* as death mask or as symbol." On the other hand, there is the image participating within an interpenetrative whole from which it cannot be divorced, although this whole is subject to rearrangements and revised "constellations" of appearances. This is at stake in Proust's idea of spontaneous, "involuntary" epiphanies of memory recall (*mémoire involontaire*) described in his novel *In Remembrance of Things Past* (1871–1922). Additionally, Aby Warburg's encyclopedic *Mnemosyne* Atlas project (begun in 1924 and left unfinished at his death in 1929) attempts to open up historical images of gestures to dynamic movement and becomings through the analogy of the "cinematic" flip-book. This latter understanding of the image forming and reforming through changing historical constellations of affect and signification, Agamben claims, is the source of ancient mythologies such as that of the statue that begins to move. Opposing the paralyzing power of the auratic image, "cinema leads images back to the homeland of gesture." Agamben believes that Samuel Beckett's 1982 TV play *Traum und Nächt* is the dream of such a gesture that both cinema and philosophy have a duty to awaken (the play is oriented around a repeated sense of awakening and desire; see sections 2 and 3).

As such, gesture is not (simply) an image, since it breaks free of the image as a representation or symbol (the reified or fetishized image). Furthermore, gesture has "nothing to say." Drawing upon the reading of Aristotle by the Roman scholar Marcus Terentius Varro (116–27 BC), Agamben argues that gesture is not a representation, nor a form of production; furthermore, it is not a means to a purposive end; nor is it autonomous (an end in its own right). Gesture cannot be assigned an origin or source in a subject, such as an author, who initiates it (*facere*). Additionally, gesture is never resolvable into a complete or completed object or performance (*agere*).

After all these qualifications concerning gesture, how can it be thought? Certainly not in terms of purposiveness as in, say, "marching . . . from point A to point B," and neither in terms of an aesthetic autonomy. Rather, the answer that Agamben offers is that each time gesture occurs it is through loss: through the forgetting (involving a fundamental loss of memory) of an action, a means and a form of signification. Both the method (the how) and the purpose are lost and forgotten, "What characterizes gesture is that . . . something is being endured and supported." It is loss and forgetting, themselves, that are endured yet supported. Thus, insofar as gesture "shows the being-in-language of human beings as pure mediality," that is, "a pure and endless mediality," this "mediality" is existence as becoming and change, the condition of which is the loss that is to be endured for the sake of the other and for others to come. Yet this loss is also "supported" by the becoming of which it is the condition. Thus, Agamben ascribes a political and ethical dimension to gesture, since language's mediality gestures toward the other.

Agamben describes the gesture as "*the exhibition of a mediality, it is the process of making a means visible as such*" (section 4). This holds true both for the porn star whose provocative look into the camera reveals that s/he prioritizes the performance itself, more than "giving pleasure to others (or themselves)," and the mime artist who estranges gestures from their "normal" context, suspending their accepted meanings and thereby reopening their potential for new and different gestural possibilities.[2] These forms of mediality exemplify Kant's notion of a "purposiveness without purpose," which the Enlightenment philosopher discusses in relation to beauty's essential form in the *Critique of Judgment*. What Agamben says about gesture with respect to the foregoing performative examples could also hold true for words; in this sense, words would have "nothing to say" except as performative gestures or acts of communicability as such. Agamben likens the gesture in this respect to a "*gag*," as both something placed in the mouth to prevent speech (since gesture says nothing) and the recourse of the performer(s) to (humorous) improvisation, and/or repetition when speech fails. Together these meanings of the term *gag* indicate a kind of silent condition of the possibility for speech to develop infinitely in infinite ways, albeit through repetition and forgetting. Each becoming of speech would involve "a gigantic loss of memory, as an incurable speech defect" that would overcome speech placed in the service of meaning as an instrumental means to an end.

Agamben explores these foregoing ideas in relation to the films of the Situationist Guy Debord. Agamben claims that Debord's use of montage exposes the mediality of film by introducing a disjunction between affect and meaning, thereby opening up new possibilities of meaning out of the material of the past and the present. Ultimately, Agamben claims that Debord's films are "imageless" since they are without ostensible purposiveness.[3] (An example of the gag in art would be Marcel Duchamp's *With My Tongue in My Cheek* (1959), a self-portrait in two modes of representation—a graphic icon and an indexical plaster cast of the artist's cheek—that "speaks" ironically of the loss of speech when placing the tongue in the cheek). In terms of cinema, Deleuze's comments about the automaton-like figures in the films of Bresson, Rohmer, and Resnais are perhaps relevant for thinking about Agamben's theory of the gag and, more generally, gesture (see Deleuze, "Cinema II: The Time-Image," *Reader* 9).

* * *

1. By the end of the nineteenth century, the Western bourgeoisie had definitely lost its gestures.

In 1886, Gilles de la Tourette, "ancien interne des Hôpitaux de Paris et de la Salpêtrière," published with Delahaye et Lecrosnier the *Études cliniques et physiologiques sur la marche* [Clinical and physiological studies on the gait]. It was the first time that one of the most common human gestures was analyzed with strictly scientific methods. Fifty-three years earlier, when the bourgeoisie's good conscience was still intact, the plan of a general pathology of social life announced by Balzac had produced nothing more than the fifty rather disappointing pages of the *Théorie de la démarche* [Theory of bearing]. Nothing is more revealing of the distance (not only a temporal one) separating the two attempts than the description Gilles de la Tourette gives of a human step. Whereas Balzac saw only the expression of moral character, de la Tourette employed a gaze that is already a prophecy of what cinematography would later become:

While the left leg acts as the fulcrum, the right foot is raised from the ground with a coiling motion that starts at the heel and reaches the tip of the toes, which leave the ground last; the whole leg is now brought forward and the foot touches the ground with the heel. At this very instant, the left foot—having ended its revolution and leaning only on the tip of the toes—leaves the ground; the left leg is brought forward, gets closer to and then passes the right leg, and the left foot touches the ground with the heel, while the right foot ends its own revolution.[4]

Only an eye gifted with such a vision could have perfected that footprint method of which Gilles de la Tourette was, with good reason, so proud. An approximately seven- or eight-meter-long and fifty-centimeter-wide roll of white wallpaper was nailed to the ground and then divided in half lengthwise by a pencil-drawn line. The soles of the experiment's subject were then smeared with iron sesquioxide powder, which stained them with a nice red rust color. The footprints that the patient left while walking along the dividing line allowed a perfect measurement of the gait according to various parameters (length of the step, lateral swerve, angle of inclination, etc.).

If we observe the footprint reproductions published by Gilles de la Tourette, it is impossible not to think about the series of snapshots that Muybridge was producing in those same years at the University of Pennsylvania using a battery of twenty-four photographic lenses. "Man walking at normal speed," "running man with shotgun," "walking woman picking up a jug," "walking woman sending a kiss": these are the happy and visible twins of the unknown and suffering creatures that had left those traces.

The *Étude sur une affection nerveuse caractérisee par de l'incoordination motrice accompagnée d'écholalie et de coprolalie* [Study on a nervous condition characterized by lack of motor coordination accompanied by echolalia and coprolalia] was published a year before the studies on the gait came out. This book defined the clinical profile of what later would be called Gilles de la Tourette syndrome. On this occasion, the same distancing that the footprint method had enabled in the case of a most common gesture was applied to the description of an amazing proliferation of tics, spasmodic jerks, and mannerisms—a proliferation that cannot be defined in any way other than as a generalized catastrophe of the sphere of gestures. Patients can neither start nor complete the simplest of gestures. If they are able to start a movement, this is interrupted and broken up by shocks lacking any coordination and by tremors that give the impression that the whole musculature is engaged in a dance (*chorea*) that is completely independent of any ambulatory end. The equivalent of this disorder in the sphere of the gait is exemplarily described by Jean-Martin Charcot in his famous *Leçons du mardi*:

> He sets off—with his body bent forward and with his lower limbs rigidly and entirely adhering one to the other—by leaning on the tip of his toes. His feet then begin to slide on the ground somehow, and he proceeds through some sort of swift tremor. . . . When the patient hurls himself forward in such a way, it seems as if he might fall forward any minute; in any case, it is practically impossible for him to stop all by himself and often he needs to throw himself on an object nearby. He looks like an automaton that is being propelled by a spring: there is nothing in these rigid, jerky, and convulsive movements that resembles the nimbleness of the gait. . . . Finally, after several attempts, he sets off and—in conformity to the aforementioned mechanism— slides over the ground rather than walking: his legs are rigid, or, at least, they bend ever so slightly, while his steps are somehow substituted for as many abrupt tremors.[5]

What is most extraordinary is that these disorders, after having been observed in thousands of cases since 1885, practically cease to be recorded in the first years of the twentieth century, until the day when Oliver Sacks, in the winter of 1971, thought that he noticed three cases of Tourettism in the span of a few minutes while walking along the streets of New York City. One of the hypotheses that could be put forth in order to explain this disappearance is that in the meantime ataxia, tics, and dystonia had become the norm and that at some point everybody had lost control of their gestures and was walking and gesticulating frantically. This is the impression, at any rate, that one has when watching the films that Marey and Lumière began to shoot exactly in those years.

2. In the cinema, a society that has lost its gestures tries at once to reclaim what it has lost and to record its loss.

An age that has lost its gestures is, for this reason, obsessed by them. For human beings who have lost every sense of naturalness, each single gesture becomes a destiny. And the more gestures lose their ease under the action of invisible powers, the more life becomes indecipherable. In this phase, the bourgeoisie, which just a few decades earlier was still firmly in possession of its symbols, succumbs to interiority and gives itself up to psychology.

Nietzsche represents the specific moment in European culture when this polar tension between the obliteration and loss of gestures and their transfiguration into fate reaches its climax. The thought of the eternal return, in fact, is intelligible only as a gesture in which power and act, naturalness and manner, contingency and necessity become indiscernible (ultimately, in other words, only as theater). *Thus Spake Zarathustra* is the ballet of a humankind that has lost its gestures. And when the age realized this, it then began (but it was too late!) the precipitous attempt to recover the lost gestures in extremis. The dance of Isadora Duncan and Sergei Diaghilev, the novel of Proust, the *great Jugend-stil* poetry from Pascoli to Rilke, and, finally and most exemplarily, the silent movie trace the magic circle in which humanity tried for the last time to evoke what was slipping through its fingers forever.

During the same years, Aby Warburg began those investigations that only the myopia of a psychologizing history of art could have defined as a "science of the image." The main focus of those investigations was, rather, the gesture intended as a crystal of historical memory, the process by which it stiffened and turned into a destiny, as well as the strenuous attempt of artists and philosophers (an attempt that, according to Warburg, was on the verge of insanity) to redeem the gesture from its destiny through a dynamic polarization. Because of the fact that this research was conducted through the medium of images, it was believed that the image was also its object. Warburg instead transformed the image into a decisively historical and dynamic element. (Likewise, the image will provide for Jung the model of the archetypes' metahistorical sphere.) In this sense, the atlas *Mnemosyne* that he left incomplete and that consists of almost a thousand photographs is not an immovable repertoire of images but rather a representation in virtual movement of Western humanity's gestures from classical Greece to Fascism (in other words, something that is closer to De Jorio than Panofsky). Inside each section, the single images should be considered more as film stills than as autonomous realities (at least in the same way in which Benjamin once compared the dialectical image to those little books, forerunners of cinematography, that gave the impression of movement when the pages were turned over rapidly).

3. The element of cinema is gesture and not image.

Gilles Deleuze has argued that cinema erases the fallacious psychological distinction between image as psychic reality and movement as physical reality. Cinematographic images are neither *poses éternelles* (such as the forms of the classical age) nor *coupes immobiles* of movement, but rather *coupes mobiles,* images themselves in movement, that Deleuze calls movement-images.[6]

It is necessary to extend Deleuze's argument and show how it relates to the status of the image in general within modernity. This implies, however, that the mythical rigidity of the image has been broken and that here, properly speaking, there are no images but only gestures. Every image, in fact, is animated by an antinomic polarity: on the one hand, images are the reification and obliteration of a gesture (it is the *imago* as death mask or as symbol); on the other hand, they preserve the *dynamis* intact (as in Muybridge's snapshots or in any sports photograph). The former corresponds to the recollection seized by voluntary memory, while the latter corresponds to the image flashing in the epiphany of involuntary memory. And while the former lives in magical isolation, the latter always refers beyond itself to a whole of which it is a part. Even the *Mona Lisa,* even *Las Meninas* could be seen not as immovable and eternal forms, but as fragments of a gesture or as stills of a lost film wherein only they would regain their true meaning. And that is so because a certain kind of *litigatio,* a paralyzing power whose spell we need to break, is continuously at work in every image; it is as if a silent invocation calling for the liberation of the image into gesture arose from the entire history of art. This is what in ancient Greece was expressed by the legends in which statues break the ties holding them and begin to move. But this is also the intention that philosophy entrusts to the idea, which is not at all an immobile archetype as common interpretations would have it, but rather a constellation in which phenomena arrange themselves in a gesture. Cinema leads images back to the homeland of gesture. According to the beautiful definition implicit in Beckett's *Traum und Nacht,* it is the dream of a gesture. The duty of the director is to introduce into this dream the element of awakening.

4. Because cinema has its center in the gesture and not in the image, it belongs essentially to the realm of ethics and politics (and not simply to that of aesthetics).

What is a gesture? A remark of Varro contains a valuable indication. He inscribes the gesture into the sphere of action, but he clearly sets it apart from acting (*agere*) and from making (*facere*):

> The third stage of action is, they say, that in which *they faciunt* "make" something: in this, on account of the likeness among *agere* "to act" and *gerere* "to carry or carry on," a certain error is committed by those who think that it is only one thing. For a person can *facere* something and not *agere* it, as a poet *facit* "makes" a play and does not act it, and on the other hand the actor *agit* "acts" it and does not make it, and so a play *fit* "is made" by the poet, not acted, and *agitur* "is acted" by the actor, not made. On the other hand, the general [*imperator*], in that he is said to *gerere* "carry on" affairs, in this neither *facit* "makes" nor *agit* "acts," but *gerit* "carries on," that is, supports, a meaning transferred from those who *gerunt* "carry" burdens, because they support them (VI VIII 77).[7]

What characterizes gesture is that in it nothing is being produced or acted, but rather something is being endured and supported. The gesture, in other words, opens the sphere of *ethos* as the more proper sphere of that which is human. But in what way is an action endured and supported? In what way does a *res* become a *res gesta,* that is, in what way does a simple fact become an event? The Varronian distinction between *facere* and *agere* is derived, in the end, from Aristotle. In a famous passage of the *Nicomachean Ethics,* he opposes the two terms as follows: "For production [*poiesis*] has an end other than itself, but action [*praxis*] does not: good action is itself an end" (VI 1140b).[8] What is new in Varro is the identification of a third type of action alongside the other two: if producing is a means in view of an end and praxis is an end without means, the gesture then breaks with the false alternative between ends and means that paralyzes morality and presents instead means that, *as such,* evade the orbit of mediality without becoming, for this reason, ends.

Nothing is more misleading for an understanding of gesture, therefore, than representing, on the one hand, a sphere of means as addressing a goal (for

example, marching seen as a means of moving the body from point A to point B)
and, on the other hand, a separate and superior sphere of gesture as a movement that has its end in itself (for example, dance seen as an aesthetic dimension). Finality without means is just as alienating as mediality that has meaning only with respect to an end. If dance is gesture, it is so, rather, because it is
nothing more than the endurance and the exhibition of the media character of
corporal movements. *The gesture is the exhibition of a mediality: it is the process of making a means visible as such.* It allows the emergence of the being-in-
a-medium of human beings and thus it opens the ethical dimension for them.
But, just as in a pornographic film, people caught in the act of performing a
gesture that is simply a means addressed to the end of giving pleasure to others (or to themselves) are kept suspended in and by their own mediality—for
the only reason of being shot and exhibited in their mediality—and can become
the medium of a new pleasure for the audience (a pleasure that would otherwise be incomprehensible); or, just as in the case of the mime, when gestures
addressed to the most familiar ends are exhibited as such and are thus kept suspended "entre le désir et l'accomplissement, la perpétration et son souvenir"
[between desire and fulfillment, perpetration and its recollection]—in what
Mallarmé calls a *milieu pur,* so what is relayed to human beings in gestures is
not the sphere of an end in itself but rather the sphere of a pure and endless
mediality.

It is only in this way that the obscure Kantian expression "purposiveness
without purpose" acquires a concrete meaning. Such a finality in the realm of
means is that power of the gesture that interrupts the gesture in its very being-
means and only in this way can exhibit it, thereby transforming a *res* into a *res
gesta.* In the same way, if we understand the "word" as the means of communication, then to show a word does not mean to have at one's disposal a higher
level (a metalanguage, itself incommunicable within the first level), starting
from which we could make that word an object of communication; it means,
rather, to expose the word in its own mediality, in its own being a means,
without any transcendence. The gesture is, in this sense, communication of
a communicability. It has precisely nothing to say because what it shows is the
being-in-language of human beings as pure mediality. However, because
being-in-language is not something that could be said in sentences, the gesture
is essentially always a gesture of not being able to figure something out in language; it is always a *gag* in the proper meaning of the term, indicating first of
all something that could be put in your mouth to hinder speech, as well as in
the sense of the actor's improvisation meant to compensate a loss of memory
or an inability to speak. From this point derives not only the proximity between
gesture and philosophy, but also the one between philosophy and cinema.
Cinema's essential "silence" (which has nothing to do with the presence or
absence of a sound track) is, just like the silence of philosophy, exposure of the

being-in-language of human beings: pure gesturality. The Wittgensteinian definition of the mystic as the appearing of what cannot be said is literally a definition of the *gag*. And every great philosophical text is the *gag* exhibiting language itself, being-in-language itself as a gigantic loss of memory, as an incurable speech defect.

5. Politics is the sphere of pure means, that is, of the absolute and complete gesturality of human beings.

Notes

1. Such legislation grants the state the irrevocable power to exceed the law and strip citizens of their legal rights, sometimes indefinitely. The most notorious outcome of this is the predicament of the prisoners at Guantánamo Bay who are reduced to an existential condition of what Agamben cablls "bare life," a life without rights.
2. Writing about Guy Debord's films, Agamben qualifies his observation about pornography, referring to it as a banal pleasure that, like advertising, "act[s] as though there were always something more to be seen." See Giorgio Agamben, "Difference and Repetition: On Guy Debord's Film," in *Guy Debord and the Situationist International: Texts and Documents*, ed. Tom McDonough (Cambridge, MA: October/MIT Press, 2004), pp. 313–19.
3. Agamben says of Debord's cinema, and cinema in general, that it has the capacity "to exhibit the image as image and . . . allow the appearance of "imagelessness," which, as Benjamin said, is the refuge of all images. It is here . . . that the ethics and the politics of cinema come into play" (p. 319).
4. Gilles de la Tourette, *Études cliniques et physiologiques sur la marche* (Paris: Bureaux de progrès, 1886).
5. Jean-Martin Charcot, *Charcot, the Clinician: The Tuesday Lessons* (New York: Raven, 1987).
6. See Gilles Deleuze, *Cinema I: The Movement-Image*, trans. Hugh Tomlinson and Barbara Habberjam (Minneapolis: University of Minnesota Press, 1986).
7. Marcus Terentius Varro, *On the Latin Language*, trans. Roland G. Kent (Cambridge: Harvard University Press, 1977), p. 245.
8. Aristotle, *Nicomachean Ethics*, trans. Martin Ostwald (Indianapolis: Bobbs-Merrill, 1983), p. 153.

CHAPTER 12

"IN HIS BOLD GAZE MY RUIN IS WRIT LARGE"

SLAVOJ ŽIŽEK

Slavoj Žižek (b. 1949) is a Slovenian philosopher and cultural critic. He is a professor at the the European Graduate School, institutional director of the Birkbeck Institute for Humanities at the University of London, and senior researcher at the Institute of Sociology, University of Ljubljana. Žižek is one of a rare number of philosophers today whose renown exceeds academe and who is widely known publicly in the media. Žižek's quick wit, combined with an idiosyncratic presentation of self, are reasons for the interest that he attracts, but his deep engagement with contemporary global politics and issues of exploitation—he is a self-proclaimed communist and radical—are equally important factors contributing to his popularity.

Žižek's philosophy is informed by two intellectual traditions: Marxism (and its Hegelian heritage) and Lacanian psychoanalysis, the latter of which is particularly evident in the analyses of the accompanying text. For Žižek, Jacques Lacan's method of *reading* texts, both oral (the patient's speech) and written, provides the impetus for what he describes as his own readings *"with* Lacan" that range over both high and popular culture, including numerous films— Hitchcock is an especial favorite but also the Marx Brothers, film noir, the films of David Lynch, as well as the *Matrix* and *Batman* series, among others. Many of Žižek's favorite films feature in two documentaries that he has presented, *The Pervert's Guide to Cinema* (2006) and *The Pervert's Guide to Ideology* (2013).[1] Written in 1992, the accompanying text by Žižek develops a singular analysis of what constitutes the horrific element in Hitchcock's masterpiece *Psycho* (1960).

Lacan proposes that the identity of the self revolves around a depthless void—the nothingness that lies behind the Symbolic order and its signs and signifiers (that encompass all socialized forms of expression and representation). The individual self displaces this void in order to maintain his/her own consistent identity as a subject-I based upon a constellation of memories, assumptions, and values formed since an infant from within, and by means of, the Symbolic order. However, according to Lacan, the subject is never fully lodged within the Symbolic order: the presymbolic element that is left over from the symbolization process remains in the subject's unconscious, "a surplus of the Real always eludes the symbolic grasp and persists as a non-symbolized stain, a hole in reality which designates the ultimate limit where 'the word fails.'" Lacan maps out two ways by means of which what is repressed "returns" within subject-object relations: first, as a symptom that is within the aegis of the Symbolic order and, second, as a stain that corresponds to the drive in the order of the Real. It should be emphasized that the capitalized term *Real* in this context does not denote so-called reality, rather it denotes the remainder that is left over from the infant's incomplete process of subjectivization: a nonsymbolizable "stain" that cannot be integrated into subjectivity. The eruption of the Real into the Symbolic order can have traumatic consequences for the subject, causing psychic breakdown. But, for Žižek, it is also a point where the figure of the superego that dominates subjectivity and the social with its moral and ethical imperatives can be caught out and recognized as an empty construct without substance.

Žižek's analysis of Alfred Hitchcock's *Psycho* moves in two directions along the axes of the Symbolic and Real orders, employing a series of terms that correspond to them. In the text the terms used that relate to the Symbolic order are as follows: the name of the Father, the big Other (another name for the symbolic order dominated by the superego), desire, symptom, signifier, *Vorsetellungs-Repräsentanz* (literally, ideational representative), hysteria; while the set of terms that correspond to the Real order are the desire of the mother, the pre-Symbolic, the unconscious, stain, the Thing, trauma, drive, psychosis, and autism. While Žižek in this text proceeds in both directions, the Symbolic and the Real, ultimately, he conceives of them together in the form of an interwoven, closed spiral in the form of a Moebius strip or band (a favorite figurative form of Lacan's), and this is reflected further in the uncanny relationship of the two halves of the film.

In the first instance of hysteria, the symptom of repression is formed through language (the Symbolic order) by means of a chain of signifiers that signify—that is, represent—the Real that subjectivity represses. In this connection, Žižek cites Hitchcock's film *The Lady Vanishes* (1938), in which the eponymous lady disappears mysteriously. And yet the lady's absence (Miss Froy played by May Whitty) is made visible through the mediation of writing (signifiers) in two scenes: Iris (Margaret Lockwood) catches a glimpse of Miss Froy's surname, which was traced in the dust on the window of the railway carriage in an ear-lier scene, and Gilbert (Michael Redgrave) sees Miss Froy's empty Harriman's herbal tea packet fleetingly attached to a carriage window after being thrown away by one of the train's cooks. Significantly, both scenes are of writing on a window, so that, in Žižek's interpretation, the windows function as a symbolic screen lining "diegetic reality" and thwarting the Real, while the writing upon the screen are signifiers (even though Žižek refers to the writing on the win-dowpane as "an apparition of a stain")—that is, symptoms—of a subjective void that cannot be framed and represented but around which signification revolves: in this instance the vanished lady. Since signification can never cap-ture absence, as such, and yet is compelled by this absence to refer to it, signi-fication, as desire, is composed of a chain or series of endless signifiers (figured as S_1, S_2, S_3, and so on) in accordance with Saussure's structuralist linguistic theory and Lacan's dictum that the unconscious is structured like a language. As Lacan says, language speaks (*ça parle*, it speaks) of an absence within itself. Žižek summarizes this Lacanian theory in the passage "Desire is a metonymic sliding propelled by a lack, striving to capture the elusive lure: it is always, by definition, 'unsatisfied' . . . it is nothing but the movement . . . from one signi-fier to another, the eternal production of new signifiers, which, retroactively, give sense to the preceding chain."

In classic Hollywood films the denouement of the film resolves the preced-ing action and narrative, but Žižek observes that the subject's fantasy is that things could always have been otherwise: events might have happened differ-ently resulting in a different "narrative closure." At bottom this belief reflects the subject's fantasy that s/he is a free agent capable of transforming their own desire, but this is to ignore the fact that desire is not the subject's "own," but rather the result of its organization within the Symbolic field. Following Hei-degger, Žižek proposes that the subject "being-of-language" is overdetermined by its "being-toward-death," that is, by the impossibility of representing the absence that s/he desires to witness and be present at: "the entire wealth of fan-tasies can ultimately be reduced to a variation on two elementary scenes: that of the subject's conception—the parental coitus—and that of the subject's death." Applying the logic of these two positions (fantasized openness of alter-natives and symbolic determination) to classic films, Žižek argues that such narratives operate within a "curved space" that preserve the sense that things could have been different even while they are incapable of actually represent-ing the transformation of subjectivity that such difference, in fact, would entail (the curve acts almost like a barrier to envisaging this possibility). With respect to this last point, Žižek notes that the hero in Phillip José Farmer's science-fiction novel *The Doors of Time* (otherwise known as *The Gates of Time*, 1966) attempts *unsuccessfully* to travel in another time dimension (unsuccessful because such travel in reality would alter fundamentally the subject-hero).

Turning to another film of a vanishing lady, Žižek observes that Hitchcock's *Psycho* could be read as two separate parts, bounded in both cases by a narrative closure that allow for an openness of possible narratives. These two parts are, first, the story of Marion Croft (Janet Leigh) up to the point of her conversation in the parlor with Norman Bates (Anthony Perkins), "who confronts her with the abyss that awaits her at the end of the road—in him, she sees a mirror-image of her own future; sobered she decides to return to normal life." And, second, "a rather traditional unraveling of the mystery of a pathological serial killer." If the film is read in terms of these independent elements, Marion's murder, which concludes the first part, could be incorporated within an interpretation that takes the view that her desire to "assume again her place in the community" simply remains unfulfilled. As with conventional Hollywood movies, the narrative closure effected by Marion's murder would allow for a degree of openness that things could have been otherwise. However, Marion's murder challenges the notion of a purported fit between inner subjectivity (Marion's resolve) and outside reality. Furthermore, "Marion's senseless murder emerges when, in terms of the inherent logic of the narrative, the story is already over, and saps the effect of closure." In effect, Žižek argues that a form of time travel takes place in *Psycho* figured through the camera dissolve of the drain "which swallows water and blood" into Marion's eye at the conclusion of the shower scene, its vortex a classic trope for time travel. Žižek asserts that at this point in the film, "one can say that we 'pass the doors of time' and enter another temporal modality." And yet, Žižek adds the proviso that this modality turns out in *Psycho* not to be a fantasized different temporal dimension supporting an ideology of an unchanged subject, but the "night of the world," an abyss that is the uncanny double of the light of the day from which Marion came. Thus, the transition from the narrative of Marion's flight to that of the mystery of Norman is the point on the reversible planes of the Moebius band or strip at which the neurotic subject of the symbolic realm crosses into a psychotic or autistic presymbolic realm dominated by the drive, that is, the desire of the mother, "if we progress far enough on one surface, all of a sudden we find ourselves on its reverse." (Žižek reminds us of the similarity between the names Norman and Marion.)

Žižek describes the drive as "*always-already satisfied*: contained in its closed circuit, it 'encircles' its object . . . and finds satisfaction in its own pulsation, in its repeated failure to attain the object." Thus, Norman Bates is not a "subject," as such, but rather a preoedipal (or antioedipal) automaton, an impersonal drive with whom "identification . . . is not possible: one can only identify with the other as desiring subject." In this regard, the "acousmatic voice" of Norman/(M)Other is especially important for Žižek, a concept he develops from Michel Chion's landmark book *The Voice in Cinema* (1982). Referring to a dictionary definition, Chion defines "acousmatic" as, "a sound that is heard without its cause or source being seen."[2] In the third section of his book, entitled "Norman; or The Impossible Anacousmêtre" and subtitled "The Impossible Embodiment," Chion proposes that "the mother's voice" in Hitchcock's *Psycho* is not embodied through human presence as "it" is never visibly identified with either Norman Bates or the dead mother, not even at the end of the film when the mother's voice speaks over an image of Norman—since his mouth remains closed. In a very literal sense this voice is unlocatable, its audio effect operating neither to the left nor the right of the space of the cinema, a trait that was supported by the fact that, at the time *Psycho* was made in 1960, Dolby stereo sound and multitracking did not exist. The upshot of this is that the mother's voice is never in its fantasized "place," but rather subsists as a free-floating and unidentifiable object. Žižek argues that once the voice-over or voice-off is eventually isolated in regard to Norman Bates in the concluding scenes of *Psycho*, this, paradoxically, only results further in Norman's desubjectivization with the consequence that he embodies the paranoiac superego figure of his Mother: "The Voice has attached itself to the wrong body, so that what we get is a true zombie, a pure creature of the Super-ego, totally powerless in itself (Norman-mother 'wouldn't even hurt a fly'), yet for that very reason all the more uncanny." Uncanny because it reveals that the subject (Norman) is essentially hollow and devoid of any positive content: a construction (built and maintained by the Symbolic order). In this context it is worth bearing in mind that Freud's use of the term *uncanny*, to which Žižek refers and which was written originally in German, contains two terms: *Heimlich* ("homely") and its prefix *un-*, meaning "unhomely" or "alien."

The murder of Marion in the infamous shower scene is not experienced as a totally unexpected shock, because her story is already over, as "she has already made a decision to return and to repay her debt to society." However, the second murder, of the detective Arbogast (Martin Balsam), Žižek considers to be truly traumatic, a "displacement" of the experience of Marion's murder and an encounter with the Real. Ultimately, the murder of Arbogast is not linked to the spectator's voyeurism and, indeed, undercuts every possible positioning of the spectator. Žižek emphasizes the point that everything conspires in the film's diegetic setup for the audience to anticipate Arbogast's murder so that his murder proceeds as of a necessity to the film's narrative drive—which is very different to the interruptive experience of Marion's murder. Even so, Arbogast's murder is experienced as a surprise; the explanation for this being that however aware the subject is of the unconscious (represented in *Psycho* by the automaton murderer), nevertheless, s/he is intent upon repressing this knowledge of an alien otherness inhabiting the subject. Bearing in mind the figure of the Moebius band or strip, this otherness is not only that of the unconscious but also the Symbolic order, too, that is responsible for constructing the subject.

Initially, leading up to the murder, the spectator identifies with the detective's curiosity as he approaches the old house and goes up the stairs, after quietly entering the front door, so as to discover the veracity of Norman's familial life. In this respect, as the subject "peers anxiously into the space in front of him/her[, s/he looks] in it for the traces of 'more than meets the eye'—for the mysterious maternal thing." In other words, in identifying with the detective Arbogast, the spectator seeks, in psychoanalytic terms, the absent maternal body. However, thereafter, Arbogast is depicted from a high point of view situated at the level of the ceiling above the landing ("God's view"). This viewpoint given to the spectator might infer an objectivity and sense of control. But such reassurance is quickly undermined by the entrance of the murderer from the side door below the God's-eye view; the murderer, Žižek observes, "moves with slow, discontinuous, intercepted, cut movements, as if what we see is a doll revivified, a living dead, not a true living person." The next edit is of Arbogast's slashed face as he expresses utter perplexity and surprise, seen in close-up from the murderer's point of view. This rapid editing of the scene of the detective's murder elides both subjective and objective points of view: the murderer is inhuman and, therefore, cannot be identified with, while neither Arbogast nor "God" can account for, or prevent "the 'stain' (the murderous Thing)" from achieving its murderous intent (an intent that, in any case, is not a desire but a drive). Thus, the subject/spectator is not governed by the gaze of the super-ego but is offered access to "the impossible gaze of the Thing . . . the gaze of the Thing itself on the subject." In short, the gaze that is operative in Arbogast's murder is an eruption of the Real (the stain) in the symbolic and visual fields; as Žižek puts it at the beginning of the text, "*Psycho* carries [the] Hitchcockian subversion of the viewer's identification to its utmost, forcing him/her to *identify with the abyss beyond identification.*"[3]

When possessed by his (dead) Mother, Norman Bates exists within a presymbolic realm; in these scenes he is not a subject as such, but rather a drive. But, with the introduction of the God's-eye view in two of the scenes in *Psycho*, a further twist of the Moebius strip occurs, which, this time, reveals the void at the heart of the Symbolic order, the "blind run of the symbolic machine." If God's view is not one of reassuring control, as might be fondly imagined, then this indicates that God's realm is "that of the dead." For Žižek, this realm is "none other than the symbolic order," an empty construction from which all enjoyment has been evacuated. Affirmation of life and enjoyment, therefore, depends upon recognizing the emptiness of the Symbolic order and the falsity of its gods (that is, the superego in all its repressive dimensions). Žižek suggests that the dream recorded by Freud of the dead son who appears to the Father in his dream and declares, "Father, can't you see I'm burning?" could be adapted to mean "*Father, can't you see I'm enjoying?*"[4] the radical possibility of the son escaping the domination of the father/superego figure so long as this figure remains—or would seem to remain—in ignorance of the son's freedom. Effectively, this means that the son overcomes his subservience to the gaze of the Other (in this context, the father/superego) and no longer attempts to cast the Other into a dialectic of stable/unstable object from his subject position of desire. By way of conclusion, it should be said that this is unlike the character Phaedre in Racine's play of the same name, from which the title of Žižek's essay, "In His Bold Gaze My Ruin Is Writ Large," is taken. As Žižek explains, "Phaedre, the wife of King Theseus, reveals her love to Hippolytus, the king's son from a previous marriage, and is cruelly rebuffed; as her husband enters, she mistakes Hippolytus's grim expression—actually a sign of his distress—for an insolent determination to betray her to the king, and takes vengeance on him, the outcome of which is her own ruin. Verse 910 of *Phaedre* . . . enunciates this misreading ('In his bold gaze my ruin is writ large')."

* * *

Psycho's Moebius Band

Psycho carries [the] Hitchcockian subversion of the viewer's identification to its utmost, forcing him/her to *identify with the abyss beyond identification*. That is to say, the key that enables us to penetrate the film's mystery is to be sought in the rupture, in the change of modality, that separates the first third from the last two-thirds (in accordance with the "golden section" whereby the ratio of the smaller to the larger part coincides with the ratio of the larger part to the whole). During the first third of the film we identify with Marion, we experience the story from her perspective, which is why her murder derails us, causing us to lose the ground from under our feet—up to the end of the film, we are in search of a new footing, clinging to the point of view of the detective Arbogast, of Sam and Lila . . . yet all these secondary identifications are "empty"or, more precisely, supplementary: in them, we identify not with subjects but with a pure, flat, investigative machine on which we rely in our effort to reveal the mystery of Norman, the "hero" who replaces Marion as the film's focal point and dominates the last part, and who is in a sense nothing but her mirror-negative (as is indicated by the very mirror-relationship of their respective names: Marion—Norman). In short: after the murder of Marion, identification with the personality who dominates the diegetic space becomes impossible.[5] Where does this impossibility of identification come from? In other words, wherein consists the change of modality generated by the passage from Marion to Norman? . . .

The relationship between these two worlds eludes the simple oppositions of surface and depth, reality and fantasy, and so on—the only topology that suits it is that of the two surfaces of the Moebius band: if we progress far enough on one surface, all of a sudden we find ourselves on its reverse. This moment of passage from one surface to its reverse, from the register of hysterical desire to that of psychotic drive, can be located very precisely: the fade-in, after the murder of Marion, of the close-up of the drain which swallows water and blood, into the close-up her dead eye. Here, the spiral first *enters* the drain, then *exits* the eye,[6] as if passing through the zero-point of an eclipse of time, a "night of the world," to quote Hegel—in terms of science fiction, one can say that we "pass the doors of time" and enter another temporal modality. A comparison with *Vertigo* is revealing here: in *Psycho*, we enter precisely that abyss which draws Scottie in *Vertigo*, yet which he is still able to resist.

As a result, it is not difficult to discern Lacanian names for the two surfaces of this Moebius band—to propose an elementary formula which regulates Marion's and Norman's universe:

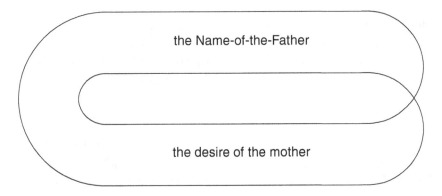

the Name-of-the-Father

the desire of the mother

Marion stands under the sign of the Father—that is, of the symbolic desire constituted by the Name-of-the-Father; Norman is entrapped into the mother's desire not yet submitted to the paternal Law (and as such not yet a desire *sensu stricto*, but rather a pre-symbolic drive): the hysterical feminine position addresses the Name-of-the-Father, whereas the psychotic clings to the mother's desire. In short, the passage from Marion to Norman epitomizes the "regression" from the register of *desire* to that of *drive*. In what does their opposition consist?

Desire is a metonymic sliding propelled by a lack, striving to capture the elusive lure: it is always, by definition, "unsatisfied," susceptible to every possible interpretation, since it ultimately coincides with its own interpretation: it is *nothing but* the movement of interpretation, the passage from one signifier to another, the eternal production of new signifiers which, retroactively, give sense to the preceding chain. In opposition to this pursuit of the lost object which remains for ever "elsewhere," drive is in a sense *always-already satisfied*: contained in its closed circuit, it "encircles" its object—as Lacan puts it—and finds satisfaction in its own pulsation, in its repeated failure to attain the object. In this precise sense, drive—in contrast to symbolic desire—appertains to the Real-Impossible, defined by Lacan as that which "always returns to its place." And it is precisely for this reason that identification with it is not possible: one can identify with the other only as desiring subject; this identification is even *constitutive* of desire which, according to Lacan, is by definition a "desire of the Other"—that is to say intersubjective, mediated by the other: in contrast to the "autistic" drive, contained in its circuit.

Norman thus eludes identification in so far as he remains prisoner of the psychotic drive, in so far as access to desire is denied him: what he lacks is the effectuation of the "primordial metaphor" by means of which the symbolic Other (the structural Law epitomized by the Name-of-the-Father) supplants *jouissance*—the closed circuit of drive. The ultimate function of the Law is to confine desire—*not the subject's own, but the desire of his/her (M)Other.* Norman Bates is therefore a kind of anti-Oedipus *avant la lettre*: his desire is alienated in the maternal Other, at the mercy of its cruel caprice.

This opposition of desire and drive determines the contrasted symbolic economy of *Psycho*'s two great murder scenes, the shower-murder of Marion and the staircase-slaughter of the detective Arbogast. The shower-murder scene has always been a *pièce de résistance* for interpreters, its power of fascination diverting attention from the second murder, the film's truly traumatic point—a textbook case of what Freud called "displacement." Marion's violent death comes as an absolute surprise, a shock with no foundation in the narrative line which abruptly cuts off its "normal" deployment; it is shot in a very "filmic" way, its effect is brought about by editing: one never sees the murderer or Marion's entire body; the act of murder is "dismembered" into a multitude of fragmentary close-ups which succeed one another in frenetic rhythm (the rising dark hand; the knife's edge close to the belly; the scream of the open mouth . . .)—as if the repeated strikes of the knife have contaminated the reel itself and caused the tearing-up of the continuous filmic gaze (or, rather, the opposite: as if the murderous shadow stands in, within the diegetic space, for the power of editing itself . . .).

How, then, is it possible to surpass this shock of the intrusion of the Real? Hitchcock found a solution: he succeeded in intensifying the effect by presenting the second murder as something *expected*—the rhythm of the scene is calm and continuous, long shots prevail, everything that precedes the act of murder seems to announce it: when Arbogast enters the "mother's house," stops at the base of the empty staircase—this crucial Hitchcockian leitmotiv—and casts an inquisitive glance upwards, we immediately know that "something is in the air"; when, seconds later, during Arbogast's ascent of the stairs, we see in close-up the crack in the second-floor door, our premonition is further confirmed. What follows then is the famous overhead shot which gives us a clear—so to speak geometrical ground-plan of the entire scene, as if to prepare us for what finally arrives: the appearance of the "mother"-figure which stabs Arbogast to death. . . .

The lesson of this murder scene is that we endure the most brutal shock when we witness the exact realization of what we were looking forward to—as if, at this point, *tuche* and *automaton* paradoxically coincide: the most terrifying irruption of *tuche* which wholly perturbs the symbolic structure—the smooth running of *automaton*—takes place when a structural necessity simply realizes itself with blind automatism.

This paradox reminds one of the well-known sophism which proves the impossibility of a surprise: the pupils in a class know they will have to pass a written test within the next week, so how can the teacher effectively surprise them? The pupils reason as follows: Friday, the last day, is out, since on Thursday evening everybody would know that the test will have to take place the next day, so there would be no surprise; Thursday is also out, since on Wednesday evening, everybody would know that—Friday already being ruled out—the only possible day is Thursday, and so on . . . What Lacan calls the Real is precisely the fact that, despite the irrefutable accuracy of this reasoning, *any day except Friday will still constitute a surprise.*

Behind its apparent simplicity, Arbogast's murder thus relies on a refined dialectic of expected and unexpected—in short, of (the viewer's) desire: the only way to explain this paradoxical economy, where the greatest surprise is caused by the complete fulfillment of our expectations, is to assume the hypothesis of a subject who is split, desiring—whose expectation is cathected by desire. What we have here is, of course, the logic of the fetishistic split: "I know very well that event X will take place (that Arbogast will be murdered), yet I do not fully believe it (so I'm none the less surprised when the murder actually takes place)." Where, exactly, does the desire reside here, in the knowledge or in the belief?

Contrary to the obvious answer (in the belief—"I know that X will take place, but I refuse to believe it since it runs against my desire . . ."), the Lacanian answer here is quite unambiguous: in the knowledge. The horrifying reality that one refuses to "believe in," to accept, to integrate into one's symbolic universe, is none other than the Real of one's desire, and the unconscious belief (that X could not actually happen) is ultimately a defense against the Real of desire: as viewers of *Psycho,* we desire the death of Arbogast, and the function of our belief that Arbogast will not be attacked by the "mother"-figure is precisely to enable us to avoid the confrontation with the Real of our desire.[7] And what Freud calls "drive"—in its opposition to desire, whose nature is by definition split—is perhaps precisely a name for the absolute "closure" where what actually happens corresponds perfectly to what one knows exactly will happen . . .

Aristophanes Reversed

Psycho is . . . a kind of hybrid of two heterogeneous parts: it is easy to imagine *two* "rounded-off" stories, quite consistent in themselves, glued together in

Psycho to form a monstrous whole. The first part (Marion's story) could well stand alone: it is easy to perform a mental experiment and to imagine it as a thirty-minute TV story, a kind of morality play in which the heroine gives way to temptation and enters the path of damnation, only to be cured by the encounter with Norman, who confronts her with the abyss that awaits her at the end of the road—in him, she sees a mirror-image of her own future; sobered, she decides to return to normal life.[8] From her standpoint, the conversation with Norman in the room with stuffed birds is therefore an exemplary case of a successful communication in the Lacanian sense of the term: she gets back from her partner her own message (the truth about the catastrophe that lurks) in a reversed form. So when Marion takes her shower, her story is—as far as narrative closure goes—strictly speaking over: the shower clearly serves as a metaphor of purification, since she has already made a decision to return and to repay her debt to society: that is, assume again her place in the community. Her murder does not occur as a totally unexpected shock which cuts into the midst of the narrative development: it strikes during the interval, the intermediate time, when the decision, although already taken, is not yet realized, inscribed into the public, intersubjective space—in the time which the traditional narrative can easily leave out (many films actually end with the moment of "inner" decision).

The ideological presupposition behind it is, of course, that of a prestabilized harmony between Inside and Outside: once the subject really "makes up his/her mind," the implementation of his/her inner decision in social reality ensues automatically. The timing of Marion's murder relies, therefore, on a carefully chosen ideologico-critical jest: it reminds us that we live in a world in which an insurmountable abyss separates the "inner decision" from its social actualization; that is, where—in contrast to the prevailing American ideology—it is decidedly *not* possible to accomplish everything, even if one really resolves to do so.[9]

The film's second part, Norman's story, is also easy to imagine as a closed whole, a rather traditional unraveling of the mystery of a pathological serial killer—the entire subversive effect of *Psycho* hinges on putting together the two heterogeneous, inconsistent pieces.[10] In this respect, the structure of *Psycho* mockingly reverses Aristophanes' myth from Plato's *Symposium* (the split of the original androgynous entity into a masculine and a feminine half): the two constituents, taken in themselves, are fully consistent and harmonious—*it is their fusion into a larger Whole which denaturalizes them*. In contrast to the abrupt ending of Marion's story, the second part seems to accord perfectly with the rules of "narrative closure": at the end, everything is explained, put in its proper place . . . Yet on a closer look, the denouement proves far more ambiguous.

As Michel Chion has pointed out,[11] *Psycho* is ultimately the story of a Voice ("mother's voice") in search of its bearer, of a body to whom it could stick; the status of this Voice is what Chion calls *acousmatic*—a voice without a bearer, without an assignable place, floating in an intermediate space, and as such all-pervasive, the very image of the ultimate Threat. The film ends with the moment of "embodiment" when we finally behold the body in which the Voice originates—yet at this precise moment, things get mixed up: within the traditional narration, the moment of "embodiment" demystifies the terrifying phantom-like Voice, it dispels its power of fascination by enabling us—the viewers—to *identify* with its bearer. (This reversal whereby the unfathomable Phantom assumes shape and body—is reduced to a common measure—is far from being limited to horror movies: in *The Wizard of Oz*, for example, the Wizard's voice is "embodied" when the little dog who follows the smell behind the curtain uncovers the helpless old man who creates the spectacle of the Wizard by means of a complicated apparatus of machinery).[12]

While *Psycho* also "embodies" the Voice, the effect of it here is the exact opposite of "gentrification" which renders possible our—the viewer's—identification: it is only now that we confront an "absolute Otherness" which precludes any identification. The Voice has attached itself to the wrong body, so that what we get is a true zombie, a pure creature of the Superego, totally powerless in itself (Norman-mother "wouldn't even hurt a fly"), yet for that very reason all the more uncanny.

The crucial feature with regard to the allegorical functioning of *Psycho* is that at this precise moment when, finally, the Voice finds its body, Norman—in the penultimate shot of the film which immediately precedes "The End"—raises his gaze and looks directly into the camera (i.e., into us, the viewers) with a mocking expression which displays his awareness of our complicity: what is accomplished thereby is the above-mentioned reversal of our gaze from I to *a*, from the neutral gaze of the Ego-Ideal to the object. We look for the "secret behind the curtain" (who is the shadow which pulls off the curtain and slaughters Marion?), and what we obtain at the end is a Hegelian answer: we always-already partake in the absolute Otherness which returns the gaze.

"A Triumph of the Gaze Over the Eye"

Let us recall our attitude when, inside a car or a house, we observe a storm outside: although we are quite close to the "real thing," the windowpane serves as a screen protecting us from immediate contact. The charm of a train journey resides precisely in this "de-realization" of the world beyond the screen: it is as if we are at a standstill, while the world beyond runs past . . . The intrusion of a stain disrupts this safe distance: the field of vision is invaded by an element which does not belong to the diegetic reality, and we are forced to accept that the pulsative stain which disturbs the clarity of our vision is part of our eye, not part of the reality we are looking at. No wonder, then, that in *The Lady Vanishes*—a film whose action takes place mostly in a train—the story pivots on such an apparition of a stain on the windowpane; yet the "stain" which emerges here is a signifier, not an object. What we have in mind, of course, is the scene in the dining-car where, in the midst of the conversation, the two crucial proofs of Miss Froy's existence (first her name written on a dusty glass, then the tea-bag with the name of Miss Froy's tea brand) appear on the "screen" itself (on the dining-car's windowpane through which the hero and the heroine observe the countryside), only to be wiped out instantly.

This phantom-like apparition of a signifier on the screen follows the logic of symptom as return of the repressed, in a kind of reversal of Lacan's formula of psychosis: "what is foreclosed from the Symbolic returns in the Real"—in the case of the symptom, what is excluded from reality reappears as a signifying trace (as an element of the symbolic order: a name, a tea brand) on the very screen through which we observe reality. In other words, the name "Froy" and the empty tea-bag on the windowpane exemplify what Lacan, in his reading of Freud, conceives as *Vorstellungs-Repräsentanz*: the signifier which acts as a representative—a trace—of the excluded ("repressed") representation, in this case the representation of Miss Froy, excluded from the diegetic reality.

In contrast to this, the intrusion of the stain in the scenes from *Birds* and *Psycho* is of a psychotic nature: here, the non-symbolized returns in the guise of a traumatic object-stain. *Vorstellungs-Repräsentanz* designates a *signifier* which fills out the void of the excluded representation, whereas a psychotic stain is a *representation* which fills out a hole in the Symbolic, giving body to the "unspeakable"—its inert presence testifies that we are in a domain where "words fail." The surplus-signifier "hystericizes" the subject, whereas the effect of the non-signifying stain is psychotic—we are thus again at the opposition hysteria-psychosis, the elementary axis of *Psycho*'s universe.

The asymmetry of these two returns (that of the stain of the Real where the word fails; that of the signifier to fill out the void that gapes in the midst of representational reality) is dependent on the split between reality and the Real. "Reality" is the field of symbolically structured representations, the outcome of symbolic "gentrification" of the Real; yet a surplus of the Real always eludes the symbolic grasp and persists as a non-symbolized stain, a hole in reality which designates the ultimate limit where "the word fails." It is against this background that *Vorstellungs-Repräsentanz* is to be conceived as an attempt to inscribe into the symbolic order the surplus that eludes the field of representation.[13] The success of what we call "sublimation" relies on this reflexive reversal of the "lack of the signifier" into the "signifier of the lack"—that is to say, on this primordial metaphor by means of which the stain—the brute enjoyment for which there is no signifier—is replaced by an empty signifier, a signifier which does not signify any reality—that is to say: a stand-in for a representation which is constitutively excluded from reality, which must fall out if "reality" is to retain its consistency:

Vorstellungs-Repräsentanz
stain

. . .

The Narrative Closure and Its Vortex

The ultimate Hitchcockian dream was, of course, to manipulate the viewer directly, bypassing altogether the *Vorstellungs-Repräsentanz* (the intermediate level of representation and its reflective redoubling in the representative). Ernest Lehman, who wrote the scenario for *North by Northwest,* recalls the following remarks by Hitchcock from the time when they were working together on this film:

> "Ernie, do you realize what we're doing in this picture? The audience is like a giant organ that you and I are playing. At one moment we play *this* note on them and get *this* reaction, and then we play *that* chord and they react *that* way. And someday we won't even have to make a movie—there'll be electrodes implanted in their brains, and we'll just press different buttons and they'll go 'oooh' and 'aaah' and we'll frighten them, and make them laugh. Won't that be wonderful?"[14]

What one should not miss here is the exact nature of the element excluded by this Hitchcockian fantasy: the "mediating" element which would become superfluous if the fantasy of direct influence on the viewer were to be realized is none other than the *signifier,* the symbolic order. This dream of a drive that could function without its representative in the psychic apparatus is what one is tempted to baptize the psychotic core of Hitchcock's universe—a core strictly homologous to Freud's dream of a moment when the symbolic procedure of psychoanalysis will be replaced by pure biology. As long as we remain within the symbolic order, however, Hitchcock's relationship to the viewer is by necessity allegorical: the symbolic order (in the case of the film: the order of diegetic reality) always contains a kind of "umbilical cord," a paradoxical element which links it to the excluded level of the interaction between Hitchcock and the public. In other words, it is true that what Hitchcock ultimately aims at is the so-called "emotional manipulation of the public," yet this allegorical dimension can be effective only in so far as it is inscribed into diegetic reality itself by means of an element whose presence "curves" the narrative space.

This element which enters the narrative space from the intermediate acousmatic domain is crucial if one is to conceive properly the problematic of "narrative closure." Narrative closure as a rule indexes the inscription of ideology into a text: the ideological horizon of a narrative is delineated by the borderline separating what can from what cannot take place in it—the extreme case is, of course, the so-called formulaic genres (the classic whodunit, for example, where one can rely absolutely upon the detective's capacity to solve the enigma). And according to Raymond Bellour, Hitchcock's films remain thoroughly within the closure that constitutes the "Hollywood matrix": the "machine for the production of the couple" where the final scene brings us back to the starting point, and so on.

The naive question "Why couldn't the denouement be different?," although it extraneates the self-evident character of the closure, is, however, far less subversive than it may seem: it remains confined to the "narrative closure" whose inherent condition is that it (mis)perceives itself as its opposite. Ideology is not the closure as such but rather the illusion of *openness,* the illusion that "it could also happen otherwise" which ignores how the very texture of the universe precludes a different course of events—in this case, the universe itself would literally "fall apart." Contrary to the vulgar pseudo-Brechtian version, the basic matrix of ideology docs not consist in conferring the form of unavoidable necessity upon what is actually dependent on a contingent set of concrete circumstances: the supreme lure of ideology is to procure the illusion of "openness" by rendering invisible the underlying structural necessity (the catastrophic ending of the traditional "realist" novel or the successful final deduction in a whodunit "works" only if it is "experienced" as the outcome of a series of [un]fortunate contingencies).

What we necessarily overlook when we move within a narrative space is the way this space is "curved": from within, the horizon always appears infinite and open. As is often the case, for a clear figuration of this one must look at a typical science-fiction narrative: the hero exerts himself to realize an "impossible" goal (change into a different time-dimension—that is, into alternative history, as in Phillip Jose Farmer's *The Doors of Time,* or something of that order), yet when he finally seems to be on the verge of attaining it, strange things begin to occur, a series of accidents prevent him from fulfilling his plan and the world we know is thus saved . . . [15] It is almost superfluous to point out the psychoanalytic resonance of such a notion of "narrative closure": what the fact of "repression" ultimately amounts to is that *the space of "what can be said," the subject's universe of meaning, is always "curved" by traumatic blanks,* organized around what must remain unsaid if this universe is to retain its consistency. The subject necessarily misrecognizes the *constitutive* nature of these blanks—s/he perceives them as something that hinges upon pure contingency, as something that easily "could not have happened"—yet when the thing *does* happen (when, for example, the meaning of a symptom is put in words), the entire universe falls apart. . . . And—to return to Hitchcock—the above-mentioned dissolve in *Psycho* (into the drain, out of Marion's eye) is precisely such a passage through "the door of time," from one closed-curved space into another.

One can see, now, how the narrative closure is closely linked to the logic of fantasy: the fantasy-scene stages precisely the irrepresentable X which curves the narrative space—which is, by definition, excluded from it. This X is ultimately the subject's birth and/or death, so the fantasy-object is the impossible gaze which makes the subject into a witness to his/her own conception or death (the entire wealth of fantasies can ultimately be reduced to a variation on two elementary scenes: that of the subject's conception—the parental coitus—and that of the subject's death).

The "curvature" of the narrative space registers the fact that the subject never lives in "his/her proper time": the subject's life is fundamentally barred, hindered; it elapses in a "not-yet" modality, in the sense of being structured as the expectation and/or memory of an X, an Event in the full meaning of the term (Henry James's name for it was the jump of the "beast in the jungle"), spent in preparation for a moment when things will "really start to happen," when the subject will "really begin to live" . . . Yet when we finally approach this X, it reveals itself as its own opposite, as death—the moment of proper birth coincides with death.[16] The being of the subject is a being-towards . . . structured in relationship to a traumatic X, a point of simultaneous attraction and repulsion, a point whose overproximity causes the eclipse of the subject. Being-towards-death is therefore, in its inherent structure, possible only with a being-of-language: the space curved is always a symbolic space; what causes the curvature of space is the fact that the symbolic field is by definition structured around a "missing link."[17]

The general lesson to be drawn from this is that a kind of fundamental "narrative closure" is *constitutive* of reality: there is always an "umbilical cord" which links the field of what we experience as "reality" with its foundation which must remain unseen; this cord which "curves" the narrative space links it to its process of enunciation. The narrative space is curved precisely in so far as its process of enunciation is always-already inscribed into it; in short: in so far as it is allegorical with regard to its process of enunciation. "Narrative closure" is therefore another name for the *subjectivization* by means of which the subject retroactively confers meaning on a series of contingencies and assumes his/her symbolic destiny: recognizes his/her place in the texture of the symbolic narrative.

Rather than directly breaking these rules which guarantee the consistency of a narrative space (the usual strategy of the avant-garde authors), Hitchcock's subversion of it consists in dispelling the lure of its false "openness"—in rendering visible the closure as such. He pretends to comply fully with the rules of closure—in *Psycho,* for example, both parts end with a closure (inner purification, catharsis, of Marion; Norman's embodiment)—yet the standard effect of closure remains unfulfilled: the surplus of the contingent real (Marion's senseless murder) emerges when, in terms of the inherent logic of the narrative, the story is already over, and saps the effect of closure; the final explanation of the mystery of the mother's identity changes into its opposite and undermines the very notion of personal identity ...

We can see, now, how the threads of our interpretation gather together. In the guise of the Other's gaze, Hitchcock registers a proximity beyond identification with *personae* from diegetic reality: its uncanniness fits perfectly the ambiguity which distinguishes the German term *das Unheimliche*—that is to say, its absolute Strangeness indexes its opposite, a threatening overproximity. This figure of "absolute Otherness" is none other than the *Vorstellungs-Repräsentanz*: it stands in, within the diegetic reality, for a representation which is constitutively excluded from its space.

Therein consists the allegorical dimension of Hitchcock's universe: the *Vorstellungs-Repräsentanz* is the umbilical link by means of which the diegetic content functions as an allegory of its process of enunciation. The place of this figure is acousmatic: it never simply partakes in diegetic reality, but dwells in an intermediate space inherent to reality yet "out of place" in it. As such, this figure "curves" the narrative space: the space is curved at precisely the point at which we approach too close to the forbidden domain of the "absolute Otherness." ... Hitchcock's entire universe is founded upon this complicity between "absolute Otherness," epitomized by the Other's gaze into the camera, and the viewer's look—the ultimate Hegelian lesson of Hitchcock is that the place of absolute transcendence, of the Unrepresentable which eludes diegetic space, coincides with the absolute immanence of the viewer reduced to pure gaze. The unique gaze into the camera which ends Norman's monologue and then dissolves into the mother's skull—this gaze which addresses us, the viewers—separates us from the symbolic community and makes us Norman's accomplices.

Lacanian theory provides a precise notion for this "absolute Otherness": the subject beyond subjectivization—beyond what Lacan, in his *Seminar* II, upon introducing the notion of the "big Other," called "the wall of language"—in other words: the subject *not* bound by the symbolic pact and as such identical to the Other's gaze (from the uncanny look into the camera of the *Lodger*'s hero to Norman's final look into the camera in *Psycho*).[18] In so far as this subject dwells "beyond the wall of language," its correlative is not a signifier representing it, marking its place within the symbolic order, but an inert object, a bone which sticks in the subject's throat and hinders his/her integration into the symbolic order (let us recall the motif of a skull, of a mummified head, which runs from *Under Capricorn*—Ingrid Bergman's confrontation with the aboriginal head—to *Psycho*—Lila's confrontation with Mrs. Bates's head).[19]

. . . The Gaze of the Thing

This dimension of the subject beyond subjectivization emerges in its purest in what is certainly the crucial shot in *Psycho,* perhaps even the quintessence of Hitchcock: the shot from above of the second-floor hall and staircase in the "mother's house." This mysterious shot occurs twice. In the scene of Arbogast's murder, the shot of Arbogast from the top of the stairs (i.e., from what is still a "normal" perspective, accessible to human eyes) all of a sudden "takes off," jumps back into the air and passes into the uppermost point from which the entire scene in its ground-plan is on view. The scene of Norman carrying the mother into the cellar also begins with an "inquisitive" shot from the bottom of the same staircase—that is to say, with a shot which, although not subjective, automatically sets up the viewer in the position of somebody striving to overhear the conversation between Norman and his mother in the room upstairs; in an extremely arduous and long tracking shot whose very trajectory mimics the shape of a Moebius band, the camera then elevates and simultaneously turns around its axis, so that it reaches the same point of "God's view" on the entire scene. The inquisitive perspective sustained by the desire to penetrate the secret of the house finds its accomplishment in its opposite, in the objective overview of the scene, as if returning to the viewer the message "you wanted to see it all, so here you have it, the transparent ground-plan of the entire scene, with no fourth side (off-field) excluded. . . ."

The crucial feature of this tracking shot is that it does *not* follow the trajectory of the standard Hitchcockian tracking shot (from the establishing plan rendering the overview of the scene to the "stain" which sticks out)[20] but obeys a different, almost opposite logic: from the ground-level gaze which invites the viewer's identification to the position of pure meta-language. At this precise moment, the lethal Thing ("Mother") enters through the right-hand door; its odd, "unnatural" character is indicated by the way it moves: with slow, discontinuous, intercepted, cut movements, as if what we see is a doll revivified, a living dead, not a true living person.

The explanation offered by Hitchcock himself in his conversations with Truffaut is, as usual, deceptive in its very disarming persuasiveness; Hitchcock enumerates two reasons for including this "God's view": (1) it makes the scene transparent and thus enables the director to keep the identity of "Mother" secret without arousing the suspicion of cheating or hiding something; (2) it introduces a contrast between the serene, immovable "God's view" and the next shot, the dynamic view of Arbogast falling down the stairs.[21]

What Hitchcock's explanation fails to provide is simply the *raison d'être* of the cut from the "normal" ground-level view on Arbogast to the ground-plan view from above—that is, of the inclusion of "God's view" (or, in the second case, the *raison d'être* of the long continuous tracking shot from the ground-level inquisitive view to "God's view"). The cut which then follows in the murder of Arbogast is even more odious: it transposes us from the level of reality (i.e., from the standpoint of pure meta-language making transparent the ground-plan of reality) into the Real, into the "stain" which sticks out from the frame of reality: while we observe the scene from "God's view," the "stain" (the murderous Thing) enters the frame, and the next shot renders precisely *the point of view of this stain.* This cut to the subjective view of the murderer himself (herself?)—to the impossible gaze of the Thing which has just entered the visual field of reality—accomplishes, in Hegelese, the reflection-into-self of the *objective gaze* into the *gaze of the object itself;* as such, it designates the precise moment of passing over into perversion.

The inherent dynamic of the entire scene of Arbogast's murder epitomizes *Psycho's* trajectory from hysteria to perversion:[22] hysteria is defined by the identification of the subject's desire with the desire of the other (in this case, of the viewer's desire with the inquisitive desire of Arbogast as diegetic personality); whereas perversion involves an identification with the "impossible" gaze of the object-Thing itself—when the knife cuts Arbogast's face, we see it through the very eyes of the "impossible" murderous Thing.[23] In Lacanian mathemes, we thus passed from \$◊ *a* to *a* ◊ \$: from the subject peering anxiously into the space in front of him/her, looking in it for the traces of "more than meets the eye"—for the mysterious maternal Thing—to *the gaze of the Thing itself on the subject.*[24]

Hitchcock's explanation according to which the function of "God's view" was to keep us, viewers, in ignorance (as to the mother's identity), without arousing suspicion that the director is trying to hide something from us, therefore imposes an unexpected yet unavoidable conclusion: if we are kept in ignorance by assuming God's view, then *a certain radical ignorance must pertain to the status of God Himself,* who clearly comes to epitomize a blind run of the symbolic machine. Hitchcock's God goes His own way, indifferent to our petty human affairs—more precisely, He is *totally unable to understand us, living humans,* since His realm is that of the dead (i.e. since symbol is the murder of thing). On that account, he is like God from the memoirs of Daniel Paul Schreber, who, "being only accustomed to communication with the dead, *does not understand living men"*[25]—or, to quote Schreber himself: "... *in accordance with the Order of Things, God really knew nothing about living men* and did not need to know; consonantly with the Order of Things, He needed only to have communication with corpses."[26]

This Order of Things is, of course, none other than the symbolic order which mortifies the living body and evacuates from it the substance of Enjoyment. That is to say, God as Name-of-the-Father, reduced to a figure of symbolic authority, is "dead" (also) in the sense that *He does not know anything about enjoyment,* about life-substance: the symbolic order (the big Other) and enjoyment are radically incompatible.[27] This is why the famous Freudian dream of a son who appears to his father and reproaches him with "Father, can't you see I'm burning?" could be simply translated into *"Father, can't you see I'm enjoying?"*—can't you see I'm alive, burning with enjoyment? Father cannot see it, since he is dead, whereby the possibility is open to me to enjoy not only *outside his* knowledge—unbeknownst to him—but also *in his very ignorance.* The other, no less well-known Freudian dream, the one about the father who does not know he is dead, could thus be supplemented with "(*I, the dreamer, enjoy the fact that*) father does not know he is dead."[28]

Notes

1. Both of these documentaries were directed by Sophie Fiennes and scripted and presented by Žižek. The earlier documentary is distributed by P. Guide Ltd. and ICA Projects (UK) and the latter is distributed by Zeitgeist Films.

2. Michel Chion, *The Voice in Cinema*, ed. and trans. Claudia Gorbman (New York: Columbia University Press, 1999), p. 18.

3. It can be seen here that Žižek's analysis of the structure of Arbogast's murder follows closely Lacan's analysis of Holbein's painting *The Ambassadors*. See Jacques Lacan, *The Four Fundamental Concepts of Psycho-Analysis*, ed. Jacques Alain-Miller and trans. Alan Sheridan (London: Penguin, 1979), pp. 88–89.

4. Žižek refers to two dreams described and interpreted by Freud concerning fathers and sons and the super-ego. The first dream concerns a father who falls asleep at the wake of his dead son and the son appears to him in a dream saying, "Father, don't you see I'm burning?" Besides the unconscious issues of guilt at stake in the father's dream, the dream was occasioned by the fact that a lighted candle had fallen onto the wrappings on one of the arms of the son lying in his coffin. Sigmund Freud, *The Standard Edition of the Complete Psychological Works of Sigmund Freud*, ed. and trans. James Strachey (London: Hogarth and the Institute of Psychoanalysis, 1981), chapter 7, "The Psychology of the Dream-Processes," pp. 509–10. The second dream is about a father who is already dead appearing to his son in a dream as if he has died a second time and, therefore, as if alive (about which the son was ignorant). Freud, chapter 6 (G), "Absurd Dreams—Intellectual Performances in Dreams," pp. 426–27.
      Lacan discusses the dream of the burning child and Freud's interpretation of it in *The Four Fundamental Concepts of Psycho-Analysis*, pp. 56–60.

5. Robin Wood formulated this change of modality clearly, yet his perspective remains that of subjectivization; for that reason, he is compelled to conceive it as a simple weakness of the film, i.e., as a lapse, a "compromise" with the standard detective-narration formula of investigating a mystery—what eludes him is the *structural impossibility* of identifying with Norman. See Robin Wood, *Hitchcock's Films* (New York: Barnes, 1977), pp. 110–11.

6. It was Robin Wood who pointed out this crucial detail: *Hitchcock's Films*, p. 112.

7. Hitchcock relied on a homologous dialectic of the (un)expected already in *Sabotage*; see Mladen Dolar's chapter on *Sabotage* in *Everything You Always Wanted to Ask About Lacan (But Were Afraid to Ask Hitchcock)*, ed. Slavoj Žižek (London: Verso, 1992), pp. 129–36.

8. Such a forerunner of the first part of *Psycho* actually exists: many of its motifs can be discerned in Hitchcock's TV film *One More Mile to Go* (1957).
9. Another strategy of subverting the classic narrative closure is at work in Ulu Grosbard's melodrama *Falling in Love,* with Meryl Streep and Robert de Niro, whose ending enacts, in a condensed form, the entire gamut of possible denouements of extramarital affairs in cinema history: the couple parts under the pressure of the environment; the woman is on the verge of committing suicide on the rails; after the break-up of the affair, they meet again by chance and realize that although they are still in love, they have missed the right moment; finally, they run into each other once again in a commuter train and (so it seems) reunite for good—the charm of the film consists in this playing with different codes, so that the viewer can never be sure if what he/she sees is already the final denouement. . . . What makes *Falling in Love* a "postmodern" film is this reflected relationship to the history of cinema, i.e., its playing-over of the different variants of the narrative closure.
10. The narrative shift has a long and respectable tradition, starting from Mozart-Schikaneder's *Magic Flute:* after the first third (where the Queen of Night charges Tamino, the hero, to deliver her beautiful daughter Pamina from the clutches of the tyrannical Sarastro, the Queen's ex-husband and Pamina's father), Sarastro miraculously changes into a figure of wise authority, so that the accent now shifts on to the couple's ordeal under his benevolent supervision. In so far as *The Magic Flute's* "production of the couple" by means of the ordeal can serve as the paradigm of Hitchcock's 1930s films, one is almost tempted to say that *Psycho* passes through the way of *The Magic Flute* backwards, in the opposite direction. A somewhat similar shift is often at work in contemporary popular culture, where it assumes the form of a sudden change of genre within the same work (Alan Parker's *Angel Heart,* for example, where the private-eye-investigation narrative changes into a tale of the supernatural). The appropriate use of narrative shift can unleash a tremendous ideologico-critical potential by rendering visible the necessity because of which the immanent logic of a narrative space throws us into discontinuous externality: say, the unexpected shift of an "intimate" psychological drama into the sociopolitical dimension, *precisely in so far as it is experienced as "unconvincing,"* reproduces, at the level of the conflict of genre codes, the discord between subjective experience and objective social processes, this fundamental feature of capitalist everyday life—here, as Adorno would put it, the very weakness of the narrative form, the "unfounded" shift in the narrative line, functions as an index of social antagonism.
11. See Michel Chion's chapter on *Psycho* in Žižek, *Everything You Always Wanted to Ask About Lacan,* pp. 195–207.
12. One of the formulaic twists of thrillers is, of course, the adding, at the very end, of a supplementary "turn of the screw" which belies the "embodiment," as in a short story from Hitchcock's TV series where a woman finally kills her neighbor, whom she has identified as the anonymous molester threatening her by phone—yet when she sits down by his body, the phone rings again and the well-known voice bursts into obscene laughter . . .
13. This reflexive redoubling is precisely what Lacan adds in his (obvious mis-)reading of the Freudian concept of *Vorstellungs-Repräsentanz.* With Freud, *Vorstellungs-Repräsentanz* designates the simple fact that drive does not pertain to biology pure and simple, but is always articulated by means of its psychic representatives (the fantasy-representations of objects and scenes which stage its satisfaction), i.e., *Vorstellungs-Repräsentanz* is the drive's representative within the psychic apparatus

(see Sigmund Freud, "Repression," in *Standard Edition*, 14:152–53, and "The Unconscious," *Standard Edition*, 14:177). With Lacan, on the contrary, *Vorstellungs-
Repräsentanz* is a representative (a place-holder [*le tenant-lieu*]) of what the representational field excludes, it stands in for the missing ("primordially repressed")
representation: "Now, that is precisely what I mean, and say—for what I mean, I say—in
translating *Vorstellung-Repräsentanz* by representative of the representation" (Lacan,
The Four Fundamental Concepts, p. 218).

14. Donald Spoto, *The Dark Side of Genius: The Life of Alfred Hitchcock* (New York: Bal-
lantine, 1984), p. 440.

15. Let us just recall—among many products of this kind—a science-fiction film about
an atomic aircraft carrier on a routine cruise near Midway in 1972; a strange cloud-
vortex suddenly appears from nowhere and transfers it thirty years back, immediately
before the Battle of Midway. After long hesitation, the Captain decides to follow his
patriotic duty and to intervene—in other words, to enter the forbidden domain and
thereby get involved in the time-snare, changing his own past—yet at this very moment,
the mysterious vortex appears again and throws the aircraft carrier back into the
present.

16. Biology offers here an almost perfect metaphor of this paradoxical status of the subject. What we have in mind is a species of worm—*Acarophenax triboli*—mentioned
by Stephen Jay Gould (see his "Death Before Birth, or a Mite's *Nunc Dimittis*, in *The
Panda's Thumb* [Harmondsworth: Pelican 1983], pp. 63–64; for a Lacanian reading, see
Miran Božovič, "Immer Ärger mit dem Körper," in *Wo Es War* 5–6 [Vienna: Hora Ver-
lag, 1988]): inside the mother's body, i.e., before his own birth, the male copulates
with and fecundates his "sisters," then passes away and is born dead—in other words,
he skips the 'living body' and passes directly from the state of foetus to that of corpse.
This limit-case of a foetus born as a corpse is the closest biological correlative to the
status of the "barred" subject of the signifier ($): never living in "its proper time," pass-
ing over "real life" . . .

17. On this notion of the "missing link," see chapter 5 of Slavoj Žižek, *For They Know Not
What They Do* (London: Verso, 1991).

18. Besides Norman, there are two more brief apparitions of absolute Otherness in *Psycho*, yet—significantly—they are later "domesticated," i.e., their Otherness proves a
lure, since they are both an agency of Law: the policeman with dark glasses perceived
by Marion as a threat to her escape (due to the hysterical distortion of her vision, Marion misperceives those who are actually trying to stop her flight to ruin as impedi-
ments on her way to happiness), and Arbogast's first appearance as the eavesdropping
intruder in the conversation between Sam and Lila (his face, shot in extreme close-
up, assumes unpleasantly obtrusive dimensions of a stain). One of the most striking
appearances of this absolute Otherness in Hitchcock's films is found in *Murder!*: when
Fane (the murderer) first enters, his outstanding feature is his fixed, quasi-hypnotic
gaze into the camera . . .

19. One should recall here Lesley Brill's crucial insight into how the contours of Hitchcock's universe are delineated by the extremes of *romance* (where the movement runs
"from outside inwards": due to an external contingency which throws them together,
the couple is forced to behave as if they were married or in love, and this imitation,
this external ritual, begets, in a performative way, "true" love—the matrix of Hitchcock's films of the late 1930s) and *irony* (where, on the contrary, communication fails,
since we do *not* succeed in "doing things with words"; i.e., where the word remains
"empty" and lacks the performative power to establish a new intersubjective link): the

romance is undermined precisely by the presence of the "absolute Otherness." Lesley Brill, *The Hitchcock Romance: Love and Irony in Hitchcock's Films* (Princeton: Princeton University Press 1988).

20. For a theory of Hitchcockian tracking shot, see Slavoj Žižek, *Looking Awry: An Introduction to Jacques Lacan through Popular Culture* (Cambridge, MA: MIT Press, 1991), pp. 93–97.

21. See Francois Truffaut, *Hitchcock* (London: Panther, 1969), pp. 343–46.

22. See Raymond Bellour, "Psychosis, Neurosis, Perversion," in Marshall Deutelbaum and Leland Poague, eds., *A Hitchcock Reader* (Chichester: Wiley-Blackwell, 2009), pp. 311–31.

23. Apropos of Jacob Boehme's mystical relationship to God as Thing, Lacan says: "To confuse his contemplative eye with the eye with which God is looking at him must surely partake in perverse *jouissance*." "God and the *Jouissance* of the Woman," in Juliet Mitchell and Jacqueline Rose, eds., *Feminine Sexuality: Jacques Lacan and the École Freudiènne* (New York: Norton, 1982), p. 147.

24. This perverse gaze of the Thing emerges for the first time in Kant's *Critique of Practical Reason;* in the last paragraph of the first part, the question is raised of why God created the world in such a way that the Supreme Good is unknowable to us, finite humans, so that we cannot ever fully realize it? The only way to elude the hypothesis of an evil God who created the world with the express intention of annoying humankind is to conceive the inaccessibility of the Thing (God, in this case) as a positive condition of our ethical activity: if God as Thing were immediately to disclose Himself to us, our activity could no longer be ethical, since we would do Good not because of moral Law itself but because of our direct insight into God's nature, i.e., out of the immediate assurance that Evil will be punished. The paradox of this explanation is that—for a brief moment, at least—Kant is forced to accomplish what is otherwise strictly prohibited in his "critical philosophy"—the reversal from $\$\lozenge\,a$ to $a\,\lozenge\,\$$—and to view the world *through the eyes of the Thing (God):* his entire argument presupposes that we position ourselves within God's reasoning.

25. Sigmund Freud, "Psychoanalytic Notes on an Autobiographical Account of a Case of Paranoia (Schreber)," in *Case Histories* II (Harmondsworth: Penguin, 1979), p. 156.

26. Freud, p. 156.

27. Cf. Abraham Lincoln's famous answer to a request for a special favor: "As President, I have no eyes but constitutional eyes; I cannot see you."

28. Therein consists, according to Lacan, the asymmetry between Oedipus and Jocasta: Oedipus did not know what he was doing, whereas his mother knew all the time who her sexual partner was—the source of her enjoyment was precisely Oedipus's ignorance. The notorious thesis on the intimate link between feminine enjoyment and ignorance acquires thereby a new, intersubjective dimension: woman enjoys in so far as her *other* (man) does not know.

CHAPTER 13

——————

AND LIFE GOES ON

Life and Nothing More

JEAN-LUC NANCY

A former student of the philosopher Paul Ricoeur, Jean-Luc Nancy (b. 1940) taught at the University of Human Sciences in Strasbourg and was a guest professor at the University of California, Berkeley, and the Freiean Universität in Berlin. Now retired from teaching, he continues to write about issues that encompass aesthetics, religion, politics, and community.

With his long-term friends and sometime collaborators Jacques Derrida and Philippe Lacoue-Labarthe, Nancy developed a deconstructive philosophy, which, in his own work, he has consistently brought to bear upon the tradition of phenomenology with the aim of reevaluating its ontology of the body and related ideas of affective experience. Whereas the phenomenology of Husserl and Merleau-Ponty (see *Reader* text 4) embraced notions of immediacy, continuity, and presence, on the contrary, Nancy stresses a phenomenology that is based on ideas of withdrawal, spacing, and separation: in this conception the subject is in touch with her-/himself and others only on condition and by virtue of their ontological separateness from presence and (the fantasy of) meaning. Nancy's model of phenomenology, therefore, is marked by perpetual difference and deferral, as he states in the introduction to *The Birth to Presence* (1993), "What is born has no form. . . . To be born is not to have been born, and to have been born." He qualifies this saying, "It is the same with all verbs: to think is not yet to have thought, and already to have thought."[1] These are axioms about birth and thought envisaged as processes of becoming that, by definition, are without identity or an envisaged purpose and are open to the future; hence, as Nancy says, "To be born is not to have been born," "to think is not yet to have thought." Nevertheless, in this conception birth and thought are *already* born—"to be born is . . . to have been born," "to think is . . . already to have thought"—since they are repetitions of the unbounded freedom and openness of past becomings. Nancy believes that this phenomenology of deferral and becoming is fundamental to a group of films that the Iranian director Abbas Kiarostami (b. 1940) made in the late 1980s and 1990s, one of which is *Life and Nothing More* (1992; the title in its French translation, Nancy notes, is "And Life Goes On").[2] The accompanying essay "And Life Goes On: Life and Nothing More" (1994) is a response to this film. The essay is one of two by Nancy on the work of Kiarostami published in the book *The Evidence of Film* (2001), which also contains a transcribed conversation between Nancy and Kiarostami (2000).[3]

Following an earthquake in the region of Manjil-Rudbar, northwest of Tehran (a devastating earthquake that occurred in 1990 affecting hundreds of villages with around forty thousand fatalities and some sixty thousand injured), the film recounts the story of a search for the local boy who featured in a previous film by Kiarostami, *Where Is My Friend's Home?* (1987) Essentially, *Life and Nothing More* is a road movie involving a quest—but with a difference, as many of the scenes, all of which take place amidst the aftermath of the earthquake, are improvised on the spot with the local people. As Nancy says, each of the film's scenes are pure inventions (like all films, the film constructs images but simultaneously it is also about "the *art* of constructing images"). The film's narrative of the filmmaker and his son seeking the missing boy is subjected to a series of delays and obstructions owing to roadblocks and earthquake damage; often, too, they are forced to stop and rest, during which time they discuss the earthquake and its aftermath with the hospitable locals whose lives have been damaged. Time, in Kiarostami's film, has no present, as such. Rather, there is, Nancy says, what precedes and what goes ahead, only the past and the future, although these categories are by no means clearly demarcated. The former is figured in the film by the discontinuity of the earthquake and its unforeseen traumatic consequences, aspects of which in all their surprising, terrible, and incomprehensible effects are part of the film's subject. While the latter, the going ahead, is most visibly represented by the yellow Renault car in a kind of Sisyphean movement ("the *automobile* as the central object and subject of the film"), sometimes forging ahead, at other times moving falteringly up the zigzag roads of the damaged Mangil-Rudbar region. At the end of the film, the slowly withdrawing camera leaves the car winding ahead into an unresolved future ("The subject has no project") while the soundtrack plays Vivaldi's *Concerto for Two Horns*, which strikes an incongruous note for a film set in northern Iraq (the music was first composed in eighteenth-century Catholic Venice). Yet discordance—in the form of oppositions between beauty and tragedy, tenderness and bitterness, distance and proximity—is the subject of the film.

To the devastation and displacement caused by the earthquake, the people of Manjil-Rudbar respond with extraordinary stoicism. One of the central themes of *Life and Nothing More*, Nancy claims, is justice; can justice be done with regard to the earthquake and its aftermath? In turn, this issue begs the question of judgment and the evidence required whereby a judgment can be formed. Some of the locals ask whether God is responsible for the earthquake, and God's intervention in the Old Testament story of Abraham's sacrifice of his son Isaac is recalled as a way of imagining a just God. The director's son repeats this question and story although, significantly, he acknowledges that his understanding of the issues in question are derived from different sources and partly made up. Can, then, the film do justice—not just to the effects of the earthquake, but to "life" as that which "discontinues continuously" and to the life of images despite, or because of, the fact that the Real (the earthquake, and life that continues) cannot be represented and understood? In one telling scene, which Nancy describes as being "at the center of the film," the filmmaker gazes briefly at a damaged genre picture that has been split down the middle by the effect of the earthquake, as if to allegorize the question of a just distance, the right distance toward the events that are the substance of the film. By way of justice, Nancy asserts that true cinema "makes evident a conspicuous form of the world, a form or a sense." And, he goes on to say that "evidence always comprises a blind spot within its very obviousness: in this way it leans on the eye. The 'blind spot' does not deprive the eye of its sight: on the contrary, it makes an opening for a gaze and it *presses* upon it to look."[4] With the word *sense* (*sens*), Nancy has several meanings in mind, which encompass both a certain sense of direction (the to'ing and fro'ing of traversals and movements in the film, something "that obeys no injunction, no destination") as well as the senses of the body. While the so-called evidence that cinema offers is actually a blind spot, this omission can only be accessed through a physical touch of some weight: "the blind spot . . . leans on the eye . . . it *presses* upon it to look." There is, therefore, no perspective or objective view of life cinema can offer. Rather, in Kiarostami's films it seems to be both a matter of gaining a sense of distance *and* proximity together: the distance of the middle-class filmmaker from the local inhabitants, the distance instantiated by Kiarostami's camera, but also the proximity gained by the visitors to the region in their encounter with the stoicism of the local people, and their pragmatism, set against the beauty and violence of the landscape.

The outside seen through the dusty screen of the car window is analogous to the camera and cinema screen to which the audience's gaze is attached. Nancy claims that Kiarostami's film is "an avoidance of interiority" as this might be embodied either by the lead actor (playing the filmmaker), who remains largely inscrutable, or by the inside of the car as an analogy for the boxlike space of the camera and the cinema. For Nancy, the dust on the window screen caused by the heat and the rebuilding operations that pervades the region's atmosphere is a form of what he calls a "*text (écrit),*" an in-tangible, blind "writing" that, in the midst of movement ("*cinema:* means continuous movement"), breaks open the "logic" of a narrative to leave in the wake of its disappearance, an excess or remainder left from the absence of presence in the form of "a sinuous, steep and dusty trace." The journey undertaken by the director and his son to Koker, their friend's village, is constantly beset by delays, discontinuities, but also spaces of rest and emotionally touching experiences. All these discontinuities and remarkable juxtapositions are "traces" in the sense that Nancy uses the term to invoke a continuous stream of discontinuities that Kiorastami's cinema offers as the evidence of life.

✳ ✳ ✳

And Life Goes On is, in its French translation ("I will come back to it"), the title of the film made in 1992 by Abbas Kiarostami.[5]

Among ordinary expressions, among current ways of speaking, that is to say, ways that have an immediately recognizable value and that can be exchanged without difficulty (that are exchanged for nothing, for their own echo and that, *therefore, are worth nothing . . .*), this one speaks of this constant and inevitable flow of life, which continues its course in spite of everything, in spite of mourning and catastrophe. In fact, the film tells us from the beginning, by means of a voice on the radio: "The magnitude of the disaster is enormous" (it's about the 1990 earthquake in Iran).

The expression says that it has to continue and it also says that it is good that it continues, that life is really, perhaps, also that: that it goes on. The expression says nothing about "life," its goal, its meaning, its quality; it does not say that it is the life of the species, or that of the universe that would unfold itself above that of individuals (no doubt, in the middle of the film, we will see a young couple getting married after the catastrophe, but we will not see the birth of a child); the expression does not imply an indifference to death, or to any form of completion or accomplishment. Quite the contrary, in a sense, the film is itself this accomplishment, it accomplishes, it shows that: the catastrophe, the continuity, and also something else, the image that the film both represents and designates at the same time—an image that is neither pure and simple "life" nor an imaginary. Neither a "realist" nor a "fictional" phantasm, but life *presented* or *offered* in its evidence.

(No doubt, I speak too quickly and say too much at a time. But that's how it goes with a film. It's about the simultaneity of succession: the paradox of what continues.)

The expression (or the title) says that in addition to accomplishments, in addition to discontinuous productions or revelations, in addition to, or by means of, them and in their center, or in their heart, as their very truth, there is the continuous *(le continu)*, that it continues. In addition to what, at times, produces meaning or non-meaning, there is that which only moves on (*fait seulement du chemin*): that is, meaning in another way, the meaning of life as something "continuing" that is not even a direction (in the film people ceaselessly look for directions), that is not really a path, not really a journey, but a traversal without attributable borders, hence, without discontinuous markers, a traversal that only passes through (this is called an experience), a passing through (*un passer*) that only continues, a past that passes in fact (this is called mourning [*un deuil*]), a passage that continues and leads only to its own passing present, or else to its non present (this could be called an eternity)—and that which remains unseizable other than in passing, that which is life itself, its meaning and its salt, its truth that obeys no injunction, no destination.

And Life Goes On speaks of a perseverance of being, in being, that makes us think inevitably of Spinoza. But it is not necessary to stop at Spinoza. Rather, one must add this: this perseverance, this continuation—which is not simply a continuity—is nothing else but being itself. Being is not something; it is that something goes on. It is that it continues, neither above nor below the moments, events, singularities and individuals that are discontinuous, but in a manner that is stranger yet: in discontinuity itself, and without fusing it into a *continuum*. It continues to discontinue, it discontinues continuously. Like the images of the film.

(On this point, it is of little importance that the original of the title in Persian says something slightly different: rather "life and nothing more," "only life," and therefore "I do not want (to show) anything else but life, simply life." Because this means: here, the film does nothing but continue, it shows a continuation, that of a story [before this film, there was another film, and they are looking for one of the young actors, they do not know if he survived], that of a journey [the search], that of the life of people after the earthquake, that of life in the film, and as film. It registers the continuation of several intertwined continuations, linked together or interlocking with one another.)

Cinema gathers itself here, it concentrates on its continuity and on its continuation. Quite deliberately, ostensibly and simply it gives itself to be seen as the uninterrupted movement of its shots and its cuts, not even interrupted at its beginning and end, continuing or straddling a space off, an outside of the film that is more than simply that, because it is yet another film that both precedes it and that will follow it (the latter in the form of a television broadcast that the child will watch). But the film outside the film, therefore, the film of the film, or the image of cinema itself is not projected into an imaginary consistency, it is not entrusted to an uncertain recalling; its continuation is assured only by the way in which the film interrupts itself at the beginning and at the end.

Before, after the film, there is life, to be sure. But life continues in the continuation of cinema, in the image and in its movement. It does not continue like an imaginary projection, as a substitute for a lack of life: on the contrary, the image is the continuation without which life would not live.

The image, here, is not a copy, a reflection, or a projection. It does not participate in the secondary, weakened, doubtful and dangerous reality that a heavy tradition bestows on it. It is not even that by means of which life would continue: it is in a much deeper way (but this depth is the very surface of the image) this, that life continues with the image, that is, that it stands on its own beyond itself, going forward, ahead, ahead of itself as ahead of that which, at the same time, invincibly, continuously, and evidently calls and resists it.

At the center of the film, there is an image, an image of an image and of the only image in the strict sense of the term (there is yet another, barely glimpsed: the photo of the young actor they look for, on the poster of the film in which he was acting): a kind of old, poor-quality color print affixed to the wall of a partially destroyed house. A crack in the wall crosses the image, tears it without undoing it. It's a traditional portrait of a man with a pipe, sitting near a table on which there is a glass and a pitcher. I don't know exactly what this image represents for an Iranian memory, and I do not try to find out (I want to remain this foreign spectator who I am, and whom the film, without explicating this image to me, lets me be). The filmmaker looks at this image. The filmmaker is the main character of the film (if one may say so: he is the gaze that moves through the film, the gaze that constitutes the film in the double sense of being its subject and object). There is, in the film, no commentary on this image in the film, which becomes, nonetheless, a kind of emblem for the entire film. The absence of commentary is filled only by the gaze of the filmmaker (actor) who looks at this image. The comment is simply, how does one pick up again the thread of images cut by the catastrophe.

And it is in relation to the image, and, more specifically, this time, to television, that the title of the film is enunciated inside the film itself, and rather late in the unfolding (*déroulement*) (around the 75th of 91 minutes). A few days, then, after the 1990 earthquake, a man installs a television antenna so that a group of refugees can watch the World Soccer Cup on television in their tents. The filmmaker (character) asks him: "Do you find it appropriate to watch television these days?" The man answers: "Truthfully, I myself am in mourning. I lost my sister and three cousins. But what can we do? The Cup takes place every four years. Can't miss it. Life goes on." The Soccer Cup is for him, for them, pure image: television screens, as well as soccer imagery for all those who kick around bad balls on terrains of fortune, while dreaming vaguely of distant fame, of the kind achieved by Maradonna. Kiarostami does not undertake to rehabilitate all this imagery that has been so much decried. He does not submit to it either (in fact, he will not show one single image of the Cup). But he does not

decry it either with the chagrined and haughty minds of those who have nothing better to do than to denounce the "spectacle" *as if there were such a thing
as a pure truth lodged in an "authentic" interiority.* He shows that life continues
first of all in an exteriority, turned toward the outside of the world, turned
toward those screens that do not function primarily as lures, but rather like eyes
open onto the outside. The antenna searches the sky, searches for the air waves
carrying these images that make people talk, bet, vibrate (children bet during
the film on the outcome of the Cup), these images that are woven into social
relations as much, if not more, than dreams (we learn that on the evening of
the catastrophe many people had gone to the house of parents or friends to
watch television, and that some have died there, while others have been saved;
in that country, in order to watch television or a film, people often have to go
elsewhere).

The entire film is thus inscribed in an avoidance of interiority. We do not
know the thoughts of the filmmaker who is looking for his young actors who
may have perished. We do not know anything about the meaning of his gaze
(that could be mistaken for being too wise, too "interiorized," precisely, if it were
signified by some discourse: but it never is, never). Interiority is avoided, it is
voided: the locus of the gaze is not a subjectivity, it is the locus of the camera as
camera obscura which is not, this time, an apparatus of reproduction, but a locus
without a real *inside* (the tollbooth at the beginning and, then, the inside of the
car, with the framing through its windows or windshield—or the inverse, the
same car shot from the outside, be it from close up or far away). The image, then,
is not the projection of a subject, it's neither its "representation," nor its "phantasm": but it is this outside of the world where the gaze loses itself in order to
find itself as *gaze* (*regard*), that is, first and foremost as *respect* (*égard*) for what
is there, for what takes place and continues to take place.

For once, *sight* is not the capturing of a subject; to the contrary, it is its deliv-
erance, its sending forth ahead of itself (*envoi devant soi*), at times in extreme
close up, thrown against large blocks of stone or rubble, heaps of ruins, the sides
of trucks; at other times, in extreme long shot, thrown toward hazardous
encampments, rocky hills; and always, toward the presence of the road, its
unfolding ribbon, interrupted by faults, its unsteady shoulders, its bends and
climbs the passage of which is in no way assured.

Here, cinema plays simultaneously, inextricably on two registers (but perhaps there is no cinema worthy of its name that does not play on these two
registers):

The first is a register of interrupted continuation, of movement (after all, that
is what *cinema* means: continuous movement, not representation animated with
mobility, but mobility as essence of presence and presence as a coming, coming and passage), of displacement, of continuation, of perseverance, of the more
or less errant and uncertain pursuit (the *automobile as* the central object and

subject of the film, its character and its obscure box, its reference and its motor, the automobile gives back its full value to "automobile": it moves by itself, it moves ahead, outside of itself, it carries what presents itself, toilet seat or stove, occasional passengers, it links all these pedestrians who are walking along difficult and cut-off roads, automobile pedestrians to whom a singular air of dignity has been restituted that makes of them *walking* more than *talking beings*). It's a register of permanent clearing: incessantly, one has to find, one has to reopen the road, one has to go back and stop, one has to pass alongside, climb, gather speed; one has to ask for directions but since the roads have been cut off, this does not make much sense; one has to evaluate distances that have been modified or lost: neighboring villages have been separated by faults. And there will be no end to this. The automobile carries around the screen or the lens, the screen-lens of its windshield, always further, and this screen is precisely not a *screen*—neither obstacle, nor wall of projection—but a *text* (*écrit*), a sinuous, steep and dusty trace.

The other register is that of the passage through the image, or to the image: cinema itself, television, the soccer game on television, the image hanging on the wall, the gaze in general: not the gaze as point of view (no or little "point of view;" the image is always closer or further away than anything that could fix a "point of view"—and it is therefore not possible for the spectator of the film to identify with a certain point of view: it is a true model of what Brecht called *distanciation,* and that names nothing but the essence of the spectacle insofar as the spectacle is nothing "spectacular"), only the gaze as carrying forward, a forgetting of the self, or rather: (de-)monstration that there will never have been a *self* (*soi*) fixed in a position of spectator, because a subject is never but the acute and tenuous point of a forward movement (*avancée*) that precedes itself indefinitely.

The subject has no *project,* it does not lead what is called a *quest* (there is no Grail here, not because there would be nothing to hope for, but because hope is something else than a draft drawn on a future that can be expected, hence imagined: to the contrary, hope is confidence in the image as that which precedes, always). That's why, besides, this "subject" is not really named. There is no subject as support of an intention, there is only tension and extreme attention of somebody—of numerous bodies (*nombreux quelques-uns*)—in the continuation of this: that it continues.

This continuation has nothing mechanical or haggard. Neither is it the brute and immanent force of the species that survives. It's everyone—*every one*—who goes to the end of the one.

Certainly, the image is not life. It is even, if necessary, shamelessly deceptive: we learn that for the film shot before the earthquake, they had used special effects. They had given one actor a false hump, another a false house. In a similar vein, the young couple who gets married the day after the catastrophe perhaps does so in an illusion, similar to that of the brilliant colors of their house, and the flowers and sheets that we see inside the house. And television remains television. Just as the film remains a film, and never lets us forget it—precisely by means of its contrasts and its insistence on the framing—always the car, its windows, its doors, and the sides of the road, always on the verge of being out of focus; but also and just as well the patient arrangement of everything, the scenes that are too sharp, too precise to have been taken from real-life situations: it all looks like reporting, but everything underscores (*indique a l'évidence*) that it is the fiction of a documentary (in fact, Kiarostami shot the film several months after the earthquake), and that it is rather a document about "fiction": not in the sense of imagining the unreal, but in the very specific and precise sense of the technique, of the *art* of constructing images. For the image by means of which, each time, each opens a world and precedes himself in it (*s'y précède*) is not pregiven (*donnée toute faite*) (as are those of dreams, phantasms or bad films): it is to be invented, cut and edited. Thus it is *evidence*, insofar as, if one day I happen to *look* at my street on which I walk up and down ten times a day, I construct for an instant a new *evidence* of my street. The film is the continuous and intertwined movement of these two registers that run parallel to each other and that overlap at the same time. It is their simultaneous continuation and the continuation of each in the other: the road, the automobile, the image, the gaze; the search that moves forward, the image that presents itself; the uninterrupted movement, the rhythm of vision, the vast, permanent expanse of the countryside and its people, the interruption of lives and of contacts. The film registers the earthquake: precisely not in its terrifying imaginary—which could be only one of two things: either a reconstitution of a catastrophe-film (phantasm), or a camera really present and toppling over in the general ruin and tearing of all the images as well as of life. But the earthquake is present here as a limit of images, as the absolute real which is also the cut in the dark whence the film accedes to its first image, a cut (*coupe*) that is prolonged a little later by the crossing of a tunnel during which the credits appear: the film emerges slowly, little by little, it finds, or finds again, the possibility of the image that, at first, when it emerges from the tunnel, will consist of close-ups of ruins, trucks, abandoned objects, mechanical shovels, dust, large rocks that had fallen onto the street. It is at the same time a question of getting out of the catastrophe, of finding the road leading to the villages that have been razed, and of getting out of the dark to find the image and its right distance.

Before the credits, during the first ten minutes, there will have been experimentation, and reference to what would not be the earthquake: the solidity of cement constructions opposed to those in terracotta that were wiped out; or emigration, evoked by means of a grasshopper: the little boy will have wanted to stop to relieve himself, and he just missed provoking an accident by putting the grasshopper in front of his father's eyes. The path of the image has not been set forward yet, even though the car is already posed as the frame of the image: the little boy pissing in the distance is shot from the inside of the car.

"To piss" will also be, in the film, a motif of life that goes on, of its evidence. The father in turn will also stop to piss, and nearby, he will find in a hammock a baby whose mother is off gathering wood. Later, they meet a man carrying a stone for a toilet (for what we call "a Turkish toilet"), they will take the man aboard and will put the stone on the roof rack. There will be a shot of the man's hand reaching through the window to hold on to the stone at each turn in the road. The father will say: "You bought this on such a day?" and the other will answer: "The dead are dead. The living need this precious stone." (High angle shot of the roof of the car moving along with its toilet.)

The image is not given, it has to be approached: evidence is not what falls in any way whatever *into meaning* (*sous le sens*), as they say. Evidence is what presents itself at the right distance, or else, that in front of which one finds the right distance, the proximity that lets the relation take place, and that opens to continuity. Similarly, we have to wait for the right moment for music to become possible: more than half an hour goes by before we hear Vivaldi's *Concerto for Two Horns,* while a high angle shot of the plain, accompanied by the father's gaze, shows in the distance people busy with a funeral. Until then, there had been only the heavy noises of cars, trucks, machinery and helicopters. These noises will persist until the end, together with that, more and more isolated and fragile, of the car that has difficulty in climbing the mountain roads ("With this car you will not make it. There are dangerous turns."). But we will also hear an Iranian flute, while seeing images of a house painted bright blue, with flowers (color too emerges little by little, by discreet touches, a few flowers, a rug, the poor-quality color print on the wall, a red, yellow and blue ceramic rooster that the child finds, and these touches will be rare, isolated among the dominant spreads of ochre, brown, gray, sable, the pale blue and green). And the concerto will start up again, it will attempt to start up twice; the slow, suppressed movement eventually gives way to a slamming of car doors, before the final allegro accompanies the last climb of the car that loses itself among the steep heights. The final rejoicing of the music is not, however, a resolution of tension: the music remains at the same time at a distance from the image, and from the noise of the motor, just as the camera stays at a distance from the car that moves away, and that the film remains at a distance from life which it continues and which continues ahead of it.

The right distance of the image is not a matter of medium distance: the extreme close-up suits it just as well as the extreme long shot, or the most narrow frame (the windows of the car) just as well as the frameless shot that fills the entire screen, the immobile shots just as well as the tracking shots going at the speed of the car. The just distance (*distance juste*) is quite exactly a matter of *justice.* If life does not continue in any way whatever, in a kind of haggard, sleepwalking manner, but if it continues while exposing itself to the evidence of images, it is because it renders justice to the world, to itself.

The question of justice accompanies the entire film: if it is just that the houses of some resist while those of others do not; if it is just that one country suffers more from natural catastrophes than another; if it is just that there are catastrophes, if they are the will of God, or his punishment ("I really do not know what crime this people has committed to be severely punished by God," says one man); if it is just that some have died and others not (those who went to watch the game, or others yet, the child of a family, and not his brothers or sisters). When the child asks his father if he can take a bottle of coke from an abandoned display shelf, the father answers: "Yes, but put the money next to it." The coke is too warm, the child is going to pour it out, someone calls him from another car: "Don't throw it away, give it to us for the baby." (We hear the baby cry.)

Justice is first of all to take the real into account. The child says to a woman whose daughter died: "God does not like to kill his children." The woman: "So, who does?" The child: "It is the earthquake." And the child goes on to tell the story of Abraham and Isaac, which is, in every tradition of the Book, the emblematic story for justice that springs forth and decides in the midst of injustice.

To say "it's the earthquake" is to speak at the level of the immediate real (*dire le réel nu*). It's to say too that, perhaps, there is no God who loves and protects his children, or else that this God has nothing to do with the real. It's to take the right distance from the belief in God. The image of life puts the imaginary at a distance.

It is not a question of rendering justice to injustice, that is to say, of submitting to it. We can build so as to reduce the effects of earthquakes. We can oppose reason to fatalistic belief. First, we have to speak correctly: a girl says, "My father says it's the wilo of God "; the father: "The what of God?," "The wilo of God," "One does not say 'wilo' but 'will.'" But it's a question of doing justice to what interrupts meaning, to what cuts off the road, to what separates people from one another, and each one from himself. It's a question of rendering justice to life insofar as it knows death. To know death is to know that there will be an absolute point of arrest (*butée*) of which there is nothing to know. But to know *that* is to do justice to the evidence of life.

The man who had been endowed with a hump in the preceding film says: "These men had put a hump on me to make me look older. I went along, but I did not like it. I thought it was unjust. What is this art that shows people older and uglier than they are? Art consists in showing people younger than they are." The father (the filmmaker) answers: "Thanks to God you survived and you seem younger. The contrary is not art." The other: "No one can appreciate youth as long as he is not old. No one can appreciate life as long as he has not seen death. If one could die and come back to life, one would live better."

There is no resurrection: there is only one life, and nothing but life, and that it continues and discontinues continuously. Old age is the continuation through which youth is what it is, that is, youth. Death is a suspended continuity by means of which life is what it is: a life that continues to the very end. Art makes up immediate reality, to make evidence visible—or, more precisely (because the film is not life), to make visible that *there is* (*il y a*) this evidence and this justice. Life goes all the way to the end—that's its right measure (*juste mesure*), and that's how it always keeps going beyond itself. Let's say: that's how it is an existence, and not only natural life, which would pass the indifference of life-and-death, it lives beyond mechanical "life," it is always its own mourning, and its own joy. It becomes figure, image. It does not become alienated in images, but it is presented there: the images are the evidence of its existence, the objectivity of its assertion. This thought—which, for me, is the very thought of this film—is a difficult thought, perhaps the most difficult. It's a slow thought, always under way, fraying a path so that the path itself becomes thought. It is that which frays images so that images become this thought, so that they become the evidence of this thought—and not in order to "represent" it.

Film may want to represent; it can also go in the direction of the phantasm, or of imagery; it may seek a "visionary" quality or to be formally "visual." But just as none of these orientations ever subsists in its pure and simple state (or else, it's a failure, a maniacal kind of cinema), in the same way, to be sure, there will always exist something of this dimension of evidence, which this film belabors for its own (*que ce film travaille pour elle-même*). The certainty not only of the accuracy (*justesse*) of an image (which can belong to the immobile image, to painting or photography), but of the accuracy and of the justice of a movement of approach of the image, of a movement that pertains at the same time to an uncovering, a revelation, a coming to, and keeping at, a distance: to see coming and passing by something true, not a truthful image, but the truth of life offering images to itself.

(*A few more remarks: could it be that Abbas Kiarostami in a discreet homage to the culture of his people, and from the distance of a non-believer, thought of suras 98 and 99 of the Koran, respectively entitled* Evidence *and* The Earthquake? *The latter begins with these words: "When the earth will have experienced a violent trembling; when it will have expelled its burdens from its bosom, man will say: 'What may this mean?'—on that day, earth will tell what it knows.")*

Post-Scriptum (March 1994)

I am reading in the *Cahiers du cinema* an interview with Kiarostami, who is making a new film, a sequel to *Life and Nothing More,* with a continuation of the story but also an uncovering of some of its artifices (for example, that the wedding celebrated a few days after the catastrophe was a fiction). Thus, cinema continues and Kiarostami continues to bring it to light as cinema. Cinema keeps going on its own, indefinitely, as if it were a virtually indefinite unveiling of itself: on the one hand, each new unveiling may conceal another artifice, and it conceals it by necessity; and on the other, what is to be unveiled is nothing "in itself." What would come back then to the proper of cinema, beyond narration and image, beyond editing and shooting, beyond script, actors or dialogues—all the elements that can be the concern of quasi literary, pictorial, even musical approaches—would be this singular manner of being nothing but the linking of evidence. Other arts can present evidence of a truth, of a presence, in brief, of a "thing in itself"—an evidence that, to mark the difference, I would rather call, a *patence* (thinking of truth according to Spinoza, that *se ipsam patefacit*—that manifests itself—*et nullo egeat signo*, and has no need for a sign). Cinema too takes up this gesture, this *presentation*. But what it adds as that which is its own, the most properly distinctive property of cinema, and, perhaps also that which can be least distinguished, the most indistinguishable property of the enormous flow of films throughout the world, is the linking, the indefinite sliding along of its presentation. Where does it slide to indefinitely? In a certain way, toward insignificance (*insignifiance*) (there where the other arts appeal to an excess of *signifiance*). Toward the insignificance of life that offers itself these images, always in movement, going toward no mystery, no revelation, only this sliding along by means of which it leads itself from one image to another (exemplary, subliminal, banal, grotesque or naive, tampered with, sketchy or overloaded). Life that invents its own cinema. What a strange story, this story of a civilization that has made this gift to itself, that has tied itself to it . . . An extreme giddiness, truly, a feverish intertwining of unveiling and of special effects, *as far as the eye can see* (*à perte de vue*), truly, an overload of effects and of semblance, all that is true. Cinema is marked by the heaviest and the most ambiguous of signs—myth, mass, power, money, vulgarity, circus games, exhibitionism and voyeurism. But all that is carried off in an endless movement (*défilement*) to such an extent that evidence becomes that of passage rather than some epiphany of meaning or presence. Cinema is truly the art—in any case the technique—of a world that suspends myths. Even if it has put itself in the service of myths, at the limit, it finishes by taking them away, it carries off all epiphanies of meaning and of immobile presence into the evidence of movement. A world that links by going from one film to the next, and that learns thus, very slowly, another way of producing meaning.

Notes

This is the text of the article published under the title "De l'évidence" in *Cinémathèque*, no. 8 (Autumn 1995), and translated by Verena Andermatt Conley with the title "On Evidence: *Life and Nothing More* by Abbas Kiarostami," published in *Discourse: Journal for*

Theoretical Studies in Media and Culture 21, no. 1 (Winter 1999). I chose not to reread it before I wrote the preceding pages five years later. Therefore there are some repetitions and perhaps also some dissonances.

1. Jean-Luc Nancy, *The Birth to Presence*, trans. Brian Holmes and others (Stanford: Stanford University Press, 1993), p. 2.
2. The other films in this group by Kiarostami that Nancy discusses in his book *The Evidence of Film: Abbas Kiarostami*, trans. Christine Irizarray and Verena Andermatt Conley, ed. Yves Gevaert (Brussels, 2001), are *Where Is My Friend's Home?* (1987), *Close-Up* (1990), *Through the Olive Trees* (1996), *A Taste of Cherry* (1997), and *The Wind Will Carry Us* (1999).
3. *The Evidence of Film* is Nancy's most sustained engagement with cinema to date. However, in addition to this book he has written essays on three films by Claire Denis: "A-religion," *Journal of European Studies* 34, nos. 1/2 (2004): 14–18; "Claire Denis: Icon of Ferocity," trans. Peter Enright, in *Cinematic Thinking: Philosophical Approaches to the New Cinema*, ed. James Phillips (Stanford: Stanford University Press, 2008), pp. 160–68; "*L'Intrus* selon Claire Denis," http://www.missingimage.com/node/250633. Nancy's other writings on film include "La Règle du jeu dans *La Règle du jeu*," in *De l'histoire au cinema*, ed. Antoine de Baecque (Brussels: Complexe, 1998), pp. 145–63; and "*La Blessure*—la cicatrice," in Elisabeth Perceval, *La Blessure: essai*, preface by Nicolas Klotz (Paris: Arte, Les Petits Matins, 2005), pp. 115–26.
4. Nancy, *The Evidence of Film*, 12.
5. The English title of Abbas Kiarostami's film is *Life and Nothing More*. Jean-Luc Nancy plays on the French title, *Et la vie continue*, literally translated as "And life goes on"—TRANS.

CHAPTER 14

CONTESTING TEARS

The Hollywood Melodrama of the Unknown Woman

STANLEY CAVELL

S
tanley Cavell (1926–2018) taught at Berkeley in the late 1950s and early 1960s, after which he lectured at Harvard, where he became the Walter M. Cabot Professor of Aesthetics and the General Theory of Value, a position he held until 1997, when he became professor emeritus. Cavell's major interests centered on the intersection of the analytical tradition of philosophy—chiefly, Austin and Wittgenstein—with the continental tradition of Nietzsche, Heidegger, and Derrida. Additionally, he was influenced by the poetic philosophies of Ralph Waldo Emerson and Henry David Thoreau, as well as Freudian and Lacanian psychoanalysis. Cavell developed these interests in combination with studies of the arts, especially Shakespeare, film, and opera. Cavell's published books on film include *The World Viewed: Reflections on the Ontology of Film* (1971), *Pursuits of Happiness: The Hollywood Comedy of Remarriage* (1981), *Contesting Tears: The Hollywood Melodrama of the Unknown Woman* (1996), and *Cities of Words* (2004).

Pursuits of Happiness: The Hollywood Comedy of Remarriage and *Contesting Tears: The Hollywood Melodrama of the Unknown Woman* form a complementary pair of books about the representation of women in two genres of Hollywood films, composed of comedies and melodramas, respectively, from the period of the 1930s and 1940s. The Hollywood films that Cavell understands as defining the genre of the comedies of remarriage are *It Happened One Night* (1934), *The Awful Truth* (1937), *Bringing Up Baby* (1938), *His Girl Friday* (1940), *The Philadelphia Story* (1940), *The Lady Eve* (1941), and *Adam's Rib* (1949). Smaller in number (four in all), the melodramas that Cavell claims in his book

Contesting Tears to form a genre of their own, and which act as a counterpoint to the comedies, are *Stella Dallas* (1937), *Now, Voyager* (1942), *Gaslight* (1944), and *Letter from an Unknown Woman* (1948). Straddling the two genres of the comedies of remarriage and the melodramas of the unknown woman is what Cavell defines as a subgenre consisting of three films: *Blonde Venus* (1932), *Show Boat* (1936), and *Random Harvest* (1942). While these films uphold marriage or social convention, nevertheless, they persist in figuring the woman's desire as unknowable and leave it undecided what she could want for the future.

In the accompanying text from the introduction to *Contesting Tears* Cavell discusses the principle characteristics of both the comedies and melodramas, their antecedents, and how they contrast with each other in their depiction of the relationship between the sexes, especially as this concerns woman's desire. The following writing develops a reading of this text while expanding upon Cavell's ideas about the specific films that he explores through both *Pursuits of Happiness* and *Contesting Tears*.

Conscious of the patriarchal prejudices that might be associated with a male author in articulating power relations between the sexes, Cavell attempts in these books to contribute to the study of gender by referring to the philosophical tradition of skepticism in support of a psychoanalytic approach. Cavell traces this tradition of skepticism to its source in Descartes's conjectures in his *Meditations* (1641) about the impossibility of knowing anything with certainty, especially about reality—which he suggests may be, indeed, a dream. For Cavell, what is important about the legacy of philosophical skepticism for contemporary thought is the question of the reality of the minds of others and whether it is possible to know the other or even create a mutuality of minds despite, or by virtue of, sexual difference. Related to this matter is Cavell's political belief in democracy and the democratic right of the underprivileged, who are, by definition, voiceless, unable to gain a voice that that can be heard and listened to, however paradoxical in terms of representation this may seem. (Cavell traces this understanding of democracy to the transcendental philosophies of Emerson and Thoreau in America in the nineteenth century and to its continuation in the work of Ludwig Wittgenstein and J. L. Austin. These later thinkers developed an interest in the foreignness germane to all language use and the experience of the so-called ordinary). Cavell's overarching contention in his two books on the comedies of remarriage and the melodramas is that they stage the related difficulties and problems of fulfilling the ambitions of democracy as this pertains to woman.

All the comedies of remarriage revolve around a narrative of the overcoming of a rift or disagreement in the relationship of a married, or formerly married, couple. Ultimately, the narrative in these films takes the form of the biblical story of Genesis, "namely the creation of the woman from the man—the story of Adam's rib . . . the creation of the woman—the new creation of the woman, the creation of the new woman." In the comedies of remarriage, the reconciliation of the couples rests upon the strategies devised by the man and/or the advice of the father of the bride to "educate" the woman into remarrying or returning to her former partner. Indeed, it transpires that the woman in the comedies is "in need of an education."[1] The education in question involves the couples relearning their way toward a revived sense of "conversation," a mutually rediscovered sense of wit, joy, and friendship: the creation of "a meet and happy conversation," as Cavell says, quoting Milton on the essential element required for a successful marriage. By the end of the respective films of remarriage, such "conversation"—scripted by some of the finest Hollywood writers of dialogue at the time—promises, Cavell says, "an entire life of intimate exchange between the principal pair. We feel that these people know one another, or risk being known, and that they know how to play together (know and accept, you may say, the role of theater in their mutuality) in a way to make one happy and hope for the best."

Cavell, however, points out that the realization of the potential of the relationships in the comedies of remarriage would seem to come at the cost of the woman's role as a mother and, furthermore, of an effective relationship that she might develop toward her own mother. Neither children nor the woman's mother feature much in these films, leading Cavell to ask whether "the absence of literal mothering is the permanent price or punishment for the woman's happiness?" Additionally, Cavell highlights the privileging of the male that remains within the relationship of apparent equality as this is developed between the sexes in the comedies. As Cavell says, much in these films' narratives turns upon the choice or agreement made by the woman with the man in question, who will take on the role of her educator so that her own desire can be affirmed. Therefore, Cavell proposes that the ending of the comedies of remarriage leave "a moral cloud,"[2] a moral question about the dependency of the female characters upon their male lovers for their recreation and development. Furthermore, Cavell questions whether the man in these comedies actually himself undergoes a transformation in his relationship with the woman whom he aims to reeducate. And whether the education that he feels is necessary to teach his female counterpart is, in part, for his own "use and pleasure and pride."[3] However charming and capable of tenderness as the lead men in the comedies of remarriage are (played by actors of such expressive gifts as Spencer Tracy, Cary Grant, James Stewart, and Henry Fonda), nevertheless, their characters possess what Cavell refers to as a taint of "villainy" about them. On the positive side, this can take the form of a talent for deception that helps the man achieve his desire to win back his ex-partner (Spencer Tracy's use of a pistol, which turns out to be made of licorice, or his fake weeping in *Adam's Rib*, for instance). But, on the negative side, the man's devious abilities allow him, ultimately, to retain his original position of male power in the relationship.

The Lady Eve might be seen as an exception to this, as all of the manipulation is on the side of Jean (Barbara Stanwyck) practiced upon the unwitting Charles (Henry Fonda), but, even so, she still looks to him as both a husband and father figure.

Like the comedies of remarriage, the melodramas Cavell discusses are also about the creation of the principal woman (apart from *Letter from an Unknown Woman*) and her metamorphosis (the image of the butterfly in *Now, Voyager* is significant in this respect). But what distinguishes this genre from the former is that the woman ends up either unmarried or isolated or, as in *Letter from an Unknown Woman*, even dead. And, furthermore, the woman remains "unknown" or at least misunderstood in her existential being by her male counterpart. It is for these reasons that Cavell suggests that the women of these films are descendants, as well as sisters, of Nora, in Ibsen's play *The Doll's House* (1879), who, at the end of the play, refuses to live with her husband any longer and instead chooses to risk a life of self-discovery outside the ties of marriage.

The creation of the woman in the melodramas is not achieved through the conversation with a man of the type that is such a central feature of the comedies. However, Cavell argues that this question of the creation of woman is central to an understanding of *Now, Voyager* and *Stella Dallas,* although it remains hanging in doubt whether it is, ultimately, of relevance to Paula (Ingrid Bergman) in *Gaslight* or Lisa (Joan Fontaine) in *Letter from an Unknown Woman,* who is already dead at the beginning of the film and whose role is more like that of the mythical departed Echo calling to Narcissus. Eventually, in *Letter from an Unknown Woman,* in a scene that particularly interests Cavell, Stefan (Charles Jourdan) will cover his eyes with his hands in a gesture of recognition of Lisa's love for him while she was alive, even while at the same time it affirms her unknownness, since Stefan never manages to break free of his narcissism. Thus, in the melodramas there is a failure to develop the type of "conversation" that characterizes the couples' achievement in the comedies of remarriage owing to the limitations of the male character.

> I notice that the male's explicit limitation in *Stella* is manifested as perceptual incompetence, in one man's affable crudeness [Ed Munn] and in another man's dulled conventionality [Stephen Dallas]. I . . . notice that in *Letter* it is manifested as a man's virtuosic self-absorption and compulsive seductiveness, and in *Now, Voyager* as his courteous but advancing irrelevance, and in *Gaslight* as old-fashioned, fixated menace.

In a climactic scene of great ironic power, Paula, in *Gaslight,* turns the tables on her cruel and greedy husband, while both Stella and Charlotte, respectively of *Stella Dallas* and *Now, Voyager,* move beyond the bonds of marriage to take their own paths in life.[4] *Stella Dallas* is often thought to be a film about self-sacrifice, but Cavell believes that the film is not simply to do with this, but rather about Stella's rediscovery of her own mother (in herself); thus, Stella enacts both the roles of mother toward her own daughter as well as daughter to her own (absent) mother. According to Cavell, a similar set of relations governs *Now, Voyager* (in one early scene, Charlotte's face is montaged with that of her mother) as well as *Camille* (1936), which is based on Verdi's opera *La Traviata*. Camille/Violetta sacrifice their love for Alfredo in order that their lover's sister may marry and, presumably, have children. In this way, Cavell believes, Camille/Violetta create themselves as mothers by proxy.

While the relationship of Charlotte and Jerry in *Now, Voyager* is often taken to be the epitome of Hollywood's story of thwarted, romantic love, Cavell reads the film differently, especially the last scene that concludes with Charlotte's infamous line, "Oh, Jerry, don't let's ask for the moon. We have the stars." For Cavell, Jerry fails to comprehend Charlotte, misrecognizing her voyage of self-realization for one of self-sacrifice in adopting his daughter, Tina. Earlier in the scene, Charlotte indicts Jerry for his conventionality in wanting to prevent her from this adoption and, a little later in the scene, struggling to keep up with her thinking, he asks somewhat lamely, "And will you be happy, Charlotte?" However, in the character of Dr. Jaquith (Claude Rains)—significantly enough, Jaquith is a psychiatrist—Cavell finds a man who, indeed, does recognize Charlotte's rebirth as a woman. Are you the same woman as before, he asks, and she answers emphatically, "No."

* * *

I claim that the four films principally considered in [*Contesting Tears: The Hollywood Melodrama of the Unknown Woman*] define a genre of film, taking the claim to mean, most generally, that they recount interacting versions of a story, a story or myth, that seems to present itself as a woman's search for a story, or of the right to tell her story. In certain ways what I have to say adjoins the manifold projects now in the intellectual arena for discovering a feminine difference of subjectivity; in certain ways it takes on what in my work I conceive of as the call for philosophy, the right to its arrogation. It is a continuous issue for me on both of these ways to understand my right to intervene in them.

I call the genre the melodrama of the unknown woman, after its perhaps most illustrious member, Max Ophuls's *Letter from an Unknown Woman* (1948, with Joan Fontaine and Louis Jourdan); the other members featured here are *Gaslight* (directed by George Cukor, 1944, with Ingrid Bergman and Charles Boyer), *Now, Voyager* (Irving Rapper, 1942, with Bette Davis, Paul Henreid, and Claude Rains), and *Stella Dallas* (King Vidor, 1937, with Barbara Stanwyck and John Boles). . . . An important pattern within their mutual connections is given in their relation as a group to another genre of film I have studied and, in the light of the new genre of melodrama, continue also to study, to which I devoted the book called *Pursuits of Happiness,* a genre I name there the comedy of remarriage. The films I take as defining for remarriage comedy, a group of films also from the Hollywood of the 1930's and 1940's, are *It Happened One Night* (1934), *The Awful Truth* (1937), *Bringing Up Baby* (1938), *His Girl Friday (1940), The Philadelphia Story* (1940), *The Lady Eve* (1941), and *Adam's Rib* (1949). Systematic connections among these comedies are much easier to see or to give credit to when they are formulated, for various reasons. They are individually more famous, or anyway more beloved . . . and they share their particular directors and their characteristic stars (Katharine Hepburn, Irene Dunne, Cary Grant, Spencer Tracy, Barbara Stanwyck). Not the least interest, by the way, of *Gaslight* in particular, is that Cukor is also the director of two of the seven central remarriage comedies, *The Philadelphia Story* and *Adam's Rib.*

Remarriage comedies begin or climax with the threatened end of a marriage, that is to say, with the threat of divorce; the drive of the narrative is to get the original pair together *again,* whereas classical comedies—at least, so-called New Comedies—concern the overcoming of obstacles to a young pair's desire to be together in the first place and in a condition called marriage. The obvious obstacle to marriage in classical comedy is the woman's father (or some senex figure, some older man), who is prepared to bring down the sternness of the law upon his daughter if she goes against his wishes, whereas in remarriage comedy, if the woman's father is present he is always on the side of his daughter's desire. Moreover, in remarriage comedy the woman's mother is never present (with illuminating exceptions that prove the rule), and the woman of the principal pair is never herself shown to be a mother and is approaching an age at which the choice of motherhood will be forced upon her or forced away from her. A constellation of what may be called further "features" are consequences or causes of these circumstances, and a number will be alluded to here. I emphasize at the outset that in both remarriage comedy and its companion melodrama of the unknown woman, new circumstances or clauses of some continuing story are not limitable in advance of critical analysis (for example, it turns out that the woman's body is emphasized in some way in each of the comedies); and since the circumstances are not well thought of as common features (for example, most, but not all, open in a city and then significantly move to a place in the country, analogous to the Shakespearean so-called green world or golden world), it is critically essential to, so to speak, account for an absence in a particular instance, a process I call articulating a compensating circumstance (for example, *His Girl Friday* lacks a green world, but it contains, with equal definitiveness, what I describe as a black world). So it is part of the idea of a genre I am working with that both the specific relevant "features" of the genre and the general candidacy of an individual film for membership in the genre are radically open-ended.

Pervading each moment of the texture and mood of remarriage comedy is the mode of *conversation* that binds or sweeps together the principal pair. I suppose that this is the feature that comes in for the greatest conceptual development in *Pursuits of Happiness*. Conversation is given a beautiful theory in John Milton's revolutionary tract to justify divorce, making the willingness for conversation (for "a meet and happy conversation") the basis of marriage, even making conversation what I might call the *fact* of marriage; and conversation in these remarriage films is concerned with what religion, in the Book of Genesis, takes as what we might call its myth of marriage, namely the creation of the woman from the man—the story of Adam's rib. In these comedies the creation of the woman—the new creation of the woman, the creation of the new woman, the new creation of the human—takes the form of the woman's education by the man; hence a critical clause in the story these films tell and retell is the discerning of what it is about this man that fits him to be chosen by this woman to provide that authorization of her, of let us say her desire. This suggests a privileging of the male still within this atmosphere of equality. The genre scrutinizes this in the ways, even in this atmosphere, the male is declared, at his best, to retain a taint of villainy. This so to speak prepares the genre for its inner relation to melodrama. And if the melodrama of the unknown woman is "derived" from the genre of the comedy of remarriage, the pervasive feature of equal conversation must have its pervasive equivalent in the melodramas.

The mechanism of "derivation" is what I think of as the negation of the features of the comedies by the melodramas. For example, in the melodrama of unknownness the woman's father, or another older man (it may be her husband), is not on the side of her desire but on the side of law, and her mother is always present (or her search for or loss of or competition with a mother is always present), and she is always shown as a mother (or her relation to a child is explicit). With these differences in the presence and absence of parents and children goes a difference in the role of the past and of memory: in the comedies the past is open, shared, a recurring topic of fun, no doubt somewhat ambiguous; but in melodramas the past is frozen, mysterious, with topics forbidden and isolating. Again, whereas in remarriage comedy the action of the narration moves, as said, from a setting in a big city to conclude in a place outside the city, a place of perspective, in melodramas of unknownness the action returns to and concludes in the place from which it began or in which it has climaxed, a place of abandonment or transcendence.

The chief negation of these comedies by these melodramas is the negation of marriage itself—marriage in them is not necessarily reconceived and therewith provisionally affirmed, as in remarriage comedy, but rather marriage as a route to creation, to a new or an original integrity, is transcended and perhaps reconceived. . . . The route to this alternative integrity is still creation, or what I might call metamorphosis—some radical, astonishing, one may say melodramatic change of the woman, say of her identity. But this change must take place outside the process of a mode of conversation with a man (of course, since such a conversation would constitute marriage). It is as if the women of the melodramas are saying to their sisters in the comedies (they are sisters because both lines of women, as I argue elsewhere, descend from identifiable heroines in Shakespeare and in Ibsen): "You may call yourselves lucky to have found a man with whom you can overcome the humiliation of marriage by marriage itself. For us, with our talents and tastes, there is no further or happy education to be found there; our integrity and metamorphosis happens elsewhere, in the abandoning of that *shared* wit and intelligence and exclusive appreciation." This elsewhere is a function of something within the melodrama genre that I will call the world of women. That there should be this alternative route to integrity and possibility is hardly surprising, since it is the one taken in characteristic films of the women who represent the highest reaches of glamorous independence registered in the idea of a star—classically, the figures of Greta Garbo and of Marlene Dietrich, that of Bette Davis at her best, and I suppose those of Barbara Stanwyck and of Ingrid Bergman. The persistence of this feature of metamorphosis indicates the cause of these genres as among the great subjects of the medium of film, since a great property of the medium is its violent transfiguration of creatures of flesh and blood, its recreation of them, let us say, in projecting and screening them.

The films represented in the melodrama of the unknown woman are among those films known to our culture, from the time of their making until the present, as "women's films" or "tear-jerkers." And even in recent years, when they are receiving more attention, particularly from feminist theorists of film, they are characteristically, as far as I have seen, treated as works to be somewhat condescended to, specifically as ones that do not know their effect, the desire that is in them, and do not possess the means for theorizing this desire, as it were, for entering into the conversation over themselves. I can believe that this is true of many, even most, of the films Hollywood dubbed and merchandized as "woman's films" and that have designs upon our tears. My experience of the films . . . disputes any such condescension, and I regard them as full companions of the remarriage comedies from which I take them to derive, hence among the high achievements of the art of film—worthy companions in intelligence, in seriousness of artistic purpose, in moral imagination, and even in a sense in wit. They are of course less ingratiating than those comedies; but then so much of film, and so much in the rest of culture, is less ingratiating. But films like *Gaslight* and *Stella Dallas* are so often the reverse of ingratiating that it becomes painful to go on studying them. A compensating profit of instruction must be high for the experience to be justified . . .

I do not know whether it will help or hurt my case for the melodramas under consideration here as worthy companions of the best of the Hollywood comedies of the sound era as I go on to describe both the comedies and the melodramas as working out the problematic of self-reliance and conformity, or of hope and despair, as established in the founding American thinking of Emerson and of Thoreau. The comedies envision a relation of equality between human beings that we may characterize, using favorite terms of Emerson's, as a relation of rightful attraction, of expressiveness, and of joy. These are terms Emerson attributes to the work of poetry (in the essay "The Poet"),[5] work which, moreover, he generally understands as that of metamorphosis. The relation as between human beings is not, in the comedies, perceived as one that pervades society as it stands, but it is shown to hold between a pair who are somehow exemplary of the possibilities of this society perceivable from its current stance. The melodramas envision the phase of the problematic of self-reliance that demands this expressiveness and joy first in relation to oneself. It is a claim of mine that in his essay "Self-Reliance"[6] Emerson explicitly (but somehow unnoticeably) affiliates his guiding idea with the self-consciousness demanded in Descartes's famous *cogito ergo sum* (I think therefore I am), his pivotal answer to skepticism, to philosophical doubt concerning the existence of the world and of oneself and others in it—the thing philosophers learned to call hyperbolic doubt: I might call it doubt to excess, to the point of melodrama. Emerson's work thus undertakes nothing less in its proposal of self-reliance than a succeeding proof of human existence, as well as a demonstration of his right to offer such a proof, namely through his inheriting of philosophy—in this instance of Descartes's *Meditations*—for America.

Why the comedies and melodramas that engage this problematic of American transcendentalism's participation in skepticism concern the achievement or the transcendence of marriage—I mean why from a philosophical, call it even a metaphysical, point of view marriage is their theme—I will merely now suggest by quoting a sentence from near the end of an essay of mine of a few years ago, "Being Odd, Getting Even,"[7] that somewhat works out both Emerson's and Poe's inheritances of Descartes's philosophizing, and goes on to relate their achievement in this regard to the criticism of Cartesian skepticism developed in so-called ordinary language philosophy, particularly in Wittgenstein's *Philosophical Investigations* (a criticism whose originality is essential to the later Wittgenstein's philosophical originality as such):

"If some image of human intimacy, call it marriage, or domestication, is [or has become available as] the fictional equivalent of what the philosophers of ordinary language understand as the ordinary, call this the image of the everyday as the domestic, then it stands to reason that the threat to the ordinary that philosophy names skepticism should show up in fiction's favorite threats to forms of marriage, namely in forms of melodrama and of tragedy."

* * *

That essay links the link between Descartes's cogito proof and the proof through melodrama to an imagination of a cultural moment, in forms of romantic writing, at which the theatricalization of the self becomes the main proof of its freedom and its existence . . .

2

Among friends the taking of pleasure is an offer of pleasure, and the showing of pleasure at pleasure offered is the giving of pleasure. My book *Pursuits of Happiness* can be taken to pose the question whether the pair of a romantic marriage—whose ambitions of intimacy are apt, outside Eden, to trail a history of pain, of misunderstanding, and, despite the mutual respect in friendship, sometimes villainous antagonism—can become and stay friends. That book studies a set of films whose answer is a conditional Yes. To name the genre "the comedy of remarriage" is to say that the complex of conditions it elaborates can be summarized as the willingness for remarriage. In the set of melodramas . . . the woman's answer to that possibility of friendship is an unreserved No. Since it follows for her that she thereby says No to marriage as such, as presently conceived (unless it is essentially for the benefit, or under the aegis, of a child under her protection), it follows further that these melodramas bear an internal relation to remarriage comedy.

The internality has to do with the principal women of both genres sharing an image of their lives—demanding, if it is to be shared, equality, mutual education, transfiguration, playfulness, etc.—which I find in the perspective I call Emersonian perfectionism. . . . In neither instance is a marriage of irritation, silent condescension, and questionlessness found more desirable than solitude or, say, unknownness . . .

A perfect negation of remarriage comedy's basis in friendship is Nora's refusal, in Ibsen's *A Doll's House,* to stay one further night under the same roof with a man to whom she is not just legally bound but, despite all, remains attracted to, but from whom she shrinks from any longer receiving pleasure . . .

A certain choice of solitude (figured in a refusal of marriage) as the recognition that the terms of one's intelligibility are not welcome to others—at least not as the basis for romantic investment in any present other whom those terms nominate as eligible—is, as suggested, what the idea of unknownness comes to in my use of the subtitle *The Hollywood Melodrama of the Unknown Woman.*

Nothing beyond this is settled about the specifics of what goes unknown apart from the investigation of the lives figured in the details of the films in question. . . . I should note the objection made to me that four films seems a small number on which to base a claim to the existence of a significant genre of melodrama, as seven films seemed small in the case of the defining films of remarriage comedy. My answer is roughly four-fold: (1) that I am interested in developing the idea of a genre as well as in defining the specific genres in question (it is the idea of genre-as-medium, as opposed to the more familiar idea of genre-as-cycle—a distinction broached in my essay "The Fact of Television"[8] which takes genre-as-cycle to characterize, for example, television series, where episodes are instances of a given set of characters and setting, and takes genre-as-medium, in contrast, to characterize groups of works in which members contest one another for membership, hence for the power to define the genre); (2) that the fruitfulness of articulating the genre of remarriage comedy lies in the specificity and the quality of the genre, the conceptual detail of what I claim is the best group of films among the comedies of the opening period of Hollywood talkies, not anything and everything that anyone may call, for example, Screw-ball Comedy; (3) that the theoretical richness is verified in the distinctness this genre gives to the related specific set of melodramas, hence potentially to further definable sets of related melodramas as well as related comedies; (4) that the idea of unknownness in the melodramas, matching the continuing demand of the woman in remarriage comedy to be known, reads back, or forward, into the various moments in which I have gone into the meeting of skepticism and tragedy at the point, or drive, of an avoidance of—terror of, disappointment with—acknowledgment; so that, again, a sense of the smallness of the number of related texts rather recedes, to my way of thinking, in the face of the number of related texts by which, and by the specificity in which, they are implied.

The melodrama of the unknown women presses the question of a woman's interest in knowledge that in the remarriage comedies is elaborated in a thematics of her demand for an education. The comedies hence raise the drama in her choice of a man to provide this education, a drama whose happiness turns on the condition that the man reciprocally craves the knowledge of (that is, by) this woman and in such a manner that the struggle between the sexes can play itself out without interruption (for example, by children, or by economic need), on the sublime level of difference mutually desired and comically overcome. In the melodramas the education of the woman is still at issue, but within their mood of heavy irony, since her (superior, exterior) knowledge becomes the object-as prize or as victim-of the man's fantasy, who seeks to share its secrets (*Now, Voyager*), to be ratified by it (*Letter from an Unknown Woman*), to escape it (*Stella Dallas*), or to destroy it (*Gaslight*), where each objective is (generically) reflected in the others . . .

To extend a little further here the interaction of the two genres, I begin by noting a puzzling feature of three films I have not discussed . . . but which I have variously announced . . . or predicted, as members of the genre of the unknown woman: the von Sternberg–Marlene Dietrich *Blonde Venus* (1932), the James Whale–Irene Dunne–Paul Robeson *Show Boat* (1936), and the Mervyn

Leroy–Ronald Colman–Greer Garson *Random Harvest* (1942) all bear a remarriage theme. I call this feature puzzling because it suggests not a participation in but rather a negation of the unknown woman genre, according to which marriage as such, as it stands, is repudiated as villanous, or prohibited, or irrelevant to the woman's desire. I treat this repudiation, after all, as perhaps the essential connection between the unknown woman melodramas and the remarriage comedies from which they derive. A point of discussion might then be to ask how this little subgenre of remarriage melodrama might be compensating for its, as it were, happy ending (negating the negation in the melodramas). This may indicate a way to understand its underscoring of the ineffectuality and irrelevance of the male (in *Blonde Venus* and *Show Boat*); or (in *Random Harvest*) leaving it unknown whether the man can live with his recovered memory that the woman who has been resourceful nurse to him, then faithful secretary, then brilliant hostess for him, is one and the same woman, the one with whom he had once bestirred himself to have a child; and unknown what precisely this woman was waiting for in awaiting this memory.

And what of this subgenre's apparent neglect of the fundamental feature of the films . . . that I formulate as the woman's search for the mother? This neglect is perhaps none too sure. In *Now, Voyager,* Charlotte Vale (Bette Davis) discovers, in her "idiosyncracy," the mother in herself, having in a sense had no mother but instead a double father. In *Show Boat,* Magnolia (Irene Dunne) discovers her mother, or her kind (her biological mother represents little more than the upholder of law, or convention, before her permissive husband), in the "negress" Julie, played by the most famous (white) torch singer of the time, Helen Morgan. Magnolia is shown playing the olio in a black-face, song-and-dance called "Galavantin' Around," having joined the acting company to replace the hunted Julie; and when she is abandoned by her husband and applies for a job singing on her own it turns out to be a job currently held by that same, still haunted Julie. When asked what kind of songs she sings Magnolia replies, "Negro songs," and then auditions with "Can't Help Lovin' That Man of Mine." Julie hears the audition from her dressing room and leaves surreptitiously to make room for Magnolia. The double replacement of Julie by Magnolia is decisive for the character of both women and for the depth to which an account of the work of this narrative of gender and race must reach. I merely assert for the moment that the truth of this motherly withdrawal (I suppose as complex as the withdrawal in *Stella Dallas)*—I mean the fact that Julie has been a true teacher of her knowledge to Magnolia—is validated by its being Paul Robeson, no less, who after establishing himself by singing "Ol' Man River" watches Magnolia dancing and remarks, "Look at that gal shimmy." Irene Dunne's casting as Magnolia plays a role in her figuring definitively in both remarriage comedy and in the genre of melodrama in which it is the accidental prevention of marriage, not the deliberate rejection of it, that provides the drama (*Back Street; Love Affair*, and its remake as *An Affair to Remember*). Deliberate rejection is more the line of the borderer Julie.

An outstanding question about *Blonde Venus* is why the woman returns to the marriage—how Marlene Dietrich could, never more attractive and independent than here, and even for the sake of her child, credibly return to conjugal life with that ordinary, vindictive, stuffed shirt. (It is Herbert Marshall for whom she leaves Cary Grant. Imagine.) It makes sense of the events to say: she has judged the world she has seen, and she has seen much of it, to be second-rate, one whose unnecessary stinginess with happiness she can do nothing to improve. But her son has, even in such a world, a chance to do something, with a mother like her to teach him what men and women can be like. Watching Marlene Dietrich as a mother in this film is a revelation. I know some who have fixed ideas of what glamorous cabaret singers are like and what nurturance is like and cannot look and see their superb, however rare, coincidence here. But where does the woman's ability to judge the world come from? In the four [melodramas] under discussion . . . it comes from the woman's being confined or concentrated to a state of isolation so extreme as to portray and partake of madness, a state of utter incommunicability, as if before the possession of speech. In *Letter from an Unknown Woman*, it would accordingly be the inability of the woman to exercise this force of judgment that causes her apparently inadvertent and absolute destructiveness.

The idea of having the power to judge the world—as a place fit to live in, disdaining its demand to live without love—became guiding for me in thinking about opera, about what causes the diva's singing, something I try to locate in the span between the primitiveness of the orality of singing and the sophistication in the ecstasy in finding and presenting a voice. It is here that a reasonable space opens within which to glimpse the power of Garbo, the most famous figure of the unknown woman of film, or I might rather say, the figure about whom unknownness is felt most intuitively, most demandingly.

Arguably her greatest, most ample, role was that in *Camille* (1936, directed by George Cukor with Robert Taylor and Lionel Barrymore), based on the Dumas play *La Dame aux Camelias*, and on the knowledge of the other great setting of that play, Verdi's (and Piave's) *La Traviata*. Without the link to opera, *Camille* seems to deny its connection with the melodrama of the unknown woman in its apparent search for the father, as well as in the film's transcendence of irony in its final, tardy, recognitions. The opera all but forces us to recognize that the drama is concentrated in this woman's power to judge the world, announced early as her declaration of freedom from the world ("Sempre libera"), expressed in her choice of the half-world (this Dumas is credited with coining the term *demimonde*). Her seduction by the young, persistent admirer turns on his getting her to question her judgment of the world as unfit for love; her counter-seduction by the young man's father turns on his returning her to her former judgment of the world (of men) as implacable, but now expanding her negation of that world, her mode of partaking of it, to include the negation of herself. Yet, as she and young Alfredo have agreed, love is mysterious, in its crossing of torture and bliss.

To accept her acceding to the father's plea, as the act of sacrifice worthy to make her acceptable to this old man and his daughter, is to take this man's view of the event as authoritative. But it is a view from which—demonically plausible as it is—I seem to see her way past. ("Demonically plausible": thus I mark, and hurry past, the obligation, if the power of this narrative is to be realized, to describe the frightening persuasiveness Verdi lends to the exchanges between old Germont and Violetta, in their sequence of duets and solos that constitute the heart of Act Two. In centralizing, or concentrating, the old force of the father, *Camille,* backed by *La Traviata,* accents the virtual absence of the woman's father in the unknown woman melodrama—a condition that intuitively fits the distinctive presence of the woman's magic father in remarriage comedy.) Following her links of conviction in freedom, in love, and in God's world as the counter to man's world, this father—in appealing to her to give up his son Alfredo to save him and his sister from ruin—appeals not to the rigor of law but to the tyranny of convention. While he imagines that his privately accepting her as a daughter will be her reward for her self-sacrifice, Violetta has already, in her words of agony at man's implacability, put aside the world of men as her judge—judged their judgment of her. This is not new; it was something her life of freedom had itself declared. What is new, with the choice to forgo love, is her judgment of her old world, hence her inability any longer to accept it as her habitat. Her new reward is that through this father she is giving children to the world, which both makes or modifies her sense of giving up Alfredo and which allows her, in the fantasy of a grateful and approving daughter, to place herself within the state of motherhood—evidently her only access to it. It does not prepare a life of happiness, but it also does not invite a death of madness. Why assume the father is of more importance in himself than this suggests? Who knows men better than she? The musical setting of the words Violetta says to herself when she contrasts man's judgments with God's begins with a sonority that shifts from a key in major (here D-flat) to that key in minor, a banality that Verdi stages to terrifying effect. The capacity for such radical shifts of mood—a capacity I assume essential to that small class of narrative artists who are at once immeasurably great and incalculably popular (Verdi, Shakespeare, Dickens, Chaplin, how many more?)—is, in the realm of film acting, the signature of Garbo.

When one senses that Garbo's body of films have failed to do justice to her powers, it is, at a guess, to this capacity for mood shift that one is chiefly responding. It would be why the reference to opera, in her case, is distinctly pertinent. George Cukor's *Camille* can certainly seem not to be Garbo's equal—I cite the coarseness of all the other women in the film, of the cardboard father (Lionel Barrymore), of the insipid love music composed for the film when *Traviata*'s "Di quell'amor" is for some reason not found repeatable. But sometimes the flaws and scars seem not to matter. At such times I think one reads these awkward supports as expressive of the isolation registered in Garbo's temperament, in the narcissism of this temperament's evolution in response to itself, to its memories and anticipations more than to the promptings of perception, whose actual objects as it were transform themselves for her favor. The opening sequence, a privileged minute or two of her shifting moods, traverses a series of moods as notable for their lucidity as for their range; it constitutes an entire course in film acting and contains a greater density of description and revelation than is likely to be found in a lifetime of respectable exposure and diligence.

It is in the figure of Garbo that the idea of the woman's unknownness most purely takes on its aspect of the desire of a man for a woman's knowledge, as if to know what she knows may be taken as the answer to the question what a man after all wants of a woman—and does not want after all. (If we thereupon take as an answer to the sublimer question, What does a woman want? that what she wants is to be known, or to know that her separateness is acknowledged, we may see the epistemological mismatch for which the genders have been headed: whatever will count as her being known—and I suppose this is quite undefined—it is precisely not to be satisfied by her having at once to tell and not to tell what she knows. At best this changes the subject.) . . .

In remarriage comedy the issue of unknownness takes on, as said, the aspect of the woman's desire to know something, to be educated, where this seems to mean to know that her desire is acceptable and what its satisfaction would look like. (The problematic is broached at its most hilarious or delirious, in the films in question, in the set of interrogations and responses that Jean [Barbara Stanwyck] in *The Lady Eve* proposes as the task of finding one's ideal, rattling the paradox that anything worthy of being held on to as an ideal is impossible to arrive at and hence is unworthy to be held on to.) To prove the radical unacceptability of the woman's desire is precisely the task of the horror story the husband tells his wife in *Gaslight* to drive her mad. In *It Happened One Night*, the puzzle of the woman's desire is elaborated by a systematic symbology of foods, that is, by the recognition of human desire as (transfigured) hunger, a reasonably straight manifestation of Freud's theory of human instinct. So, I suppose, is it manifested in *Genesis,* in the apple, . . . blatantly so in the remarriage comedies, and not just because the names of Adam and of Eve appear among the seven titles of the comedies I have taken into account.

Notes

1. Stanley Cavell, *Contesting Tears: The Hollywood Melodrama of the Unknown Woman* (Chicago: University of Chicago Press, 1996), p. 116.
2. Cavell, p. 115.
3. Cavell, p. 116.
4. See especially the chapters "Ugly Duckling Funny Butterfly: Bette Davis and *Now Voyager*" and "Stella's Taste: Reading *Stella Dallas*" in Cavell, *Contesting Tears,* pp. 115–50 and 197–222, respectively.
5. "The Poet" is an essay written between 1841 and 1843, published in Ralph Waldo Emerson, *Essays: Second Series* in 1844.
6. "Self-Reliance," published in Ralph Waldo Emerson, *Essays: First Series* in 1841.
7. Stanley Cavell, "Being Odd, Getting Even: Threats to Individuality," *Salmagundi,* no. 67 (Summer 1985): 97–128.
8. Stanley Cavell, "The Fact of Television," *Daedalus* 111, no. 4 (Autumn 1982): 75–96.

CHAPTER 15

FROM ONE MANHUNT TO ANOTHER

Fritz Lang Between Two Ages

JACQUES RANCIÈRE

J acques Rancière (b. 1940) taught at the University of Paris VIII from 1969 to 2000, occupying the chair of aesthetics and politics from 1990 until his retirement. He is a former student of the prominent Marxist intellectual and member of the French Communist Party Louis Althusser (1918–1990), who taught at the École Normale Supérieure. Following his association with Althusser and the publication of *Reading Capital* in 1965,[1] which marked a watershed in his philosophical development,[2] Rancière developed his political thought by exploring the structure and form through which political dissent (*dissensus*) is brought about and actuated. For Rancière, dissensus occurs at the level of what he calls the distribution of the sensible, involving a disturbance of the normalized, consensual sociopolitical relations of subjects and bodies that effectively limit the possibilities of perceptual experience. Politics and art can in certain circumstances and in different ways create a dissensus that disrupts these established ways of seeing, hearing, and understanding and, thereby, bring about a redistribution of the sensible. Specifically, dissensus is located, and emerges from, the irreducible disparity that exists between signification and perceptual experience, a disparity that Rancière calls in French *un écart*, meaning variously fissure, gap, difference, deviation, and interval. Throughout his work since the 1970s, Rancière has endeavored to embrace this disparity as fundamental to both his political theory and philosophy of art.

Cinema has been a subject of ardent interest for Rancière since an early stage in his intellectual life. While his writings on cinema date from the late 1990s,[3] Rancière's enthusiasm for it can be traced back to the 1960s when he was infected by the wave of cinephilia aroused by Henri Langlois's Cinémathèque Française, the Parisian ciné-clubs, and the rise of the filmmakers of the *Nouvelle Vague*. Rancière describes his own cinephilia as an amateur's passion, by which he does not mean a hobbyist's passion, but rather one who upholds a form of sensibility—the aesthetic experience of the cinematic spectator—that eschews categorization and belongs neither to a world of pregiven meanings and classifiable designations or to a romanticized world of autonomous experience.

Rancière claims that the structure of cinema's stories still adhere to the principles of narrative logic and dramatic tension that were originally laid down by Aristotle in his ideas about *muthos* in the *Poetics* (ca. 335 BC). However, in the films that Rancière is attracted to the narrative logic is, on occasion, stopped, redirected, and "thwarted" by sensible affects (*opsis*) that are irreducible to the film's character or the principle of cause and effect governing the plot. According to Rancière, such affects act in combination with the narrative drive of the film to create a resistant—that is, dissenting—otherness beyond prescribed forms of identity and reason.

Informed by Kant's idea of an aesthetic experience that is disinterested and free of instrumental purpose, described in the *Critique of Judgment* (1790) in relation to both beauty and the sublime, Rancière, in his discussion of Lang's *M* (1931) in the accompanying text (2001), analyses certain moments in the film that suspend its narrative drive, however briefly. Rancière observes that Beckert's murderous intentions, around which the first part of the film revolves, can be supplanted at certain times by another kind of sensibility that gives his character a psychological complexity and depth irreducible to a single interpretation of his motivations: this is the "obstinacy" in Beckert's character, his "aberration," of which Rancière speaks. Wandering the city's streets, the murderer, Beckert, melts into the crowd like an "anonymous flâneur," whereupon he enjoys eating an apple and becomes absorbed in the spectacle of a hardware shopwindow consisting of a display of alluring art nouveau patterns and shapes. After a few moments of gazing at the display, the murderer switches his abstracted gaze from the shopwindow to the child who only then becomes an object of his murderous intentions. A little later in the film, the murderer stands like a parent beside a young girl in front of a further shopwindow. Rancière claims that, for a few moments, these scenes in front of shopwindow displays are not simply pauses or moments of rest in the narrative but an "empty time, the lost time of a stroll or the suspended time of an epiphany" that changes the very meaning of the notion of an "episode." The scenes in *M* of disinterested aesthetic appreciation that Beckert enjoys breaks with the classical idea of a narrative following a linear trajectory. Ultimately, Rancière claims that the empty time of these scenes "lends power to the narrative," allowing for the depiction of a complex sensibility (that of Beckert's) pitted against the powers of rationalism that is the real subject of *M*.

Rancière observes that in *M* two kinds of the law are at stake: first, there is "the law pure and simple. The order that protects honest, as well as dishonest, people," but there is a second form of the law in the film that particularly interests Rancière. This law is "the *mimesis* of the social comedy": "The way social roles have of living off imitation . . . [the law] that one must imitate, perform, what, whether true or false, is not there or not known." This question of mimesis is raised in the film by the last scene of the murderer's "trial" by the members of the underworld. Rancière notes that the tone of the voice of the woman representing the bereaved mothers exactly matches that of the murderer when he comes to express his own emotional distress later in the "trial." Both the murderer and the prostitute speak of what they do not know; the former since he has a split personality and remembers nothing of the murders that he commits, although he is haunted by them, and the latter because she is not one of the bereaved mothers grieving for their murdered daughters but someone who purports to "know" their grief. Each finds equivalences for experiences that they do not actually possess through the mimetic strategies of speech, the tones of their voice, and their bodily movements and gestures; Beckert, himself, performs his speech like a classical actor on the stage. In this way Beckert fictionalizes his life, attempting to persuade the jury of the "truth" of which he speaks, of what it is like to have an-other self. As he says, "I have no control over this evil thing inside me . . . it's following me, silently. . . . Afterwards I read about the crime. But I can't remember anything about it." And, for some moments the criminals in the audience are convinced by his "performance," nodding their heads in empathy as if they can feel, too, what it is like to have other voices threatening their normative selves. In these few moments, barely lasting more than a couple of edits in the film, the consensual fabric binding together the criminals under Shränker's stern leadership that affirms an otherness to (their) identity is temporarily undone.

Lang's *While the City Sleeps*, made in Hollywood in 1956, replays the hunt for a psychopathic killer that was the subject of the director's earlier film *M*, previously released in Germany in 1931. Comparing these films, Rancière believes that they represent "two different ages of the visible,"[4] as these pertain to the Weimar Republic and the postwar era in the U.S. and, more generally, the West, respectively. Rancière shows that in *M* the Weimar Republic is characterized by a rationalist mentality, exemplified by both the police and the underworld and the instrumental methods by which they map the city and its buildings in their hunt for the killer. In contrast, postwar America is characterized in *While the City Sleeps* by a regime of control based upon the construction of the subject's identity through a set of statistical categories that purport to identify and always already "know" the subject.

Rancière observes that there are different methods for bringing the serial killer to light in each of the respective films directed by Lang; in *M* the police's methods for capturing the murderer are by means of "maps and magnifying glasses, inventories and drag-nets,"[5] whereas in *While the City Sleeps* the police no longer figure as agents of apprehension, but rather the television monitor is utilized as a form of surveillance that places Mobley, a TV broadcaster and investigative journalist, "'face to face' with the murderer" in his own bedroom,[6] "transforming an imaginary capture into a weapon for a real capture."[7] By going on television with an Identikit of the murderer's profile and confronting the murderer through this medium, "Mobley adds to the knowledge of the police-man the knowledge of the clinical doctor, the supposed knowledge of the psy-choanalyst, the knowledge of the professor, and many other types of knowl-edge besides." Mobley draws upon these professions to constitute himself as a subject of sovereign knowledge that "knows" who the murderer is, what his motivations are, and where he goes, even though, in actual fact, his "knowl-edge" is inferred from clues and traces of the subject left at the murder scene. Rancière argues that, as one who speaks from "the position of one who knows and sees you," Mobley exemplifies the regime of power dominant in Western democracies today, a power that is all pervasive. In *M* the murderer manages to find refuge in a warehouse, thereby, if only briefly, evading the traps laid by both the mob and the police. Blind spots like this within the system of control and surveillance are no longer available to the murderer in *While the City Sleeps*; by analogy, the subject today exists only insofar as s/he is always already appre-hended as an a priori object of statistical knowledge and power.

In *While the City Sleeps* the mimetic elements of *M* demonstrated in the trial scene have changed significantly because now the performance has become entirely identified, through the character of Mobley, with an authoritarian fig-ure claiming to possess knowledge of the murderer that he does not know. Such a persona no longer relies upon performative qualities of rhetorical persuasion, as does the murderer and the prostitute in *M*; now there is no room for doubt or uncertainty as to personality or motivation—or for a possible exchange of identifications. Mobley "confiscates" this power of mimesis, and with it all ideas of psychological depth or complexity. Indeed, "the tele-visual image" that Mob-ley represents, "calls into question the very *gestus* of acting." Reflecting the effect of this Identikit model of knowledge and power upon the murderer in *While the City Sleeps*, the actor (John Drew Barrymore) playing his part can only put on a monotonous performance of a pathological stereotype: "the same snarl, the same eyes widening in alarm, the same sequence of gestures." In this scenario, "knowledge" is conveyed as if face to face, but the televisual medium or technical apparatus is not what organizes the new regime of visibility con-gruent with the film's production. Rather, it is the changed "scientific," statisti-cal approach to mimesis that characterizes this new power of the visible.

Rancière draws attention to the correspondence between the murderer and Mobley in *While the City Sleeps*, both of whom use, in different scenes, the same technique of placing the doors' security locks on the latch to reenter the apartments of women they are attracted to. By this means, the murderer regains entry into the apartments of his intended victims, while Mobley returns to his fiancée's apartment after she has sent him packing, reminding him that they are not yet married. For Rancière, it is as if, after reentering his fiancée's apartment, Mobley gives a distant-learning lesson to the murderer showing him how to seduce a woman and, by implication, what kind and degree of social normalization is required to carry this out successfully. Rancière suggests that, in performing this pedagogical lesson for the murderer, Mobley takes on the role of an older brother. This role corresponds to Mobley's ideas about himself as a broadcaster, instead of as a father figure representing American democracy, freedom, and the rights of the press, as do the Kynes who run the news empire. Mobley has no inclination to take on that role, even though the elder Kyne wishes him to do so. Rather, what interests Mobley is the power that can be gained through utilizing the TV broadcast, with himself in the role of a tele-instructor identifying what the public seems to want and appearing to know how to satisfy it, much as an older brother might want to appear toward his sibling. In Lang's vision of American democracy, this fraternal figure, who speaks from "the position of one who knows and sees you," has superseded the power of both the oedipal father and George Orwell's Big Brother, both of whom allowed for momentary transgressions and spaces for anarchic thinking. According to Lang, power now resides in the capacity to construct subjects through Identikit categories of identification so that who you are is always already given. In this respect, Rancière disputes Deleuze's reading of America as a land of brethren and freedom assured by virtue of its immigrant background.[8] As Rancière states, the dissensus expressed in *M* by the mimetic values of Beckert and the prostitute at the former's trial is emptied of its power for affirming alterity by the regime of the older brother in *While the City Sleeps*, "Fritz Lang's fable confronts the fraternal utopia of American democracy with a counter-utopia: the world of older brothers is not the 'high road' of the emancipated orphans but its opposite, a world with no escape. It is not the father and the law but their absence that closes all the doors. It is the destitution of social *mimesis* . . ."

* * *

Since its release in 1955, Fritz Lang's *While the City Sleeps* has been seen as an expression of radical pessimism by an artist who had grown disenchanted with democracy and with the art of cinema through the combined forces of the American people and Hollywood. If that is the case, then what is really the object of Lang's pessimism, and how does he turn it into fable? It is standard to assume that the heart of the plot is the all-out competition between the big shots of Amos Kyne's news empire: the editor, the head of wire services, and the manager of picture services fight it out to see who gets the position of managing director of the empire when its founder dies and the business is turned over to his spoiled and incompetent son. The son gets the competition going by promising the position to the one who succeeds in unmasking the maniacal woman-killer whose crimes are at that moment terrorizing the city. A whole web of feminine intrigues is deployed for the service of the competitors. As for the visual space of the film, it seems to be entirely composed of the bodily movements and exchange of glances that cast these schemers into always unstable relationships of inferiority or superiority; in the huge glass office, they spend their days spying on what is happening on the other side of the corridor in the hopes of catching a meaningful smile or motion by surprise, all the while hiding what they themselves are doing, fashioning a mask meant to deceive the others about the power relationships at play. The assumption, in short, is that everything revolves around the competition and the secrets permanently lodged in the bowels of the immense machinery whose business is to bring to the people the light of information. Lang's pessimism consists in observing, and making us observe, that all these people hunting down the murderer are as unpleasant as he is, perhaps even more so.

But it could be that the show put on by these schemers is only a comforting illusion, and that the plot's black heart is really made up of the actions of the only two honest members of Kyne's empire, the reporter Ed Mobley and his fiancée Nancy, a secretary. Mobley is not angling for a promotion, nor is he interested in getting tangled up in any schemes. All he really wants to do is unmask the murderer, and he has his own idea about how he's going to do that: he'll lead the murderer to reveal himself by talking to him. Mobley's project is, a priori, contradictory. To speak to the murderer, he must first know who the murderer is, and if he knows who he is, it is because he has already been caught. Even the Machiavellian examiner Porphyry would be powerless if Raskolnikov hadn't bitten the bait and come out to meet him. Mobley is no examiner though, he's a television reporter, and speaking face to face with people he doesn't know is what he does every night at eight o'clock. On the night in question, he goes to the television studio ready to speak to his viewers, as he always does, and to speak to one viewer in particular, the murderer. Armed with the insubstantial pieces of evidence he got from a policeman friend, Mobley sketches the murderer's Identikit, tells him he has been identified and that soon it'll be all over for him. Without seeing the murderer, Mobley looks at him, he summons him with his voice to meet this gaze. And suddenly, mid-sentence, a spectacular camera movement anticipates the effect with a shot reverse-shot that places the camera in front of the murderer and the television monitor in the reverse angle. This literal rendition of the "face to face" that introduces the reporter into every home is at the same time a trope that inverses the very meaning of the word "television." The *televised* is no longer the one seen on television, but the one seen by it. In this scene, the televised is the murderer, who is told to recognize himself as the one of whom, and to whom, Mobley speaks.

Lang performs with this camera movement a standard theatrical operation, well known since Aristotle as recognition, the change from ignorance to knowledge. But, more than simply the process that leads from ignorance to knowledge, recognition is the operation that brings the identified and unidentified persons into alignment. The paradigmatic example is to be found in *Oedipus Rex*, where Oedipus learns that he himself is the murderer he's been looking for when the messenger, pointing at him, tells the herdsman: "here's the man that was that child." There is recognition in a nutshell, in the junction of the two demonstratives the herdsman had tried so hard to prevent. Indeed, all the other characters in the play who either know or suspect the secret spare no efforts to prevent the alignment of the two identities, to postpone the moment of recognition when Oedipus gets caught in his own trap—a trap set by the one who knew nothing and who above all had had to remain ignorant, though he was, at the same time, the only one who insisted on knowing.

This is what our scene in the film is all about. Evidently, though, Lang has inverted everything in Aristotle's schema of recognition. For one, the audience has known the murderer's face ever since he was shown in action in the opening shots of the film, quite some time before this scene. For another, the moment of recognition is not the moment when the trap closes, but when it is set, when the character who does not know pretends to know and tells someone he doesn't know: "I know you're him." Feigning to know more than one does to get the suspect to fall into the trap and cough up the missing evidence is nothing new, but elementary police work. But that's not what's happening here, as is shown, *a contrario*, by an episode a little earlier on in the film, when the police arrest the unfortunate super of the building for seeming the ideal suspect and take him back to the station, where they put him through the usual treatment: the bright lights projected on the face, the harassing questions, the intimidation, etc. This whole show, Mobley tells his friend Lieutenant Kaufman, is useless and bound to get him nowhere. Mobley puts what he knows and doesn't know to a completely different use. There are no light projectors shining in the suspect's face, no questions, there's no harassment or intimidation. Mobley is not out to make the suspect on hand confess to having committed the crime, but to bring the unidentified criminal to the recognition that he has been recognized. That requires an apparatus that institutes a different kind of face to face: a face to face with someone who is closer to you than any policeman can ever be, precisely because he is farthest away, because he only sees you from far away; a face to face with someone who is instantly on intimate terms with you, who speaks to you while speaking to everyone else, and to you just as to everyone else.

What does Mobley do in this scene, then? Two things at once. While his words sketch the Identikit that tells the criminal what he is, his eyes lock the criminal in their gaze and direct him to where he must recognize himself: in the Identikit. The problem, of course, is that Mobley's Identikit is an insubstantial illusion, an amalgam of two heterogeneous elements: the set of individuating traits (age, physical strength, hair color) Mobley uses to describe *who* the murderer is, though these never suffice to individuate anyone; and a standard and well-known clinical portrait that says only *what* he is, to what category of criminal pathology he belongs. The police would have no use for such an Identikit, nor is it intended for them. The only person who can find it useful is the person who has to recognize himself in it: the one assumed to be there facing Mobley, the one instructed to identify his *who* to this hotchpotch of distinctive traits. The murderer, by the same token, is the only one who can expose himself, who can go where he is expected through the mediation of the pleasure of having been recognized for *what* he is, and the terror of having been recognized for *who* he is. The visual counterpart to this double mediation is the double grimace of Robert Manners, played by John Barrymore Jr. Whether in front of the fictional screen of the television or in front of the real screen of the camera, the double register of the actor's expression is absolutely stereotypical. The initial feeling of satisfaction—a broad smile, eyes shining—is superseded by a growing sense of panic—a snarl, eyes widening in alarm, and hands that move into action and clutch the crossbar of the chair, just as later on they'll clutch the mother's neck and, toward the end, Dorothy Kyne's neck. The actor's performance exhausts itself in the variations on this double register, particularly the snarl. It is all he can do to convey the distress mechanically triggered in him by the sight of a woman's legs, his feverishness before the projected action, his ambivalent feelings toward his mother, or his attitude when confronted by Mobley's imaginary gaze. The stereotypy of Barrymore's performance cannot but remind us of a performance of much higher caliber from a quarter of a century earlier, also by an actor playing the role of a psychopathic killer, a sort of brother of Robert Manners. His stereotyped grimaces remind us of all the expressive nuances—the transitions from carefree stroller to savage beast to prostrate victim—that Peter Lorre brings to his role in *M*, another manhunt story, for which *While the City Sleeps* is, in some ways, the American remake.

It is of course possible to explain away the difference between the two by appealing to the quality of the actors, and it is well known that Lang had nothing but harsh words for the young Barrymore. But what is also well known is that Lang left a very small margin of initiative to the personal talent of his actors: when he discovered during the filming of *M* that Peter Lorre couldn't whistle, he did the whistling for him instead of dropping it from the film. In other words, even if John Barrymore Jr. couldn't act as well as Lang might have wanted, it is reasonable to think that he acted as Lang told him to. He may not have known how to give a *stereotyped performance*, but that is what he was asked to do. The expressive simplification has nothing to do with the incompetence of the actor, but is integral to the very apparatus of the *mise-en-scène*; this apparatus is what has changed since *M*. If it has changed, it isn't because Lang has lost his creative touch, but because an apparatus of cinematographic *mise-en-scène* is a way of playing with a political and social apparatus of visibility, a way of using one of its tacit resources, of rendering its implicit activity explicit. The stereotypy of Robert Manners' grimace is the polar opposite of *M*'s savage and conquering whistling because Lang is working with different apparatuses of visibility in *M* and in *While the City Sleeps*.

It would be worthwhile then to backtrack and consider for a moment the episode in *M* that corresponds to the remote face to face between Mobley and the murderer that launches the manhunt. Midway through *M*, the police, following a microscopic search of psychiatric hospitals, identify the murderer and his whereabouts. Armed with a magnifying glass, a policeman examines the windowsill of his lodgings, where he finds, as he runs his fingers on the wood-grain, shavings from the red pencil the murderer had used to write his taunting messages. While they are searching his lodgings, the murderer is out and about. He is standing in front of a shop window with a little girl he has just met. Both are visibly quite happy: happy with what they are looking at, happy with being together. His eyes follow the child's hand as she points to the toy of her dreams. He loves being a *flâneur*, he loves looking at shop windows, he loves little girls, he loves pleasing them. He seems to have momentarily forgotten the goal of the operation: he is just delighting in the present. She, too, is happy, since she loves toys and adults who are kind to little girls. A little later, when she sees the chalk mark on his shoulder, all she thinks about is cleaning up the stain on the "poor old man." The manhunt is about to begin, and once it does there'll be no respite, so that this scene is the hero's last moment of grace, and we must understand "grace" in the strong sense of the term. It is not a last moment of respite, but something more like a grace granted to the character, the grace he has been allotted as a character. It was but a moment earlier that a masterfully arranged composition had shown us his transition from normal person to furious and pitiless beast hunting its prey; and it is but a moment later that the hunt against him will be in full swing. But for now, there is a moment of grace when the murderer is allowed to delight in a spectacle, a touch, a sensation, and to delight in it aesthetically, disinterestedly. Before the scenario condemns the character, before he is left with no chance of survival, the *mise-en-scène* grants him his chance at being human. Not at being a sick man in need of protection, but his chance at being a carefree *flâneur* in a crowd, nothing more than a peaceful image seen through a shop window. It grants him his photogenic chance, in Jean Epstein's sense of the term.

The issue here is not one of narrative suspension, but of poetics. Aristotle's requirement that the narrative must lead the criminal to the point where he'll be caught and unmasked runs into a new, and conflicting, requirement: the *aesthetic* requirement for suspended shots, for a counter-logic that at every turn interrupts the progression of the plot and the revelation of the secret. In these moments, we experience the power of empty time, the time of goals held in abeyance when young Cosettes contemplate the dolls of their dreams, and when those condemned to "misery" delight in a simple moment of reconciliation with a world wholly indifferent to them and from which all one really wants is the chance to share in a novel quality of the sensible. "Action too has its dreamy moments," says the author of *Les Misérables,* and rightly so. The important point is not that the progression of the episodes has to be punctuated with moments of rest, but that the very meaning of episode has changed. The new action, the aesthetic plot, breaks with the old narrative plot by its treatment of time. In the aesthetic plot, it is empty time, the lost time of a stroll or the suspended time of an epiphany—and not the time of projects, of goals realized or frustrated—that lends power to the narrative. Literature came upon this pure power of the sensible between Flaubert and Virginia Woolf, and Jean Epstein, along with a handful of others, dreamed of making this power the very fabric of the language of images. True, the allures of this language never fully seduced Fritz Lang, nor did he ever embrace the notion that cinema was the new art of *aisthesis* that would supplant the old arts of *mimesis.* Lang understood very early on that cinema was an art insofar as it was the combination of two logics: the logic of the narrative structuring the episodes and the logic of the image that interrupts and regenerates the narrative. Lang also noticed early on that the combined logic of cinematographic *mimesis* bore close ties to a *social* logic of *mimesis,* that it developed as much in reaction to that social logic as under its shelter.

Let's take a closer look at the moment of aesthetic happiness, which is also a moment when places are exchanged. While the police are searching his room, the murderer is casually wandering the streets. There is something strangely complementary between M's brief moment of peace as a man of the crowds and the punctilious organization of the police, its unflagging efforts to find in the visible what it hides by tracing circles on a map with a compass, by meticulously searching every bush, and by descending into the dingiest dives to subject their every nook and cranny to the magnifying glass. M's chance to exist as a character, both for himself and for us, paradoxically depends upon all these circles that spread the news of the murder while concentrically closing in on the murderer, who manages nonetheless to inch his way and trace his own path across the circles traced by the police, the mob, public opinion, and the anarchic spread of suspicion. He is sheltered, somehow, at the heart of the trap, much as the happiness of the scene in front of the shop window is embedded in an alternating montage that stresses that the hunt for the criminal is only gaining momentum. All the circles that close in on him in the scenario of the trap, all the social circles that imitate each other, preserve him as a character and give him his chance.

To grasp the principle of this chance, we must take a look at a singular moment in the murderers already singular trial in the makeshift courtroom set up by the mob. What is so strange about this trial isn't that the members of the mob act out every single one of the roles that make up a real trial, down to the defense attorney who, his Penal Code in hand, so stubbornly defends the murderer that no one is quite sure how to ascertain "what he really thinks." It is, more profoundly, that the murderer's fate seems caught between two laws: the law pure and simple, the order that protects honest, as well as dishonest, people; and a second law: the *mimesis* of the social comedy, the way social roles have of living off of imitation, of being fueled by the social's penchant for the theatrical—for diffusing, performing, and reversing roles. The crime boss appoints himself the representative of the bereaved parents and honest citizens and confronts the murderer with photos of the young girls he has killed; the con man of the group plays the attorney for the defense. A prostitute interrupts the proceedings to voice the anguish and pain of the mothers. Is she herself a mother? Or is she playing the role of mother as the others play at being attorneys? It doesn't much matter. What does matter is the sudden change of tone in her voice: midway into her angry tirade against the murderer, her voice falters, and when she resumes, after a brief silence, she speaks more slowly, more tenderly, as if she were trying to express the ineffable pain of these mothers and to make us believe that she too has felt it. A woman caresses her shoulder while she speaks, a silent display of the solidarity of these bereaved mothers. "How could you know what it feels like? You should ask the mothers": that's the gist of what their "representative" has to tell him. The initial anger, the faltering voice, the continuation in a lower tone of lamentation, the simple words, we had heard all of it but a minute before—in the murderer's testimony. He, too, starts out by launching an angry tirade against his accusers, comes to a halt midway through, and then resumes his speech in the same lower register, the expression of his pure pain. And he, too, concludes by asking his prosecutors: "What do you know? How could you possibly know what I feel?" In both instances, the same "voice of pain" breaks the silence to invoke what the other does not know. There is something that remains unknown and that can only be imitated, vocalized, performed, something that can only be felt through an equivalent.

The murderer's chance and the happiness of the *mise-en-scène* both rest on the possibility of weaving the cry of distress and the appeased countenance into a *mimetic* fabric that is, simultaneously, a paradigm of how society functions. The *social* law of *mimesis* is that one must imitate, perform, what, whether true or false, is not there or not known. Sincerity and hypocrisy are equal before this imperative. The counterpoint to the naked order, to the social order of the law, is what we might call the freedom or chance of *mimesis,* which here grants an equal chance to the fictive mother and the fictional murderer. This is what protects M, and is precisely what has disappeared in *While the City Sleeps.* If there is a paradox in the relationship between the schemes going on inside Kyne's empire and the fate of the psychopathic killer, it isn't that these supposedly "honest people" seem more sordid and low than the criminal they are hunting down. It is rather that this empire of the democratic press and of public opinion has blotted from the field all public opinion, even the one that assumes the terrifying form of the lynching mob in *Fury.* No one is too concerned with Robert Manners in *While the City Sleeps,* no one makes the rounds of the psychiatric clinics to find out if any patients have been released, no one tries to find out the murderer's whereabouts. Even stranger, nobody reads the *New York Sentinel,* save for the journalists and the murderer. And it seems that nobody watches television either, except for Nancy, to admire her hero and, once again, the murderer. There is no list of the usual suspects and places, no need to pick up the scent of the murderer and track him down. The murderer himself, the televised, will of his own accord go where he is expected, and he'll do so because an image has come to him and directed him to sit down in front of it and to recognize himself in the imaginary Identikit of the murderer. He has to recognize himself in the Identikit and feel flattered that the identity of his case has been recognized, happy that his lipstick message worked and that his hateful glee has been recognized. But, at the same time, he must also recognize that he is trapped, that he has been recognized as the murderer. This double capture hurls the murderer into the trap and incites him to want to do what, till then, he had only done by automatic compulsion. He's now to do it as if he had been programmed to do it, either through the desire for vengeance or because he's been challenged. He has no choice but to respond in the same exact manner to every situation: he must equate his simple incapacity to bear the sight of a woman's legs with the deeper motivations of vengeance, hate, and challenge. Indeed, all of this yields only one symptom, it is all expressed in the same snarl, the same eyes widening in alarm, the same sequence of gestures.

The stereotypy of his performance, rather than reflecting the shortcomings of a deplorable actor, reflects the apparatus of visibility that sustains the character. The structure that would protect him from his pursuers is gone, and with it is gone also his chance for a moment of grace when he might be allowed to express something besides this simple facial automatism. The other's vocal address and binding gaze have locked him in this imaginary shot reverse-shot, and there is no escape. A murderer can elude the police; a man of the crowds can, like M, merge into the crowds. That is totally different from having to elude someone who looks you in the face from far away in order to make you coincide with what he knows about you, someone who, in and through you, brings what he knows and doesn't know into alignment. Face to face with the murderer, Mobley adds to the knowledge of the policeman the knowledge of the clinical doctor, the supposed knowledge of the psychoanalyst, the knowledge of the professor, and many other types of knowledge besides. He gathers all these types of knowledge under the aegis of one fundamental knowledge: he can pass himself off for the savant that he isn't. Put more generally, he knows how to act out what he is not. This is, essentially, the knowledge of the actor, and it is as an actor that the journalist combines in himself all these roles. Mobley confiscates the power of *mimesis* and its performances and identifies them with the position of the one who knows. He chains this power down to the place filled by his image, the place of the one who sees and knows.

A quick look at the classical formulation of the problem, Plato's in particular, will shed some light on the identification going on here between science and *mimesis*. The sovereign knowledge Mobley deploys in his broadcast is the ability to identify what he knows with what he doesn't know, what he is with what he isn't; in short, he deploys the knowledge of being what he is not. This defines, in Plato, the knowledge of the mimetician: a non-knowledge that passes itself off for knowledge. We're all familiar with how Plato calls this "knowledge" into question. There is Socrates, in the *Ion*, asking how the rhapsode Ion could possibly know everything he sings about in his epic poems. How could he know how to "do" everything he narrates, everything he identifies himself with? And, in the *Republic*, Socrates asking ironically if Homer knows everything his characters know. After all, his characters rule states, wage war, and so on. Does he, Homer, know how to do all that? If he doesn't, we must then conclude that his fabrications are just simulacra, appearances suitable only for nurturing the social comedy of appearances.

This social comedy of appearances, as we saw a minute ago, obliges the mob to parody both the pain of honest people and the impartiality of justice, and, in the same stroke, gives the character his chance at the very heart of the death hunt. Things have changed by the time we get to Edward Mobley, and what Homer could not do, he can. With his one iconic performance, Mobley actually manages to be everything at once: policeman, public prosecutor and judge, professor, doctor, interlocutor, and general commanding the battle. Mobley is all of these as an actor, which explains why he is no longer limited by the obligation to mimic justice or the police. The actor, having forged the imaginary synthesis of every type of knowledge, arrives in the place of the one who knows and imposes an imaginary face to face that banishes from the field every social space protecting the character, every social space granting the character the chance to be something other than what he is to knowledge, that is, a sick man, a well-documented clinical case, something akin to a Charcot photograph or an overhead projection in a pedagogical conference—a puppet of knowledge.

The apparatus of Ed Mobley in his TV studio, and the ruse used by his journalist colleague Casey Mayo in *The Blue Gardenia*, another film by Fritz Lang, are not at all alike. Mayo, angling for a spectacular story, also traps his victim by using the press to address himself directly to her. With his "Letter to an Unknown Murderess," he leads her to believe that she has already been identified and offers her his help as a ploy to get her to come out into the open. Mayo's trap, however, displays all the classical traits of seduction: set by a man for a woman, by a successful journalist for a petty switchboard operator, it trades on traditional hierarchies of sex and class. Nothing could be further from Ed Mobley's trap in *While the City Sleeps.* He offers no assistance to allure the weak one to come to him, but imposes his assistance upon the murderer in a different sense. He imposes his image, his presence, his identification of what he knows with what he doesn't know, of what he is with what he isn't. Mobley's trap trades only on the imaginary knowledge borne by the image that speaks to the televised and instructs him to act strictly in accordance with what it knows about him all the way up to where the trap engulfs him. This is no seduction, but an execution in some senses more radical than the one in the fictive trial: a scientific execution that robs the subject of the ability to be different than he is known to be. It is an execution in effigy at the same time that it is the setting of an effective trap.

This is something entirely different from Casey Mayo's *trick,* and also from the intrigues and schemes—the withholding of information, the adulteries, the hallway romances—that go on in Kyne's empire. That the honest and disinterested Mobley should despise all that is perfectly understandable. Here, at least, things are still as they were in Plato: to despise power one must know something better than power. And clearly Mobley knows something better than being the managing director of the empire: the thrill afforded by this play of knowledge that absorbs all relationships of domination and that ends up being an apparatus of execution. But, to get to the bottom of this face to face, we must look into the nature of the image Mobley places before the murderer, the nature of the power he exerts and that allows him to impose this face to face. We need a detour here, leaving behind Mobley king of the screen to follow Mobley as a man about town.

A truly peculiar love scene sheds light on our problem. Mobley downs a few shots of whiskey at a bar to muster up some courage and, a little tipsy, goes to call on Nancy. She won't let him in, but Mobley very stealthily manages to release the door's security lock so he can sneak back into the apartment unannounced and impose upon his beloved the embrace of reconciliation. This scene is, interestingly enough, modeled point for point on the murder scenes of the psychopathic killer. Everything is the same: the staircase, the fascination with women's legs, the quick side look at the released security lock, the intrusion into the apartment, the ensuing scuffle, and even the insistent inscription of the maternal signifier: "Didn't you ever ask your mother?" Nancy's reply to one of her suitor's saucy questions echoes the message the maniacal killer writes on the wall with his victim's lipstick: *Ask Mother.* Lang's camera develops a sustained analogy between the love scene and the murder scene. Where, then, is the difference? The answer visually suggested by these shots is simple: Mobley strikes the right flow, the proper motor coordination of speech, gaze, and hands. The point is to know the right way to use physical violence, to hold the neck with one hand while wrapping the waist with the other, to close one's eyes instead of rolling them or staring wide-eyed, to use vulgar language and saucy pitches instead of mute lipstick inscriptions. Mobley, in short, shows that with women there are things to do and say—they just have to be performed in the right order and with the proper timing. None of this, incidentally, requires a whole lot of subtlety: it works even when the motions and intonation are those of a man who's had a few too many whiskeys. It all comes down to starting off on the right foot, which means renouncing the position of papa's boy—à la Walter Kyne—and of mama's boy—à la Robert Manners; it means renouncing the superfluous question: are you what your parents wanted you to be? That's the price to pay for starting off on the right foot and for mastering the fluid coordination of one's motor skills, the price to pay if one hopes to turn out a good behaviorist and not a psychoanalytic Identikit.

The spectator no doubt feels that he too would fall for this mediocre pitch were he in Nancy's shoes, and that in spite of the fact that this is clearly less a love scene than a pedagogical one. Rather than making a show of his affections for Nancy, Mobley is giving the sexual psychopath a distant-learning lesson on the normal libido, on the libido that has gone through all the stages of infantile fixation and found the right objects to suck on—glasses of booze and the lips of secretaries. We're now in a position to explain Mobley's peculiar power, what he brings to this place, to the image the murderer has no chance of escaping. It is not the father, the law, order, or society that one cannot escape. Recall Mobley's attitude when Amos Kyne was going off about the duties of the press in a democracy, about the sovereignty of the people, the need to keep it abreast of all it is interested in, and so on. Mobley just turns his back to him. He is thinking about his imminent broadcast, and his silence seems to be saying: "Oh! come off it! The people, democracy, the free press, information. That's all a bunch of stuff and nonsense. What really matters is what I'm about to do. Yes, me, sitting in front of the camera and entering everybody's living room. The people don't exist. There are only tele-spectators and people like me unto infinity, people I can instruct, not as a father, but as an older brother."

This older brother is not a terrifying image of the "big brother" variety. The older brother is just someone who can project a normal image, an image of the norm, someone who has gone through all the stages of infantile fixation and "matured" his libido. Mobley faces the murderer as he would face his kid brother who never left the stage of intellectual and manual masturbation and of papa and mama stories, and is still wondering whether it was for wanting him that a man and a woman performed the series of movements known as making love. In short, he faces the murderer as an older brother, the image of the normal. The knowing actor occupies the place of the older brother, that image of the normal, the place of a fully absorbed, yet self-denied, *mimesis.* This is the new couple that replaces the duo of *mimesis* and the law. The actor has taken over the place of the expert, absorbed all of *mimesis,* and identified it from then on with the position of the one who knows and sees you. In Mobley's televised broadcast, the authority of the brother trumps the authority of the father. There are, as we know, two ways of understanding this substitution. Discussing Melville's *Bartleby, the Scrivener* and *Pierre,* Deleuze concocts a theoretical fable, an America of brothers and sisters founded on the destitution of the image of the father.[9] Fritz Lang's fable confronts the fraternal Utopia of American democracy with a counter-utopia: the world of older brothers is not the "high road" of the emancipated orphans but its opposite, a world with no escape. It is not the father and the law but their absence that closes all the doors. It is the destitution of social *mimesis* to this relationship between a knowing and seeing image and an image known and seen; its destitution to the benefit of the television image, of the played image of the one who is, and knows, normality itself, the "sexually mature" older brother.

More than a German *émigré*'s expression of disillusionment with American democracy, *While the City Sleeps* is the *mise-en-scène* of democracy's identification with the tele-visual. But this identification is not just an object for Fritz Lang. It is a new apparatus of the visible that cinema as such has to confront. We've seen its effects on the fable and on the character of the murderer, so it should come as no surprise to find that the expressions of his vanquisher, the ubiquitous god of tele-visual presence, are also marked by the same stereotypy. We continue to follow Mobley about town, in his role of lover. Close to the denouement, just as the murderer bites the bait of the tele-viser and is about to fall into the trap, Mobley finds himself the victim of a lover's quarrel with his fiancée Nancy. She is angry with him because of his escapade with the provocative Mildred, a columnist working for one of the schemers. Put on the spot by Nancy's accusations, the actor-professor Mobley is singularly incapable of speaking, of finding the tone of conviction. He tells Nancy he would be devastated if she left him, but we don't believe him. It isn't that we think he isn't being sincere. He just comes across as someone who doesn't know how to imitate, how to strike the tone and assume the image of someone overcome by his feelings. Earlier on in the film we had seen the adulterous Dorothy Kyne dupe her husband and the wily Mildred put on a third-rate performance to seduce the reporter. But Mobley, it seems, either doesn't know or has forgotten how to act out even his sincere feelings for Nancy. A sincere feeling, after all, must be performed just as much as a feigned one. The prostitute in *M* knew how to express the pain felt by the mothers, making the question—is she a mother?—redundant. Mobley, conversely, is only capable of expressing two feelings: a vain and idiotic beatitude—self-satisfied smile, mouth wide open, eyes inspired—and exasperation—eyes rolling, hands fidgeting incessantly. "Don't bother me with all this," his hands seem to be saying at first; then they tighten up, recalling the hands of the murderer, and at any rate miming the thought: "I could strangle you"; finally clenched, his two fists bang on the table in the most commonplace of angry gestures. The stereotypy of these two expressions, inane beatitude and exasperation, of course mirrors the stereotypy of the murderer's two expressions. Perhaps Mobley, too, is a captured image, perhaps the mimetician's identification with the image-that-knows has rendered him inept at the old theatrical and social games of *mimesis*, inept at expressing a sentiment through performance. Mobley is reduced to stereotypy and made a prisoner of his own exclusive knowledge: to speak from far away, in the image of the one who knows, to those who are absent.

Faulting the actor in Mobley's case would be much harder than in the case of the murderer. For all the unkind words Lang had for Dana Andrews, he must have known at least two things about him long before he got the cameras rolling. Playing the passionate lover was never this actor's speciality. In *Laura*, his big romance film, he cut a strange figure for a lover. Conversely, the one thing he always played to perfection is impassiveness. In *Laura*, again, he let the humiliations the radio star and worldly socialite Waldo Lydecker hurls at the plebeian policeman Macpherson roll off of his supremely indifferent shoulders. He was certainly capable of investing Mobley's exasperation with all the nuances and half-tones Lang might have wanted. The problem isn't with Dana Andrews' performance, but with the strange sort of actor he plays, an actor who calls into question the very notion of mimetic performance. In *While the City Sleeps,* the policeman has become the journalist and the plebeian taken the place of the worldly socialite. He has taken over the position of the writer and replaced Lydecker's radio voice with his voice and tele-visual image. But this appropriation costs the promoted plebeian a double price: he loses the ability to speak and perform Lydecker's unending love, and he loses Macpherson's patience. He is now a prisoner of his new identity, that of the image-that-knows and that speaks to you from afar. It would seem that, outside of that relationship, there was nothing left to perform but insignificance or a grimace. The image-that-knows can no longer be a character that performs. The tele-visual image, by calling into question the social performance the actor is supposed to represent, calls into question the very *gestus* of acting.

As we watch the grimaces, the rolling eyes, and the exasperated hand gestures that characterize Mobley's performance with Nancy, we may be reminded of a statement by Dziga Vertov from the heroic days of the cinema: "The machine makes us ashamed of man's inability to control himself, but what are we to do if electricity's unerring ways are more exciting to us than the disorderly haste of active men and the corrupting inertia of passive ones?"[10] The disorder of active men, the inertia of passive ones, that is exactly what Dana Andrews gives us here, like a big kick in the face of this great cinematographic ideal. Lang never really shared the ideal of the exact mechanical man captured by the electric eye. Unlike Vertov, Lang was never very enthusiastic about a society where humans were as exact as machines, and equally devoid of psychology. Nor did Lang ever think, like Epstein, that a feeling could be x-rayed and that thought impressed itself in bursts of amperes upon the brows of spectators. Lang always believed that a feeling had to be performed, imitated, and if expressionism (a term Lang disliked) means anything at all, it is that. He always opposed the anti-mimetic Utopia dear to the avant-garde of the 1920s; he always confronted it with that critical mode of *mimesis* that pits one of its modes against the other. Lang stuck to this personal credo from the days of the auteur cinema—the days of *M*, when he was master of the game—all the way through Hollywood, when he had a limited say in a process where actors, like scripts, were dictated by the producer and imposed by the industry. But he always managed to preserve a personal mimetic apparatus and to play his own art of mimesis against the art imposed upon him by the industry. The problem, though, is that in *While the City Sleeps* Lang confronts something other than the industry's financial constraints. He confronts one of the industry's other faces, this other version of the Utopia of electricity, though one that is indeed quite real and called television. This new machine recasts the terms of the relationship between art and industry by redefining the very meaning of *mimesis*. It settles the quarrel between the utopists of the mechanical eye and the artists of a thwarted *mimesis* by replacing both of them, by fixing the status of the mechanical image of the masses as a self-suppressed *mimesis*.

What role does Dana Andrews play? He plays the tele-visual man, he performs the relationship between his ability and inability. He performs the tele-visual man's ability to perform only one thing: the position of the one who knows, the one who, speaking and seeing from far away, summons those who are far off to come and sit themselves down in front of him. This ability is of course a challenge to the mimetic arts in general, and to cinema in particular. We might then think of *While the City Sleeps* as the *mise-en-scène* of the tele-visual man. This explains why the trio—murderer, journalist chasing him down, and his aide—is more important than the schemes and intrigues that run rampant in the news empire. This trio is none other than the tele-visual trio: the tele-visual couple and its witness, Nancy. Mobley knows that at the heart of Kyne s news empire, at the heart of this enterprise of bringing information to the people and of this counter-enterprise of schemes and illusions, there is ultimately only one important thing: the TV studio. The all important thing is the apparatus that puts Mobley "face to face" with the murderer and that is of no interest at all to anyone in the place except for Nancy. I suggested earlier that this trio, and not the show put on by the schemers in the rat-race for the position, is what gives the film its formula. A more precise formulation is perhaps in order. The whole film turns on the threshold that separates the tele-visual trio from the world of schemes and schemers. The trio is set apart because it knows where the serious things are happening. That is the privilege it has over the others. The price the members of this trio pay for this privilege is a deficit in mimetic ability, a deficit in the ability to do what an actor is normally asked to do, since it is, after all, what is also done in real life: imitate feelings, regardless of whether they are felt and experienced.

It makes little sense, then, to spend a lot of time trying to determine what is more interesting, the hunt for the murderer or the schemes that surround it. The real point of interest is this threshold, this relationship between the tele-visual scenario and the old scenario of representation. No matter how sordid the ambitions and means that reign supreme in Kyne's empire, the ostentatious parade of interests, passions, ambitions, deceit, lies, seductions, that old scenario of representation is still what infuses appearances with a great mimetic glow. Besieged by the new power of the image-that-knows, *mimesis* deploys all its old charms, including the most hackneyed, as in Mildred's seduction scene, played by Ida Lupino. Through this huge glow, Lang shows us what is lacking in the image-that-knows, the loss of the mimetic power of seduction that goes hand in hand with its very authority. When he is not in front of the cameras, when he is not looking at a spectator from far away but rather seeing her up close, when he must act out a feeling, the tele-visual character is reduced to this grimace. The film dramatizes this relationship between ability and inability, each side criticizing and mocking the other. Lang's *mise-en-scène* seems to capture the filmmaker's foreboding that perhaps, in art as in this story, the tele-viser will carry the day and the weak image triumph over the strong one. Perhaps it was Lang's premonition of this fate, coupled with his desire to play with it, to drag it back into the very core of the art of appearances, that led him to insist on a short scene not originally in the script, a scene that, paradoxically, the producers wanted to suppress on the grounds that it was a touch coarse: the gag of the slide-viewer with whose secret the wily Mildred sparks Mobley's interest, though all it really hides is a crawling baby. All the powers of illusion are contained in this tiny and insignificant slide-viewer.

Let's not forget the silent commentary of the bartender who picks it up: a smile, a shake of the head. In his smile we see the smile, at once mocking and disenchanted, of the director, who senses that it may very well be the end of the line for the old box of illusions, but wants to play a bit anyway with what has supplanted it.

Notes

1. The book is based on a seminar that Althusser ran on *Capital* with his students Étienne Balibar, Roger Establet, Pierre Macherey, and Jacques Rancière. The complete edition is published as Étienne Balibar, Roger Establet, Pierre Macherey, and Jacques Rancière, *Reading Capital*, trans. Ben Brewster and David Fernbach (London: Verso, 2016).

2. In his following work, Rancière rejected Althusser's claims for Marxism as an objective science capable of speaking on behalf of the proletariat. Rancière felt this to be patronizing and found a similar attitude in the writings of Marx. Rancière's early published work in *The Nights of Labor: The Workers' Dream in Nineteenth Century France* (1989) and *The Ignorant Schoolmaster: Five Lessons in Intellectual Emancipation* (1987) was meant as a counterforce to this attitude expressed by Marx and Althusser and opened up a discourse articulated by the proletariat that was irreducible to Marxist notions of (class) identity and work.

3. Rancière has published several books on cinema in recent times: *Film Fables*, trans. Emiliano Battista (Oxford: Berg, 2006), from which the accompanying text is taken, and *The Intervals of Cinema*, trans. John Howe (London: Verso, 2014). It's interesting to note the original French in the titles of these books for the multivalence of the words *cinema* and *intervals*, respectively; the former is entitled, *La fable cinématographique*, while the latter is entitled *Les écarts du cinema*. Additionally, Rancière has published a book on the Hungarian film director, Béla Tarr: *Béla Tarr, the Time After*, trans. Erik Beranek (Minneapolis: Univocal, 2013).

4. See Jacques Rancière, "Prologue: A Thwarted Fable," in *Film Fables*, p. 18.

5. Rancière, p. 18.

6. Rancière, p. 18.

7. Rancière, p. 18.

8. See Gilles Deleuze, "Bartleby; or the Formula," in *Essays Critical and Clinical*, trans. Daniel W. Smith and Michael A. Greco (Minneapolis: University of Minnesota Press, 1997), pp. 68–90.

9. Deleuze, pp. 68–90.

10. Dziga Vertov, "We: Variant of a Manifesto," in *Kino-Eye: The Writings of Dziga Vertov*, ed. Annette Michelson, trans. Kevin O'Brian (Berkeley: University of California Press, 1984).

CHAPTER 16

CINEMA AS PHILOSOPHICAL EXPERIMENTATION

ALAIN BADIOU

Alain Badiou (b. 1937) is a former chair of the École Normale Supérieure and founder of the faculty of philosophy of the Université de Paris VIII with Gilles Deleuze, Michel Foucault, and Jean-François Lyotard. Radicalized by the writings of Marx and Mao during the political upheavals in Europe in the 1960s, Badiou conceives of his philosophy as integral to his commitment to the communist cause. Communism, Badiou claims, is nothing less than "the destiny of the human species[, the belief] that a different collective organization is practicable, one that will eliminate the inequality of wealth and even the division of labour."[1] For Badiou, the struggle for equality is supported by a philosophy that affirms an ontology of epistemological ruptures and breaks, which, in effect, demonstrate that given notions of knowledge and praxis are not fixed permanently but can be changed with the advent of new epistemes. According to Badiou, systems of knowledge, including traditions of art—*worlds* as he calls them—are subject to "incessant transformations."[2] Some of these transformations do not necessarily have large consequences, but there are others of such maximal intensity that they can overturn the prevailing order of discourse, in turn, inaugurating new and unforeseen worlds of experience and knowledge.

Such paradigmatic changes Badiou refers to as "events," recalling both the radical political events of 1968 and the idea of epochal change as a change in epistemology. In a similar vein he uses the term *truth-event*, since such an event is comparable ontologically to Plato's Idea of absolute truth. However, Badiou's concept of the event is not as a unified origin of a world in a Platonic, metaphysical sense. Rather, for Badiou, the event is true in an absolute sense because it is radically multiple, irreducible to its causes and conditions. On account of this irreducibility the truth-event is only traceable through its subsequent generic "subsets" or "procedures" and "configurations" of knowledge. Badiou has explored these ideas in depth in his major works *Being and Event* (1988) and its sequel *Logics of Worlds* (2006); they are also fundamental to his work on cinema, a subject about which he has written since he was a student in the 1950s, which to date comprises a body of some thirty texts. Many of these texts are about individual films, others, such as the accompanying essay, are more extensive in offering a comprehensive philosophy and interpretation of cinema.

Badiou follows Plato in describing four categories of human experience and praxis: science, politics, love, and art. With regard to the history of Western art, Badiou cites a number of cases of seminal initiating events: Greek tragedy, the classical style of music, the novel, atonal music, and abstract art (which Badiou associates with Kazimir Malevich's withdrawal from figuration prior to the revolution in Russia in 1917). Invented in the nineteenth century, but anticipated millennia before,[3] Badiou considers the birth of cinema as a comparable event to the foregoing revolutions in art. Heterogeneous and "impure," cinema is born from a combination of the vestiges of the other arts, particularly those of painting, literature, theater, and music. In the process of this irreducible fusion, an art form was created: a new "world" known as the "seventh art" of cinema.

Badiou's intention in the accompanying text, first given as a seminar in French in 2003,[4] is to delve into what ways cinema as an art form *thinks,* so that "it is able to interrupt opinion and suddenly propose something else." Specifically, this involves an inquiry into the means by which cinema treats its subjects and themes (love, justice, moral conflicts, and so on) such that it can contest the assumptions of the social imaginary and the rule of state power. Badiou's claim is, first, that cinema is capable of thinking discontinuity; this is on account of the fact of cinema's evental and radically multiple beginnings. Second, cinema has the capacity to synthesize the disjunction between nonart and art. As cinema is a popular form of entertainment, a "mass art" loved by millions, its subjects and themes are integrally bound up with the fantasies, the obscene and violent tendencies of the social imaginary; thus, cinema is shot through with "banal images, trite materials, stereotypes, images that have already been seen elsewhere, clichés." Nevertheless, cinema has the capacity to transform the fantasies and stereotypes of the social imaginary. Indeed, Badiou claims that much of the wonder of cinema, and the pleasure of watching its affects, is to witness its ability to discover an element of purity in such impure material (Badiou cites Orson Welles's *The Lady from Shanghai* [1947] as an example of this for its conscious, reflexive treatment of woman as an evil seductress).

The achievement of this "disjunctive synthesis" between the dominant fantasies of the social imaginary and art, along with other syntheses—temporal, spatial, generic—all these are the hallmark of cinema as a "procedure" that remains true to its evental origins. Additionally, Badiou remarks upon the fidelity that cinema frequently demonstrates as a "truth-procedure" of love. In this context, Badiou discusses a number of remarkable films that are centrally concerned in their different ways with the transformative effects of love; these are, first, as a resistance to state power (Mizoguchi's *The Crucified Lovers* [1954]); second, as intimate love stories that, nevertheless, possess a prescient historical dimension (Douglas Sirk's *A Time to Love and a Time to Die* [1958] and Alain Resnais's and Marguerite Duras's *Hiroshima mon amour* [1959]); and, third, as an experience that converts the religious sense of a miracle into a secular context (Rossellini's *Journey to Italy* [1954]). Ultimately, because of its capacity to create "disjunctive syntheses" between conventionally opposed paradigms and terms, cinema can be equated to a "philosophical experimentation" expressed in the title to Badiou's essay. Here the term *synthesis* does not mean, in the classic Hegelian sense, a unification of opposing tendencies (thesis—antithesis—synthesis), but, rather, as a *disjunctive* synthesis, it denotes an open-ended sense of experimentation, the status of which is yet to be defined. In this respect, cinema offers a sense of hope: the continuing affirmation that "thought can prevail," even if each time this is only momentarily sustainable in the resistant struggle against oppression.

* * *

Cinema has a unique relationship with philosophy: we could say that it is a philosophical experiment. This raises two questions. First, "How does philosophy regard cinema?" Second, "How does cinema transform philosophy?" The relationship between them is not a relationship of knowledge. Philosophy does not enable us to know cinema. It is a living, concrete relationship, a relationship of transformation. Cinema transforms philosophy. In other words, cinema transforms the very notion of idea. Cinema basically consists in creating new ideas about what an idea is. To put it another way, cinema is a philosophical situation. Expressed abstractly, a philosophical situation is the relationship between terms that usually have no relationship with each other. A philosophical situation is an encounter between terms that are foreign to each other.

Cinema Is a Philosophical Situation

The Crucified Lovers, by the Japanese director Kenji Mizoguchi . . . is possibly one of the most beautiful films about love ever made. The story is simple. A young woman has been married off for financial reasons to the owner of a small workshop, a decent man but one whom she neither loves nor desires. Enter a young man with whom she falls in love. You can see how banal the story is. The story takes place in the Japan of the Middle Ages. Adultery is punishable by death. The adulterous lovers must be crucified. They end up fleeing to the countryside. They take refuge in a sort of poetic nature. Meanwhile, the good husband tries to protect them because he doesn't want there to be any violence and because he himself is guilty in the eyes of the law if he doesn't report them to the police. He tries to buy time, explaining that his wife has gone off to the provinces. He's really such a good husband. But the lovers are nevertheless captured and taken to be tortured. Then there are the final images of the film. The lovers are riding on a mule, tied back to back. The shot frames this image of the two lovers heading to an atrocious death, with the hint of a smile on their faces. It is truly an extraordinary smile. This isn't the romantic idea of the fusion of love and death. They never wanted to die. Quite simply, love is also what resists death, as Deleuze and Malraux said about the work of art. No doubt this is what true love and the work of art have in common.

The lovers' smile is a philosophical situation, for it shows us that between the event of love and the ordinary rules of life—the laws of the city, the laws of marriage—there is no common measure. What will philosophy say to us now? It will say: "We must think the event." We must think the exception. We must know what we have to say about what is out of the ordinary. We must think change in life.

We can sum up the tasks of philosophy as regards situations. . . . The most profound philosophical concepts always tell us something like this: "If you want your life to have meaning, you must accept the event, you must remain at a distance from power, and you must stick resolutely to your decision." In this sense, philosophy is that which helps you change your life. Rimbaud said: "The true life is absent." At heart, philosophy makes the true life become present, because the true life is present in the choice, in the distance, and in the event.

. . . Philosophy is the thinking of ruptures or of relationships that are not relationships. But this can be put another way: philosophy is what creates a synthesis, what invents a synthesis where the latter is not given. Philosophy creates a new synthesis in the very place where there is a rupture. It does not just involve observing differences but inventing new syntheses, which are constructed where there is difference. If I take the example of Mizoguchi's *Crucified Lovers* again, a synthesis also occurs with that image of the lovers being taken to be tortured. Naturally, the lovers are in conflict with social law, but in the unity of their smile another possible society is being heralded. It is not just a matter of the disjunction with social law; it is the idea that social law can change. There is the possibility of a social law that would integrate, rather than exclude, love. These lovers are universal because that synthesis, the synthesis between their status as exceptions and the ordinary law, exists. We understand that every exception, every event, is also a promise for everyone. And if it weren't a promise for everyone, that artistic effect of the exception wouldn't exist.

So we can say that whenever philosophy thinks the rupture, whenever it thinks the choice, whenever it thinks the distance, whenever it thinks the exception or the event, it invents a new synthesis that of course forces you to choose. Nevertheless, there is something in your choice that preserves the other possibility. Of course, you are for distance. Truth is completely different from power. But there is a power of truth. And of course you are for the exceptional event, but there also exists a universal promise. This is what I call the new syntheses of philosophy. "What is universal about a rupture?" is essentially the great question of philosophy. The question of rupture is fundamental, but what philosophy tries to discover is the universal value of rupture . . . If philosophy is really the invention of new syntheses, of syntheses within rupture, then cinema is very important because it alters the possibilities of synthesis . . .

What Is a Mass Art?

I'd like to enter into this question in a very simple way and begin with a fact, namely that cinema is a "mass art." An art is a "mass art" if its masterpieces—great, indisputable works of art—are seen and loved by millions of people, at the very time they were created . . . We have indisputable examples of this in the cinema: Charlie Chaplin's great films, for instance. This is a well-known but interesting example. Chaplin's films were seen all over the world, even by the Eskimos. And everyone instantly understood that these films were speaking about humanity, were speaking in a profound and crucial way about humanity, about what I would call "generic humanity"—in other words, about humanity beyond its differences. Charlie's character, although perfectly situated in a particular context, is representative of generic humanity for an African, a Japanese or an Eskimo. This is a striking example, but there are others as well, which are not limited to comic, slapstick, or romantic films. For example, Murnau's *Sunrise*, an extraordinarily condensed, innovative film, which remains to this day one of the greatest poems ever created in the cinema, was in its own time a hit comparable to *Titanic*. We know that all sorts of very great films, films by Lang, Hitchcock, Ford, Hawks, Walsh, and many others, were loved this way by millions of people.

. . . Cinema is unsurpassable as a mass art. But "mass art" implies a paradoxical relationship. It is not at all an obvious relationship, because "mass" is a political category, a category of political activism, whereas "art" is an aristocratic category. This isn't a judgment, merely a statement of the fact that "art" encompasses the idea of creation and requires our having the means for understanding that creation, requires some proximity to the history of the art in question and therefore a particular kind of education. All this accounts for why "art" remains an aristocratic category, while "mass art" is typically a democratic category. In "mass art" you have the paradoxical relationship between a purely democratic element and a historically aristocratic element . . .

The Five Ways of Thinking Cinema

First, the question of the image. To explain why cinema is a mass art—let's not forget our question—we will say it is an art of the image: it has the ability to captivate everyone. In this case, we are regarding cinema as the fabrication of a semblance of the real, a sort of double of the real. We are trying to understand cinema's ability to captivate people in terms of the ability of images to captivate. To put it another way, cinema is the high point of an art of identification. No other art allows for such a force of identification. That is the first possible explanation.

The question of time was fundamental for Deleuze, but it was so for many other critics of cinema as well. We could basically say that cinema is a mass art because it changes time into perception. It makes time visible. Cinema is basically like time that can be seen: it creates a feeling of time that is something other than the lived experience of time. Naturally, we all have an immediate lived experience of time, but cinema changes that lived experience into representation. It shows time.

. . . The third possibility involves comparing cinema with the other arts. We could say that cinema retains from the other arts precisely everything that is popular in them, and that cinema, the seventh art, takes from the other six what is most universal, what seems addressed to generic humanity. What does cinema retain from painting? The possibility of the beauty of the world of the senses. It does not retain the intellectual technique of painting or the complicated modes of representation but rather a sensory, well-regulated relationship with the outside world. In that sense, cinema is a painting without painting, a world painted without paint. What does cinema retain from music? Not the difficulties of musical composition exactly, nor ultimately the great principles of musical development or of the theme, but the possibility of accompanying the world through sound: a certain dialectics of the visible and the audible, hence the charm of sound when it is placed in existence. We all know that there is a musical emotion in cinema that is connected with subjective situations, a sort of accompaniment of the drama, like a music without music, a music without musical technique, a music borrowed from, then given back, to existence. What does cinema retain from the novel? Not the complexities of psychology but the form of the narrative: telling great stories, telling stories to humanity as a whole. What does cinema retain from the theater? The figure of the actor and the actress, the charm, the aura that has transformed them into stars. We can say that cinema is that which changes the actor into a star. So, when all is said and done, cinema does indeed take something from all the arts, but it is usually what is most accessible in them. I would even say that cinema *opens up* all the arts, strips them of their aristocratic value and delivers them over to the image of life. As painting without painting, music without music, the novel without psychology, the theater with the charm of the actors, cinema is like the popularization of all the arts. That is why it has a universal calling. This, then, is a third hypothesis, which would make the seventh art the democratization of the other six.

The fourth hypothesis involves examining the relationship between art and non-art in cinema. Cinema is always located on the edge of non-art; it is an art affected by non-art, an art that is always full of trite forms, an art that is always *below* or *beside* art with respect to certain of its features. In every era cinema explores the border between art and what is not art. *That is where it is located.* It incorporates the new forms of existence, whether they are art or not, and it makes a certain selection, albeit one that is never complete. And so, in any film at all, even a pure masterpiece, you will find banal images, trite materials, stereotypes, images that have already been seen elsewhere, clichés.

. . . There is one last hypothesis for thinking cinema: its ethical significance. Cinema is an art of figures. Not just figures of space, not just figures of the outside world, but great figures of humanity in action. It is like a sort of universal stage of action. Powerful, embodied forms, great values are debated at any given moment. Cinema conveys a unique sort of heroism. And, as is well known, it is the last bastion of heroes today. Our world is so unheroic, and yet cinema continues to feature heroic figures. It is impossible to imagine cinema without its great moral figures, without the battle between Good and Evil. There is obviously an American aspect to this, the political perspective of the ideology of the Western, which is sometimes disastrous. But there is also an amazing side to this capacity for heroism, amazing in the way that Greek tragedy could be: presenting typical characters of the great conflicts of human life to an enormous audience. Cinema deals with courage, with justice, with passion, with betrayal. The major genres of cinema, the most coded ones, such as the melodrama and the Western, are in fact ethical genres, genres that are addressed to humanity so as to offer it a moral mythology. In this respect, cinema is heir to certain functions of the theater, of the theater at the time when it was a theater for citizens.

From the Question of Time to the Question of Metaphysics: A Round Trip via Love

I'd like to give a few examples to illustrate these five different ways of thinking cinema philosophically. Let's consider the question of time, which has always been a great question about synthesis . . . There are countless examples of this, one of the most classic being Eisenstein's *The Battleship Potemkin,* in which the temporal construction of the event (the uprising, the repression, and so on) is entirely organized by montage. It is a construction of time because it rearranges things that are happening simultaneously. What we have in this case is a unique kind of time, constructed and imbricated time. But there are also temporal constructions in the cinema that are totally different from that one, the opposite of it, even: for example, a time that is obtained by being stretched out, as if, space being immobile, it were space itself that were stretched out in time. This is the case in long sequences where the camera is either still or rotating in space as if it were unwinding the spool of time.

One example that has always struck me occurs in Alfred Hitchcock's *Rebecca. Rebecca* is built on a mystery, which will eventually be resolved by a confession. The hero, played by Laurence Olivier, confesses to a crime, owing to Hitchcock's extraordinary fondness for confession. Hitchcock loves it when someone relates a crime, because he only likes guilty characters and he especially likes telling us that we're all guilty. The most cunning element in Hitchcock's films is that the innocent character is guiltier than the guilty character, which is the case in *Rebecca* since the crime turns out to have been justified. So the guilty character is innocent. But the scene that concerns us is the confession itself. It is a long sequence, a long story, and the camera revolves around the story. The time of the story is a sort of long virtuoso scene stretching out, without any montage, without any divisions, very similar to the pure flow of duration. Here we encounter a different conception, a different thinking of time. It would seem that cinema basically proposes two conceptions of time: time as construction and montage, and time as an immobile stretching out. There is something of Bergson's distinctions here, since Bergson essentially contrasted an external, constructed time, which is ultimately the time of action and science, with a pure, qualitative, indivisible duration, which is the true time of consciousness: *The Battleship Potemkin,* on the one hand, and the confession in *Rebecca,* on the other.

Just as an aside with regard to the confession in *Rebecca:* what is utterly fascinating is that there is a parallel scene in another Hitchcock film, *Under Capricorn,* where there is a long confession scene with a very similar temporality. The only difference is that it is a woman speaking, not a man. If you watch both scenes very carefully, you could even go so far as to say that Hitchcock filmed the difference between male and female duration.

But cinema's greatness doesn't lie in reproducing Bergson's division between constructed time and pure duration; it lies in showing us that a synthesis between the two is possible. What cinema offers is precisely the ability to combine these two types of time. In the greatest films—I'm thinking of Murnau's *Sunrise,* for example—you can absolutely show how moments of pure duration are inscribed within the "assembled" construction of time. There is an absolutely extraordinary scene in *Sunrise,* a trolley car coming down a hill. This pure movement filmed from inside the trolley car is an utterly intense feeling of duration, at once fluid and poetic. But the film is otherwise very much constructed, very much assembled in terms of montage. In the final analysis, what cinema offers, and I think it is the only art that does so, is the possibility of the presence of pure duration within temporal construction, which can really be termed a new synthesis.

Metaphysics has often been defined in terms of the use of opposite categories, basically in terms of a dualism, of major oppositions: finite and infinite, substance and accident, soul and body, sensible and intelligible, and so on . . . What is the difference, in cinema, between the sensible and the intelligible? There isn't any, in actual fact. The intelligible, in cinema, is only a heightening of the sensible, a color or a light of the sensible. This is also why cinema can be an art of the sacred, as it is an art of the miracle. I'm thinking of Rossellini's or Bresson's films. Do Rossellini and Bresson separate the sacred or the intelligible from the sensible? No, they don't, because cinema makes it possible for the sacred or the intelligible to appear as the purely sensible.

Look at Rossellini's film *Journey to Italy.* It is another film about love. (I wonder what cinema would do without love, and what we ourselves would do without love.) It is the story of a couple that is falling apart; we're all familiar with that situation. They take a trip to Italy in the vague hope that things will improve, but of course they don't. The man is tempted by other women. As for the woman, she seeks isolation, solitude, in the city of Naples or in nearby nature, around Mount Vesuvius. But the film ends with their love really being revived, which is actually a sort of miracle . . . Basically, what Rossellini is trying to tell us comes down to a radical proposition: love is not a contract; it is an event. If it can be saved, it will be saved by an event. In the last scene, Rossellini films the miracle. You can film a miracle in cinema, and it may even be the case that cinema is the only art that has the potential to be miraculous.

. . . I think there is an intimate relationship between cinema and love, first of all because love, like cinema, is the eruption of the miraculous in life. The whole problem is whether or not that miracle can last. As soon as you say "It can't last," you fall into a cynical and relativistic conception of love. But if you want to have a positive conception of love you have to maintain that the miracle can last forever. . . . Let me suggest a definition of love to you: "Love is the silence that follows a declaration." You say "I love you," and then all you have to do is keep quiet, because, in any case, the declaration has created the situation. This relationship to silence, this presentation of bodies is tailor-made for cinema. Cinema is also an art of the sexual body. It is an art of nudity. That creates an intimate relationship between cinema and love.

And so I think that cinema is a movement from love to politics, whereas theater is a movement from politics to love. The two trajectories are opposite ones, even if the problem is ultimately the same: What is a subjective intensity within a collective situation? To illustrate this, let's take some examples involving World War II and the question of the relationship between the situation of love and that of war. There are two very different, paradigmatic films on this topic: a classic film, a melodrama, *A Time to Love and a Time to Die,* by Douglas Sirk and a modern film, *Hiroshima, mon amour,* by Alain Resnais and Marguerite Duras. In *A Time to Love and a Time to Die* there are some extremely powerful scenes dealing with the war on the Russian front and the ruins of Berlin. In *Hiroshima, mon amour,* the atomic bomb that was dropped on that Japanese city is the issue and so is the German occupation of France. The historical and political situation is very important. But you enter into these figures through the words of love, through the encounter of bodies, through the intensity of intimacy. And that, I think, is cinema's real movement. Theater's movement is different, because the theater must ground the general situation in language and construct individuals on that basis.

You can also see that when you go from love to politics, when you go from love to History, the technique of the image is twofold. On the one hand, you have the image of intimacy, which is necessarily a compact image, a tightly framed image, and, on the other hand, the image of History with a capital H, which is an epic image, an open image. Cinema's movement involves opening up the image, showing how, within this intimate image, there is the possibility of the larger image. This trajectory of opening up is typical of cinema: its genius lies in such opening up. It could be shown that the problem of theater is associated with condensation while the problem of cinema has to do with opening language up.

Cinema and the Invention of New Syntheses

Finally, let's take the question of the multiplicity of the arts: cinema proposes new syntheses. Even before people began to talk about multimedia, the cinema was itself a kind of multimedia. For example, there has always been a problem with regard to the relationship between visual and musical values. It is a problem that runs through the whole history of art. How can there be a synthesis of visual and musical values? That is the whole problem of opera as a genre. Cinema does in fact propose such a synthesis, however: it is the great resource of slapstick films, for example. Go see or see again the Marx Brothers in *A Night at the Opera* . . . Or Visconti's *Death in Venice,* especially the beginning of the film when the character arrives in Venice. We don't know a whole lot about him. We see him arrive with his luggage, get in the boat, and move through the canals of Venice. Naturally, we experience intense visual values, associated with the esthetic relations existing between Visconti and Venice. But these are not just beautiful images of Venice; it is already a sort of mortal poem, a magnificent, melancholy journey. And Visconti incorporates into the sequence what will become the musical leitmotif of the film, the *Adagio* from Mahler's *Fifth Symphony*. Now, what is extraordinary is that at no time is it ever just decorative. Between the character sitting motionless in the boat, whose face we see, and the impression we feel (Venice, the canals, the buildings, and Mahler's *Fifth Symphony*) there is a synthetic fusion that produces a unique effect belonging to no other art. It is not an isolated musical impression, it is not just a pictorial impression, it is not a psychological or literary impression; it is really a cinema idea, and that idea is a synthesis . . . This sequence in *Death in Venice* in no way involves eliminating the difference between music and painting—that would be meaningless. On the contrary, we see the difference, but we also see a synthesis within this difference, and this is really something created purely by cinema.

When we consider the question of the relationship between art and non-art, we also encounter new cinematic syntheses, in particular via cinema's use of the great popular genres and its transformation of these unique forms into artistic materials. Let's talk about the circus, for example, which gives rise to a real cinematic transfiguration that deserves to be examined closely. Whether in Chaplin's *The Circus* or in Browning's *The Unknown*, Fellini's *The Clowns* or Tati's *Parade*, or actually in many other films as well, the circus is treated as a popular genre, but it is simultaneously integrated into a new artistic synthesis. These films aren't mere documentaries about the circus; they aren't just a copy. They feature a synthetic integration of circus techniques into a different, more cinematic context. The same goes for cabaret or variety shows, which were legion at the dawn of the seventh art. Thus, the Marx Brothers were at first associated with a variety or cabaret-type show. But if the Marx Brothers had only put on a cabaret show, we would probably not remember them now at all. There is a unique operation in cinema that consists in providing cabaret with a universal stage, integrating it into a new synthesis. It is the same for the detective novel, the crime thriller, or even the sentimental novel, which were all materials that enabled the cinema to produce masterpieces. Cinema can show the open nature of the question of the popular. The clearest example of this is Orson Welles' *The Lady from Shanghai*. This film shows the woman's darkness, her negative image, but it also shows her reflection. Basically, cinema is capable of showing metaphysics and of showing (by taking it apart) its deconstruction as well. All of Orson Welles' films are open to that twofold, open-ended, poetic interpretation of showing both a metaphysical mythology and the destruction of that mythology by the same cinematic process. That is incidentally why Welles used all the resources of montage as well as all the resources of still frames. He is both the great montage director and the great sequence-shot director, not for formal reasons but because he is at once someone who proposed mythologies and someone who proposed the inner destruction of mythologies. And with that, I believe, we have something absolutely novel for contemporary philosophy.

I'll complete this overview with the moral role of cinema. There are basically two apparent possibilities in cinema for staging great ethical conflicts. On the one hand, there is what could be called the "wide horizon form," in which the moral conflict is set in an adventure, in a sort of epic, the Western, the war movie, or a great story. In this case, the conflict is enlarged: the role played by the setting—nature, or space, as in Kubrick's *2001: A Space Odyssey,* which is a metaphysical Western—allows the values to be visible against the backdrop of the immensity of nature in exactly the same way as the heroes in Westerns stand out against the horizon. This cinematic possibility amplifies the conflict.

. . . The other possibility, on the contrary, is the "confined setting," the closed circle, the little group. In this microcosmic case, everyone stands for one value or position. Cinema can also work in a stifling space, and certain cinematic techniques make it possible to flatten space. Orson Welles often used this kind of technique: filming very near the ground so that there was no horizon, with all the characters flattened in space. And yet, he, too, filmed conflict. He achieved the intensity of the conflict by means of confinement. In this respect as well, cinema is capable of synthesis: it can move from enlargement to confinement, from an infinite horizon to the flattening of a confined setting. In some great classic Westerns a combination of this sort can be found. Take Anthony Mann's *The Naked Spur,* for example. It is a classic Western, an iconic story. A small group of characters, with two sworn enemies in its midst, has to move from one place to another. The film makes the trip, the space opening onto the magnificence of nature in the American West (the waterfalls, the streams, the mountains) coexist with the confinement in a little group, along with the heightening of tension and violence, the duel within the microcosm.

. . . What does cinema bring with it that is new? Now, I think that cinema brings an upheaval with it. At the heart of this upheaval new syntheses are created, syntheses of time, syntheses among the arts, syntheses with what is not art, syntheses in the operations by which morality is represented. I venture the hypothesis that the passage between cinema's ideas and philosophy's concepts always poses the question of syntheses. If we are able to create philosophical concepts from cinema, it is by changing the old philosophical syntheses by bringing them into contact with the new cinematic syntheses.

Let me give an example of that process. Cinema shows that there is no real opposition between constructed time and pure duration since it can install one within the other, something that is always done by the great filmmakers, really only the greatest ones—Murnau, Ozu, or Welles, for example—because it is very difficult to do. Only the greatest poets of the cinema are capable of doing it. It is an extremely important question because it poses the idea of a rupture in time. And since the question of philosophy is the question of ruptures, the relationship between ruptures and time is a fundamental one. It is also a political question. For instance, it is the question of revolution. Revolution was the very name of the rupture in time, like a new synthesis within temporal ruptures. It is also a philosophical idea, in particular the idea of a new existence, of a new life. Now, cinema in its turn tells us: there are new temporal syntheses. For example, there is no complete opposition between constructed time and pure duration. And also: there is no complete opposition between continuity and discontinuity. Or: discontinuity can be thought within continuity. And also: the event can be thought immanently; it is not necessarily transcendent. Naturally, cinema doesn't *think* this; it *shows* it, or even better, it *does* it. It is an artistic practice, an artistic thinking; it is not a philosophy. There is no theory of continuity and discontinuity in cinema but rather the creation of new relationships between continuity and discontinuity.

I think this may be the most important point: cinema is an art in which what happens is both continuous and discontinuous. In mediocre works, it is neither continuous nor discontinuous; it is merely a matter of images. But in great works, there is something undecidable between continuity and discontinuity. Continuity is created with discontinuity. Or, if you prefer, cinema is a promise, a promise that may have no equivalent: we can live within discontinuity. And that gives rise to a new image, an absolutely new one, which is the continuation of the poem by images. Cinema exists for that very reason, on account of that reason. You could take numerous examples, such as those great films whose continuity is indisputable but which still make room for sudden appearances, for complete surprises, for bolts out of the blue. I'm thinking of Ozu's *Tokyo Story,* the story of an old man. (This is a big theme in cinema, as is the case with *Death in Venice* or *Wild Strawberries,* and old men should be grateful to cinema, which has given them so much.) In *Tokyo Story* the basic pace is particularly slow, and this makes the old people's temporality, which is stretched out but ultimately secretly fast, visible. Ozu shot it wonderfully: a few still frames, a patch of sky, train tracks, telephone poles, and electric wires. This next-to-nothing quality constitutes the sudden appearance of the new. It is an extraordinarily simple, exactly right symbol of the synthesis between continuity and discontinuity. The sudden appearance of something is always possible, and cinema tells us that the possibility of that miracle really does exist: such is the promise it makes to the film viewer. Cinema is the miracle of the visible as an enduring miracle and as an enduring rupture. This is without a doubt the greatest thing we owe to cinema, and philosophy should try to understand it with its own devices.

. . . I'd like to illustrate the ethical thinking of cinema by way of its relationship with the figure of the lawman, which is a basic theme in cinema. . . . This figure is so iconic that the lone lawman may often kill more people than the criminal does. That is because redressing the crime is difficult: to kill the real bad guy you first have to kill dozens of other people. This is a special culture, with a delicate balance between law and retribution. Now, what strikes me is that this problem of the relationship between law and retribution also happens to be the oldest problem in theater, since it is precisely the subject of Aeschylus' great trilogy, the *Oresteia*. In the latter, Aeschylus tells how the law must replace retribution, through the creation of a public tribunal. Theater begins pretty much with the idea that retribution has to be replaced by the law. The cinema, at least a certain American cinema, tells how retribution can replace the law, via the figure of the lone lawman . . .

One major hypothesis of Deleuze's is: cinema thinks with images, "image" meaning the presence of time. But does cinema *really* have to be thought on the basis of the category of images? That is the problem I'd like to raise, although not to criticize Deleuze, because his work on cinema is essential, introducing as it does creativity and freedom into philosophy. Not to criticize Deleuze, then, but simply to wonder if there isn't something else in cinema, another philosophical resource, a broader possibility than that of the image as transformation of the thinking of time. I'd like to examine the exact role of the notion of "image" in cinematic creation, to investigate the conditions of production of the cinema image.

Cinema, an Absolutely Impure Art

Cinema is an absolutely impure art and is so right from its conception, because the system of its conditions of possibility is an impure material system.

. . . Malraux explained the essence of the image; he also explained why Charlie Chaplin's films were shown in Africa, and he compared cinema to the other arts. But the last sentence of the text was this: "In any case, the cinema is an industry." But is it really a question of "in any case?" In actual fact, the cinema is *first and foremost* an industry. And it is an industry even as concerns the great artists of cinema. The vast majority of them worked in the industrial system of the cinema. And so money, the industry, implies something about cinema itself, not just about the social conditions of cinema. This means: cinema begins with an impure infinity. Art's task is to make a few fragments of purity emerge from that impurity, a purity wrested, as it were, from a fundamental impurity. So I would say that cinema is about purification: it is a work of purification. With only slight exaggeration cinema could be compared to the treatment of waste. You start out with a bunch of different things, a sort of indiscriminate industrial material. And the artist makes selections, works on this material. He'll condense it, he'll eliminate some things, but he'll also gather things together, put different things together, in the hope of producing moments of purity.

... Where the other arts are concerned, the artist doesn't have *enough* things; he has to create out of nothing, out of absence, out of the void. Where cinema is concerned, there are too *many* things, absolutely and always too many.

... Let's take a few examples. First, the question of sound. The contemporary world is the world of a confused jumble of sounds; that is one of its major features. Terrible noises, different kinds of music that you can't even hear anymore, engine noises, disparate conversations, loud-speakers, and so on. What is cinema's relationship with this sonic chaos? Either it reproduces the sonic chaos (but in that case it is not a creation) or else it cuts through it in order to rediscover, to give birth to a new simplicity of sound. This is once again a synthesis. For the idea is not to deny the sonic chaos—if you deny it, you give up talking about the world as it is—but to recreate a pure sound out of this sonic chaos, out of today's terrible musics, out of that sort of typical loud beat. The best example of this work on sound can be found in Godard. In a Godard film, you come up against the sonic chaos: for example, several people all speaking at once (and, what's more, you can't really understand what they're saying). You've got bits of music, you've got cars going by ... But the chaos is gradually organized, as if there were a hierarchy of noises in Godard's work. Godard transforms the sonic chaos into a murmur, like a sort of new silence made from the noises of the world. It is the invention of a silence contemporary with the sonic chaos, as if we could then hear a secret the world were confiding.

A second example is the use of cars. The use of cars is one of cinema's, or even television's, big clichés ... That is why the great artists, our contemporaries, have come up with another use of the car. Let me give you two examples. In Kiarostami's films, the car becomes a place of speech. Instead of being an image of action, as with gangsters' or police cars, it becomes the closed place of speech about the world; it becomes a subject's destiny. The impurity of the image of the car creates a new purity here, which is basically that of contemporary speech. What can we say to one another within this absurd world of the car? ...

My third example is sexual activity. The image of sex is a staple in the cinema: naked bodies, embraces, even sexual organs have become a commonplace of the screen, as uninteresting as cars. This is what the audience has always hoped to see, but it has never, even today, seen anything ... except disappointing things. This disappointment can actually be called "pornography" ... I think there are three ways of transforming the pornographic image. The first is to change it into an image of love, where the light of love is internal to the sexual figure. The second way is to stylize it, to make it almost abstract, to transform the bodies into a sort of ideal beauty without, however, giving up the sexual representation. Some remarkable scenes in this vein could be mentioned, in Antonioni's films, for example. The third way amounts to being even more pornographic than pornography: this could be called "super-pornography," a kind of meta-pornography. It can be found in some of Godard's scenes: for example, in the big daisy chain scene in *Sauve qui peut (la vie)* (*Every Man for Himself*). Once again, the artist starts with the impurity of the image, its banal and obscene nature, and reworks it from within, gearing it toward a new simplicity.

Now for my fourth and last example: shoot-outs, gunshots, gun-fights. In this case, too, it is hard to find anything more conventional and clichéd. The number of gunshots fired in the cinema is truly extraordinary. A Martian watching our films would think that human activity boiled down to using guns. Will the great artist give up guns? Of course not. There are shoot-outs in some very great films. But, once again, the artist reworks things differently. In *The Lady from Shanghai* the gunshots are also images that explode, and in John Woo's and Takeshi Kitano's films the gun battles turn into a kind of dance, a very visual choreography. They, too, accepted the rule of the gangster film and took the material with all its triviality but transformed it through a unique stylization.

. . . At bottom, when we see a film we are seeing a fight: the struggle against the material's impurity. And the battle is won at times and lost at others, even in the same film. A great film is one in which there are a lot of victories, only a few defeats for a lot of victories. That is why a great film always has something heroic about it. It is also why the relationship with cinema isn't one of contemplation but of participation, solidarity, admiration, or even jealousy, irritation, or hatred. Cinema's hand-to-hand combat amazes us. We take part in it; we assess the victories; we assess the defeats; we admire the creation of a few moments of purity. Those victorious moments are so extraordinary that they account for cinema's emotional power. There is an emotion of combat: all of a sudden the purity of an image seizes us and, similarly, so does the outcome of a battle. That is also why cinema is an art that makes you cry. You cry from joy; you cry from love, from fear, from rage; you cry on account of the victories and sometimes on account of the defeats. Something almost miraculous happens when cinema manages to extract a little bit of purity from all that is worst in the world.

So we can now return to the question of the relationship between cinema and philosophy. What they have in common is the fact that they both begin with the contemporary real: thanks to them, that real is no longer missing from thought. The other arts start with the purity of their own histories; science starts with its own axioms, with its own mathematical transparency. Cinema and philosophy start with impurity: the opinions, images, practices, and events of human existence. And they both choose to believe that an idea can be created out of this contemporary material, that an idea doesn't always come from an idea, that it can come from its opposite, from ruptures in existence, and that an image is made from the imagery of the world, from its infinite impurity. In both cases, the work is a cross between a struggle and a sharing. The work of philosophy involves creating conceptual syntheses where there is rupture; the work of cinema involves creating purity out of the most trivial conflicts in the world. That is the real connection between cinema and philosophy; that is what they share.

What's more, cinema is a real piece of luck for us philosophers because it shows the power of purification, the power of synthesis, the possibility that something can happen even though the worst may prevail. Basically, cinema teaches philosophy a lesson of hope. Cinema tells philosophers "All is not lost," precisely because it deals with the greatest abjection: violence, betrayal, obscenity. It tells us that it is not because such things exist that thought is done for; thought can triumph even in a milieu like that. It won't always triumph, it won't triumph everywhere, but victories do exist.

The idea of potential victory strikes me as being a very important issue today. For a long time, with the idea of revolution there was the hope of a great potential victory, a definitive, irreversible victory. And then the idea of revolution disappeared. We are the orphans of the idea of revolution. As a result, we often think that no victory is possible anymore, that the world has lost its illusions, and we eventually become resigned. Cinema, however, says in its own way: "There are victories even in the worst of worlds." Naturally *the* victory probably doesn't exist any longer, but there are individual victories. To be faithful to these individual victories already means a lot for thought. So let's watch films philosophically, not just because they create new figures of the image but because they tell us something about the world, something as simple as can be: "The worst of worlds shouldn't cause despair." We should not despair. That is what cinema tells us, I think, and that is why we should love it. It can keep us from despair if we know how to look at it, to look at it as a struggle against the impure world, to look at it as a collection of precious victories.

Notes

1. Alain Badiou, *The Meaning of Sarkozy*, trans. David Fernbach (London: Verso, 2008), pp. 97–98.
2. Lauren Sedofsky, "Matters of Appearance: An Interview with Alain Badiou," *Artforum International*, November 2006, p. 253.
3. Indeed, Badiou represented a widespread idea of the association between a movie theater and Plato's image of the cave in book 7 of *The Republic* in his own interpretation of the text, Alain Badiou, *Plato's Republic: A Dialogue in Sixteen Chapters, with a Prologue and an Epilogue*, trans. Susan Spitzer (London: Polity, 2012), p. 212ff.
4. The text of this essay is transcribed from an unpublished seminar, "Penser le cinéma," Buenos Aires, Alliance Française, September 24 and 25, 2003.

CHAPTER 17

CINEMATIC TIME AND THE QUESTION OF MALAISE

BERNARD STIEGLER

Bernard Stiegler (b. 1952) is the head of the Institut de Recherche et d'Innovation (IRI), which he founded in 2006 at the Centre Georges-Pompidou. He is president and cofounder in 2005 of the political and cultural group Ars Industrialis and the founder in 2010 of the philosophy school École de Philosophie d'Épineuil-le-Fleuriel. Stiegler's work has explored questions of technology and epistemology through phenomenology, evolutionary biology, political economy, and the critique of consumer capitalism. He is a prolific writer whose best-known publications are *The Lost Spirit of Capitalism: Disbelief and Discredit* (2004) and the five-part volumes of *Technics and Time (La Technique et le temps)* (1994–), from which the present text is taken (volume 3, 2011).

In *Technics and Time,* Stiegler argues that humanity is distinguished from animal life by its reliance upon technology; material circumstances are changed by technology that, in turn, bring about changes in the organization of consciousness and experience. The term *technics* refers to the way in which humankind has entered a new stage in evolution, that of "epiphylogenesis," in which the genetic heritage of humankind gives way to new forms of existence and being through technological innovation and practice.

Stiegler begins his account of cinematic time by stating that stories are perennial and appeal to every generation helping forge "the link between the generations." Their power lies in the promise that they hold out "of the writing of new episodes of future life, yet to be invented." However, as Adorno and Horkheimer analyzed in "The Culture Industry Enlightenment as Mass Deception"

(*Reader* text 3), the power to invent stories today lies largely in the interests of instrumental Capitalism as controlled by U.S. global industries. Given that both cinema and television have a leading responsibility for the global transmission and dissemination of stories today, with the ultimate effect, Stiegler says, of getting the whole world to adopt "the American way of life," there is the need for a thoroughgoing critique of the invention and use of stories by capital. While Stiegler recognizes the importance of Adorno's and Horkheimer's work in this area, he believes that their critique needs to be developed through an analysis of "[the] *uniqueness* of the techniques that appeared specifically with cinema."

Such cinematic technics, Stiegler says, have their own capacity to produce an "extraordinary belief effect" in the spectator that is testified to by the experience of watching a film and feeling reinvigorated to the point that "indeed, if the film is good, we come out of it less lazy . . . full of emotion and the desire to do something, or else infused with a new outlook on things." Cinema, in other words, is an inspirational force for life, and Stiegler's quest, therefore, is to inquire into the source of this vital energy. This involves Stiegler in an application of Roland Barthes's theory of analog photography to cinema and in rethinking Husserl's phenomenological principle of memory retention with regard to melody to theorize the temporal flux at stake in cinema.

In his book *Camera Lucida* (1980), Barthes highlights the uncanny nature of analog photography, which not only presents to the viewer what is past, but does so by means of direct, indexical traces of light that existed at the time the photograph was taken and compose the photographic reproduction itself, "a photograph's *noëme* [meaning a photograph's essence] is its 'that-has-been' . . . *I can never deny the thing has been there.*" There is the indisputable fact that what is present in the photographic image is made visible through traces of light directly connected to the past. This is the uncanny effect of the past breaking through into the present *as* the past and *as* what has disappeared. Such an affect has the intense power, Barthes claimed, to disarm the viewer with a sublime sense of finitude and mortality, "Every photograph is this catastrophe: 'every photograph declares this future anterior, whose stakes are death.'" Referring specifically to photography, Barthes subsequently oriented this experience around the emotional effect of the *punctum*, meaning a piercing or wounding that opens the subject to a sense of mortality. These ideas of Barthes inform Stiegler's account of cinema, especially regarding his discussion of the scene from Fellini's *Intervista* (1987) in which Marcello Mastroianni and Anita Ekberg watch themselves performing in *La Dolce Vita* (1960), a film that was made nearly thirty years earlier:

> No-one looking at herself again, from thirty years later, having aged those thirty years, could not *not* feel the terrible reality of time passing through the photographic "that has been," through the "conjunction of reality and the past,"

the silvery coincidence re-animated by cinema's temporal flux. . . . In Anita's case, she is not merely saying this to herself: as image, she is dead *and* she is going to die. She must say to herself: "I am going to die: I am dying." This *present participle* is *precisely that of flux.*

Stiegler's notion of flux, thought grammatically as the present participle "dying," opens life to finitude and death but also to the possibility of change and becoming, as this might be generated by "the writing of new episodes of future life, yet to be invented."

Developing this idea of temporality and loss (together, they define the term *flux*), Stiegler critiques Husserl's ideas about a pure or direct form of phenomenological perception. The key example that Husserl offers in this regard is that of listening to a melody and the particular way in which the preceding (absent) notes continue to inform the present so that nothing is lost in memory as the notes of the melody build on one another, forming an entire ensemble over the flow of time. This is referred to as "primary retention": "When I hear a melody, as a temporal object it presents itself to me as it unfolds. . . . Because the sonorous *now* retains all the notes preceding it, the present note can sound melodic, can be 'musical,' whether it is harmonious or unharmonic: it continues to be properly a *note* and not merely a sound or a noise."

However, Stiegler argues that the perception of the temporal object such as music or recorded music, or, indeed, cinema, is never pure in Husserl's sense, even though it has a certain pertinence for a common understanding of the function of melody in music (especially when it is experienced over the course of the music's duration rather than remembered, say, the next day—this is a distinction that Husserl tries to make between primary and secondary forms of retention). However, for Stiegler, the flow of temporality involved in listening to music or watching a film is *always* a matter of "imaginative" and selective recombinations of experience through what Stiegler refers to as a tertiary form of retention that is, in actual fact, constitutive of primary and secondary forms of retention. Such shifts in consciousness depend on the important fact that memory is a process of forgetting; Stiegler here means not so much everyday forms of forgetting but rather fundamental experiences of change that involve "loss" and form the condition for new becomings of identity and consciousness (in which the notion of consciousness is thought of in temporal terms rather than as a fixed entity). For, if forgetting did not occur, then everything would be retained in memory at the same time in an infinite regress, "If 'to memorize' did not mean already 'to have forgotten' . . . Time has ceased to exist." For Stiegler, phenomenological experience is never the same twice, and this is supported by, and exteriorized through, the technology of reproduction in which to experience the same event (possibly through numerous recordings) is to experience it always differently and otherwise. Stiegler argues that the technics of forgetting and loss in memory is the very condition by which new selections of thought, and therefore new stories, can take place. Given this understanding of memory as loss, and the fact that reproducibility is the condition that means the same never reoccurs, Stiegler is able to mount a critique of American mythmaking that seeks to disavow such difference. To help substantiate his critique Stiegler points out the genealogical link between the psychotic Blanche Dubois in Elia Kazan's *A Streetcar Named Desire* (1951) and the Southern belle Scarlett O'Hara from *Gone with the Wind* (1939), both characters being played by the actor Vivien Leigh. The last step of this critique is Stiegler's quotation, *America, America*, that refers to Elia Kazan's eponymous film of 1963. This reference serves as a prescient reminder that insofar as America is a symbol of freedom and hope, it is by virtue of being a land of emigrants who do not have a mythical shared origin upon which a regulated, common future can be founded.

* * *

Desire for Stories / Stories of Desire

The propensity to believe in stories and fables, the passion for fairy tales, just as satisfying in the old as in the very young, is perpetuated from generation to generation because it forges the link between the generations.[1] Insatiable, they hold out the promise, to generations to come, of the writing of new episodes of future life, yet to be invented, to be fictionalized [*fabuler*].

This ancient desire for narrative(s) still orders modern society: it animates the most complex, and most secret, of social movements. But the conditions of this desire's satisfaction have been radically transformed; it has become the object of a global industry.

What Horkheimer and Adorno call "cultural industries" now constitute the very heart of economic development, whose most intimate power is clearly always the most ancient desire of all stories, and the key to (all contemporary) desire in general . . .

Global commerce now develops by mobilizing techniques of persuasion owing everything to the narrative arts. There is no event, no moment, independent of the desire for stories. Media networks and the programming industries exploit this fictionalizing *tendency* by systematizing the specific resources of audiovisual technics. And within the horizon of these immense technological and social issues, *cinema* occupies a unique place. Its technics of image and sound—now including informatics and telecommunications—re-invent our belief in stories that are now told with remarkable, unparalleled power. But at the same time, these technical powers cast doubt on and sow incredulity into the future of a world to whose disruption they have already greatly contributed.

If cinematic narratives' influence on the public results at its most fundamental level from a desire for the most ancient stories, and if this is a desire that can be found in every age, and if that underlies every era of the arts and all techniques for making such stories believable, it is all the more necessary that we analyze—and in detail—the *uniqueness* of the techniques that appeared specifically with cinema, techniques that more than any others in history have organized the programming industries' production practices, and we must do this in order to account for the incomparable efficacy of "the animated sound-image," to understand the extraordinary belief-effect it produces in the spectator: to explain how and why the cinema, in *becoming television* (i.e., the technical network as producer and diffuser of symbols through a global industry), combines the universal desire for fiction and, through it, conditions the entirety of humanity's evolution, though always at the risk of exhausting its desire for stories.

This analysis is all the more necessary since that cinematic singularity in turn reveals another singularity: that of the "human soul" as such; the cinematic techno-logically exhumes the "mechanism" of "hidden art" in its "depths."[2]

Boredom

Which one of us, on a gloomy autumn Sunday afternoon, one of those afternoons when one feels like doing nothing, bored even with not wanting to do anything, has not had the desire to watch some old film, no matter which, either at some nearby movie house, if it is in town and there are a few dollars to waste, or on video or DVD at home—or (last resort) just turning on the television where in the end there is no film but some very mediocre series, or indeed *anything?* Just to be lost in the flow of images.

* * *

Why don't we turn it off and pick up a book—a book, say, in which we could find a really good story, strong and well written? Why, on such a Sunday afternoon, do those moving images win out over written words in beautiful books?

The answer is that we need only look. And even if what we are looking at is completely inane but the filmmaker has somehow been able to exploit the video-cinematographic possibilities, the cinematic will attract our attention to the passing images, no matter what they are, and we will prefer to see them unfold before our eyes. We become immersed in the time of their flowing forth; we forget all about ourselves watching, perhaps "losing ourselves" (losing track of *time),* but however we define it, we will be sufficiently captured, not to say captivated, to stay with it to the very end.

During the passing ninety minutes or so (fifty-two in the case of the televisual "hour") of this *pastime,* the time of our consciousness will be totally passive within the thrall of those "moving" images that are linked together by noises, sounds, words, voices. Ninety or fifty-two minutes of our life will have passed by *outside* our "real" life, but *within* a life or the lives of people and events, real or fictive, to which we will have conjoined our time, adopting their events as though they were happening to us as they happened to them.

If by some lucky chance the film is a good one, we who are watching it in complete lethargy, the core validation of the animated sound-image by which we can leave everything behind and still be completely uninvolved—not even (as with a book) following written sentences and turning pages, careful not to lose the gist of the story; indeed, if the film is good, we come out of it less lazy, even re-invigorated, full of emotion and the desire to do something, or else infused with a new outlook on things: the cinematographic machine, taking charge of our boredom, will have transformed it into new energy, transubstantiated it, made something out of nothing—the nothing of that terrible, nearly fatal feeling of a Sunday afternoon of nothingness. The cinema will have brought back the expectation of *something,* something that must come, that will come, and that will come to us from our own life: from this seemingly non-fictional life that we re-discover when, leaving the darkening room, we hide ourselves in the fading light of day.

Cinema's Two Fundamental Principles

In cinema we never have to be wary of losing a text's development: there is no text. And where there is none, it enters us without our having to look for it. Cinema weaves itself into our time; it becomes the temporal fabric of those ninety or fifty-two minutes of unconscious consciousness that is characteristic of a being, a film viewer, strangely immobilized by motion.

This is true because of cinema's two fundamental principles:

1.   Cinematographic recording is an extension of photography; photography is an analog recording technique (which I analyze in *Technics and Time, 2* [12]), like the reality effect Roland Barthes describes in showing that a photograph's *noëme* is its "that-has-been":

I call "photographic referent" not the *optimally* real thing to which an image or a sign refers but the *necessarily* real thing which has been placed before the lens, without which there would be no photograph. Painting can feign reality without having seen it. . . . In Photography, I can never deny that *the thing has been there.* There is a superimposition here: of reality and the past. . . .

Looking at a photograph, I inevitably include in my scrutiny the thought of that instant, however brief, in which a real thing happened to be motionless in front of the eye. I project the present photograph's immobility upon the past shot, and it is this arrest which constitutes the pose.[3]

The instant of the snap coincides with the instant of *what is* snapped, and it is in this co-incidence of two instants that the basis of the possibility of a conjunction of past and reality allowing for a "transfer" of the photograph's immobility in which the spectator's "present" coincides with the appearance of the spectrum.

2.   The cinema adds sound by including *phono*-graphic recording. The phonogram, like the photo, results from an analogic technique of artificial memorization, which is why what is true of the photo is also, to a large extent, true of all phonograms: listening to a recorded concert, I must include in my listening experience the fact that the concert "has been," has already taken place. But the photo's truth is only the same as that of the phonogram to a certain point, since in the phonogram I am dealing with a fluid object, with an unfolding that changes the terms of analysis: the aural object is itself a flux in which it is impossible to isolate a moment of sound: it does not have a Barthesian "pose"; it emerges from the phenomenology of what Husserl calls "temporal objects."

Cinema can include sound because film, as a photographic recording technique capable of representing movement, is itself a temporal object susceptible to the phenomenological analysis proper to this kind of object. A film, like a melody, is essentially a flux: it consists of its unity in and as flow. The temporal object, as flux, coincides with the stream of consciousness of which it is the object: the spectator's.

The power of these two cinematic principles, and thus of the singularity of cinematic recording techniques, results from two other co-incident conjunctions:

> —on one hand, the phono-photographic coincidence of past and reality ("there is a double conjoint position: of reality and of the past," which induces this "reality effect"—believability—in which the spectator is located, in advance, by the technique itself);
>   —on the other, the coincidence between the film's flow and that of the film spectator's consciousness, linked by phonographic flux, initiates the mechanics of a complete adoption of the film's time with that of the spectator's consciousness—which, since it is itself a flux, is captured and "channeled" by the flow of images. This movement, infused with every spectator's desire for stories, liberates the movements of consciousness typical of cinematic *emotion* . . .

The Kuleshov Effect

Working through the concept of the temporal object in the fifth section of *Logical Investigations*, Husserl attempts to account for the temporality of all consciousness as a structure of flux. The question is thus to analyze the phenomenological conditions constituting this flux. But it is impossible for Husserlian phenomenology to engage in such an analysis of consciousness: its structure being intentional, consciousness is always consciousness *of* something; it is only possible to account for the temporality of consciousness by analyzing an "object" that is itself temporal.

Husserl discovers this object in 1905: melody. A melody is a temporal object in the sense that it is constituted only in its duration. As a temporal object its phenomenality is flow. A glass—say, a plain glass of water—is clearly a temporal object in the sense that it exists *in time* and is thus subject to universal physical laws and to entropy: it is temporal because it is not eternal. This is true of all "real" objects. But a properly temporal object is not simply "in time": it is *formed* temporally, woven in threads of time—as what appears in passing, what happens, what manifests itself in disappearing, as flux disappearing even as it appears. And the properly temporal object is the ideal object constituting the temporal fabric of the stream of consciousness itself, since the flux of the temporal object precisely coincides with the stream of consciousness of which it is the object. To account for the structure of the temporal object's flux is to account for the structure of the stream of consciousness of which it is the object.

In the temporal object as melody, Husserl discovers *primary retention*. Primary retention is a kind of memory, but it is nonetheless not the aspect of memory involving recall. Husserl sometimes calls this "re-memory," sometimes "secondary memory."

Primary retention is what the *now* of an unfolding temporal object retains in itself from all of its previous *nows*. Even though they have passed, these preceding *nows* are maintained within the temporal object's current *now*, and, in this respect, they remain present even while perpetually becoming past; they remain present as having happened and in being sustained as having happened in the current *now*—they are maintained as *both* present and absent in the currently occurring *now* and insofar as the temporal object is not completely unfolded, completely past but still *passing* (i.e., temporal).

When I hear a melody, as a temporal object it presents itself to me as it unfolds. In the course of this process each note that is presented *now* retains in itself the preceding note, which itself retains the preceding one, etc. The current note contains within it all the preceding notes; it is the "now" as the maintainer of the object's presence: the temporal object's presence is its passing maintenance. This continuity is the temporal object's *unity*. Because the sonorous *now* retains all the notes preceding it, the present note can sound melodic, can be "musical," whether it is harmonic or unharmonic: it continues to be properly a *note* and not merely a sound or a noise.

Properly understood, for Husserl these primary retentions cannot be seen as memories in the sense that one can remember, for example, a melody one heard yesterday. That would only be a matter of recall, the recall of something that happened but is no longer present; primary retention, on the contrary, is an originary association between the *now* and what Husserl calls the "just-past," which remains present in the now. Maintaining the just-past in an ongoing present provides continuity to what is making itself present *now,* the most obvious example of which is melody in which a note can clearly only occur through an association with the notes that preceded and will follow it (those to follow being the ones that will resonate as a retention in the *current* note, which will be retained in its turn, but with which it will then share space as a protention concealed and sustained from preceding retentions). This is what has been called the "Kuleshov Effect,"[4] though it is considered by François Albera to be nothing more than a myth since Kuleshov himself never fully described it, and since the experience that catalyzes it can, as Albera emphasizes, be initially attributed to Pudovkin.[5] In any case, historically, the Kuleshov Effect consists of inserting the same image of the actor Mozzhukhin's face numerous times into a series of sequences constructed around the image,[6] in which each time the actor's face appears it does so with three other quite different images. The image of Mozzhukhin's face, though it is always the same, is nonetheless perceived by viewers as three different images, each seeming to produce a different version of the same face.

In fact, it is this cinematic *effect* that ceaselessly produces a particular consciousness, projecting onto its objects everything that has preceded them within the sequence into which they have been inserted and that only they produce. And in fact this is the very principle of cinema: to connect disparate elements together into a single temporal flux.

Husserl's principle of primary retention is the most productive conceptual basis through which to analyze this "generalized cinema." Though Franz Brentano was the first to attempt to think through the primary retention of the just-past, according to Husserl he had failed, in that Brentano claimed that primary retention, as the past originarily engendered by the present now of perception, was a product of the *imagination,* originarily associated—as the past—with this perception. In Brentano's version, it is the imagination that both provides retention with the index of the past and that simultaneously connects the present now to its retentions in an out-flowing in which the passing temporal object finally disappears. But for Husserl such a viewpoint is inadmissible in that it amounts to saying that the time of a temporal object is *imagined, not perceived*—and that as a consequence, temporal objects are not realities but effects of the imagination: this would mean the negation of the reality of time itself.

However, in claiming that primary retention is not a product of the imagination but the phenomenon of the *perception* of time par excellence, Husserl must not only distinguish primary from secondary retention, which would obviously be necessary, but in fact *oppose* them.[7] Opposing primary memory to secondary memory, primary retentions of perception to re-memories, is to initiate an absolute difference between perception and imagination, to propose that perception owes nothing to the imagination, and that what is perceived is in no case imagined; further, this claim must absolutely not be contaminated by the persistent fictions produced by the imagination: life is perception, and perception is not imagination.

In other words, life is not cinema. Nor philosophy.

Life-as-perception of the living present, for Husserl, *does not tell us stories.*

Selections, Criteria, and Recordings

The Kuleshov Effect in particular and cinema in general nonetheless show that as an interdependence among just-past retentions in the ongoing present of a temporal object, and as the re-memory of the past in general, this primary/secondary opposition is a phantasm.

And if it were possible to demonstrate that lived reality is always a construct of the imagination and thus perceived only on condition of being fictional, irreducibly haunted by phantasms, then we would finally be forced to conclude that perception is subordinated to—is in a transductive relationship with—the imagination; that is, there would be no perception outside imagination, and vice versa, perception then being the imagination's projection screen. The relationship between the two would be constituted of previously nonexistent terms, and this in turn would mean that life is *always* cinema and that this is why "when one loves life one goes to the cinema," as though we go to the cinema in order to find life again—to be somehow resuscitated by it.

Philosophy would first have to ask: "Where do these phantasms come from?" And then: "What is a life that is in need of being constantly resuscitated?"

I have attempted to confront these questions in exploring the nature of a third kind of memory, not primary or secondary, but tertiary: a memory resulting from all forms of recordings—a memory Husserl designates as *consciousness of image.* Turning our attention to Freud later on,[8] we will see why these tertiary retentions are equally the support for the *protentions* constituting the expectation that animates a consciousness built on archi-protentions: death, desire for reproduction and expenditure—whose core is the unconscious.

Primary retention, says Husserl, is grounded totally and uniquely on perception. The primary retentions constituting a temporal object are not the product of conscious selection, since if consciousness of time's unfolding were to select what it retained from that process, and if as a result it did not retain all of it, then it would no longer be a function purely and simply of perception, but already a kind of imagination, at least by default.

However, it is enough to have heard a melody twice through in order to be able to state that in these two hearings consciousness had not been listening with the same ears: that something happened between the first and second hearing. This is because each provides a new phenomenon, richer if the music is good, less rich if bad, that the melomane (the melody *maniac)* takes in heavy doses. This difference obviously results from an alteration in the phenomena of retention—i.e., from a variation in selection: consciousness does not retain everything.

From one hearing to another it is a matter of different ears, precisely because the ear involved in the second hearing has been affected by the first. The same melody, but not the same ears nor, thus, the same consciousness: consciousness has changed ears, having experienced the *event* of the melody's first hearing.

Consciousness is affected in general by phenomena presented to it, but this affect occurs in a special way with temporal objects. This is important to us in the current investigation because cinema, like melody, is a temporal object. Understanding the singular way in which temporal objects affect consciousness means beginning to understand what gives cinema its specificity, its force, and its means of transforming life leading, for example, to the global adoption of "the American way of life." An inquiry such as this presupposes an analysis of the specifics and the specificity of the recording techniques producing cinematic flux and the effects it engenders in consciousness, especially in that consciousness is *already cinematographic* in its principles of selection for primary memories, a selection that relies on criteria furnished by the play of secondary memory and associated tertiary elements, the combination forming a montage through which a unified flux is constructed (as "stream of consciousness"), but which is identical in form to the cinematic flux of an actual film, as a temporal object and as the result of a constructed montage.

These are some of the preconditions for the association of primary, secondary, and tertiary retentions, of an associated-montage-of-retentions we will explore . . .

Consciousness has altered between two subsequent experiences of a melody, and this is why the same primary memories selected from the first hearing are not selected in the second, the object being the same, the phenomenon being different. But we must then ask how it is possible to say that "one consciousness can listen to the same temporal object twice." And this is in fact, and indeed, impossible without the existence of analog techniques for recording a melody phono-graphically. In other words, the fact of the consciousness's selection of primary retentions, and thus the intervention of the imagination at the heart of perception, is only made *obvious* by tertiary retention—by a phonogram, in that for the first time it makes possible the identical repetition of the same temporal object, within the context of a multiplicity of phenomena seen as so many diverse occurrences of one and the same object.

Let us examine this remarkable possibility more closely.

I hear, for the first time, a melody recorded on some mechanism, some phonographic support medium, analog or digital. Then later on I listen to the same melody again, from the same disc. Clearly in this new second hearing the sound just-past, insofar as it is now a primary retention into which other, previous primary retentions have been and are being incorporated, *in that it is past* and is no longer passing, yet in some fashion it did not happen *again* in precisely the same way as the first time. If this were not true, I would never hear anything other than what I had already heard. But the sound just-past, combining with other sounds just-past before it, and that pass each time differently from that first time, is absolutely new in its data, the phenomenon being a different phenomenon, the experience of the same piece of music giving me an *other*(ed) experience of that music despite my consciousness of the fact that it was the same music, played a second time, from which two different experiences occurred in me; at the same time, the passing of sound just-past, the primary retention constituting this unfolding in its original, unique construction—all of this "owes" something, in its very passage, to a previous passing that has disappeared, owes something to the preceding hearing: owes *that* hearing its modification.

In its passing, retention is modified and thus itself becomes past: retention-as-passage is essentially self-modification. But this modification is clearly *now* rooted in the secondary memory of the first hearing, even though on the other hand it precisely surpasses (is different from) that first hearing. In the melody's second hearing, what I hear results from the fact that I have previously heard it, yet it results from that previous hearing precisely and paradoxically in that I hear *something else* the second time: the first time, I never actually heard the melody; the second time, the already-known led me miraculously (back) to that unknown. In that second hearing, what is present is already known, but presents itself differently, such that the expected appears as unexpected.

Inscribed in my memory, the anteriority of the melody's first hearing arises from secondary memory, i.e., from the imagination and from fiction. What is strange is obviously that this already gives rise to the *not-yet*; that the already-heard gives way to the not-yet-heard, echoing a protentional expectation that has entered into a play of archi-protentions. Between the two hearings, consciousness has changed because a *clearing away* has taken place: primary retention is a selection process brought about through criteria that have been established during previous clearings away, which were themselves selections resulting from other, prior clearings. This occurs because as memorization, primary retention is also a primary memory *lapse,* a reduction of what *passes by* to *a past* that retains only what the criteria constituting the secondary retentions allow it to select: secondary retentions inhabit the process of primary retention in advance.

This is the case when I have already heard a melody and am hearing it again, but it is also the case when I have never heard it, since then I hear from the position of an expectation formed from everything that has already musically happened to me—I am responding to the Muses guarding the default-of-origin of my desire, within me. And this occurs because of a memory lapse, *a forgetting,* and because this forgetting occurs only as a function of certain criteria: my ability to construct the object of a critique. If "to memorize" did not mean already "to have forgotten," nothing could be retained, since nothing would have passed, nothing would have happened.

Imagine hypothetically that I have an infinite memory and that I can remember what happened yesterday. I thus remember every second and fraction of a second exactly identically. When I come to the end of the day, I remember that at that moment I am remembering the entire day, which I begin to do again in remembering myself remembering anew, each second exactly and identically, etc. There is no longer any difference, because there has been no selection: time has not *passed.* Nothing has happened nor can happen to me, neither present (in which something new always presents itself to me, including boredom with the absence of the new) nor past: the present no longer passing, no longer happening; no passage of time is possible. Time has ceased to exist.

In fact, remembering yesterday, having a *past,* means reducing yesterday to less than today, diminishing yesterday, having no more than finite memories of it. This retentional finitude is the grounding condition of consciousness-as-temporal-flux. And what is true of secondary memory is true of all memory, including primary memory; thus primary retention can only be a selection, brought about according to criteria that are themselves the products of selections. However, in the case I have laid out here, i.e., understanding how we hear a melody recorded on any phonographic support mechanism, this secondary memory, indissociable (though different) from primary memory, is also indissociable from tertiary memory, "consciousness of image"—the phonogram as such.

And that is precisely what is at stake.

Phonographic Revelation

Husserl's examples of "consciousness of image," of what I call tertiary memory, are the painting or the bust. For Husserl, this "configuration through image," the object of a consciousness of image, plays absolutely no role in the constitution of a temporal object—nor, consequently, in the constitution of the flux of consciousness itself. Not only does such a memory type not appear to perception; it does not even appear to the past flow of consciousness, in contrast to secondary memory, which, though it no longer arises from perception, is inscribed in the flow of consciousness's past and appears to this living consciousness as its own past, since it was perceived.

For Husserl, the consciousness of image is not a *memory* of that consciousness; it is an artificial memory of what was not perceived nor lived by consciousness. A nineteenth-century painting is certainly a kind of memory, but one could not say, according to Husserl, that it is a memory of someone looking at it *now*. It is, rather, a memory trace of the painter, who has in some fashion exteriorized and frozen his memory, thus allowing, a century later, another consciousness to contemplate it as an image of the past—but in no case as a memory of his own lived past. In Husserlian phenomenology, only that which arises from conscious, *lived experience,* is, strictly speaking, unquestionable and should be taken into account in any analysis of the constituting conditions of phenomena. Husserl's phenomenological attitude consists of positioning consciousness as the constituter *of* the world, not something constituted *by* it. Since tertiary memory is a reality *in the world,* it cannot be constitutive of consciousness but must necessarily be derivative of a consciousness that has no real need of it.

However, since the unique event that is the advent of the technical possibility of analogic recording of a *temporal* musical object, and the ability to repeat it technically, the link between primary and secondary retentions has become obvious: clearly, even though each time it is repeated it is the same temporal object, it produces two different musical experiences. I *know* that it is the same temporal object, because I know that the melody was recorded by a technique producing a co-incidence between the stream of what was being recorded and that of the machine doing the recording. I know that the recording mechanism's time coincided with the melodic flux. And this co-incidence of machinic flux and that of the temporal object produces, for the flow of consciousness of both the object and its recording, a conjunction of past, reality, and this effect of the real that Barthes identifies in photography and that is replicated in the realm of sound, the difference being that as Barthes points out in the case of photography there is the *pose,* whereas in the case of phonography, of recorded sound (as in cinema), there is *flux.*

Consciousness of image, in the case of the phonogram (though it could also be said of cinematic recording), is what finally roots the primary and the secondary in one another, through the technical possibility of the temporal object's repetition (and it cannot be emphasized strongly enough that before the *phonograph,* as before the cinema, such repetitions were strictly impossible). At the same time it becomes obvious that the grounding of the *second primary* is in the memory of the *first primary*. It is obvious only because of the *fact* of recording: it is the phonographic *revelation of* the structure of all temporal objects.

Returning to *Intervista*

The consequences of this revelation are considerable: the criteria according to which consciousness selects primary retentions, passes them by consciousness, and distills them no longer applies solely to secondary retentions of lived, conscious memory, but equally to tertiary retentions; cinema shows us this most clearly.

To explore this point further, I must return to and extend the analysis I have already begun of a scene in Federico Fellini's *Intervista*.[9]

In the film, Fellini appears in a scene with Marcello Mastroianni, with whom he pays a visit to Anita Ekberg. In the course of the evening the three of them watch the Trevi Fountain scene [of Mastroianni and Ekberg] from *La Dolce Vita*. Thus, in *Intervista* we see an actress watching herself playing a character, and the scene's extreme tension results from its undecidability: Anita is appearing in a film by Fellini, but she is playing watching herself portraying a different character thirty years earlier, and no viewer of the second film, *Intervista*, could escape being certain that as she watches the earlier film—watches her *past* life, her *past* youth—Anita cannot simply play watching herself without knowing that this is a matter of the Quintessential Performance, the most serious one of all, the first and the last engagement, the play of all plays:[10] no one looking at herself again, from thirty years later, having aged those thirty years, could not *not* feel the terrible reality of time passing through the photographic "that has been," through the "conjunction of reality and the past," the silvery coincidence re-animated by cinema's temporal flux. *We* see an actress playing an actress watching an actress playing a "real" character in a fictional film, but we know that she is "playing" at watching herself *having been,* that what she is doing is no longer a simple portrayal, a pure performance any actor might be required to give (to play this or that character), but the absolutely tragic staging of *her own* existence, insofar as that existence is *passing by* irremediably and forever—-forever, except for what concerns this silvery image she has left on a reel of film: an image in which she has been preserved.

Watching herself performing thirty years earlier, Anita must feel the future anterior so striking to Roland Barthes as he looks at the photograph of Lewis Payne taken several hours before Payne's hanging:

In 1865, young Lewis Payne tried to assassinate Secretary of State W. H. Seward. Alexander Gardner photographed him in his cell, where he was waiting to be hanged. The photograph is handsome, as is the boy: that is the studium. But the *punctum* is: *he is going to die*. I read at the same time: *This will be* and *this has been;* I observe with horror an anterior future of which death is the stake. By giving me the absolute past of the pose (aorist), the photograph tells me death in the future. What *pricks* me is the discovery of this equivalence. In front of the photograph of my mother as a child, I tell myself: she is going to die: I shudder, like Winnicott's psychotic patient, *over a catastrophe which has already occurred.* Whether or not the subject is already dead, every photograph is this catastrophe (*Camera Lucida,* p. 96).

"Every photograph is this catastrophe;" every photograph declares this future anterior whose stakes are death—and the dramatic outcome of every narrative, every play, every cinemato-graphic emotion.

In Anita's case, she is not merely *saying* this: as image, she is dead *and* she is going to die. She must say to herself: "I am going to die; I am dying," This *present participle* is *precisely that of flux*—that of her past life, of the film on which she has been recorded, and of her current consciousness of this film that, in unfolding, carries her along and makes her pass by, placing her in a time that leads toward the absence of time: non-passing, infinite memory that will no longer be special, where everything will be retained forever in its instant: *"The Instant of my Death."*[11]

But all of that is, in this scene in *Intervista,* the result of the fact that film is a temporal object in which "the actor's body is conflated with the character's; where the film's passing is necessarily also the actor's past, the moments of life of a character are instantly moments of the actor's past. That life is merged, in its being filmed, with that of its characters" (*Technics and Time,* 2:22).

This confusion of the actor's life with the filmed one is that of primary, secondary, and tertiary retentions coinciding in a single event: the properly cinemato-graphic event. In this filmic coincidence, which Fellini stages in an extraordinary way by including the fact that, for any viewer of *Intervista* who has already seen *La Dolce Vita,* the latter necessarily also becomes part of the viewer's past, and a reference to the earlier film is not simply a reference made to one fiction in the course of another fiction, which would merely be a citation: this first fiction, *La Dolce Vita,* cited in the second fiction, *Intervista,* is simultaneously

1. a *tertiary retention* (an artificial memory presented in a support medium, of which an extract, a piece of film, is projected into another film and recorded on another piece of film);
2. a *temporal object* that has been seen and re-seen, and that is currently being seen by the viewer of *Intervista;* and further,
3. as a temporal object, the film is a secondary memory for this viewer, a part of his or her past stream of consciousness, then re-activated;

4. ninety minutes of the viewer's past life, the running time of *La Dolce Vita*, have been lived as the extended retention of primary retentions in the *now* of an elapsed narrative entitled (in its entirety) *La Dolce Vita*, and of which a particular sequence is then re-lived (i.e., the section included in *Intervista*); and

5. included in *Intervista's* cinematic flux; that is, in Anita's passing stream of consciousness as well.

Additionally, *La Dolce Vita* is no longer simply a fiction for someone viewing *Intervista*: it has become its past, such that watching Anita watching herself perform the scene in *La Dolce Vita*, the viewer sees himself or herself passing by. This is true even if *La Dolce Vita* is not part of the viewer's past in the same way it is in Anita's, Mastroianni's, and Fellini's past; all three have actually lived what the spectator sees "in the cinema." *Intervista*, as a temporal object, is temporal in making the temporal object *La Dolce Vita*, lived by the characters in *Intervista* just as by its current viewers—each in a particular role—re-appear.

Consequently, the viewer (of *Intervista*) faced with the impossibility of distinguishing between reality and fiction, between perception and imagination, while (each in his or her particular role) *all must* also say to themselves, "*We are passing by there.*" . . .

America, America

It would be a simple matter to show that this scenario could only result in the most general of structures, structures of haunting and phantasmatic spectrality already predicted by Socrates to the Athenians regarding the immortality of the soul.[12]

"The immortality of the soul" is the screen—confusing perception and imagination, doxa and epistëmë, sensible and intelligible, which must always be distinguished without ever being placed in opposition—onto which that structure will then be projected and dissimulated: as projection screen "the immortality of the soul" is the opening of a great "film," *metaphysics*, introducing the extravagant Socrates played by Plato.

Fellini stages this spectacle's machinery most clearly at *Intervista's* conclusion showing how metaphysics "functions" and beyond that, the "consciousness" that is its product. This structure is revealed in its greatest force, the force of direct evidence, in cinema, and because cinema is a temporal object.

In a similar frame, we might *remember* the characters in Resnais's *My American Uncle*, in which memory is a dense fabric of cinematographic citations. As he set out on the project, Resnais had imagined making a film consisting entirely of citations but had to abandon the idea for economic reasons:

> The idea of only using extracts from existing films existed from the very first scenario. At one point we even thought of making a film exclusively based on scenes drawn from the millions of films that make up the history of cinema. The novel, the cinema, and the theater contain every possible behavior. With enough time and patience, perhaps it might happen. But financially it would be a mad undertaking.[13]

The great French actor Jean Gabin appears in the memory of René Ragueneau, being played by Gerard Depardieu. Gabin was a cinematic presence, "in the limelight" as would have been said before World War II. In that cinematic era there were "stars." Stars: inaccessible, untouchable, *impassive,* yet visible, perceptible beings; beings balanced between, on the one hand, the intelligible, where they seemed to be fabricated in the spirit of a Greek ideality (and in the pre-philosophic spirit of divinities), and on the other hand, the corruptible, sublunary world of the viewer's eye beholding them, an eye so fragile, so obviously predisposed to vanishing, so flawed: an eye merely passing by.

By the very fact of this juxtaposition of the cinematographic temporal object as between the real life of actors and that of their fictional characters, the Hollywood star could only *become* a star through a play of hauntings in which reality and fiction, perception and imagination become confused together—and along with them primary, secondary, and tertiary memory.

The great case in point that we still remember is Vivien Leigh's Blanche Dubois in *A Streetcar Named Desire,*[14] Blanche is a faded Southern belle who has lost the family house, a "house with colonnades," one of those residences that the Scarlett O'Hara of *Gone with the Wind* would not abandon at any price.[15] Watching Vivien Leigh playing Blanche, how could one avoid saying to oneself that she, and director Elia Kazan, and all the viewers of *Streetcar,* are haunted by Scarlett: by her extraordinary beauty, her brilliant and unbearable coolness as a mad young Southern woman—how could one avoid it? Who has not seen, loved, and detested Scarlett? *Gone with the Wind* was made a dozen years before *A Streetcar Named Desire* and is, of course, among the greatest successes in cinema history; it is a film that has been seen—that has *passed by,* unfolded, been unrolled—literally everywhere, and with it, Scarlett O'Hara, as played by Vivien Leigh, loved and hated by the entire world. Kazan could neither ignore nor neglect this when he cast his later film. How not to shudder before such a psychotic, at the catastrophe that has unfolded when we see Blanche taken away forever from her "sanctuary" with Stella and Stanley? How not to feel insane ourselves, carried along by this exemplar of the great, mad

American destiny—that never fails at the same time to sell us, through making us laugh and cry in the face of our own fate, the American Way of Life?
America, America!

Notes

1. For a further reading of this theme, see Stiegler's recent *Taking Care of Youth and the Generations* (2010), from Stanford University Press. "Taking care" for Stiegler means caring of/for the continuity of generational (collective) individuation possible only through technics—through grammatization. The discussion makes extensive use of Kant's "Answering the Question: What Is Enlightenment?" and the history of European public education since its advent in the late eighteenth century to interrogate the way in which pedagogy, and the educational tradition, has "grammatized," shifting from the oral/familial to the written/public—though grammatization is "writing" in the largest sense; "exteriorized" onto programmed (semiotic) media that, as Derrida points out, has always been the case with "language," is all the more so in an age of icons, logos, text-messaging, and a general grammatization. The entire notion of the "tertiary" is predicated on its lack of dependence on the "human," but rather on techniques of recording that "transcend" the human in the sense that they are not dependent on any life or life experience but on a collective (i.e., "super" individual) medium of ex-pression, in a number of forms, ranging from writing to music to images to sounds.—TRANS.

2. "This schematism of our understanding in regard to phenomena and their mere form, is an art, hidden in the depths of the human soul, whose true modes of action we shall only with difficulty discover and unveil." Immanuel Kant, *Critique of Pure Reason*, trans. Norman Kemp Smith (New York: Macmillan, 1965). Henceforth CPR.

   The standard French translation used by Stiegler, by Treinesaygues and Pacaud, contains different language: "Ce schématisme de notre entendement, relativement aux phénomènes et à leur simple forme, est un art caché dans les profondeurs de l'âme humaine et dont il sera toujours difficile d'arracher le mécanisme."—TRANS.

3. Roland Barthes, *Camera Lucida*, trans. Richard Howard (New York: Hill and Wang, 1981), pp. 76, 78. Henceforth CL.

4. Xavier Lemarchand first compared this analysis to the Kuleshov Effect in his dissertation, "Différance et audiovisuel numérique," at the Université de technologie de Compiègne, 1998.

5. Cf. François Albera, "Introduction to Lev Koulechov," in *L'Art du cinema et autres écrits*, vol. 2 (Lausanne: L'Age d'homme, 1994). Henceforth FA.

6. Ivan Ilyich Mozzhukhin (1889–1939) was a leading actor in Russian cinema. In 1910 he left law school at Moscow University to join a traveling theater troupe. His is the face of Lev Kuleshov's experimentation with image perception employing a film-as-image psychological montage alternating Mozzhukhin's face with other unrelated images; the effect was that Mozzhukhin's face itself seemed to undergo alterations related to the surrounding images, produced by fading memory.

   Mozzhukhin left Russia during the Revolution, arriving in Paris in 1919 and quickly becoming a star of French silent cinema, his hypnotic stare appearing on many European film magazine covers. Mozzhukhin wrote his own films in which he experimented with the perception of reality, for example, building sets that made the actors seem much smaller than normal, and juxtaposing incongruous visual elements in scenes (e.g., the camera entering a detective's office to find a chorus line of men in tuxedos waltzing about the room).

Novelist Romain Gary claimed to be Mozzhukhin's son; on a final cinematic note, Gary's novel *La promesse de l'aube (Promise of Dawn),* which fictionalizes the story of his mother and Mozzhukhin, was adapted into a screenplay and then a 1970 film directed by Jules Dassin (who plays Mozzhukhin).—TRANS.

7. Jean-Michel Salanskis, in his very meticulous assessment of the first two volumes of *Technics and Time* ("Ecce faber," *Les temps modernes,* no. 608 [April–May 2000]), seems to me not to have understood this concluding chapter of volume 2, saying that in it I denounce Husserl's distinction between primary and secondary memories (that is, it must be noted, between perception and imagination). On the contrary, my goal there is precisely to reaffirm this distinction, asserting that it is weakened by the fact that Husserl himself understands it as an opposition. My claim is quite simply that a distinction is not an opposition, and further that this confusion is the origin of metaphysics—to which we will return at length. In this volume, and in volume 5 of *Technics and Time,* we will also return to a number of matters addressed in my good friend Salanskis's article.

8. In Bernard Stiegler, *Technics and Time, 4: Symbols and Diabols, or the War of the Mind,* forthcoming.

9. This analysis was first presented in Rome in 1985 at the invitation of Jean Lauxerois and published in *La Revue Philosophique* in 1990 under the title "Mémoires gauches." I returned to it in the first chapter of *Technics and Time, 2.* Here I will extend those analyses, addressing their consequences for the temporal object, initiated in the last chapter of *Technics and Time, 2* . . .

10. "Il s'agit du Grand Jeu, du plus sérieux: du premier au dernier enjeu, de l'enjeu de tous les jeux"—TRANS.

11. Stiegler is playing a *double jeu* here, not only taking Barthes's future anterior to its conclusion but relating it directly to that other multilayered *punctum:* Maurice Blanchot's "L'instant de ma mort," in which Blanchot recounts the real or fictional narrative of his own "pricking," the reportedly transfiguring experience of having been placed before a German firing squad, only to face a *mock* execution. Blanchot himself is recalling Dostoevsky's 1848 experience of just such a "theatrical" event. The layers of "play" and "playing" involved in "the instant of my death," particularly in light of that impossible first-person pronoun, are parallels to Stiegler's citation of "reality and the past" in Fellini's film and its relation to the temporal object.—TRANS.

12. Cf. Stiegler, *Technics and Time, 4.*

It should be remembered that *âme,* here clearly "soul," was not for Socrates, nor for Aristotle, what the word has meant in the modern era. The Greek ψυχή, generally rendered in Latin as *anima,* is closer to "life force" or *élan vital.*—TRANS.

13. Alain Resnais, "La vie est un roman," *L'Avant-Scène Cinema,* no. 263 (March 1981): 7.

14. Elia Kazan's 1951 film released in France with the title *Un tramway nommé Désir.*

15. *Gone with the Wind:* Victor Fleming, 1939; in French, *Autant en emporte le vent.*

CHAPTER 18

THE MIRACLE OF ANALOGY

or, The History of Photography, Part 1

KAJA SILVERMAN

K aja Silverman (b. 1947) is Keith L. and Katherine Sachs Professor of Contemporary Art at the University of Pennsylvania. Silverman's early work was inspired by a combination of interests in semiotics, psychoanalysis, and gender theory, which she brought to bear upon the subject of cinema in her books *The Acoustic Mirror: The Female Voice in Psychoanalysis and Cinema* (1988), *Cinema and Male Subjectivity at the Margins* (1992), and *Speaking About Godard* (1998), coauthored with the German artist and filmmaker Harun Farocki. In subsequent work, beginning especially with the publication of *World Spectators* (2000) and then *Flesh of My Flesh* (2009), Silverman initiated a rethinking of her earlier reading of semiotics and psychoanalysis through the philosophical tradition of phenomenology, particularly the work of Martin Heidegger and Maurice Merleau-Ponty. Silverman's reading of these thinkers allowed her to challenge the dichotomy between the subject and object and, more broadly, the assumption of differences, rather than resemblances, similarities, and correspondences, governing all relations of human subjectivity and the world. Seeking to displace the emphasis upon relational organizations of difference, Silverman's more recent writing embraces Merleau-Ponty's idea that the subject's interwoven mode of existing *in* the world overlaps or "crosses" with the mode of existence *of* the material world and, as such, is the condition for the subject's perception. For Silverman, this idea chimes with Walt Whitman's statement in a famous passage from his poem *Leaves of Grass* (1855) that "a vast similitude interlocks all," leading her to declare that "each of us is connected through similarities that are neither of our making or our choosing to countless other beings. We cannot extricate our-selves from these relationships because there is no such thing as an individual; the smallest unit of Being is two interlocking terms. . . . *Everything matters.*"[1] Such ontological equality, Silverman maintains, does not negate dissent, con-flict, or finitude, but she insists that there are forms of relationality in the world that "destabilize all of our hierarchies, and undermine all of our antith-eses." Silverman's thesis in her most recent book, *The Miracle of Analogy: or, The History of Photography, Part 1,*[2] from which the accompanying text is taken, is that photography discloses the relationality of the world through forms of "analogy." At their simplest these forms are conceived of as binary pairs that are mutually related and informing. Silverman proposes that the rel-evant binary sets at stake in photography are those of the image and the refer-ent, the negative and the positive (in analog photography), the relationship of photography with other media (for instance, with painting), and the correla-tion between the photographic image and variations of the image produced later over time that includes the development of the analog image to the digital image. These pairs, Silverman argues, are held together in a relation, however slight or apparently imperceptible, in which each transform the other in a con-stant back and forth movement that Silverman describes as a process of "reversible reversals" structured in the form of a "chiasmus." Chiasmus is a term that Silverman adopts from Merleau-Ponty's phenomenology,[3] the model for which is based upon the subject's mode of visual perception that is realized by means of the optic chiasm, the crossing of optic nerves at the base of the brain, a crossing that produces a blind spot where these nerves coincide with the retina. In the accompanying text Silverman adapts this model, whereby the invisible is the condition of the visible, to discuss the analogies or crossovers underlying the relations between perceiver and perceived, subject and image, as these are explored by Chantal Akerman in films such as *Je, tu, il, elle* (1974) and in her adaptation (Silverman refers to it as a "renovation") of Proust's novel *The Captive,* which was released in 2000.[4]

In order to counter the traditional, metaphysical conception of the relation between the perceiver and the perceived, the seer and the seen, Silverman ini-tially refers to Sartre's discussion of *The Look* in his book *Being and Nothing-ness* (1943),[5] where an account is given of a dialectic between the subject and object that she wishes to critique and overturn. In this passage on *The Look,* Sartre imagines himself standing alone in a park commanding the view of the surrounding lawn and benches. As the account develops, however, Sar-tre's subjective sense of sovereignty is radically diminished with the entrance of another man into the park. As a consequence, Sartre finds that he is no longer able to position himself at the imaginary center of the scene, for it is as if the lines of visual control over the park, those that Sartre perceived him-self formerly to dominate, were drained away and taken over by the visitor.

Once the subject of the scene, Sartre feels reduced to one among a number of objects.

Silverman argues that in the opening scene of *The Captive* Chantal Akerman radically redistributes the power relations of the seer and the seen, which Sartre describes in *Being and Nothingness,* through a series of formal and gestural interchanges between the film's protagonists. This is despite the fact that, at first, Simon (Stanislas Merhar) would appear to be attempting, as Silverman says, "a sort of arrestation" of the moving image as "the ego attempts to stabilize itself and master the world." In this opening sequence, Simon gazes at home film footage of a group of women playing at the seaside and, in particular, at two women, Ariane (Sylvie Testud) and Andrée (Olivia Bonamy). Silverman claims that, ultimately, this scene cannot be read in terms of the gaze of the male voyeuristic subject, but rather as an analogy that encompasses Simon, Ariane, and Andrée in a circuit of looks and a series of amorous relations (relations that are taken up later by the film). Foregrounding and, at the same time, expanding the "reversible reversals" of looks and interrelations between the three protagonists is Akerman's filming of the projected film, thus creating the effect of a mise en abyme, a film within a film that, in principle, extends ad infinitum across every projection of *The Captive*. As the shadow of Simon's head falls upon the projected screen, a blind spot is formed, the chiasmatic crossing point between the negative of the shadow to the positive of the film footage that simultaneously brings together Simon (that is to say, his unconscious) with the women, as well as all three with the audience as Ariane and Andrée gaze toward the camera and out at us. This, then, is not just an exchange between the protagonists within the film but also an exchange between Akerman's film and the audience who, in being touched by the analogies explored in the opening scene, are also incorporated into a phenomenology of giving and receiving.

Finally, a further set of interrelations is acknowledged by Kaja Silverman, who dedicates her text to her friend, the art historian Mieke Bal, as they share a mutual love for Proust; Bal herself has written a book on Proust that helped prompt Silverman's own reading.[6] In particular, Silverman cites Bal's analogy between the bodies of the two lovers, Simon and Ariane, pressed together, yet not interpenetrating, and "the image of the breasts of two women pressed flat against one another" that Marcel sees while watching Albertine and Andrée dance together" in a previous encounter. While in the novel this arouses Proust's jealousy, the reuse of its visual form in the film in the sex scenes of Simon and Ariane would suggest that the relations between them are a kind of bond, a chiasmus of amorous desire crossed with the need for autonomy.

* * *

From Chapter 4, A Kind of Republic

According to *The Oxford English Dictionary*, a chiasmus is "a rhetorical or literary figure in which words, grammatical constructions, or concepts are repeated in reverse order, in the same or a modified form,"[7] such as John F. Kennedy's "Ask not what your country can do for you—ask what you can do for your country." But chiasmus is also operative in other domains. The brain is able to fuse the two-dimensional images that light inscribes on the retinas of two-sighted people into one three-dimensional image because half of the optic nerve fibers carrying visual "information" from each retina to the brain cross at the optic chiasm.[8] "Chiasmus" is also Merleau-Ponty's name for the ontological thread stitching the seer to what is seen, the toucher to what is touched, and sight and visibility to touch and tactility.[9]

We are all both seers and part of the spectacle of the world, the philosopher argues in *The Visible and the Invisible*. Each of us also touches, and is touched, and there is a "reciprocal insertion and intertwining" of the visual in the tactile, and the tactile in the visual.[10] Since these faculties belong to the same body, we cannot separate them, but we also cannot weave them into a seamless whole by exercising all of them at once, or by being simultaneously the seer and what is seen, the toucher and what is touched. We shuttle back and forth between these aspects of our Being, at one moment a seer or toucher, and at the next moment what is seen or touched.

If we were alone in the world, there would be no communication between these "selves," and our non-identity would be a source of perpetual unhappiness. Since, however, we share this world with others, who also see and are seen, and touch and are touched, they provide the "rejoinder" for which we would otherwise wait in vain, and we do the same for them. We see because they are visible, and we are visible because they see us. Through their gaze, we are also able to see our own, and when gazing at them, to experience our own visibility. Merleau-Ponty metaphorizes this relationship as "two mirrors facing one another [in which] two indefinite series of images [. . .] arise which belong really to neither of the two [mirror] surfaces. "Through the images reflected in them, he adds, these mirrors form a "couple," which is "more real" than either of them could be alone.[11] This couple has no fixed constituency, and its members belong to many other couples. I invoke it here not to suggest that it is the building block of society, but rather to make the following point: we are not "ourselves" when we are isolated from others. Two is the smallest unit of Being.

Chiasmus is also operative within a closely related domain: that of personhood. "Consciousness of self is only experienced by contrast," Emile Benveniste writes in *Problems in General Linguistics*. "I use *I* only when I am speaking to someone who will be a *you* in my address. It is this condition of dialogue that is constitutive of *person*, for it implies that reciprocally *I* becomes *you* in the address of the one who in his turn designates himself as I."[12] Personhood consequently depends on the utterance of these two reversible and mutually defining pronouns. This pronominal chiasmus is closely related to the one described by Merleau-Ponty. Giving and receiving the "you," as Martin Buber puts it,[13] is one of the most important means we have for affirming our ontological kinship with another human being.

From Chapter 5, Je/Vous

In the paragraph [of Proust's *The Guermantes Way*][14] after the one in which Marcel compares Albertine to a constantly changing photograph, he talks about photographs into which multiple viewpoints have been crammed, presumably so as to overcome the limits of human vision. He emphasizes the absurdity of this project by comparing it to his own attempt to get behind Albertine's eyes by kissing her, and by suggesting that the photographic image has a directly contrary effect upon the human eye. "I can think of nothing that can to so great a degree as a kiss evoke out of what we believed to be a thing with one definite aspect the hundred other things which it may equally well be," he wryly observes, "since each is related to a no less legitimate perspective."[15]

Proust also tries to make room for others in the last volume of his novel by abstracting away from sensory experience to universal laws, but this leads to a generalization of the first-person pronoun, rather than a greater accommodation of the second.[16] A new Marcel also emerges in some passages in *Time Regained*—one whose perceptual coordinates are closer to "radiography" than to photography. As the narrator suggests in *Within a Budding Grove,* this is a mortifying optic; it peels away the "tiny particles of epidermis whose varied combinations form the florid originality of human flesh" to reveal the "joyless universality of a skeleton."[17] Marcel recoils from this kind of looking in the second volume of *In Search of Lost Time,* but he later justifies it as the necessary condition for art making. A book is "a huge cemetery in which on the majority of the tombs the names are effaced," he writes in *Time Regained.*[18]

There is one passage in the last volume of Proust's novel, though, where the narrator not only acknowledges that the world reveals different aspects of itself to every seer but also expresses the desire to leave his cork-lined room, and re-enter the "loud, clamoring, semi-visible world."[19] He stops talking about art as the purveyor of universal truths and begins thinking of it as the agency through which looks that would otherwise remain completely sealed off might somehow communicate with one another. "Through art alone are we able to emerge from ourselves," Proust writes in *Time Regained,* "to know what another person sees of a universe that is not the same as our own and of which, without art, the landscapes would remain as unknown to us as those that may exist on the moon."[20] And although he is no closer to uttering the second-person pronoun here than he is when he characterizes Albertine as "a product of [his] temperament," he is clearly trying to make the first-person pronoun a lot more capacious.

The reverse field that was disclosed through the negative/positive distinction did not disappear after the industrialization of photography; it remained stubbornly in place, and although neither Sartre nor Merleau-Ponty links it to the so-called "medium," they are obsessed with it. Both philosophers also respond to the passage in which Proust attempts to make room for other landscapes and looks. In chapter 3 of *Being and Nothingness*, Sartre tells a story about a man who visits a public park. The man is alone at first, and everything seems to radiate out from his look, but then someone else enters the park, who perceives it from a different position, and toward whom the "raw green" of the lawn turns a different "face."[21] The "whole universe" slides away from him, and toward the interloper.[22] The man tries to recover his equilibrium by reasoning that since he sees the latter, he is still the perceiving subject, and the Other the object of his look, but he is prevented from doing so by an even more distressing realization: the realization that the Other is also looking at him. What is true of the "raw green" of the lawn is also true of him; he turns a different face to the Other than he does to himself, and it will forever elude him.

This is a reversible but not a reciprocal relationship; either one sees or one is seen. The same principle obtains at the level of language; Sartre narrates the story from the first man's perspective, in direct discourse, and he refers to the second man with the third-person pronoun. At the outset, "I" means "the one who sees," and "he" means "the one who is seen," but at a certain point the speaker realizes that "the truth of 'seeing-the-Other'" is "'being-seen-by-the-Other.'" Since this is an unavoidable objectification, "I" must signify the one who is seen. "Thus I, who in so far as I am my possibles, am what I am not and am not what I am—behold, now I am somebody!" he exclaims.' "And the one who I am—and who on principle escapes me—I am he in the midst of the world in so far as he escapes me."[23] But the first-person pronoun is nothing without the second, and it soon devolves into the third.

Merleau-Ponty responds to this section of *Being and Nothingness* as well as to the passage which Sartre attempts to rebut in *The Visible and Invisible*. He begins by not only agreeing with a number of Sartre's claims but strengthening them. If two men entered a park, he writes, the "raw green" of the landscape would indeed turn a different "face" to each of them, since we all have our "own depth," and this depth is "backed up" by what we see. We "espouse" the aspects of the visible world with which we are in "pre-established harmony"—with the things that are the equivalent "on the outside" of what we are "on the inside."[24]

What the second man saw when he entered the park would also escape the first. The face that the world turns toward us is "only for our vision and our body"; it cannot be seen by anyone else. And since it shows different aspects of itself to other seers, what each of us sees is only the "surface of an inexhaustible depth."

But once he has detailed these points of commonality, Merleau-Ponty parts company with Sartre and aligns himself with Proust. He extends what the novelist says about art to speech, and he makes this linguistic mediation one of the cornerstones of his phenomenology. Our perceptions are not hermetically sealed, Merleau-Ponty argues, because language allows us to share them with one another. When I look at a landscape with someone else, and each of us describes what we see to the other, "the individual green of the meadow under my eyes invades his vision without quitting my own," and I "recognize" his green in mine. Our landscapes "interweave," and we realize that "it is not *I* who sees, or *"he"* who sees," but rather a "vision in general" that sees, and that "inhabits" both of us.[25]

Merleau-Ponty clearly grasps the significance of the pronominal antithesis that figures so prominently in Sartre's account of the look, because he emphasizes it here. He also makes dialogue the agency of its resolution. Oddly, though, he does not utter the word on which all dialogue depends; instead of replacing the third-person pronoun with the second, he leaps to "vision in general." He thus inadvertently promotes *impersonality*, instead of *relationality*, just as Proust does in the final volume of his novel. I want to end this chapter with a work that satisfies all three definitions of the chiasmus, and that will help us to see how interdependent they are: Chantal Akerman's filmic "renovation" of *In Search of Lost Time, The Captive* (2001).[26]

The Captive opens with credits over a 35mm nocturnal shot of the sea. This shot—which comes slowly and moodily into focus—is accompanied by the sound of crashing waves. The transition from it to the film "proper" is unusually smooth, since the first scene also begins with a frontal shot of a seascape, accompanied by the sound of waves. Now, though, the sun is high in the sky, and a group of girls are playing in the water. This shot is also grainier than the one that precedes it, and it is followed by a series of handheld and equally grainy shots of the girls and the water. The sound of a film projector competes with— and eventually replaces—the sound of waves, and from time to time we hear the "click" of a still camera.

Two girls leave the water and approach the camera: Ariane and Andrée, Akerman's Albertine and Andrée. They pause briefly in front of the camera, allowing the photographer to study their faces, and their friends gather around them. Then the girls begin playing with a soccer ball on the beach, and the image becomes once again hard to read. The photographer attempts to follow their movements, but the jerkiness of his handheld camera renders them even less intelligible. Eventually he manages to isolate Ariane from the others, and he moves from a close-up to an extreme close-up of her face.

Akerman cuts away from this close-up to a 35mm shot of Simon, the counterpart in her film for the narrator in Proust's novel. He stands beside a projector, which he is using to screen a film. It is a home movie, presumably shot by him, and the source of the grainy images at which we have been looking. The projector permits us to identify the mechanical "whirr" that competes with and eventually drowns out the crashing waves. At first, it also seems responsible for the mysterious "click," since Simon repeatedly stops the projector and rewinds a bit of film, and each time he does so, we hear this sound. Before long, though, it becomes evident that the "click" is the auditory exteriorization of a *mental* camera. Akerman also treats the amateur camera and the film projector as perceptual metaphors. She uses the blur that results when unpredictable movements are filmed with a handheld camera, and then re-photographed with a higher-resolution camera, to depict the "spectacle of forms undergoing an incessant process of change";[27] the clicking sound to dramatize Simon's perception, which transforms this mobile beauty into a series of still photographs; and the stopping and starting of the projector to suggest another sort of arrestation—that through which the ego attempts to stabilize itself, and master the world.[28]

As the camera holds on Simon, he says, *"Je . . . je . . . je . . . vous."* Since he looks at Ariane as he utters these words, she is obviously the referent for one of them, but it is impossible to determine which, since he could be speaking either for her or for himself. These pronouns become even shiftier when the camera cuts back to the home movie. Ariane and Andrée stand together on the beach, against the backdrop of the sea. They are wrapped in towels, and lean into each other like lovers, but—because they stand with their backs to the sun—their faces are difficult to make out. As we look at this ambiguous shot, we hear Simon utter the following words, from an off-screen position: *"je . . . je vous . . . je vous . . . je vous aime bien."*

Since *"vous"* is the plural as well as the formal version of the second-person pronoun in French, its field of possible referents now expands to include Andrée. Initially, this expansion seems to secure Simon in the position of the *"je,"* but before long another possibility emerges: the possibility that the first—and second—person pronouns are reversible designators for Ariane and Andrée. The camera returns to Simon, who repeats these words, but this time he smiles as he speaks, and there is a lilt to his voice. It then cuts back to the home movie, and remains facing in this direction until the end of the scene. Simon approaches the screen, sits down in front of it, and presses his face against Ariane's image. His head forms an oversized shadow in the lower-left frame. From this strange position, which is simultaneously inside and outside the home movie, Simon again says, *"Je vous aime bien."* The emphasis now falls as much upon the last two words as the first two. In this iteration, *"aimer bien"* means not only "to love a lot," but also "to love well."

In *The Captive,* as in the novel it analogizes, the central male character derives erotic gratification from pressing against the female body. Proust represents this as a masturbatory sexuality, but in *The Mottled Screen* Bal links it to "the image of the breasts of two women pressed flat against one another" that Marcel sees while watching Albertine and Andrée dance together, and that "plunges" him into "jealous rage."[29] As we have already seen, physical contact is also an important part of . . . Merleau-Ponty's chiasmus, which is tactile as well as visual. Akerman retains this aspect of the Proustian narrative, but she makes it a source of female as well as male pleasure.

Simon climaxes twice while pressing against Ariane's body, and both times she also manifests extreme sexual pleasure. She enjoys this activity, she explains later in the film, because it is non-invasive—because it does not encroach upon her physical or (even more importantly) her psychic interiority. She is therefore free to think about Andrée while experiencing corporeal pleasure with Simon, i.e., to be with both of them at the same time.[30] The second time he says *"Je vous aime bien,"* he acknowledges that his own pleasure derives from the same source—that he loves Ariane because she and Andrée love each other. The third time, he goes even further: he affirms their right to address these words to each other. And since by doing this, he loves them *well,* he also finds his own way back to the *"je."*

This scene relies heavily upon the shot/reverse shot formation. Since this device is often used within normative cinema to construct sexual difference and conceal the presence of the camera, Akerman ostentatiously avoids it in two of her most celebrated films, *Jeanne Dielman* (1975) and *News from Home* (1976). This is not, however, the role for which it is "destined." The shot/reverse shot is structurally linked to the recto and verso of the camera obscura's image stream and [Fox] Talbot's double reversals, and it houses the same power. Akerman mobilizes this power here, through another "renovation." Ariane and Andrée are separated from Simon by the fourth wall, so they shouldn't be able to return his look, but they miraculously do. After he acknowledges the interdependence of his desire for Ariane, and hers for Andrée, and affirms the girls' right to say *"je vous aime bien"* to each other, they respond by smiling first at each other, and then at him. And when Simon walks over to the screen, and presses his head against Ariane's image, he responds to *their* response.

Akerman often signals her authorial presence by correlating the height of the camera to her own look—i.e., by positioning it lower than usual.[31] She follows this practice when filming Simon, but because these shots establish him as the source of the home movie, this is easy to miss. However, in the last shot of this scene, Akerman alerts us to the fact that there is a second focalizer in a number of ways: by not moving her camera when Simon does; by continuing to film the screen from a standing position after he sits down; by dramatizing the lateral distance separating him from the camera by situating his head in the left corner of the image; and by showing Ariane and Andrée looking away from him, toward another seer.

We recognize this focalizer from other Akerman films—not just as a formally rigorous eye, but also as a person named "Chantal," who is Jewish, Belgian, and a lesbian. The parallels between *The Captive* and *Je tu il elle* (1974) are particularly striking. In the latter film, Akerman plays a lesbian who seduces a former girlfriend, and during their lovemaking the two women press their bodies passionately together. The title of the film also consists entirely of pronouns. Chantal is the only character who appears in every scene, which might seem to entitle her to the *"je,"* but there are also two other claimants to this position, and times when she is more closely aligned with one of the other pronouns. In the second part of the film, she is picked up on the side of a road by a truck driver. He commandeers the first-person pronoun by doing most of the talking, thereby assigning the second-person pronoun to her. Chantal later gives him a "hand-job," at which point she could be a "you," a "she," or an "I," and he a "you," a "he," or an "I." In the scene in which she visits her former girlfriend, each exercises power, and then has it wrested away from her by the other. The "I" and "you" shift positions at a dizzying rate, both literally and metaphorically, and the surprisingly frank way in which Akerman films their lovemaking marks both of them as a "she." As Ivone Margulies so elegantly puts it, the four pronouns in the title of the film "seem to be on call, performing rituals of abeyance."[32]

Things are every bit as labile in *The Captive*, both within the fiction and at the level of the enunciation. Here, however, Akerman is less contestatory. She emphasizes the impossibility of replacing Simon's look with hers by depicting it as a blind spot within her own field of vision. She also presents her look as a *second* vantage point from which to observe and desire the band of girls, rather than an alternative to it. Last, but not least, Akerman shows these two looks meeting at the site of Ariane's body, like the landscape invoked by Proust, Sartre, and Merleau-Ponty. If we were to translate this meeting into language, it would read: *"je . . . vous . . . je vous."* This chapter is the site of a similar exchange. In it, two old friends meet each other through a book they both love, and give and receive the "you."

Notes

1. The Miracle of Analogy nonsite.org.
2. Kaja Silverman, *The Miracle of Analogy: or, The History of Photography, Part 1* (Stanford: Stanford University Press, 2015).

3. Maurice Merleau-Ponty's concept of the chiasmus is developed fully in his later book, *The Visible and the Invisible*, trans. Alphonso Lingis (Evanston: Northwestern University Press, 1968 [1964]). However, it already makes appearances in his earlier work such as *The Structure of Behavior* of 1942, trans. Alden Fischer (Pittsburgh: Duquesne University Press, 1963).

4. Marcel Proust's novel, *The Captive* (*La Prisonnière*), the fifth volume of the seven-volume work *In Search of Lost Time* (*À La Recherche du Temps Perdu*), was published in 1923 and is principally concerned with Proust's obsessive relationship with Albertine (and Andrée). Akerman's film casts Simon as Proust and Ariane as Albertine in a modern setting.

5. Jean-Paul Sartre, *Being and Nothingness: An Essay on Phenomenological Ontology*, trans. Hazel E. Barnes (London: Routledge, 2001).

6. Mieke Bal, *The Mottled Screen: Reading Proust Visually*, trans. Anna-Louise Milne (Stanford: Stanford University Press, 1997).

7. *Oxford English Dictionary Online*, s.v. "Chiasmus," accessed December 2013, http://oxforddictionaries.com/definition/english/chiasmus?q=chiasmus.

8. David G. Stork, Dieter R. Brill, and David Falk, *Seeing the Light: Optics in Nature, Photography, Color, Vision, and Holography* (New York: Wiley, 1982), p. 182.

9. I am drawing here on the last chapter of Merleau-Ponty's *The Visible and the Invisible*, especially pp. 137–39.

10. Merleau-Ponty, p. 138.

11. Merleau-Ponty, p. 139.

12. Emile Benveniste, "Subjectivity in Language," in *Problems in General Linguistics*, trans. Mary Elizabeth Meek (Coral Gables: University of Florida Press, 1971), pp. 224–25.

13. Martin Buber, *I and Thou*, trans. Walter Kaufmann (New York: Simon and Schuster, 1970), p. 84.

14. Marcel Proust, *In Search of Lost Time*, vol. 3: *The Guermantes Way*, trans. C. K. Scott Moncrieff, Terence Kilmartin, and D. J. Enright (New York: Modern Library, 1993), p. 498.

15. Proust, pp. 498–99.

16. In a chilling passage in *Time Regained*, Proust maintains that "matter is indifferent" and that "anything can be grafted upon it by thought." Marcel Proust, *In Search of Lost Time*, vol. 6: *Time Regained*, trans. Andreas Major, Terence Kilman, and D. J. Enright (New York: Modern Library, 1993), pp. 320–21. He invokes this axiom as proof of his "idealism."

17. Marcel Proust, *In Search of Lost Time*, vol. 2: *Within a Budding Grove*, trans. C. K. Scott Moncrieff, Terence Kilman, and D. J. Enright (New York: Modern Library, 1992), p. 648.

18. Proust, *Time Regained*, p. 310.

19. I take this phrase from Ralph Ellison, who uses it to describe a chiasmus that is closely related to those I discuss in this book, and to which I will return in *The Promise of Social Happiness*. See his *Invisible Man* (New York: Vintage International, 1995), p. 574.

20. Proust, *Time Regained*, p. 299.

21. Sartre, *Being and Nothingness: A Phenomenological Essay on Ontology*, trans. Hazel E. Barnes (New York: Citadel, 1956), p. 231.

22. Sartre, p. 231.

23. Sartre, p. 239.

24. Merleau-Ponty, *The Visible and the Invisible*, pp. 132–33.

25. Merleau-Ponty, pp. 141–42.

26. Akerman introduces a narrative element into *The Captive* that is not present in Proust's novel and that suggests that the former is a renovation of the latter, rather than an "adaptation": workmen are constantly painting and plastering the walls of Simon's apartment.

27. Proust, *Within a Budding Grove,* p. 661.

28. Proust claims in *Time Regained* that "nothing is further from what we have really perceived than the vision that the cinematograph presents" (p. 279), but it is difficult to place much credence in this assertion, since associational montage works the same way Proustian analogy does; both privilege resemblance over temporal contiguity. As Bal argues in *The Mottled Screen, In Search of Lost Time* also evokes a certain kind of avant-garde film: the kind where the diegesis is based on vision rather than narrative (p. 213). *The Captive* provides both an instantiation of, and a reflection upon, this last sort of cinema.

29. Bal, p. 8.

30. Simon is later overcome by the desire to know what Ariane is thinking about, and this desire proves fatal for her.

31. Akerman reflects upon this practice in an interview with the editors of *Camera Obscura:* "Delphine [Seyrig] said, 'Why do you use such a low angle?' I said, 'That's my size.' She said, 'It's better from a little higher up.' And I said, 'No, I don't want to do that. That's not how I see the world.' [*Jeanne Dielman*] was never shot from the point of view of the son or anyone else. It's always me." Chantal Akerman, "*Jeanne Dielman, 23 Quai du Commerce, 1080 Bruxelles,*" *Camera Obscura,* no. 2 (1977): 119.

32. Ivone Margulies, *Nothing Happens: Chantal Akerman's Hyperrealist Everyday* (Durham: Duke University Press, 1996), p. 116.

SELECTED BIBLIOGRAPHY

Adorno, Theodor. *Aesthetic Theory*. Edited by Robert Hullot-Kentor. Minneapolis: University of Minnesota Press, 2006.

Adorno, Theodor, and Walter Benjamin. *The Complete Correspondence, 1928–1940*. Edited by Henri Lonitz. Translated by Nicholas Walker. Cambridge: Polity, 1999.

Adorno, Theodor, and Max Horkheimer. *Dialectic of Enlightenment*. Translated by John Cumming. London: Verso, 1997.

Agamben, Giorgio. *The Coming Community*. Translated by Michael Hardt. Minneapolis: University of Minnesota Press, 2007.

——. "Difference and Repetition: On Guy Debord's Film." In *Guy Debord and the Situationist International: Texts and Documents*. Edited by Tom McDonough. Cambridge, MA: October/MIT Press, 2004.

——. *The Man Without Content*. Translated by Georgia Albert. Stanford: Stanford University Press, 1999.

——. *Means Without End: Notes on Politics*. Translated by Vincenzo Binetti and Cesare Casarino. Minneapolis: University of Minnesota Press, 2000.

Althusser, Louis. *Essays on Ideology*. London: Verso, 1984.

Althusser, Louis. *For Marx*. Translated by Ben Brewster. London: Verso, 1986.

Artaud, Antonin. *Antonin Artaud: Selected Writings*. Edited by Susan Sontag. Berkeley: University of California Press, 1976.

Badiou, Alain. *Being and Event*. Translated by Oliver Feltham. New York: Continuum, 2005.

——. *Cinema*. Translated by Susan Spitzer. Cambridge: Polity, 2013.

——. *Handbook of Inaesthetics*. Translated by Alberto Toscano. Stanford: Stanford University Press, 2005.

——. *Logics of Worlds: Being and Event II*. Translated by Alberto Toscano. New York: Continuum, 2009.

Bal, Mieke. *The Mottled Screen: Reading Proust Visually*. Translated by Anna-Louise Milne. Stanford: Stanford University Press, 1997.

Balibar, Etienne, and John Rajchman with Boyman Anne. *French Philosophy Since 1945: Precepts, Concepts, Inventions. Postwar French Thought*, vol. 4. New York: New Press, 2011.

Barthes, Roland. *Camera Lucida*. Translated by Richard Howard. New York: Hill and Wang, 1981.

Baudrillard, Jean. *The Consumer Society: Myths and Structures*. London: Sage, 1998.

——. *The Gulf War Did Not Take Place*. Translated by Paul Patton. Bloomington: Indiana University Press, 1995.

——. *The Mirror of Production*. Translated by Mark Poster. St. Louis, MO: Telos, 1975.

——. *Seduction*. Translated by Brian Singer. London: Macmillan, 1990.

——. *Simulacra and Simulation*. Translated by Sheila Faria Glaser. Ann Arbor: University of Michigan Press, 1994.

——. *Symbolic Exchange and Death*. Translated by Ian Hamilton Grant. London: Sage, 1993.

Baudry, Jean-Louis. "Ideological Effects of the Basic Cinematographic Apparatus." In *Film Theory and Criticism: Introductory Readings*. Edited by Leo Baudry and Marshall Cohen, pp. 355–65. Oxford: Oxford University Press, 2004.

Baudry, Jean-Louis. "The Apparatus: Metapsychological Approaches to the Impression of Reality in the Cinema." In *Film Theory and Criticism: Introductory Readings*. Edited by Leo Baudry and Marshall Cohen, pp. 206–23. Oxford: Oxford University Press, 2004.

Bazin, André. *What Is Cinema?*, vol. 1. Berkeley: University of California Press, 1967.

——. *What Is Cinema?*, vol. 2. Berkeley: University of California Press, 1971.

Benjamin, Andrew, ed. *The Lyotard Reader*. Oxford: Basil Blackwell, 1991.

Benjamin, Walter. *Illuminations*. Ed. Hannah Arendt. Translated by Harry Zohn. London: Fontana/Collins, 1982.

——. *One-Way Street and Other Writings*. Translated by Edmund Jephcott and Kingsley Shorter. London: Verso, 1992.

——. *Selected Writings*, vol. 1: *1913–1926*. Edited by Marcus Bullock and Michael W. Jennings. Cambridge, MA: Belknap Press of Harvard University Press, 1997.

——. *Selected Writings*, vol. 2: *1927–1930*. Edited by Michael W. Jennings, Howard Eiland, and Gary Smith. Translated by Rodney Livingstone and others. Cambridge, MA: Belknap Press of Harvard University Press, 1999.

——. *Selected Writings*, vol. 3: *1935–1938*. Edited by Howard Eiland and Michael W. Jennings. Translated by Edmund Jephcott, Howard Eiland, and others. Cambridge, MA: Belknap Press of Harvard University Press, 2006.

Bergson, Henri. *Creative Evolution*. Translated by Arthur Mitchell. Lanham, MD: University Press of America, 1984.

——. *Duration and Simultaneity*. Translated by Robin Durie and Mark Lewis. Manchester: Clinamen, 1999.

——. *Matter and Memory*. Translated by Nancy Margaret Paul and W. Scott Palmer. New York: Zone, 1991.

Bersani, Leo, and Ulysse Dutoit. *Forms of Being: Cinema, Aesthetics, Subjectivity*. London: British Film Institute, 2004.

Bogue. Ronald. *Deleuze on Cinema*. London: Routledge, 2003.

Bowman, Paul, ed. *Rancière and Film*. Edinburgh: Edinburgh University Press, 2013.

Bresson, Robert. *Notes on Cinematography*. Translated by Jonathan Griffin. New York: Urizen, 1977.

Buck-Morss, Susan. "Aesthetics and Anaesthetics: Walter Benjamin's Artwork Essay Reconsidered." *October* 62 (Autumn 1992): 3–41.

Burch, Nöel. *Theory of Film Practice.* Translated by Helen R. Lane. London: Secker and Warburg, 1973.

Butler, Judith. *Senses of the Subject.* New York: Fordham University Press, 2015.

Cahiers du Cinéma. *The 1950's: Neo-Realism, Hollywood, New Wave,* vol. 1. Edited by Jim Hillier. Cambridge, MA: Harvard University Press, 1985.

——. *1960–1968: New Wave, New Cinema, Reevaluating Hollywood,* vol. 2. Edited by Jim Hillier. Cambridge, MA: Harvard University Press, 1992.

——. *1969–1972: The Politics of Representation,* vol. 3. Edited by Nick Browne. Cambridge, MA: Harvard University Press, 1990.

——. *1973–1978: History, Ideology, Cultural Struggle,* vol. 4. Edited by David Wilson. London: Routledge, 2000.

Carroll, Noël. *The Philosophy of Motion Pictures.* Oxford: Blackwell, 2008.

Cavell, Stanley. *Cities of Words: Pedagogical Letters on a Register of the Moral Life.* Cambridge, MA: Belknap Press of Harvard University Press, 2005.

——. *Contesting Tears: The Hollywood Melodrama of the Unknown Woman.* Chicago: University of Chicago Press, 1996.

——. *Pursuits of Happiness: The Hollywood Comedy of Remarriage.* Cambridge, MA: Harvard University Press, 1981.

——. *The World Viewed: Reflections on the Ontology of Film.* New York: Penguin, 1971.

Caygill, Howard. *Walter Benjamin: The Colour of Experience.* London: Routledge, 1998.

Chion, Michel. *The Voice in Cinema.* Edited and translated by Claudia Gorbman. New York: Columbia University Press, 1999.

Cixous. Hélène. "The Laugh of the Medusa." Translated by Keith Cohen and Paula Cohen. *Signs* 1, no. 4 (Summer 1976): 875–93.

Coleman, Felicity. *Film, Theory and Philosophy: The Key Thinkers.* Edited by Felicity Coleman. Durham: Acumen, 2009.

Constable, Catherine. *Thinking in Images: Film Theory, Feminist Philosophy, and Marlene Dietrich.* British Film Institute, 2005.

Debord, Guy. *Society of the Spectacle.* London: Rebel Press Aim, 1987.

De Lauretis, Teresa, and Stephen Heath. *The Cinematic Apparatus.* London: Macmillan, 1980.

Deleuze, Gilles. *Bergsonism.* Translated by Hugh Tomlinson and Barbara Habberjam. New York: Zone, 1991.

——. *Cinema I: The Movement-Image.* Translated by Hugh Tomlinson and Barbara Habberjam. London: Athlone, 1986.

——. *Cinema II: The Time-Image.* Translated by Hugh Tomlinson and Robert Galeta. London: Athlone, 1989.

——. *Kant's Critical Philosophy: The Doctrine of the Faculties.* Translated by Hugh Tomlinson and Barbara Habberjam. Minneapolis: University of Minnesota Press, 1984.

——. *Negotiations, 1972–1990.* Translated by Martin Joughin. New York: Columbia University Press, 1995.

——. *Nietzsche and Philosophy.* Translated by Hugh Tomlinson. London: Athlone, 1983.

——. "Postcript on the Societies of Control." *October* 59 (Winter 1992): 3–7.

Deleuze, Gilles, and Félix Guattari. *Anti-Oedipus: Capitalism and Schizophrenia.* Translated by Robert Hurley, Mark Seem, and Helen R. Lane. London: Athlone, 1984.

——. *A Thousand Plateaus: Capitalism and Schizophrenia.* Translated by Brian Massumi. London: Athlone, 1988.

——. *What Is Philosophy?* Translated by Hugh Tomlinson and Graham Burchell. New York: Columbia University Press, 1994.

Doane, Mary-Ann. *The Emergence of Cinematic Time: Modernity, Contingency, the Archive.* Cambridge, MA: Harvard University Press, 2002.

——. *Femmes Fatales: Feminism, Film Theory, Psychoanalysis.* London: Routledge, 1991.

Duras, Marguerite. *Hiroshima mon amour.* Paris: Gallimard, 1994.

——. *The Lover.* Translated by Barbara Bray. London: Flamingo, 1986.

Eisenstein, Sergei. *Towards a Theory of Montage: Selected Works,* vol. 2. Edited by Michael Glenny and Richard Taylor. Translated by Michael Glenny. London: I. B. Tauris, 2010.

Flaubert, Gustave. *Madame Bovary.* Edited and translated by Paul de Man. New York: Norton, 1965.

Frampton, Daniel. *Filmosophy.* London: Wallflower, 2006.

Freud, Sigmund. *The Standard Edition of the Complete Psychological Works of Sigmund Freud.* Translated and edited by James Strachey. London: Hogarth and the Institute of Psychoanalysis, 1981.

Giunta, Carrie, and Adrienne Janus. *Nancy and Visual Culture.* Edinburgh: Edinburgh University Press, 2016.

Gregg, Melissa, and Gregory J. Seigworth, eds. *The Affect Theory Reader.* Durham: Duke University Press, 2010.

Groys, Boris. *Art Power.* Cambridge, MA: MIT Press, 2008.

Gustafsson, Henrik, and Asbjørn Grønstad, eds. *Cinema and Agamben: Ethics, Biopolitics, and the Moving Image.* New York: Bloomsbury, 2014.

Harvey, James. *Jacques Rancière and the Politics of Art Cinema.* Edinburgh: Edinburgh University Press, 2018.

Heath, Stephen. *Questions of Cinema: Theories of Representation and Difference.* Basingstoke: Macmillan, 1981.

Hegel, Georg Wilhelm Friedrich. *Hegel's Aesthetics: Lectures on Fine Art,* vols. 1 and 2. Translated by T. M. Knox. Oxford: Clarendon, 1988.

——. *Introductory Lectures on Aesthetics.* Translated by Bernard Bosanquet. London: Penguin, 2004.

——. *Phenomenology of Spirit.* Translated by A. V. Miller. Oxford: Oxford University Press, 1977.

Heidegger, Martin. *Basic Writings.* Edited by David Farrell Krell. London: Routledge, 2004.

——. *Being and Time.* Translated by John Macquarrie and Edward Robinson. Oxford: Blackwell, 2006.

Hui, Yuk. *On the Existence of Digital Objects.* Minneapolis: University of Minnesota Press, 2016.

Husserl, Edmund. *On the Phenomenology of the Consciousness of Internal Time.* Translated by John B. Brough. Boston: Kluwer Academic, 1991.

Irigaray, Luce. *This Sex Which Is Not One.* Translated by Catherine Porter with Carolyn Burke. Ithaca, NY: Cornell University Press, 1985.

Kaes, Anton. *Shell Shock Cinema: Weimar Culture and the Wounds of War.* Princeton: Princeton University Press, 2009.

Kant, Immanuel. *Critique of Judgment.* Translated by Werner S. Pluhar. Indianapolis: Hackett, 1987.

——. *Critique of Practical Reason.* Translated by Werner S. Pluhar. Indianapolis: Hackett, 2002.

——. *Critique of Pure Reason.* Translated by Norman Kemp Smith. London: Macmillan, 1990.

Kracauer, Siegfried. *From Caligari to Hitler: A Psychological History of German Film.* Princeton: Princeton University Press, 1947.

———. *The Mass Ornament: The Weimar Essays.* Edited and translated by Thomas Y. Levin. Cambridge, MA: Harvard University Press, 1995.

Kristeva, Julia. *Black Sun: Depression and Melancholia.* Translated by Leon S. Roudiez. New York: Columbia University Press, 1989.

———. *Intimate Revolt: The Powers and Limits of Psychoanalysis.* Translated by Jeanine Herman. New York: Columbia University Press, 2001.

———. *Powers of Horror: An Essay on Abjection.* Translated by Leon S. Roudiez. New York: Columbia University Press, 1982.

Kul-Want, Christopher, ed. *Philosophers on Art from Kant to the Postmodernists: A Critical Reader.* New York: Columbia University Press, 2010.

Lacan, Jacques *Écrits: A Selection.* Translated by Alan Sheridan. London: Routledge, 2006.

———. *The Four Fundamental Concepts of Psychoanalysis.* Edited by Jacques-Alain Miller. Translated by Alan Sheridan. London: Penguin, 1991.

Lyotard, Jean-François. *The Inhuman: Reflections on Time.* Translated by Geoff Bennington and Rachel Bowlby. Cambridge: Polity, 1993.

———. *Libidinal Economy.* Translated by Iain Hamilton Grant. London: Athlone, 1993.

———. *The Postmodern Condition: A Report on Knowledge.* Translated by Régis Durand. Manchester: Manchester University Press, 1986.

Marx, Karl. *Capital: A Critique of Political Economy,* vol. 1. Translated by Ben Fowkes. London: Penguin, 1990.

McMahon, Laura. *Cinema and Contact: The Withdrawal of Touch in Nancy, Bresson, Duras, and Denis.* London: Modern Humanities Research Association and Maney, 2012.

Merleau-Ponty, Maurice. *Phenomenology of Perception.* Translated by Colin Smith. London: Routledge, 2006.

———. *Sense and Non-Sense.* Translated by Hubert L. Dreyfus and Patricia Allen Dreyfus. Evanston, IL: Northwestern University Press, 1964.

———. *The Visible and the Invisible.* Edited by Claude Lefort. Translated by Alphonso Lingis. Evanston, IL: Northwestern University Press, 1968.

Metz, Christian. *The Imaginary Signifier: Psychoanalysis and the Cinema.* Bloomington: Indiana University Press, 1982.

Mullarkey, John. *Philosophy and the Moving Image: Refractions of Reality.* Basingstoke: Palgrave Macmillan, 2009.

Mulvey, Laura. *Death 24x a Second: Stillness and the Moving Image.* London: Reaktion, 2006.

———. *Visual and Other Pleasures.* Basingstoke: Palgrave Macmillan, 1989.

Nancy, Jean-Luc. *The Birth to Presence.* Translated by Brian Holmes and others. Stanford: Stanford University Press, 1993.

———. *The Evidence of Film: Abbas Kiarostami.* Translated by Christine Irizarray and Verena Andermatt Conley. Brussels: Yves Gevaert, 2001.

———. *The Inoperative Community.* Edited by Peter Connor. Translated by Peter Connor, Lisa Garbus, Michael Holland, and Simon Sawhney. Minneapolis, Minnesota: University of Minnesota Press, 1991.

———. *The Muses.* Translated by Peggy Kamuf. Stanford, California: Stanford University Press, 1996.

Nietzsche, Friedrich. *The Birth of Tragedy and The Case of Wagner.* Translated by Walter Kaufmann. New York: Vintage, 1967.

———. *The Birth of Tragedy and The Genealogy of Morals.* Translated by Francis Golffingklj. New York: Doubleday Anchor, 1956.

———. *The Gay Science, with a Prelude in Rhymes and an Appendix of Songs.* Translated by Walter Kaufmann. New York: Vintage, 1974.

——. *The Portable Nietzsche*. Edited and translated by Walter Kaufmann. New York: Penguin, 1976.

——. *The Will to Power*. Edited by Walter Kaufmann. Translated by Walter Kaufmann and R. J. Hollingdale. New York: Vintage, 1968.

Pearson, Keith Ansell. *Philosophy and the Adventure of the Virtual: Bergson and the Time of Life*. London: Routledge, 2002.

Pearson. Keith Ansell, and John Mullarkey, eds. *Henri Bergson: Key Writings*. New York: Bloomsbury, 2014.

Plato. *The Portable Plato*. Edited by Scott Buchanan. New York: Penguin, 1977.

——. *Sophist*. Indianapolis: Hackett, 1993.

Proust, Marcel. *In Search of Lost Time*, vol. 1: *Swann's Way*. Translated by C. K. Scott Moncrieff, Terence Kilman, and D. J. Enright. New York: Modern Library, 1992.

——. *In Search of Lost Time*, vol. 2: *Within a Budding Grove*. Translated by C. K. Scott Moncrieff, Terence Kilmartin, and D. J. Enright. New York: Modern Library, 1992.

——. *In Search of Lost Time*, vol. 3: *The Guermantes Way*. Translated by C. K. Scott Moncrieff, Terence Kilmartin, and D. J. Enright. New York: Modern Library, 1993.

——. *In Search of Lost Time*, vol. 4: *Sodom and Gomorrah*. Translated by C. K. Scott Moncrieff, Terence Kilmartin, and D. J. Enright. New York: Modern Library, 1993.

——. *In Search of Lost Time*, vol. 5: *The Captive, the Fugitive*. Translated by C. K. Scott Moncrieff and Terence Kilmartin. New York: Modern Library, 1993.

——. *In Search of Lost Time*, vol. 6: *Time Regained*. Translated by Andreas Major, Terence Kilmartin, and D. J. Enright. New York: Modern Library, 1993.

Rancière, Jacques. *Béla Tarr, the Time After*. Translated by Erik Beranek. Minneapolis: Univocal, 2013.

——. *Film Fables*. Translated by Emiliano Battista. New York: Berg, 2006.

——. *The Future of the Image*. Translated by Gregory Elliott. London: Verso, 2007.

——. *The Intervals of Cinema*. Translated by John Howe. London: Verso, 2014.

——. *The Philosopher and His Poor*. Translated by John Drury, Corinne Oster, and Andrew Parker. Durham: Duke University Press, 2003.

——. *The Politics of Aesthetics: The Distribution of the Sensible*. Translated by Gabriel Rockhill. New York: Continuum, 2005.

Rodowick, David Norman. *Gilles Deleuze's Time Machine*. Durham: Duke University Press, 1997.

——. *Reading the Figural; or, Philosophy After the New Media*. Durham: Duke University Press, 2001.

Rohdie, Sam. *Montage*. Manchester: Manchester University Press, 2006.

Rosen, Philip, ed. *Narrative, Apparatus, Ideology: A Film Theory Reader*. New York: Columbia University Press, 1986.

Sartre, Jean-Paul. *Being and Nothingness: An Essay on Phenomenological Ontology*. Translated by Hazel E. Barnes. London: Routledge, 2001.

Saussure, Ferdinand de. *Course in General Linguistics*. Translated and annotated by Roy Harris. London: Duckworth, 1983.

Sedofsky, Lauren. "Being by Numbers, Lauren Sedofsky Talks with Alain Badiou." *Artforum* (October 1994): 84–87.

Shaviro, Steven. *Post-Cinematic Affect*. Winchester: Zero, 2010.

Silverman, Kaja. *The Acoustic Mirror: The Female Voice in Psychoanalysis and Cinema*. Bloomington: Indiana University Press, 1988.

——. *Flesh of My Flesh*. Stanford: Stanford University Press, 2009.

——. *Male Subjectivity at the Margins*. New York: Routledge, 1992.

——. *The Miracle of Analogy: Or, The History of Photography, Part 1.* Stanford: Stanford University Press, 2015.

——. *World Spectators.* Stanford: Stanford University Press, 2000.

Silverman, Kaja, and Harun Farocki. *Speaking About Godard.* New York: New York University Press, 1998.

Sobchack, Vivian. *The Address of the Eye: A Phenomenology of Film Experience.* Princeton, New Jersey: Princeton University Press, 1992.

Spinoza, Benedict de. *Ethics.* In *A Spinoza Reader: The Ethics and Other Works.* Translated by E. Curley. Princeton: Princeton University Press, 1994.

Stiegler, Bernard. "Automatic Society: Londres, février 2015." *Journal of Visual Art Practice* 15, nos. 2–3 (2016): 192–203.

——. *Technics and Time, 1: The Fault of Epimetheus.* Translated by Richard Beardsworth and George Collins. Stanford: Stanford University Press, 1998.

——. *Technics and Time, 2: Disorientation.* Translated by Stephen Barker. Stanford: Stanford University Press, 2008.

——. *Technics and Time, 3: Cinematic Time and the Question of Malaise.* Translated by Stephen Barker. Stanford: Stanford University Press, 2011.

Tannenbaum, Eugen. "Der Großfilm." In *Der Film von Morgen.* Edited by Hugo Zehder. Berlin: Kämmerer, 1923.

Vertov, Dziga. *Kino-Eye: The Writings of Dzigo Vertov.* Edited and with an introduction by Annette Michelson. Translated by Kevin O'Brien. Berkeley: University of California Press, 1984.

Virilio. Paul. *Speed and Politics: An Essay on Dromology.* Translated by Mark Polizzotti. New York: Semiotext(e), 1986.

——. *War and Cinema: The Logistics of Perception.* Translated by Patrick Camiller. London: Verso, 1989.

Weber, Samuel. *Benjamin's -abilities.* Cambridge, MA: Harvard University Press, 2010.

——. *Mass Mediauras: Form, Technics, Media.* Edited by Alan Cholodenko. Stanford: Stanford University Press, 1996.

Whitford, Margaret, ed. *The Irigaray Reader.* Oxford: Blackwell, 1991.

Žižek, Slavoj, ed. *Everything You Always Wanted to Know About Lacan (But Were Afraid to Ask Hitchcock).* London: Verso, 1992.

——. *Looking Awry: An Introduction to Jacques Lacan Through Popular Culture.* Cambridge, MA: MIT Press, 1991.

——. *The Parallax View.* Cambridge, MA: MIT Press, 2006.

——. *The Pervert's Guide to Cinema.* Directed by Sophie Fiennes. Distributed by P. Guide Ltd. and ICA Projects, 2006.

——. *The Pervert's Guide to Ideology.* Directed by Sophie Fiennes. Distributed by Zeitgeist Films UK, 2013.

——. *The Sublime Object of Ideology.* London: Verso, 1989.

——. *Trouble in Paradise: From the End of History to the End of Capitalism.* London: Allen Lane, Penguin, 2014.

INDEX